Library of
Davidson College

Stability and Change in American Politics:
The Coming of Age of the Generation of the 1960s

Stability and Change in American Politics: The Coming of Age of the Generation of the 1960s

Michael X. Delli Carpini
DEPARTMENT OF POLITICAL SCIENCE
RUTGERS UNIVERSITY

NEW YORK UNIVERSITY PRESS
NEW YORK AND LONDON
1986

Copyright © 1986 by New York University
All rights reserved
Manufactured in the United States of America

Library of Congress Cataloging-in Publication Data

Delli Carpini, Michael X., 1953–
   Stability and change in American politics.

   Bibliography: p.
   Includes index.
   1. Political participation—United States.
   2. United States—Politics and government—1945–
   3. Baby boom generation—United States.   I. Title.
   JK1764.D45   1985   323'.042'0973   85-15348
   ISBN 0–8147–1780–2 (alk. paper)

Clothbound editions of New York University Press books are Smyth-sewn and printed on permanent and durable acid-free paper.

Designed by Ken Venezio

*This book is dedicated to my parents, Domenick and Frances;
my brothers, John, Dominic, and Joseph;
and my sister, Lisa.
For teaching each other well.*

Contents

TABLES	ix
FIGURES	xvii
ACKNOWLEDGMENTS	xix
INTRODUCTION	xxi

PART ONE
Generational Change, Periods, the Life Cycle, and the Sixties

CHAPTER 1	Generations and Politics	3
CHAPTER 2	The Sixties and the Sixties Generation: An Overview	23
CHAPTER 3	Data and Methods	55

PART TWO
The Effects of Generation, Periods, and the Life Cycle on Mass Political Orientations

CHAPTER 4	Diffuse Political Support	75
CHAPTER 5	The Political Agenda	95
CHAPTER 6	Issue Stands	120
CHAPTER 7	Political Involvement	141

Contents

CHAPTER 8	Political Decision Making	159
CHAPTER 9	Political Participation	177
CHAPTER 10	Partisan Support	196
CHAPTER 11	Political Stability	219

PART THREE
Situations and Structures: The Impact of the Social, Cultural, and Economic Environments on Generational Change

CHAPTER 12	Demographic Change	243
CHAPTER 13	The Political Impact of the Socioeconomic Environment	269
CHAPTER 14	The Political Impact of the Sociocultural Environment	295
CHAPTER 15	Generations, Periods, and Political Change	322
APPENDIX A	Variable Means	342
APPENDIX B	Question Wording and Coding	343
APPENDIX C	Model Parameters	358
APPENDIX D	Description of Methods Used in Part III	362
INDEX		365

Tables

TABLE 1.1	Description of Generations and Subgenerations	18
TABLE 2.1	Percentage of the Electorate Made Up by and Mean Age of the Sixties Generation	50
TABLE 3.1	NES Surveys Used and Ns of Each Survey	56
TABLE 4.1	Description of Measures of Diffuse Support	80
TABLE 4.2	Effects of Life Cycle, Generation, and Period on Diffuse Support	85
TABLE 4.3	Interaction Effects on Diffuse Support	86
TABLE 4.4	Subgenerational Effects on Diffuse Support	88
TABLE 4.5	Interaction Effects between Subgenerations, Life Cycle, and Periods on Diffuse Support	89
TABLE 5.1	Description of Measures of the Public's Political Agenda	99
TABLE 5.2	Life Cycle, Generation, and Period Effects on the Political Agenda	106
TABLE 5.3	Interaction Effects on the Political Agenda	109
TABLE 5.4	Effects of Subgenerations on the Political Agenda	111

TABLE 5.5	Interaction Effects between Subgenerations, Life Cycle, and Periods on the Political Agenda	114
TABLE 6.1	Descriptions of the Measures of Issue Stands	124
TABLE 6.2	Effects of Life Cycle, Generation, and Period on Issue Stands	129
TABLE 6.3	Interaction Effects on Issue Stands	131
TABLE 6.4	Effects of Subgenerations on Issue Stands	133
TABLE 6.5	Interaction Effects between Subgenerations, Life Cycle and Periods on Issue Stands	134
TABLE 6.6	Main and Interaction Effects for Life Cycle, Generation, and Period on Opinions towards Korea and Vietnam	136
TABLE 6.7	Effects of Subgenerations on Opinions Concerning Korea and Vietnam	137
TABLE 7.1	Descriptions of the Measures of Political Involvement	145
TABLE 7.2	Effects of Life Cycle, Generation, and Period on Political Involvement	149
TABLE 7.3	Interaction Effects on Political Involvement	152
TABLE 7.4	Effects of Subgenerations on Political Involvement	153
TABLE 7.5	Interaction Effects between Subgenerations, Periods, and Life Cycle on Political Involvement	153
TABLE 8.1	Description of Measures of Decision-making Cues	164
TABLE 8.2	Effects of Life Cycle, Generation, and Period on Political Decision Making	169
TABLE 8.3	Interaction Effects on Political Decision Making	171

Tables

TABLE 8.4	Effects of Subgenerations on Political Decision Making	172
TABLE 8.5	Interaction Effects between Subgenerations, Life Cycle, and Period on Political Decision Making	173
TABLE 9.1	Description of the Measures of Political Participation	180
TABLE 9.2	Effects of Life Cycle, Generation, and Period on Political Participation	186
TABLE 9.3	Interaction Effects on Political Participation	187
TABLE 9.4	Effects of Subgenerations on Political Participation	188
TABLE 9.5	Interaction Effects between Subgenerations, Life Cycle, and Period on Political Participation	189
TABLE 9.6	Generational and Subgenerational Differences in Alternative Forms of Participation	192
TABLE 10.1	Description of the Measures of Partisan Support	203
TABLE 10.2	Effects of Life Cycle, Generation, and Period on Partisan Support	209
TABLE 10.3	Interaction Effects on Partisan Support	211
TABLE 10.4	Subgenerational Effects on Partisan Support	213
TABLE 10.5	Interaction Effects between Subgenerations, Life Cycle, and Period on Partisan Support	214
TABLE 11.1	Description of Measures of Political Stability	224
TABLE 11.2	Effects of Life Cycle, Generation, and Period on Political Stability	230
TABLE 11.3	Interaction Effects on Political Stability	232
TABLE 11.4	Effects of Subgenerations on Political Stability	233

TABLE 11.5	Interaction Effects between Subgenerations, Life Cycle, and Period on Political Stability	235
TABLE 12.1	Description of the Measures of Demographic Characteristics	249
TABLE 12.2	Effects of Life Cycle, Generation, and Period on Demographic Characteristics	257
TABLE 12.3	Interaction Effects on Demographics	260
TABLE 12.4	Effects of Subgenerations on Demographic Characteristics	262
TABLE 12.5	Interaction Effects between Subgenerations, Life Cycle, and Period on Demographic Characteristics	263
TABLE 13.1	Description of Summary Measures of Political Orientations	270
TABLE 13.2	Summary of Effects of Life Cycle, Generation, and Period	272
TABLE 13.3	Effects of Socioeconomic Factors on Political Support within the Sixties Generation	275
TABLE 13.4	Effects of Socioeconomic Factors on Selection of a Sixties Agenda within the Sixties Generation	277
TABLE 13.5	Effects of Socioeconomic Factors on Selection of an Economic Agenda within the Sixties Generation	277
TABLE 13.6	Effects of Socioeconomic Factors on Selection of a Social Welfare Agenda within the Sixties Generation	279
TABLE 13.7	Effects of Socioeconomic Factors on Selection of a Foreign Agenda within the Sixties Generation	279
TABLE 13.8	Effects of Socioeconomic Factors on Domestic-issue Stands within the Sixties Generation	280

Tables

TABLE 13.9   Effects of Socioeconomic Factors on Foreign-issue Stands within the Sixties Generation   280

TABLE 13.10   Effects of Socioeconomic Factors on the Level of Political Involvement within the Sixties Generation   282

TABLE 13.11   Effects of Socioeconomic Factors on Ideological Decision Making within the Sixties Generation   283

TABLE 13.12   Effects of Socioeconomic Factors on Cue-specific Decision Making within the Sixties Generation   283

TABLE 13.13   Effects of Socioeconomic Factors on Party-based Decision Making within the Sixties Generation   284

TABLE 13.14   Effects of Socioeconomic Factors on Nonpolitical Decision Making within the Sixties Generation   284

TABLE 13.15   Effects of Socioeconomic Factors on the Level of Political Participation within the Sixties Generation   285

TABLE 13.16   Effects of Socioeconomic Factors on Diffuse Party Support within the Sixties Generation   286

TABLE 13.17   Effects of Socioeconomic Factors on Short-term Party Choice within the Sixties Generation   286

TABLE 13.18   Effects of Socioeconomic Factors on Long-term Party Choice within the Sixties Generation   288

TABLE 13.19   Effects of Socioeconomic Factors on Stability in the Amount of Political Participation within the Sixties Generation   288

TABLE 13.20   Effects of Socioeconomic Factors on Stability in the Long-term Choice of Party within the Sixties Generation   289

Tables

TABLE 13.21	Effects of Socioeconomic Factors on Stability in the Short-term Choice of Party within the Sixties Generation	289
TABLE 13.22	Effects of Socioeconomic Factors on Stability in the Choice of Party during a Campaign within the Sixties Generation	290
TABLE 14.1	Effects of Sociocultural Factors on Political Support within the Sixties Generation	298
TABLE 14.2	Effects of Sociocultural Factors on Selection of a Sixties Agenda within the Sixties Generation	300
TABLE 14.3	Effects of Sociocultural Factors on Selection of an Economic Agenda within the Sixties Generation	300
TABLE 14.4	Effects of Sociocultural Factors on Selection of a Social Welfare Agenda within the Sixties Generation	301
TABLE 14.5	Effects of Sociocultural Factors on Selection of a Foreign Agenda within the Sixties Generation	301
TABLE 14.6	Effects of Sociocultural Factors on Domestic-issue Stands within the Sixties Generation	304
TABLE 14.7	Effects of Sociocultural Factors on Foreign-issue Stands within the Sixties Generation	304
TABLE 14.8	Effects of Sociocultural Factors on the Level of Political Involvement within the Sixties Generation	306
TABLE 14.9	Effects of Sociocultural Factors on Ideological Decision Making within the Sixties Generation	308
TABLE 14.10	Effects of Sociocultural Factors on Cue-specific Decision Making within the Sixties Generation	308

Tables

TABLE 14.11	Effects of Sociocultural Factors on Party-based Decision Making within the Sixties Generation	309
TABLE 14.12	Effects of Sociocultural Factors on Nonpolitical Decision Making within the Sixties Generation	309
TABLE 14.13	Effects of Sociocultural Factors on the Level of Political Participation within the Sixties Generation	311
TABLE 14.14	Effects of Sociocultural Factors on Diffuse Party Support within the Sixties Generation	312
TABLE 14.15	Effects of Sociocultural Factors on Short-term Party Choice within the Sixties Generation	313
TABLE 14.16	Effects of Sociocultural Factors on Long-term Party Choice within the Sixties Generation	313
TABLE 14.17	Effects of Sociocultural Factors on Stability in the Amount of Political Participation within the Sixties Generation	316
TABLE 14.18	Effects of Sociocultural Factors on Stability in the Long-term Choice of Party within the Sixties Generation	316
TABLE 14.19	Effects of Sociocultural Factors on Stability in the Short-term Choice of Party within the Sixties Generation	317
TABLE 14.20	Effects of Sociocultural Factors on Stability in the Choice of Party during a Campaign within the Sixties Generation	317

Figures

FIGURE 4.1	Patterns of Change in Diffuse Support, 1952–1980	81
FIGURE 5.1	Patterns of Change in the Political Agenda, 1960–1980	100
FIGURE 6.1	Trends in Selected Issue Stands, 1952–1980	125
FIGURE 7.1	Trends in Political Involvement, 1952–1980	146
FIGURE 8.1	Trends in Decision Making, 1952–1980	166
FIGURE 9.1	Trends in Political Participation, 1952–1980	181
FIGURE 10.1	Trends in Partisan Support, 1952–1980	204
FIGURE 11.1	Trends in Political Stability, 1952–1980	225
FIGURE 12.1	Trends in Demographic Characteristics, 1952–1980	250

Acknowledgments

There are many people who assisted in the completion of this project. I would like to thank Rutgers University for a generous leave policy, which provided me with the time to complete much of this research. I would also like to thank the University for several sources of financial aid, including a University Fellowship and two Research Council Grants. The staff of the Center for Computer and Information Services were of great assistance in the technical aspects of this project, and I would like to thank Gert Lewis, Don Robertson, and Chris Jarocha-Ernst particularly in this regard.

Several people provided a variety of levels of encouragement, advice and criticism. I would like to thank Patrick Cotter, Norman Luttbeg, Roberta Sigel, and Lee Sigelman for their comments on parts of this research presented as convention papers. I am also grateful to Gerry Pomper and Roberta Sigel for their more general encouragement and support. And I would like especially to thank Scott Keeter and Cliff Zukin for their careful reading of early drafts of much of this work, and for being such good colleagues and friends.

The staff of the New York University Press have been invaluable. Colin Jones saw the merit of this project at a stage when it might easily have been missed and helped tremendously in seeing it through to completion. Despina Papazoglou and Robert L. Bull, III made the process of turning a rough manuscript into a much more comprehensible book an easy one. Thanks also to Kathleen Daly for her administrative assistance.

Finally I would like to thank Jane Whittaker. From the point at which this project was no more than incoherent ramblings to its final edit Jane has been my harshest critic and my strongest supporter. The extent to which there is value to the ideas discussed in this book and force to the way in which they are argued and defended is substantially due to her careful readings and her insightful advice.

Introduction

This is a book about political change. More specifically, it is about changes in the political attitudes, opinions, and behaviors of the American public which were brought about (and which are still being brought about) by the "coming of age" of people raised in the tumultuous years known as "The Sixties." More than that it is about the relationship between change and continuity; between evolutionary and revolutionary change; between attitudinal change and structural change; and, perhaps most importantly, about the relationship between political change and political progress in mass democracies. These are issues of importance to anyone who has ever voiced an opinion about a political or social issue, or voted, or worked for a party, or signed a petition, or stood in a picket line. These are issues of importance to anyone who has *not* done these things (or stopped doing them) because they seemed to be futile. And these are issues of importance to political systems that are based on concepts of political power that are dependent on some notion of the will of the people.

In essence, this book is a detailed case study of the political impact of generational replacement. This is an important area of inquiry for a number of reasons. An examination of the

Introduction

sixties generation seems a useful endeavor in and of itself, since that group stands out (in popular perceptions at least) as one that experienced uniquely intense and nontraditional politics. What is the legacy of that decade? Did the cultural, social, economic, and political environment of those years have a lasting impact on mass politics in general, or on the generation raised during this time in particular? This second question is of particular importance today. The sixties generation consists of the largest age cohort in the history of the United States, and now represents a majority of the adult population in this country. Members of this generation now dominate middle management positions in business. They are the educators of the next generation (as well as of younger members of their own generation) in schools from kindergarten to college. They are the pool from which political leaders at all levels are increasingly being selected. In short, we are currently witnessing the passing of power from one generation to another. For at least the next half century, the direction of the United States will be decided, in part, by the generation that is presented in these pages.

Beyond providing an explication of our recent past and an educated glimpse into our immediate future, this case study is also an examination of the more general process of generational change. Ultimately this book is about the possibility that fundamental, coherent, and long-term political change evolves from the replacement of one generation with another. Are generations politically different? Do they remain politically distinct over time? What aspects of a generation's unique political attitudes, opinions, and behaviors seem most likely to survive the situational, structural, and biological changes which occur with age? These are questions that this research helps answer, not only as they apply to the sixties generation, but also to the process of generational politics as a whole.

Introduction

The thesis of this book consists of two general arguments (both of which are developed more fully in Chapter Two, and refined throughout the book). The first is that in the 1960s, values, norms, and ideas were more likely to be disseminated from peripheral subcultures to the dominant or hegemonic culture, which is not normally the case in advanced industrial societies such as the United States. This "reversal" in the spread of social change took place for a variety of reasons, but it was possible in part because the large cohort of young, middle-class Americans served as a conduit of sorts. As a result, the sixties generation developed a set of political orientations that were distinctive. Second, however, we argue that this generational change in political attitudes, opinions, and behaviors was not accompanied by the structural changes that are necessary to provide both longevity and coherence. Indeed, we ultimately conclude that the very nature of generational replacement makes such meaningful change unlikely.

The picture of the sixties generation that emerges from this book is a complex and often disconcerting one, but it is one that supports both of the arguments outlined above. You will see that this generation is politically distinct in a number of ways. It is less supportive of the political system; it is likely to have different political priorities. It is politically more liberal than preceding generations and more Democratic in its vote, though not in its overall support. It is less psychologically or behaviorally involved in electoral politics. You will also see that this distinctiveness is greatest in the generation's rejection of traditional politics, and least dramatic in terms of providing alternative agendas, solutions, or structures. In addition, this distinctiveness is eroding with time, as members of the generation find themselves occupying roles not too different from those filled by their parents and grandparents.

Introduction

In the remainder of this book we explore how life cycle, period, and generational changes have affected the nature of mass political attitudes, opinions, and behaviors in the United States over the past three decades. Part One (Chapters One through Three) is an introduction to the key concepts used in this study, to the sixties and the sixties generation, and to the data and methods. In Chapter One we introduce and discuss the idea of mass-based political change, focusing on the specific role played by the impact of generational change, contemporary events, and the life cycle. Once defined, these concepts are used to develop a working definition of both the sixties and the sixties generation. In the next chapter, a brief description of the 1960s is presented, along with some thoughts on why one should expect change in political orientations, and what kind of change would be most likely. Chapter Three presents a discussion of the data to be used in the empirical analysis and an explanation and justification for the methodology employed.

Part Two (Chapters Four through Eleven) contains the heart of this analysis, with each of the eight chapters devoted to a different aspect of political orientation, ranging from deep-seated attitudes through particular opinions to actual behavior: diffuse support, political agendas, stands on issues, political involvement, decision-making cues, political participation, partisan support, and attitudinal and behavioral stability. In each of these chapters we examine both the logic behind the expectation of change as well as the empirical evidence for the effects of generation, life cycle, periods and their interaction. The distinct political patterns of subgenerations are also explored.

Part Three (Chapters Twelve through Fifteen) explores some structural and situational explanations for the patterns of change uncovered. It examines the extent to which attitudinal and behavioral change both affect and are affected

Introduction

by specific characteristics of the socioeconomic and sociocultural environment. Chapter Twelve examines the extent to which the sixties generation is socially, culturally, and economically different from preceding generations. Chapter Thirteen estimates the effect of the generation's socioeconomic environment on its political distinctiveness, while Chapter Fourteen estimates the impact of the sociocultural environment. Finally, Chapter Fifteen summarizes the findings and relates them not only to mass political change as it concerns the sixties generation, but also to the larger issue of the possibility of progressive development which both originates from the mass citizenry and which has a lasting and fundamental impact on the workings of the political, social, and economic systems in which it takes place.

PART ONE

Generational Change, Periods, the Life Cycle, and the Sixties

CHAPTER 1

Generations and Politics

The focal point of this study is the sixties and the sixties generation. Knowing which aspects of those years to emphasize, and what age groups to include as part of the generation, requires that they first be put into a more general context of political change and generational replacement. In this chapter we begin to explore these issues by considering the nature of mass political change. The next section looks at the distinction between sudden, episodic change and that which is more gradual or evolutionary. Section three discusses the difference between aggregate change that emanates from within individuals and aggregate change that results from generational replacement. Section four further differentiates political change in light of the influence of generations, distinct political periods, the life cycle, and their interaction. In section five we begin to apply these concepts to the 1960s and the sixties generation. Finally, section six briefly summarizes the chapter.

RATES OF POLITICAL CHANGE

The concept of mass political change can refer to a wide variety of occurrences. In the history of the United States, one need only consider the revolt from England and the attempted revolt of the South from the North, the sudden changes in voting patterns that marked the 1890s or the 1930s, or the gradual decline in partisan support in the twentieth century to see the range that it can include. While there are many dimensions along which mass political change can be distinguished, an important one is the rate at which it takes place. One of the first students of American politics to emphasize rates of political change was V. O. Key, Jr. In 1955 Key wrote his seminal piece on critical change in U.S. politics. In it he noted the tendency in the electorate for sudden, radical shifts in support for competing political elites. Five years later he published a second article in which he emphasized the importance of gradual demographic change and its incremental impact on mass opinions and behaviors. While Key was focusing on electoral politics exclusively, his basic distinction between change that is steady and gradual and change that is episodic and sudden is applicable more generally to the study of opinions and behaviors.

Sudden, dramatic alterations in the established opinions and behaviors of a population are, of course, usually the easiest to detect and often the most interesting to study. It is, therefore, not surprising that most research on mass political behavior tends to emphasize this type of change. Perhaps the best example of this kind of research is the work on critical elections (Key, 1955; Sundquist, 1973; Burnham, 1965; 1970). These studies concentrate on brief, intense periods during which fundamental shifts in mass support for particular elites and/or particular agendas take place. Such shifts are triggered by the advent of new issues that challenge established coalitions in both the mass population and among political elites. Often a particularly intense event (such as a war or a depression) serves as the catalyst for the emergence of new political coalitions, agendas, and opinions. Such realignments can be considered periodic (Burnham) or coincidental (Sundquist), but they are the exceptions that define the rule. That is, they are occasional adjustments to the political system that are both distinct from more normal patterns and that ultimately define those patterns.

At the other end of the spectrum is the study of evolutionary change. Such change is often more difficult to detect, especially over short periods of time. It results not from clear reactions to brief periods of intense politics but from gradual economic, social, and political development. The work of Nie, Verba, and Petrocik (1979) or Inglehart (1977) best exemplifies research of this genre, though much of Burnham's work could be placed here as well. These studies emphasize changes in demographics, such as education, income, or occupation, or in technological developments, such as those of the mass media or the workplace and how these changes lead to parallel shifts in political attitudes and actions. Again, these alterations can be seen as essentially discrete (Nie, et al.) or as part of more systematic developments (Inglehart). However, all these studies, whatever their differences, consider incremental changes in attitudes, opinions, and behaviors.

While distinguishing between episodic and evolutionary political change is a useful technique for studying mass politics, and does reveal some very real distinctions among types of change, one must be careful (as the authors cited here have been) not to lose sight of the links between them. In particular, these extreme types of political change are interconnected in two ways. First, incremental change can be seen as the condition that exists between periods of more dramatic, intense activity. That is, rather than conceptualizing the normal pattern within political periods as one of stasis, it is perhaps more realistic to characterize it as a period of gradual change, with the rate and nature of the shift determined by the social, economic, and political parameters set during the more dramatic periods of upheaval.

Second, and perhaps more importantly, the nature of critical change is almost certainly determined in part by the nature of

Generational Change, Periods, and the Life Cycle

the evolutionary shifts in mass politics that preceded it. While issues and events no doubt trigger such change, the reaction to those issues and events (indeed sometimes their very occurrence) can only be fully understood in light of the more subtle movements that have occurred since the last such "eruption." In short, the political orientations of a population over time can best be understood by considering not only episodic change and incremental change, but also the interaction between the two.

INDIVIDUAL VERSUS AGGREGATE CHANGE

The discussion above of both episodic and incremental change revolved around the impact of issues, events, and social and economic developments on the pattern of mass political attitudes and behaviors. These patterns necessarily occur over time, however, and over time the individuals who make up a population also change, due to the natural cycles of birth and death, as well as to immigration and emigration patterns. If we are interested in going beyond cataloguing the patterns of change to try to explain their sources, a distinction must be made between aggregate change that results from parallel shifts within individuals who already are a part of the population and that which results from the replacement of one set of individuals with another.

Consider the concept of incremental change which was discussed above. If one were to find a gradual loss of support for the Democratic party over a 20-year span, that loss could be the result of either former supporters becoming slowly disenchanted with the party, or older citizens dying and being replaced with a new generation that is less enamoured of the Democratic party right from the start (or some combination of both processes). Determining the actual reason for the loss of support is critical both for understanding the nature of the change and for speculating on its long-term consequences. In addition, while such competing explanations are more obviously relevant in discussions of evolutionary change, even more dramatic shifts can be the result of alterations in the makeup of the population. Andersen, for instance, finds that most of the rapid rise in support for the Democratic party in the 1930s can be attributed to first-time voters and not to disenchanted Republicans (1979; 1979b).

Distinguishing between change resulting from the succession of generations and change attributable to other sources is both methodologically and theoretically more difficult than it would at first seem. We consider methodological issues in Chapter Three. Here we would like to consider some theoretical issues. It is important that we clearly distinguish between an "age cohort" and a generation. An age cohort is a group of individuals who all fall into the same age group at a particular time: all individuals who are between the ages of 18 and 28 in 1984 for example. Nothing is implied concerning the individuals who make up this cohort beyond the similarity in ages. A generation, in contrast, implies some shared experiences, some common bond that is "imprinted" on a particular age cohort within a population (Mannheim, 1928). This imprinting results from a process that lies somewhere between the socialization of an individual and the development of an entire political culture. Unique personality development results from the interaction of the self, the socializing experiences of family, peers, school, the mass media, and other social agents, and the idiosyncratic experiences derived from one's daily routine. A common national culture, on the other hand, is the summation of those personal traits, socializing experiences, and historical occurrences that most individuals within the society in question have experienced. Generations represent a similar development, but only for a particular age cohort within the population. That is, generations result from a socialization process that is less general than it is for an entire culture, but more general than the unique experiences of particular individuals.

The logic behind the importance of the concept of generation lies in the assumption that there is an interaction between age and experiences. This interaction occurs in two ways. First, there is a tendency for people within the same age cohort to be exposed to similar historical, social, cultural, and political experiences. The rise of mass education, the Vietnam War, the development of the home computer—all have affected the entire society in many ways, but they have also provided unique experiences to different age cohorts. Certain age cohorts were the first to enjoy the opportunity to be gained from extensive public education; certain age cohorts were required to fight in Vietnam; certain age cohorts are growing up with computers as part of their daily routine. The sum of these common experiences, opportunities, and situations creates a "Zeitgeist" or historical spirit that bonds the individuals who are a part of it (Mannheim, 1928; Lambert, 1972).

The second assumption that underlies the age-experience link is that different age groups are likely to perceive and react to the same experience in different ways, precisely because of the particular stage of personal and social development they have reached when the events occur. That is, not only is one generation likely to have a unique set of experiences that distinguish it from past and future ones, but each generation is likely to react to the same experiences in different ways. A family sits around the television watching the aftermath of the assassination of John F. Kennedy. All are affected by that experience, but the particular nature of the impact is likely to be strongly related to age. Similarly, a family stands for the playing of the national anthem before the start of a baseball game. The feelings (or lack of them) engendered by that experience will no doubt differ markedly from the elderly grandparents, to the middle-aged parents, to the teenage son and to the eight-year-old niece.

Generations and Politics

A third assumption concerning the link between age and experience is that a generation's personality is shaped by the experiences that occur during a particular stage of its members' development. There is some disagreement on the actual years involved, but generally the years between the late teens to mid-twenties are considered critical. For Mannheim (1928), the crucial years are from 17 to 25, while Lambert (1972) finds the years from 18 to 26 are (see also, Jennings and Niemi, 1974, 1981 on this issue). The logic behind this assumption is clear enough. It is the age at which individuals begin to step out into the world as independent adults that is central to the formation of each generation's unique personality. While there is much that is attractive about this notion, we reject it as a general rule for several reasons.

First, since the idea of a generational personality is based on the idea of individual personalities that share common world views, it seems overly simplistic to select one stage of early development as necessarily dominant in the process. Developmental theorists such as Erikson (1968), Maslow (1962), and, to an extent, even Freud (1964) would agree that early adulthood is an important stage, but certainly it is not the only, not the first, and not the last stage at which such development takes place. To the extent that generational development is based upon the commonalities found in the development of individual personalities, then, it too must be forming at various stages.

One might argue that while it is analogous to individual development, generational development is a distinct process that follows distinct patterns. In particular, since generational development involves the impact of larger social and historical forces, it stands to reason that the age at which one first steps out into the world as a somewhat independent adult would be critical to that process. Even if one did accept that the two processes are largely unrelated (something we reject), it still does not follow that early adulthood must be the critical stage.

One certainly would not want to argue that historical, cultural, economic, and social forces do not affect the development of individuals prior to their emergence from the family, nor that such forces do not act in similar ways on similar age groups. In addition, the particular age at which one begins to outgrow childhood ties is also culture and time bound. The point at which one first feels the grasp of the outside world was arguably well before the age of 17 or 18 in the England of the mid-1800s, in the United States of the 1930s, and, for very different reasons, the contemporary era of the United States.

A final objection to the emphasis placed on young adulthood is the implication that, beyond this age, change that has a unique impact on an entire generation and which becomes part of that generation's personality is unlikely. Again, it is not the case that socialization at the individual level ends with young adulthood (Sigel and Hoskin, 1977), nor that historical forces, among others, stop affecting a generation as a group. Why, then, should we assume that a generation's personality will not form its most distinctive characteristics later in life?

Yet another conceptual hurdle must be negotiated before we can begin to piece together a workable definition of generations, a hurdle that exists for anyone who assumes that a particular age range is critical in determining a generation's character. This assumption is based on a static notion of age, although aging is a continuous process. Consider that you have defined "The Depression Generation" as one in which its members were between 17 and 26 during the Depression, and the "World War II Generation" as one in which members fell in that age cohort during that war. Aside from the problem of establishing cutoff dates for periods such as a depression, you have the added problem that a good portion of one generation falls into the age group of the other. In other words, the idea of labeling particular generations and distinguishing them from others is really an artificial division of a dynamic process into a categorical one to gain a deeper understanding of the consequences of such processes. This problem is exacerbated by the notion put forth above that generations develop their personalities at various ages.

Does all this mean that generational analysis cannot or should not be done, that it is too fluid a process to allow characterizations beyond the most qualitative discussions? We believe not, though the issues raised above do change the way in which such research should be laid out. The key lies in returning to the underlying premise of the idea of a generation: the summation of the juncture of historical events and experiences and of age cohorts through time. Proper analysis should therefore start with the question: a generation in regard to what? If one is interested in studying the ramifications of the Depression, then one can talk about the Depression Generation. One cannot necessarily distinguish it entirely from other generations that might, under other circumstances, be equally worthy of study. It is, in a sense, only a useful fiction.

Beyond this, however, the points raised above suggest that not only must a researcher choose from among alternative boundaries, he or she must consider the age cohort (or cohorts) most likely to be affected by the events selected. Again consider the Depression. While all Americans alive were affected by it in some way, it would seem plausible to argue that it was an experience which most directly affected those who were of an age to be in the work force (people between the ages of 19 and 60 for instance). World War II, however, might better be considered as having its most direct impact on those who were of an age to have experienced (either by serving in the armed forces or having a spouse who served) the war directly, those between the ages of 17 and 35 perhaps.

The point just made raises yet another question that must be answered by the researcher: affected in what way? More specifically, there are at least two types of experiences that need to be distinguished: direct and indirect socialization. By direct socialization is meant the learning and imprinting that occurs by being in the age cohort centrally involved in the events under consideration (a member of the work force during the Depression, for example). By indirect socialization is meant being from a cohort that was affected, but through a more passive process (being a child during the Depression). Both have important ramifications for the development of each generation's profile, but the dynamics of that impact may very well be different.

What does all this suggest in concrete terms for the empirical study of generations? Fundamentally, it suggests that one cannot look at a population at a particular point in time, neatly divide it into equal age groups, and call each a generation. Generational analysis requires either starting with a particular age group and considering the key forces that would act as direct and indirect socializing agents in the development of its unique personality, or starting with a particular set of events or a period and examining the way in which it directly or indirectly affects the personality of different generations. In addition, it suggests that the problem of overlap makes a definitive analysis of multiple generations in a single study extremely difficult in the best of circumstances and impossible in many situations. One can do such analysis on age cohorts but not on generations.

GENERATIONS, LIFE CYCLE, AND PERIODS

Armed with this understanding of generation, we can now return to the notion of individual change beyond that attributable to generation. In particular, we are interested in the effects of age that are not due to its interaction with historical and societal forces, but that are more directly associated with the aging process and change related to the passage of time.

Generations and Politics

Many changes take place within an individual as he or she grows older. Many of these changes are not likely to affect how one views the social and political world, but some will. In particular, processes, such as cognitive development, the routinization of attitudes and behaviors through repetition, and the continuous refinement of those attitudes and behaviors through personal life experiences and contact with the social and political world, can clearly lead to changes over time (Campbell, et al., 1960; Milbrath and Goel, 1977; Wolfinger and Rosenstone, 1980; Nie, et al., 1974; Hudson and Binstock, 1976; Abramson, 1983; Jennings and Niemi, 1981). One's attitude about the effectiveness of elections for choosing political leaders, for example, is determined in part by the capacity of an individual to grasp the theory underlying the electoral process, in part by the gathering of specific information about the actual mechanics of the process, and in part by one's repeated experience with the process over time. All of these elements are related to the life cycle. While the specific way in which the life cycle affects attitudes, opinions, and behaviors depends in part on the particular attitudes, opinions, and behaviors involved, several general observations can be made about how it does so.

First, there does not appear to be any theoretical or empirical reason to assume that one ever stops the iterative process of learning and reevaluating. Second, when the entire life cycle from birth to death is considered, the rate of learning and changing appears to slow (Dennis, 1973; Dawson, et al., 1977). However, when only adulthood is considered, the rate of change directly attributable to the effects of the life cycle should be considered essentially linear. That is, once the rapid cognitive and educational developments associated with childhood and adolescence have occurred, there are no solid biological or experiential arguments to suggest that there should be less change and development in one's forties than in one's thirties, or in one's sixties than in one's fifties, etc. (short of the physical and mental infirmities that can be associated with very old age). Third, the pattern of change associated with the life cycle should be relatively constant from one generation to another, when other factors are controlled for. The concept of the life cycle assumes a process that is similar for all groups and for all age cohorts over time. While members of one generation may hold different attitudes from members of another one, the independent effects of aging on those attitudes should be the same.

In addition to the effects of the life cycle described above, there is one other independent effect on the development of attitudes, opinions, and behaviors that needs to be considered: period effects. By period effects is meant social, political, cultural, and economic events that affect all generations and all age cohorts in a similar manner. Watergate may have had some important generational effects that impressed those who were children at the time in one way, those who were relatively new participants in the electoral process in a somewhat different way, and those who were long-time participants in yet a third way, but it also (most likely) had a more-general effect that operated in a constant manner across all generations and all age groups. This would be considered a period effect. The effect of mass-media campaigns on the loosening of partisan ties for all cohorts in a society, or the increased participation across the board that might result from a particularly important or interesting election are also examples of period effects. Such effects can be short-lived (as with the increased participation due to the dynamics of a particular election) or more long lasting (as with the loosening of partisan attachments), but the defining characteristic is its uniform impact.

The final set of effects to be discussed are those that result from the *interaction* of generation, life cycle, and period effects. While each of the three former concepts are theoretically and methodologically distinct, it is possible for additional effects on

Generations and Politics

political attitudes, opinions, and behaviors to result from the interaction of two (or more) of them. For example, a man who is 25 years old in 1984 might hold certain attitudes towards civil rights that are in part determined by his age, in part determined by his generation, and in part determined by the political atmosphere of the period, but his attitudes will also be in part determined by the unique interaction of his age and generation, or his age and the period, which distinguish them from attitudes of 25 year olds in 1980 or members of his generation who are 20 or 30. Such interactions can prove important to a more complete understanding of the interrelationships among generation, life cycle, distinct periods, and political orientations.

DEFINING THE SIXTIES GENERATION

We would now like to begin to apply some of the general concepts discussed in this chapter to the specific case to be studied in this book: the 1960s and the sixties generation. Consistent with the approach discussed above, we begin by identifying the bounds of the general period under investigation. There is a fair amount of discretion in such a selection process. Despite the common term used to describe the period, "the sixties" began some time after 1960 and ended some time in the early seventies. While there are, no doubt, other reasonable points at which the period could be considered to have begun, in this study 1963 is used. The year 1963 was chosen for several reasons. It was in 1963 that the civil-rights movement thrust itself into the public consciousness with the massive march on Washington (a year later the inner cities erupted in a less organized and civil expression of blacks' concerns). It was in 1963 that involvement of the United States in Vietnam began to accelerate, that public concern over that involvement began to crystallize, and that the Congress renewed the Selective Service

Act (the next year would bring the Gulf of Tonkin Resolution and the first large demonstrations at Berkeley). It was also in 1963 that the Students for a Democratic Society (SDS) became a force in campus politics, it being the year after the release of the Port Huron Statement. The "British Invasion" of pop music and pop culture was also launched in 1963, with the Beatles making their first appearance in the United States the very next year. American music was also changed forever with Bob Dylan's (and others') electrifying performance at the Newport Folk Festival. Finally, it was in 1963 that Kennedy was assassinated, an event considered by many to mark the end of "America's Eden" (Jones, 1980; p. 77).

Identifying the end of the sixties as a sociopolitical period is also somewhat of a judgment call, though two dates seem the most likely candidates. The first would be that of the end of the direct involvement of the United States in the Vietnam War, which came with the signing of the peace treaty in 1973. The second would be the year of the resignation of Nixon, in August of 1974. Since much of the Watergate revelations involved issues that directly or indirectly tied into the important issues of the sixties, and since, for many people, Nixon had come to symbolize "the establishment" during that period, we chose the latter year as representing the end of the sixties.

Having demarcated the period of the sixties, the events of which served as socializing agents, it is now necessary to identify the cohorts that were most likely to be affected by them. Consistent with the arguments made in the previous section, we must consider both whom the events of the sixties most revolved around, and whether cohorts were directly or indirectly affected by them. Again these decisions have an arbitrariness to them and should be considered as tendencies rather than hard-and-fast rules. Despite this, however, certain characteristics of the period do suggest possible groupings. If the events and experiences of the 1960s revolved around anyone,

Generations and Politics

they revolved around the young. It was a period, for better or worse, when ideas, trends, music, etc., seemed to flow from young to old, rather than in the more-traditional direction. It was the young who gathered at Newport, Monterey, and Woodstock, who crowded Yankee Stadium to scream and faint over the Beatles; it was the young who marched in the streets and on the campuses; it was the young who died in the battlefields. More specifically, we would argue that the age group that most directly experienced the events of the period ranged from the beginnings of the teen years (13) when one was first likely to immerse oneself in the music, clothing, culture, and ideas of the period, to the midtwenties (24), when one was either finished with college and/or beginning to face the harsh realities of earning a living, raising a family, and the other responsibilities that come with growing older.

Beyond this age cohort, we also define the cohorts that immediately precede and follow it. Recall that periods like the sixties not only affect those who directly experience the events of the time, but also those who are indirectly socialized by them. In this case, individuals who were alive during the period from 1963 to 1974 but who were too young to become involved directly (ages one to 12) were being affected by such a socialization process. In addition, the cohort immediately preceding the "experienced" segment of the population, who were young enough to be attracted to the events of the period, but whose generational profile and position in the life cycle made full immersion into its culture unlikely, is also defined. The ages for this "ambivalent" group start with 25 and end, somewhat arbitrarily, at 36 (chosen in part because it seems a transitional age from young adult to middle age and in part because it adds some symmetry to the categories).

With the three divisions described above we have now identified the age cohorts that, to varying degrees, constitute the sixties generation. Individuals over the age of 36, while likely to have been affected by the period in some way, are not considered to have had their generational character fundamentally altered by it. Instead, they are treated as a collection of various generations that reacted to rather than were socialized by or truly experienced those events. These generational subdivisions are summarized in Table 1.1.

TABLE 1.1
Description of Generations and Subgenerations

Generation	Subgeneration	Description	Age*
Sixties		Individuals who were socialized in, who experienced, or who were ambivalent to the events of 1963 to 1974.	1–35
	Socialized	Individuals who were old enough to be alive in the 1960s but too young to have directly experienced it.	1–12
	Experienced	Individuals who were of an age to have directly participated in the culture of the 1960s.	13–24
	Ambivalent	Individuals who were of an age to have been torn between the norms of the participants of the 1960s and the norms of previous generations.	25–36
Reactive**		The portion of the population which, while affected by the 60s, were unlikely to have their (undefined) generational characteristics significantly altered.	37 +

*Age during the period from 1963 to 1974.
**Residual category of many generations.

We have, so far, spoken of the sixties as a point in time, and of age cohorts as static entities, each identified by its own static relationship to the period (children were socialized by it; teenagers and adolescents experienced it; and young adults were ambivalent towards it). In reality, however, the sixties as defined here extend over a 12-year span, during which individuals moved from childhood to adolescence to adulthood at distinct times. In order to preserve the utility of the concepts of generation, life cycle, and period, but still acknowledge their dynamic qualities, it would be better to conceive of the sixties as a flow of events and the "static relationships" as *processes*. That is, individuals, and individuals aggregated into age cohorts, are distinguished by their unique combinations of ambivalence towards, experience of, and socialization by the events of the sixties rather than by a more artificial "either/or" classification. At the individual level, this would mean, for example, that someone who was 13 in 1963 and who, therefore, spent all of the critical years from 13 to 24 "experiencing" the sixties would be distinguished from someone who was 8 in 1963, and who, therefore, was partly socialized by the period and who partly experienced it more directly. Similarly, it allows us to distinguish both of the above from someone who was 20 in 1963 and so partly experienced the sixties directly, but also was old enough to be in an ambivalent situation in the latter half of the period. These finer distinctions can then be combined into age cohorts in a way that captures more fully the dynamic interaction which is occurring at the individual level (how this is made operational empirically is discussed in Chapter Three).

SUMMARY AND CONCLUDING REMARKS

In this chapter we have outlined the basic elements that underly the notion of change in the political attitudes, opinions, and behaviors of democratic publics and have begun to apply some of them in defining the parameters of the 1960s and the sixties generation. The concept of mass political change has several dimensions that must be distinguished. It can occur suddenly and dramatically or gradually; it can occur because groups and individuals within the population undergo transformations, because the population itself is changed by the death of the members of one cohort and their replacement by the members of new cohorts, or by some combination of both. Finally, it can be dissected and understood only with an understanding of the differences among the effects of generation, life cycle, and distinct historical periods.

A generation is a cohort of similarly aged individuals who have been exposed to historical, social, cultural, economic, and political events in such a way as to imprint the personality and world view of that cohort permanently, giving it a unique character. Properly identifying a generation requires, first, a realization that the development of a generational profile is a fluid process akin to individual socialization; second, a careful identification of the period(s) deemed most critical in this socialization process; and third, sensitivity not only in choosing which age cohorts are most likely to be affected by the events in question but also in identifying whether that impact is direct or indirect. Even with these precautions, one must remain aware that, in many ways, the concept of generation is an artificial cataloguing of what is essentially a dynamic process.

Beyond change that results from generational replacement, change can also result from the life cycle and from the effects of particular periods. Effects of the life cycle result from changes associated with aging and the cognitive and experiential development which accompanies it. Such change is assumed to be relatively constant for all generations and to be essentially linear in adulthood. Period effects are those that result from particular events, but that, unlike generational effects, have an impact on the entire population in a similar way. Finally, interaction effects are those that result from the unique combinations of the influence of generation, periods, and/or the life cycle which different cohorts experience at particular times.

Applying these observations to "the sixties" first requires defining what one means by that term. The sixties are defined in this research as the period beginning in 1963 and ending in 1974. These endpoints were chosen because they encompass most of the social, political, and cultural elements that have become emblematic of that period. The population was then divided into the sixties generation (and its subgenerations) depending on whether the interaction of age and history was seen as being largely one of indirect socialization, direct experience, ambivalence, or some combination of them. Cohorts not falling into any of these categories are considered members of other, undefined generations. While this latter group was clearly affected by the sixties, they are assumed to be *reacting* to the period rather than having their generational profiles fundamentally shaped by it.

REFERENCES

Abramson, Paul R. *Political Attitudes in America*. San Francisco: W. H. Freeman, 1983.

Andersen, Kristi. "Generation, Partisan Shift, and Realignment: A Glance Back at the New Deal." In Nie, et al., *The Changing American Voter*. Cambridge, Mass.: Harvard University Press, 1979, pp. 74–95.

———. *The Creation of a Democratic Majority*. Chicago: University of Chicago Press, 1979.

Burnham, Walter Dean. "The Changing Shape of the American Political Universe." *American Political Science Review,* 59 (1965), pp. 7–28.

———. *Critical Elections and the Mainspring of American Politics*. New York: Norton, 1970.

Campbell, Angus, Philip E. Converse, Warren E. Miller, and Donald E. Stokes. *The American Voter*. New York: John Wiley, 1960.

Dawson, Richard E., Kenneth Prewitt, and Karen S. Dawson. *Political Socialization*. Boston: Little, Brown, 1977.

Dennis, Jack (ed.). *Socialization To Politics*. New York: John Wiley, 1973.
Erikson, Erik H. *Identity, Youth and Crisis*. New York: Norton, 1968.
Freud, Sigmund. *New Introductory Lectures on Psychoanalysis*. Translated by James Strachey. New York: Norton, 1964.
Hudson, Robert H., and Robert H. Binstock. "Political Systems and Aging." In Robert H. Binstock and Ethel Shanas (eds.) *Handbook of Aging and the Social Sciences*. New York: Van Nostrand, 1976.
Inglehart, Ronald. *The Silent Revolution*. Princeton: Princeton University Press, 1977.
Jennings, M. Kent, and Richard G. Niemi. *The Political Character of Adolescence*. Princeton: Princeton University Press, 1974.
——. *Generations and Politics*. Princeton: Princeton University Press, 1981.
Jones, Landon Y. *Great Expectations*. New York: Ballantine Books, 1980.
Key, V. O., Jr. "A Theory of Critical Elections." *Journal of Politics*, 17 (1955), pp. 3–18.
——. "Secular Realignment and the Party System." *Journal of Politics*, 21 (1959), pp. 198–210.
Lambert, T. Allen. "Generations and Change: Towards a Theory of Generations as a Force in Historical Processes." *Youth and Society*, 4 (September, 1972), pp. 21–46.
Mannheim, Karl. "The Problem of Generations." In Philip G. Altbach and Robert S. Laufer (eds.). *The New Pilgrims*. New York: David McKay, 1972.
Maslow, Abraham. *Towards a Psychology of Being*. New York: D. Van Nostrand, 1962.
Milbrath, Lester W., and M. L. Goel. *Political Participation*. Chicago: Rand McNally, 1977.
Nie, Norman H., Sidney Verba, and Jae-On Kim. "Political Participation and the Life Cycle." *Comparative Politics*, 6 (1974), pp. 319–340.
Nie, Norman H., Sidney Verba, and John R. Petrocik. *The Changing American Voter*. Cambridge, Mass.: Harvard University Press, 1979.
Sigel, Roberta S., and Marilyn Brookes Hoskin. "Perspectives on Adult Political Socialization—Areas of Research." In S. A. Renshon (ed.). *Handbook of Political Socialization*. New York: The Free Press, 1977, pp. 259–293.
Sundquist, James L. *The Dynamics of the Party System*. Washington, D.C.: Brookings, 1973.
Wolfinger, Raymond E., and Steven J. Rosenstone. *Who Votes*. New Haven: Yale University Press, 1980.

CHAPTER 2

The Sixties and the Sixties Generation: An Overview

In the previous chapter we began to define the boundaries of both the era known as "the sixties" and the generation that, in a variety of ways, was most likely to have its unique personality shaped by that era. In this chapter we take a closer look at the period and the generation, focusing on the elements that made both unique and the elements that were likely to have political ramifications. The next three sections present cultural, economic, and political dimensions of the period respectively and examine the events and trends that make it distinct. Section five theorizes on the connection among the cultural, economic, and political aspects of the period and the development of political attitudes, opinions, and behaviors within both the sixties generation and the rest of the population. Section six extends this discussion to the periods since 1974, describing change both in the cultural, economic, and political environments, and in the sixties generation itself. The final section is a summary and conclusion.

THE CULTURE OF THE SIXTIES

Any attempt to summarize the culture of the sixties, especially in a few pages, is bound to fall short of its mark. This is so because the events of the period are often contradictory and, initially, directly affected only subcultures that were loosely connected to each other and to mainstream society. Nonetheless, one of the dominant characteristics that separates this brief period from others in the history of the United States was the tendency for subcultural rituals, ideas, and lifestyles rapidly to become part of the dominant, hegemonic culture (though often in distorted ways). This characteristic is critical to the underlying structure of the sixties and warrants a closer look.

Large, diverse societies such as the United States consist of discrete subcultures the norms of which differ markedly from each other. These cultures spring from a variety of sources: ethnicity, race, sex, region, class, or age, for example. Overarching these subcultures, however, is a dominant, hegemonic culture (Gramsci, 1971; Williams, 1973; Sahlins, 1976; Gitlin, 1980), which is representative of the mainstream of society. This macroculture reflects the values and norms of the segment of society that dominates all others economically, politically, and socially. While there is an exchange relationship that exists between this culture and the various subcultures, for the most part it is the former that dominates the relationship: the values of the latter are discarded as members of a subculture are assimilated. This assimilation is neither complete nor universal. Furthermore, the hegemonic culture does incorporate aspects of some subcultures, but by and large the exchange is weighted in favor of the mainstream (much in the same way that colonialist nations dominate the cultures of the subjugated nations, yet rarely fail to incorporate aspects of those cultures into their own).

The Sixties and the Sixties Generation

In the sixties, however, it appears that the weighting of this exchange shifted in dramatic ways. While the dominant culture of white, middle-class and middle-aged male America never lost control of the society's norms, it did seem to momentarily lose its grip. For a brief while, the values that came to public dominance were not flowing exclusively from the hegemonic center, but instead seeped in from several distinct subgroups. In particular, but not exclusively, this new influence came from black America and black Africa, from parts of the Orient, from working-class America and England, and primarily from the youth cultures of America and England.

Black America has always had a distinctiveness that is based in part on its African heritage, in part on its class position, and in part on the unique and unfortunate circumstances of its history. Four factors in the 1960s changed the relationship of this subculture with the prevailing culture of middle America. The first factor was demographic. Beginning in the late fifties and early sixties blacks increased both in absolute numbers and as a percentage of the overall population. Their average income relative to the white population rose; and due to migration, their numbers greatly increased outside of the South (and especially in urban areas of the Northeast).[1] The second factor was a heightened sense of black consciousness and cultural pride, which led to an exploration of both their American and ancestral African roots (Blake, 1980). The third factor was the rise to prominence of black leaders and the related increase in the number and variety of demands made by the black community. Finally, political victories in the courts, the Congress, and the streets led to an environment that increased the possibility of blacks having a political say more commensurate with their numbers (Boskin, 1980). All of these factors were of course interrelated, and all led to greater visibility for blacks and issues of black concern. The combination of greater visibility, greater power, and a concern for understanding, preserving, and developing a unique black culture caused that subculture to have an unusually powerful influence on the values of white middle-class Americans. This influence could be seen in the music, dress, and language of the period, and as is discussed later, in the attitudes and opinions that were prevalent during the period as well.

At the same time that Afro-American culture was influencing the norms of the larger society, an interest in things Oriental was also blossoming in the West (Myerhoff, 1980). Superficial trappings of the East were quick to catch on. Incense, jewelry, gauze clothing, and the like were pervasive, as were various forms of Oriental art. The teachings of Eastern philosophers and religious leaders were extremely popular during this period, and books like the *Tibetan Book of the Dead*, the *Koran, Bhagavad Gita, Be Here Now,* and *Siddhartha*, as well as Oriental poetry, became best sellers. The Beatles' celebrated visit to India and their association with the Mahesh Yogi greatly enhanced an interest in the East. Western rock music often took on a decidedly Eastern flavor, and musicians such as Ravi Shankar enjoyed unprecedented popularity in the West, both in their own right and as the musical gurus of many Western rock stars. A generation that had by most accounts rejected organized religion found itself in the ashrams of various religious movements that directly or indirectly based their teachings on the philosophies of the Orient. Transcendental meditation, practically unheard of a few years earlier, was widely practiced from desert communes to corporate board rooms. Again, the music, dress, and language of the sixties came to reflect this influence, as did the attitudes, opinions, and world views of a large segment of American culture.[2]

Other ethnic and religious subcultures also found their way into mainstream thought and action. Various aspects of Native American culture were popularized for instance, from jewelry and dress, to the struggle of A.I.M. (The American Indian Movement), to the writings of Carlos Casteneda. Values and lifestyles of long-isolated groups like the Quakers, Mennonites, and Amish also were popularized in unexpected places. In an almost bewildering number of ways these subcultures would be intertwined and reshaped into a culture unrecognizable as any one tradition or ideology, but clearly arising from various aspects of all of them.

In addition to the ethnic and religious influences, a less-obvious, but no-less-important change in the traditional flow of values was taking place. America's idols were coming not from the movies, as they once had, but from music; not from Hollywood but from Philadelphia, Detroit, San Francisco, and Liverpool; and not from the glamorous upper class and from high society but from the working class, from the "wrong side of town." It was the decade of the antihero, of the workingman's uniform of dirty blue jeans and a denim shirt. The voices of the sixties generation were to a surprising degree the voices of the children of the working class.[3]

This reversed flow of values was evident between age groups as well as between classes (Friedenberg, 1980). Middle America found itself following the lead of middle America's children. There was a tremendous and well-publicized chasm between the attitudes, opinions, and values of the young and old ("The Generation Gap"). The social and cultural agenda itself was dominated to an unusual degree by the issues of the young. While differences between young and old have been noted since the time of Plato, never before had the rebellious, energetic, experimental, and undisciplined nature of youth been given such free rein and commanded so much attention. To older generations, the youth movement was either a threat to the traditional values of America or a lifestyle to be emulated, but it was a force to be reckoned with and not just a stage to be tolerated.

Given that these subcultures, and foreign cultures, have

existed for years, decades and even centuries before, what was it about the sixties that partly reversed the usual relationship between them and the hegemonic culture in the United States? The answer lies partly in the unique circumstances of that decade. First and foremost, it was during this decade that members of the baby boom came of age. In absolute numbers and in relative percentages, there were more teenagers around than ever before (Lipset and Ladd, 1972). This acted both to increase the possibilities of interaction among the young themselves, among the young of different subcultures, and among different generations and to draw more attention to their activities. Part of the strength of this generation was due to strength in numbers (see Table 2.1 below).

Second, in the sixties, universal and instantaneous communications were first made possible through television. Between 1950 and 1970 the number of television stations increased 500 percent, while the percentage of households with TV sets jumped from 10 percent to almost 100 percent. Whether through entertainment or the news, mainstream America was inundated with information about the world and about itself. And often to the dismay of parents, it was the children who, "glued to that damn box" hour after hour, night after night, took it all in. Information that once had to be sought out actively could now be taken in passively and in the privacy of one's own home (Zukin and Snyder, 1984). Events, situations, and lifestyles that were limited to certain strata of society or certain parts of the world could now be indirectly experienced by the entire population. The visual nature of TV added both to its appeal and to its impact (McCluhan, 1964). The intermingling of cultural biases, social norms, and the information and entertainment qualities of television often juxtaposed unrealistic notions of life in middle America with images of poverty, of cities in flames, of a war without meaning, and of students in protest against "the establishment."

Much like a social magnifying glass, the media focused national attention on many aspects of American life, bringing a variety of subcultures to popular attention. This increased visibility of new and often exotic ideas and behaviors helped to increase the likelihood of further innovation and experimentation. Magnifying glasses can also distort one's perspective, however, especially if the lens is flawed or if the user is unable to also view the object with the naked eye. The popularity of fads and the strength of movements and subcultures were often distorted as the media exaggerated their importance by the mere fact of their attention. This increased the chances that events pertaining to a small segment of the population would have ramifications well beyond those it would have had otherwise. Also, it often led to the artificial growth of some movements, as well as their rapid and occasionally untimely decline (Gitlin, 1980).

A third factor in the shifting of values was the increase in public education during this period, and in higher education in particular (Laufer, 1972). Greater educational opportunities meant that 75 percent of 17-year-olds graduated from high school in 1970, as opposed to 55 percent in 1950 and almost a third of the 18- to 24-year-old population went to college in 1970, whereas only 15 percent did so in 1950. Over the period the median number of school years completed jumped from a little over nine to over 12. The results of these trends were nothing short of revolutionary. Even more than television, education introduced the young to ideas, traditions, and values previously unknown to them. These new ideas both gave this generation a choice in how they would live and demonstrated the relativity of the values they had held as incontrovertible and universal. Education also made this generation aware of the differences (as well as the inconsistencies) between social norms and values taught to them as children, and those actually practiced all around them (Eisen and Steinberg, 1980).

The increase in higher education also provided a forum for direct interaction between members of different cultures and subcultures. Individuals who had rarely stepped outside their own subculture, be it a city neighborhood, a rural community, or an upper-middle-class suburb, suddenly found themselves face to face with representatives of cultures literally and figuratively foreign to them. Again this intermingling offered its participants new options in lifestyles and challenged the inherent logic of the ideas on which they were raised.

Besides introducing students to new cultures both in and outside the classroom, the educational process also offered an incubator in which these various cultures and their hybrids could grow. College campuses became not only places to learn sciences and the liberal arts, but also laboratories for personal experimentation. Students could try alternate lifestyles in an environment where the costs of such experimentation were minimized and in which the influx of new blood and new ideas was constant.

In summary, the sixties owed its unique cultural character primarily to the unprecedented number of young people, to the impact of television, and to the effects of the increased availability of higher education.

THE ECONOMICS OF THE SIXTIES

The late fifties and the 1960s were a period of almost unprecedented growth in the United States. Almost any measure of personal or national wealth demonstrates this. Family income nearly doubled between 1950 and 1970 (in constant 1981 dollars). In addition, while this growth was not universal, there were encouraging signs that many on the lower rungs of the economic ladder were slowly closing the gap between themselves and their wealthier neighbors. For example, the percentage of people living below the poverty line decreased from 25 percent in 1960 to about 15 percent in 1970. This decline in poverty was even more dramatic for blacks.

What did the favorable economic environment mean for the generation that grew out of it? First, it was partly responsible for the size of the sixties generation. The optimism generated by the economic boom that followed World War II led both to the personal confidence that one could support a large family and the sense that these children would find themselves in a situation that would be worth inheriting. This personal decision was bolstered by the more general sense that more children now would mean an even stronger economy in the future because the number of consumers and producers would be increased. So, corporations awarded shares of stock to employees as they had new children; *Time* magazine heralded the increased birth rate as the addition of millions of "new consumers"; public service signs in New York subways proclaimed "Every day 11,000 babies are born in America. This means new business, new jobs, new opportunities"; and a *Life* magazine cover story was titled "Kids: Built-in Recession Cure" (Jones, 1980, pp. 40–41). In short, if it was the size of the new generation that in part led to its unusual cultural impact, it was economic prosperity and a desire to keep it going that led to the size of the generation.

The economics of the time were also responsible for a very large percentage of this new generation's being raised in the comfortable, middle-class environment. This was so because more and more families were moving into the middle class from lower classes. As one indication of this trend, the percentage of the population with white collar occupations increased from just over 35 percent in 1950 to close to 50 percent by 1970. Most of the economic incentives for larger families described above were aimed at this middle segment. The late fifties and early sixties were, in Jones' words, the era of "the big barbecue" (pp. 40–53).

Economic conditions were not only responsible for the size of the middle-class "baby boom" generation, but also for its cultural distinctiveness. They accounted as well for the cultural distinctiveness of the other classes and subcultures in American society. This was so for several reasons. First, as Inglehart argues (1971, 1976, 1977, 1981), there seems to be a tendency for generations raised in an environment of economic security to seek out lifestyles and to develop values that are "postmaterialist" in their orientation. That is, such individuals are less likely to have to deal with issues of material survival and accordingly are free to pursue personal and social fulfillment. While Inglehart's thesis is based upon Maslow's concept of a need hierarchy, one need not subscribe to Maslow to see the connection between economic security and personal lifestyle. The notion can be accepted that attention is more likely to be turned to issues of the quality of life as basic material needs are satisfied without also accepting the fact (as do Maslow and Inglehart) that, once such a shift in attention is made, it is resistant to change in the face of new economic situations. The developmental theory of Rogers (1961) takes just such an approach. The idea of a hierarchy of needs can be discarded altogether if it is assumed that, when basic needs are satisfied, the costs of more esoteric pursuits are reduced, making such pursuits more likely. The main point remains unchanged no matter which level of theory is used to underpin it: the economic prosperity in which the sixties generation was raised allowed it to develop values and behaviors that extended beyond the constant search for economic security, which characterized their immediate predecessors.

Related to this argument is a crucial distinction between a generation that seeks economic security and eventually achieves it, and a generation that finds itself raised in such an environment. Most of the sixties generation falls into the latter category. Its members were raised in a family and social environment that lauded the virtues of the work ethic at the same time that the family and society wanted something more, something better for its young. As a result, this new generation received the benefits of this ethic without paying its costs, and therefore found it hard to accept as a way of life. Some of its members also saw certain limits of this ethic, since material comfort did not guarantee personal happiness or fulfillment. In short, the children of the sixties were in many ways no different from the generations that preceded them: they sought to improve their condition. However, where their parents looked around and saw the costs of poverty and a lack of economic security, this new cohort looked around and saw the costs of too great a preoccupation with personal wealth and security. And since the values of the hegemonic culture extolled wealth and security, it was natural for this generation to look outside that culture for new values and role models (see Flacks, 1967).

At the same time that the children of middle-class America were looking for an ethic to call their own, numerous subcultures were also feeling the impact of the prosperity of the times, though in somewhat different ways. To the extent that economic improvements did reach into segments of the society such as the black community, the working-class community, or the poor community, it generated a desire for more, having given them a taste of what was possible and of what was due them. In a manner akin to international theories of relative deprivation and the "J-Curve" theory of protest and rebellion, these groups began to increase their demands for more social and economic rewards after they had received a little of both. In addition, the tremendous visibility of the prosperity of white middle-class America fueled this desire to be included and to be included quickly (Bell, 1975; Hirschman, 1982).

Several related, but more specific effects of the economic conditions also played a part in defining the nature of the times. First, relative economic security increased the amount of leisure time and the amount of personal income that could be spent on entertainment. In 1950 $10 billion was spent on leisure and pursuits, while this was increased to over $40 billion by 1970. Second, this ability to spend money on leisure pursuits increased the likelihood that entrepreneurs would seek to capitalize on it. Any marketable ideas, especially those aimed at the large and growing sixties generation, were likely to be spread throughout the country very quickly in an attempt to sell them to as large a segment of the population as possible. Whether in the record industry, the clothing industry, or the media, there was money to be made in the culture of the sixties. Third, the economic prosperity of the period was largely responsible both for the boom in public higher education and for the greater availability of financial support for college tuition. As a result, the contribution of education to the unique character of the sixties discussed in the previous section can be traced in part to economic roots.

Perhaps the most important effect of economic conditions was felt after the counterculture began to take hold. The alienated middle-class young, militant blacks, and the rebellious poor and members of the working class often vocally and physically challenged the norms, values, and property of the dominant members of society. While this challenge engendered violence on both sides, one must marvel in ret-

The Sixties and the Sixties Generation

rospect at the relative tolerance demonstrated by members of the mainstream, especially in their official capacity (the elected government, the courts, the military and police). Their tolerance can be attributed (in part) to the economic conditions of the time. Were resources scarcer, or security more tenuous, rhetoric and behavior protesting the system would have been more harshly dealt with. In addition, the middle-class "heart" of this rebellion made it hard to draw clear battle lines, making retribution less acceptable, less likely, and less severe.

THE POLITICS OF THE SIXTIES

To this point we have discussed the environment of the sixties in general cultural, social, and economic terms. While all contribute to the development of political attitudes, opinions, and behaviors, there are also political influences that colored the character of the period. First and foremost was the war in Vietnam.

The war in Vietnam politicized everyone to some extent, but the sixties generation to the greatest degree, supplying a rallying point for already developing political sentiments (Keniston, 1968). For the sixties generation itself, the most immediate impact was the draft. Vietnam-related drafts were begun in 1965, and by December over 40,000 young men were being called up each month (Jones, p. 107). By the war's end, 1.6 million American draftees had seen combat in Vietnam, and over 50,000 never returned, with hundreds of thousands returning disabled. Practically everyone we have classified as a member of that generation had a relative or a friend, or knew of a peer, who had been drafted, and most knew of someone who had been wounded or killed. Every male who turned 17 between 1965 and 1974 was required to register for the draft, and faced the decision of whether or not to do so. As a matter of simple self-interest, therefore, the Vietnam War forced members of this generation to think politically and to consider their relationship to the larger political forces that were intruding into their lives.

The extent to which the protests against the war were motivated by pure self-interest can be exaggerated, however. The fact remains that the sheer size of the sixties generation meant that the probability of any individual's being drafted was relatively small. During the war, 27 million men were of draft age, and 11 million were actually called up, but the 1.6 million that saw combat in Vietnam represented only 6 percent of the eligible population. In addition, half of the generation—the women—were not subject to the draft, though they were active in many protest movements against the war. The large pool of potential draftees which this huge cohort provided also afforded the luxury of generous deferments for college and graduate study, meaning that many of the most vocal opponents of the war were not only the least likely to be drafted, but, given the threat of being drafted if expelled from school, were actually endangering their deferments by protesting. Finally, the fact that the Korean war did not inspire equivalent mass protests in the fifties, despite the numerous political parallels, adds further evidence that more was involved in the Vietnam protests than simple self-interest.

The politicizing effects of the war seem, therefore, to stem from a more complex interaction of events and circumstances. Vietnam was a televised war. Every evening the American public could watch the fighting, see the suffering not only of American soldiers but of the Vietnamese men, women and children. Romantic notions of war could not stand up to this visual documentary of the day-to-day horror in Vietnam. And as the media brought the *personal* anguish of the war into sharper and sharper focus (training their attention on an individual town obliterated in a fire fight, an individual family routed, an individual American soldier dying in his friend's arms, an individual child burnt and mutilated by napalm) the reasons justifying the debacle receded into a hazy obscurity. No rational political or moral imperative could justify the carnage. Out of all this emerged no cause worth dying for, no rallying point for public support.

The inequities of the draft system raised further questions concerning what values were actually being demonstrated by the war. This was a war fought by America's underclass: "Only 9% of college graduates saw combat duty. High school dropouts were twice as likely to see combat and four times as likely to be drafted. One study in Chicago discovered that men from low-income neighborhoods were three times as likely to die in Vietnam as men from upper-income neighborhoods" (Jones, p. 109). Blacks, while representing less than 11.6 percent of the combat soldiers in Vietnam, accounted for 24 percent of the combat deaths in 1965 (p. 110).

In addition, the draft deferment for students meant that their eligibility, while protected at one level, ran "over a minefield of eight years, from their nineteenth birthday until their 26th" (Jones, p. 108). In short, the draft combined a real concern for personal safety with obvious moral inequities and then allowed the resulting guilt, resentment, and fear to fester over as much as an eight-year period. The "revamping" of the draft in 1967 and 1968 into a lottery system simply added fuel to the fire, since the already obvious inequities were not forgotten, and the personal threat to students was increased. By this time, the war itself was the issue.

As much as the war was a catalyst for political action, it was also the perfect windmill for this Don Quixote of a generation to tilt at. This was a generation already suspicious of the values of the nation; a generation already active on campuses through such organizations as the SDS; a generation attracted to such liberal organizations as Vista and the Peace Corps; a generation already battle trained from its alliance with the civil-rights movement. The Vietnam war was an issue that, more than the others, could mobilize and interest a larger percentage of the generation, but it could do so in part because this was a generation looking for a cause. The war came to symbolize more than just a bad policy, but a bankrupt social order, and the protests and rallies and meetings became the new centers for community spirit, much in the same way that campuses, or concerts, or coffee houses did. The melding of social, cultural, and political alienation could be seen in the music, which combined an unsophisticated, often bizarre mixture of personal, social, and political revolution and independence; it expressed a celebration of individual uniqueness and common bonds that never coalesced into a consistent ideology but which reappeared in different guises depending on the circumstances (see Orman, 1984; Rosenstone, 1980. For a discussion of this blending of politics and culture in literature, see Dickstein, 1977).

While the war in Vietnam came to dominate political concerns, politics suffused the entire period. The roots of this generation lie in the optimism of the social programs of Kennedy and Johnson, such as the Peace Corps, Vista, the War on Poverty, and Civil Rights legislation. It was, therefore, this generation that was most uprooted by the assassination of Kennedy and by Johnson's perceived betrayal through Vietnam. What began as a search for something beyond personal security by developing a sense of social responsibility and community quickly grew into a more militant, undisciplined force as the acceptable avenues of behavior proved futile and as the more moderate, mainstream leaders of this cohort such as Eugene McCarthy, Robert Kennedy, and later George McGovern were prevented from achieving their goals.

The sixties was also the decade of political violence at all levels. Malcolm X, Medgar Evers, George Jackson, John and Robert Kennedy, and Martin Luther King all died because of their political beliefs or positions. Violence permeated many of the campus demonstrations, sometimes planned, sometimes the result of tension between opposing sides, or between demonstrators and the police. Domestic insurgency by militant groups such as the Weathermen or the Symbionese Liberation Army were common. While the extent of the actual violence remains unclear (Cobb and Elder, 1972; Epstein, 1975), the Black Panthers found themselves in the midst of political unrest and violent rhetoric. Finally, at Jackson State and Kent State student protestors and onlookers were killed by members of the National Guard. Relative to the domestic political violence in other nations, or even to the nonpolitical violence in the United States, the number of deaths and casualties might seem small, but in a nation where political battles seldom take such extreme forms, these events in so short a span of time suggest a highly politicized period. When one adds the indirectly political violence of the strikes and picket lines during the period, the inner-city violence and rioting in major cities throughout the country, and the violence against blacks in the South, the tenor of the times becomes quite clear. Even the tragic deaths of the generation's rock heros such as Hendrix, Joplin, and Morrison suggest something about the undercurrent of violent nihilism that lay just beneath the surface of the times.

Between the acceptable behavior of "Kennedy's Children" (Patrick, 1976) and the violent outbursts of revolution and counterrevolution lay the most distinctive political aspects of the period. Patterned on the nonviolent but disruptive tactics of Ghandi, Martin Luther King, Jr., and the Berrigan brothers, the sit-ins and protest marches of the campuses and cities, whether aimed at issues of civil rights, the war, or narrower issues of campus politics, became emblematic of a new approach to political involvement in the United States.

All of this is not to say that most Americans, or even most members of the new generation, were *directly* involved in these political activities (though clearly the number of people who did was greater than in recent times before or after). Rather it is to suggest that during this period politics permeated the times in ways that made not thinking about and being affected by it next to impossible. The lines between politics and education, or entertainment, or work or any of the other dimensions of society became blurred. The classroom was a political forum, as was the workplace and the concert hall. Woodstock was as much a political and social statement as it was a musical event. The lyrics of the Jefferson Airplane, Bob Dylan, the Who, the Beatles, and hundreds of other popular musicians and groups were filled with political and social commentary. Events like "Earth Day" combined entertainment, communalism, and politics in ways that paralleled partisan rallies of the late nineteenth century. Politics was not just in city hall; politics was not just in Washington; politics was not just in the voting booth—politics was in the air.

THE IMPACT OF CULTURE, ECONOMICS, AND POLITICS OF THE SIXTIES ON MASS ATTITUDES, OPINIONS, AND BEHAVIORS

The development of political attitudes, opinions, and behaviors, whether in an individual or in a class of individuals, is closely linked both to the structure of the society in which they are developed and the pattern of experiences that result from such social structures. While we will explore these relationships in detail for particular attitudes, opinions, and behaviors as they are introduced in subsequent chapters, a general discussion of the overall connection between the culture, economics, and politics of the sixties and mass political orientations is in order now.

By "political attitudes" is meant deep-seated feelings about the political system, the way it works, and one's relationship to it. Trust in government, a sense of political efficacy, and support for the political system are typical examples of political attitudes. One's political ideology is also an example of a deep-seated political orientation. Attitudes differ from opinions in that they usually are developed earlier, are more resistant to change, and are the general stuff upon which specific opinions are based (Bem, 1970; Triandis, 1971; Bennett, 1980).

In what way might the culture, economics, and politics of the sixties have affected the development of political attitudes? The answer to this is rather complicated, both because we must distinguish between the sixties generation, its subgenerations, and the presixties cohorts, and because the elements of the period itself were often pulling in very different directions. The popular attraction to mysticism and to Eastern philosophies (as well as certain aspects of the drug culture) led to a kind of removed attitude that emphasized tolerance and learning to live within the bounds of certain situations rather than struggling to change them. It emphasized passive rather than active interactions with one's environment. The socializing impact of such a philosophy might be to distance one completely from the world of politics, developing a kind of self-imposed alienation. Existentialism, popular during this period in the writings of Sartre, Brecht, and Pinter among others, also generated a sense of alienation, though characterized more by resignation than by acceptance. However, mysticism and existentialism also engendered a passive resistance to conformity that differentiated this form of nonparticipation from that of the more traditional apolitical citizens of Berelson (1952). The strong influence of black and working-class youth cultures would add to this sense of isolation a strong dose of mistrust of the political system, as well as a more rebellious, aggressive edge to the alienation and a heightened sense of group consciousness.

These subcultures and tendencies, combined with the middle-class predispositions of most of young white America, produced the unique characteristics of the generation's political profile. Raised in an environment that fostered a sense of personal and political efficacy together with a naïve trust in the fairness of the system, such a cohort would normally fall into the role of "model" citizen, one that participated at levels and in ways that kept the system legitimate while never disrupting the fundamental power relationships (Erikson, et al., 1980). All this changed, however, when this cohort, which held a high trust for society and which enjoyed personal and political power, encountered black America and young working-class America, which held little trust in society but had little power, while also being exposed to the philosophies of existentialism and Eastern religions. The result was a highly unstable set of attitudes which, depending on the combination that was displayed in any particular situation, could produce a generation of supportive, highly involved individuals, supportive, but uninvolved individuals, mistrusting and politically involved individuals, or mistrusting and politically inactive individuals. To some extent these types represent different segments of the generation, depending on the circumstances of their subgroup's socialization. But they also represent conflicting forces within individuals, tensions that released themselves in radically different ways at different times, depending on the symbols that activated certain combinations of attitudes (Bennett, 1980).

The economics of the times produced similar tensions. The prosperity of the period should have led to positive support and a sense of efficacy. However, the inequities that were made apparent as a result of the mingling of subcultures also produced envy or guilt depending on the group involved. Finally, the rejection of materialism, part of the Eastern view, added an element of indecision concerning the importance of such feelings (especially for those who already had material security). Again, the result is a highly volatile generation, capable of radically different views, both within individuals and across subgroups.

The politics of the period offered no easy solution to the diverse tendencies discussed so far. In part, "the system" worked. The civil-rights movement, the youth movement, the antiwar movement produced tangible and symbolic benefits that undoubtedly resulted in feelings of efficacy and support, and some level of trust. The sixties were also years of failure and disillusionment, however. The political violence and assassinations, the failed protests and the electoral defeats, the betrayal and lies of elected leaders produced feelings of disillusionment. Whether one was supportive or not, efficacious or not, trusting or not depended on one's perception of the system, one's political sympathies and causes, and one's sense (both on balance and in specific cases) of whether or not their goals were achieved.

The development of specific opinions (what issues are important, what solutions should be implemented, who should pay the costs, etc.) inasmuch as they are based on the same cultural, economic, and political environments, and to some extent, on the attitudes that result from those environments, are filled with the same conflicting pressures and inconsistencies as those discussed above. The open exchange between the various subcultures no doubt works to produce a more liberal orientation, as the problems, needs, and wants of different groups become better understood. The tendency of the young to champion more liberal causes adds to this orientation. For example, support for civil rights, economic aid for minorities and the poor, and aid to education seem natural positions to adopt. Opposition to the Vietnam war also seems an obvious stand to expect from the sixties generation.

To what extent the specific issues mentioned above led to concern over other issues by the sixties generation is difficult to determine even now. Did concern for minorities lead to a general interest in health care and employment? Did anti-Vietnam war feelings lead to an antimilitarist view? How was the mistrust of the government engendered by the war effort reconciled with a desire for government involvement in civil rights, desegregation, etc.? Answers to these questions are complicated by the crosspressures the middle-class segment of the generation was exposed to. How these issues were resolved ultimately depended on the relative strengths of the socialization effects of generation, race, class, and other associations with which an individual is involved.

As with the development of attitudes and opinions, the effect of the sixties on political behavior was also linked to a myriad of competing forces. The same pressures of culture, economics, and politics that push attitudes sometimes towards greater political support, sometimes towards an isolation from politics, and sometimes towards active rejection of the system can also lead to equally contradictory behavioral manifestations. The images of the representative of the sixties generation as political dropout, as social worker or campaign worker for progressive candidates, or as radical demonstrator and protestor all have a certain legitimacy to them precisely because the forces that move people in one

The Sixties and the Sixties Generation

(or more) of these directions were all present in that period (Gilmour and Lamb, 1975). From the black subculture came the lessons learned from the resistance of the civil-rights movement against the system and, later, from the more radical protests and violence of the urban riots and the militant organizations. From the East came further notions of passive resistance. From the middle class came an involvement in mainstream electoral politics. From youth came a rebellious unpredictability. And from all of them came experiences with failure that kept dropping out as an always viable alternative.

While the sixties generation was having its attitudes, opinions, and behaviors shaped in an inconsistent, often unpredictable manner, the generations dating from before the sixties also were reacting to the period. To some extent, these older cohorts were subject to the same pressures that their children and grandchildren endured. We therefore would expect some similar, though less extreme patterns of behavior to be displayed by the former groups. However, the events of this period were undoubtedly seen as a challenge to the norms and values that these earlier generations not only helped establish, but under which a large number of that group flourished. Thus, these older people could be expected to "dig in," to cling more strongly to long-held attitudes, opinions, and behaviors, and perhaps even move more strongly in the opposite direction of the sixties generation (Koeppen, 1980). That is, to become more supportive of the traditional system, more conservative in their political opinions, and more active in mainstream politics. Again, the specific form which the reaction of members of this group took depended upon the strength of the competing effects of prior socialization, the effects of the times, and of aging.

Finally, the sixties generation itself would be expected to show differences in attitudes, opinions, and behaviors depending on whether the cohorts were socialized by or directly experienced the events of the sixties. This difference, interacting with the cross pressures described above, adds additional combinations of political orientations to the already complex picture. Those socialized to be favorably inclined to nontraditional forms of behavior, but entering the adult population in a period when such participation had waned, might be more likely to drop out, for example. Alternately, someone who participated in the politics of the sixties and felt, on balance, that the costs outweighed the benefits might become alienated, while a younger member of the generation may enter the electorate invigorated by the indirect experiences of the sixties, but unscathed by aborted efforts and failed visions. Similarly, being raised and entering the adult population during times of economic prosperity, or during periods of political upheaval such as the Vietnam era should produce a different reaction than being raised during a period of economic prosperity or the Vietnam era but entering the world of politics directly when times have become economically more uncertain and politically more stable. In short, while the forces that form attitudes, opinions, and behaviors were present for the entire sixties generation, the specific influence which they exert would be different for different age cohorts within that generation.

PATTERNS OF CHANGE SINCE THE SIXTIES

Were attitudinal and behavioral patterns frozen and completely internalized at some point in an individual's or a group's development, we could end our general discussion at this point. But the changing tenor of the times and the continuous effects of aging make events that occur after a generation's character is essentially established important for understanding that generation's attitudes and behaviors. Two events clearly established the end of the sixties: the end

The Sixties and the Sixties Generation

of direct American involvement in Vietnam and the Watergate conspiracy. These provided both a real and a symbolic close to a period that had already showed signs of burning out on its own. The end of the war served both as a symbol of the effectiveness of the antiwar movement, which by this time had become the only unifying political force for the generation, and a death knell for any real chance of future generation-based political change. Without a common cause the movement was unable to refocus its energies in a new direction. The Watergate era briefly appeared to offer a new opportunity for activism against the system, but the nature of the issues and of Nixon's handling of them quickly precluded such ideological or generational politics. Instead, the issue became the removal of a corrupt group of politicians, a removal eventually sought by all but the most die-hard partisans. Watergate became a public cleansing of the disarray of the sixties, taking on a different meaning for different groups. For the sixties generation it was as close as they would get to a trial: old crimes and wrongdoings were unearthed or publicly relived, the guilty parties were rounded up, publicly humiliated, and sentenced or "exiled." Not all the "criminals" were caught, and not all were sentenced to everyone's satisfaction, but more was on trial (symbolically, at least) in those televised hearings and court cases than the break-in of the Democratic National Headquarters.

For different members of the presixties generation the ritual embodied different things. For Democrats it was the removal of a corrupt and uncooperative Republican administration that had bullied them for six years; for middle America it was the tragic removal of a public servant who had betrayed his oath; for ideological conservatives it was further evidence that Nixon in particular and the Republican party in general was failing as a mouthpiece for their political views; and for liberals it was further evidence of the corruption of the right. Finally, for Nixon supporters it was the last hurrah of the new left, the final blow from a generation that had disrupted the political scene for a decade.

For everyone, however, Watergate stood for two things. First, it was evidence of the failure of politics, a reason to move back to the pursuit of private goals in private ways (Hirschman, 1982). The tumult of the decade had already begun to show signs of wearing the population's political vigor thin. Watergate provided the final shove back to the pursuit of self-interest, to a more-encompassing, yet traditional alienation from politics. Second, Watergate signalled the end of the sixties. There would be no more talk of generation gaps, no more protests, riots, or even political candidates who were ideologically to the left, no more demands for immediate social change. Subcultures advocating alternate lifestyles, alternate political agendas, and alternate social structures still existed, but the ears and the eyes and the minds of mainstream America had turned away from them. What they did or said was no longer relevant, no longer newsworthy, and no longer entertaining.

The era of Ford and the campaign, election, and administration of Carter all typified this return to a consensual, middle-of-the-road political environment. The economic recession added to the closing of ranks around one's personal possessions and the quiet hoping that social, economic, and political problems would simply go away. When, instead, they worsened, and were added to by international incidents such as the Iranian Embassy takeover, the Soviet invasion of Afghanistan, and the subsequent grain embargo and Olympic boycott, the American public was forced back into the political world. But this was an older, battle-worn public still stinging from the events of the sixties. Change now meant change to the right, not because the population was so conservative but because it was so untied from any clear ideo-

The Sixties and the Sixties Generation

logical moorings. Carter was viewed as soft, indecisive, and a Democrat, so an individual viewed as tough, decisive, and a Republican was elected. The 1980 election did not demonstrate a public galvanized into decisive action. It demonstrated how difficult it had become to mobilize the public into political action even in the midst of economic and political disarray.

The mid- to late seventies were not without their social movements. During this period the women's movement, largely ignored during the sixties, reemerged as a force, and numerous citizen-action groups also developed during this decade (Boyte, 1980). But we had returned to group politics, where influence is wielded through campaign contributions, and strategic publicity and lobbying. The failure of the one attempt at public mobilization—the ERA—demonstrated the inability of vocal, active members of subcultures to capture the vocal, active support of mainstream America during this period.

And what of the sixties generation during these years? Three factors are important in considering its role. First, in terms of sheer numbers, it was during this era that they came to dominate the American electorate. As can be seen in Table 2.1, generational replacement was rapidly changing the composition of the adult population. In 1956, when the first segments of the cohort which would be ambivalently affected by the sixties entered the electorate, they comprised about 13 percent of that electorate. This percentage has been slowly increasing so that by 1976 the sixties generation accounted for over half the electorate, and by 1980 65 percent. In the sixties, by comparison, they accounted for an average of 39 percent. Ironically, this generation became a majority as its most distinctive behavior was disappearing.

Part of the explanation for this declining distinctiveness may lie in the average age of the members of that generation

TABLE 2.1
Percentage of the Electorate Made Up by and
Mean Age of the Sixties Generation

Year	1956	1960	1964	1968	1972	1976	1980
% of the electorate	13	22	29	39	48	55	65
Mean age	22	25	27	28	28	30	32

in the electorate. In 1956 this average age was about 22. In 1980 the average age was 32 (the fact that the generation aged ten years over a 24-year period is not due to the theory of relativity. It is the result of larger and younger subgenerations within the sixties generation entering the electorate and slowing down the aggregate aging process). By 1980 the age span of the sixties generation ran from 18 to 43. In terms of its age and its composition of subgenerations, the sixties generation has been undergoing internal change throughout the period under investigation.

The third and final point to note is that toward the end of the seventies a large percentage of this generation began to reach the age at which their social situation changed markedly. Marriage, children, occupational responsibilities, etc., all began to have a stronger grip on them, perhaps leading to related changes in political orientations. But these are issues to be dealt with later. Suffice it to say for now that it is in the mid- to late seventies that this generation established itself as the new mainstream in American politics.

SUMMARY AND CONCLUDING REMARKS

In this chapter we have briefly outlined some of the distinctive characteristics of the decade of the 1960s and established a link between that distinctiveness and the development of political attitudes, opinions, and behaviors. Central to this unique character was a tendency for the hegemonic culture of middle-class white America to become unusually responsive to subcultures and foreign cultures. This responsiveness, in which the youth culture of middle-class America served as a sort of repository for the various elements, resulted in both an exploration of a wider variety of lifestyles and values and in a questioning of the norms of the culture in which most Americans had been raised. It also resulted in an inconsistent, unstructured, and often superficial melding of these subcultures into the mainstream. The economic prosperity of the times served as a driving force for the Wanderlust of the middle class, as an inducement for more peripheral cultures to demand their share of that prosperity, and as a buffer against a reactionary stifling of the countercultural movement. Finally, the politics of the period combined events that forced society to question the nation's political priorities, that served as a focal point for more general disenchantment with the nation's social, cultural, economic, and political systems. Eventually, distinctions among these systems were blurred, as, for example, cultural events became political, and political events became cultural.

All of the events of the sixties acted on the development of mass political attitudes, opinions, and behaviors less by moving the country in a particular direction than by expanding the possible range and intensity of such orientations. Extremes in the levels of alienation, support, efficacy, and trust; in the choice of agendas and on particular issue stands; and in the level and type of participation: all seem to be likely effects of the cultural, economic, and political changes that characterized this period.

The political, social, cultural, and economic environments have been greatly changed since 1974, as have the composition and the social position of the sixties generation. The extent to which the effects of the sixties survive these environmental and demographic changes depends upon how

Generational Change, Periods, and the Life Cycle

deep-seated they were ingrained into the personality of the generation (and more importantly, into the social, economic, cultural, and political institutions of the nation), and how powerful and contradictory the effects of aging and becoming "settled" are. The extent to which the competing forces of aging, politically distinct periods, generation, and demographic change are responsible for changes in attitudes, opinions, and behaviors will be the subject of the empirical analysis to follow.

NOTES

1. All demographic trends discussed in this chapter were obtained from the *Statistical Abstract of the United States, 1982–83* and from *The Historical Statistics of the United States*, both published by the U.S. Census Bureau.

2. This is not to say that this was the first time in which the Western world found itself attracted to the East. Late nineteenth- and early twentieth-century England bears a certain (though we would argue superficial) similarity to what was happening in the 1960s. There are differences between these two situations, however. While there was some interest in the East in both eras, in the sixties there was a definite sense of searching, of exploring. People were not reading the *Koran* as dilettantes. There was a genuine and more widespread desire to expand one's personal horizons. This was, we think, a far more significant cultural borrowing than a fad for Egyptian headgear, or Victorian aristocrats sporting saris and silk smoking jackets.

3. One might argue that the 1950s also was the decade of the antihero and the working-class hero. While this is true, it does not conflict with our argument for several reasons. First, the fifties in fact served as a socializing experience for many of the people we identify as members of the sixties generation, so that the former decade serves to reinforce and perhaps even to initiate the latter in this regard. Second, the extent of an antihero motif was much greater in the sixties than the fifties, moving from one of a number of types to the dominant type. Finally, the antihero of the fifties was best characterized as the rugged individual who still accepted most aspects of the American dream (consider James Dean in *Giant*). The antihero of the sixties often had a more alienated, meaningless or anarchist quality (Peter Fonda in *Easy Rider*, Dustin Hoffman in *The Graduate* or *Midnight Cowboy*).

The Sixties and the Sixties Generation

REFERENCES

Bell, Daniel. "The Revolution of Rising Entitlements." *Fortune* (1975).
Bem, Daryl J. *Beliefs, Attitudes, and Human Affairs.* Belmont, Cal.: Brooks/Cole Publishers, 1970.
Bennett, W. Lance. *Public Opinion in American Politics.* New York: Harcourt Brace Jovanovich, 1980.
Berelson, Bernard. "Democracy Theory and Public Opinion." *Public Opinion Quarterly,* 16 (Fall, 1952), pp. 313–330.
Blake, J. Herman. "The Resurgence of Black Nationalism." In Joseph Boskin and Robert A. Rosenstone (eds.). *Seasons of Rebellion: Protest and Radicalism in Recent America.* Washington, D.C.: University Press of America, 1980, pp. 39–54.
Boskin, Joseph. "The Revolt of the Urban Ghettos." In Boskin and Rosenstone (eds.), op. cit., pp. 15–38.
Boyte, Harry C. *The Backyard Revolution.* Philadelphia: Temple University Press, 1980.
Cobb, Roger W., and Charles D. Elder. *Participation in American Politics.* Boston: Allyn and Bacon, 1972.
Dickstein, Morris. *Gates of Eden.* New York: Basic Books, 1977.
Eisen, Jonathan, and David Steinberg. "The Student Revolt against Liberalism." In Boskin and Rosenstone (eds.), *Seasons of Rebellion,* pp. 177–195.
Epstein, Edward Jay. *Between Fact and Fiction.* New York: Random House, 1975.
Erikson, Robert S., Norman R. Luttbeg, and Kent L. Tedin. *American Public Opinion.* New York: John Wiley, 1980.
Flacks, Richard. "The Liberated Generation: An Exploration of the Roots of Student Protest." *Journal of Social Issues,* 23 (July, 1967), pp. 52–75.
Friedenberg, Edgar Z. "The Oppression of Youth." In Boskin and Rosenstone (eds.). *Seasons of Rebellion,* pp. 221–236.
Gilmour, Richard, and Richard Lamb. *Political Alienation in Contemporary America.* New York: St. Martin's Press, 1975.
Gitlin, Todd. *The Whole World Is Watching.* Berkeley, Cal.: University of California Press, 1980.
Gramsci, Antonio. *Selections from the Prison Notebooks,* edited and translated by Quintin Hoare and Geoffrey Smith. New York: International, 1971.
Hirschman, Albert O. *Shifting Involvements.* Princeton: Princeton University Press, 1982.
Inglehart, Ronald. "The Silent Revolution: Intergenerational Change in Post-Industrial Societies." *American Political Science Review,* 65 (1971), pp. 991–1017.
——. "The Nature of Value Change in Post-Industrial Societies." In Leon

Lindberg (ed.), *Politics and the Future of Industrial Society.* New York: McKay Press, 1976, pp. 57–99.

———. *The Silent Revolution.* Princeton: Princeton University Press, 1977.

———. "Post Materialism in an Environment of Uncertainty." *American Political Science Review,* 75 (December, 1981), pp. 880–900.

Jones, Landon Y. *Great Expectations.* New York: Ballantine Books, 1980.

Keniston, Kenneth. *Young Radicals.* New York: Harcourt, Brace, Jovanovich, 1968.

Koeppen, Sheilah R. "Anger on the Right." In Boskin and Rosenstone (eds.). *Seasons of Rebellion,* pp. 146–171.

Laufer, Robert S. "Sources of Generational Consciousness and Conflict." In Philip G. Altbach and Robert S. Laufer (eds.), *The New Pilgrims.* New York: David McKay, 1972, pp. 218–237.

Lipset, Seymour Martin, and Everett Carl Ladd, Jr. "The Political Future of Activist Generations." In Altbach and Laufer (eds.), op. cit., pp. 63–84.

Maslow, Abraham. *Towards a Psychology of Being.* New York: D. Van Nostrand, 1962.

McCluhan, Marshall. *Understanding Media.* New York: Signet Books, 1964.

Myerhoff, Barbara G. "Youth Culture: New Styles of Humanism." In Boskin and Rosenstone (eds.), op. cit., pp. 237–259.

Orman, John. *The Politics of Rock Music.* Chicago: Nelson Hall, 1984.

Patrick, Robert. *Kennedy's Children.* New York: Samuel French, 1976.

Rogers, Carl L. *On Becoming a Person.* Boston: Houghton-Mifflin, 1961.

Rosenstone, Robert A. "The Times They Are A'Changin'." In Boskin and Rosenstone (eds.), op. cit., pp. 317–336.

Sahlins, Marshall. *Culture and Practical Reason.* Chicago: University of Chicago Press, 1976.

Triandis, Harry C. *Attitude and Attitude Change.* New York: John Wiley, 1971.

Williams, Raymond. "Base and Superstructure in Marxist Cultural Theory." *New Left Review,* 82 (1973), pp. 3–16.

Zukin, Cliff, and Robin Snyder. "Passive Learning. When the Media Environment Is the Message." *Public Opinion Quarterly.* 48 (Fall, 1984), pp. 629–638.

CHAPTER 3

Data and Methods

While a number of different attitudes, opinions, and behaviors are examined in the following chapters, and on occasion different data and methods are introduced to illuminate specific points, the bulk of what follows depends heavily on a single data source and a single method of analysis. The next section discusses the data to be used, illuminating its strengths and weaknesses; section three describes the methods to be employed; section four explains how to interpret the findings to be presented; section five is a summary and conclusion.

THE DATA

For our study we relied upon the series of National Election Studies (NES) from 1952 to 1980, designed and carried out by the Inter-University Consortium for Political and Social Research at the University of Michigan. Only the presidential election year surveys are used. Table 3.1 presents a list of the surveys employed, along with their respective sample sizes.

The choice of the NES was relatively easy once the criteria for this study were established. First, it was necessary to find a set of surveys that would provide a national sample. Sec-

TABLE 3.1
NES Surveys Used and Ns of Each Survey

Year	N	Year	N
1952	1899	1968	1673
1956	1762	1972	2705
1960	1181	1976	2248
1964	1834	1980	1614

ond, it was necessary that these surveys include a wide array of both political and social variables, as well as demographic characteristics. Third, the questions asked at various times had to be comparable. Fourth, the surveys had to span a period that began prior to the sixties and the entry of individuals who were part of the sixties generation into the electorate, and that continued beyond the years designated as the sixties. Only the NES surveys met all these requirements.

The choice of these surveys is not without its drawbacks, however. In many cases, the survey questions that are available do not address the attitudes or actions that most distinguish the sixties generation and the 1960s from what preceded them. This is especially true in the area of anti-system or untraditional behavior. While this always poses a difficulty for the secondary analysis of data, it is a particular problem when the goal of the research is to uncover change. Surveys, especially surveys repeated over time, are designed within the context of a particular system and a particular period. In addition, they are designed by individuals who are themselves part of that environment. As a result, the surveys themselves are bounded by that dominant perspective: for it to be any different would require a prescience that it is impossible to expect. This means, however, that while we can hint at the outer bounds of opinions and behaviors of the new generation, we had to be content to show how this generation differed from preceding citizens relative to the political structure that already existed. For example,

Data and Methods

while we show that the new generation is less likely to vote than prior generations, we could only speculate on whether this represented a movement away from participation in politics, or a shifting of political modes from voting to, for instance, involvement in grassroots organizations. Where possible we supplemented the main analysis with supporting ones, but the nature of the conclusions drawn from such less-systematic analyses must necessarily be more tentative. In short, this study will focus on how the mass political system which existed prior to the sixties has been changed due to the sixties and to the sixties generation.

A second and related set of issues concerns the reliability and the validity of the political items used. Chapters Four through Eleven each center on a different level of political consciousness and involvement, running from deep-seated attitudes that form early in one's political development (diffuse support) to more immediate, visible and/or specific behaviors such as vote choice. This approach is loosely modeled on the notion of a "funnel of causality" (Campbell et al., 1960). The specific items selected for analysis within each chapter are based upon both the face validity of those items and their use in prior research. However, we are at times forced to use items that may only partially or indirectly measure the larger concept being investigated in the chapter. In addition, different items are more or less reliable in their measurement of such concepts, an issue of particular importance in an analysis that depends upon multiple surveys. As a result, in each chapter of Part II we use multiple items to measure the underlying concept, and present the estimates of generational, period, life cycle, and interaction effects on each item separately. This allows us to examine the limits of and exceptions to our generalizations, while still being able to uncover systematic patterns, where they exist. Only after such general patterns are established are multiple-item indices constructed and used in Chapters 13 and 14. (For the specific items used, question wording, and details of scale construction, see Appendices B and D).

METHODS

Political change arising from generational replacement, the life cycle, and/or period effects has been studied empirically in many different ways. Methods of analysis have ranged from straightforward comparisons of attitudes and behaviors across time and groups (Cutler and Bengston, 1974; Cutler, 1977; Glenn and Hefner, 1972; Glenn, 1977; Jennings and Niemi, 1981) to more complex multivariate designs based upon linear regression (Converse, 1976; Abramson, 1979; Claggett, 1981), categorical regression (Kritzer, 1983), and dynamic modelling (Markus, 1983). In the choice of a method of analysis, each researcher attempts both to document time- and age-related change and to reduce it to its causal components, doing so in a way that introduces the greatest fit between the assumptions underlying the methodological and substantive theories involved. Central to this notion of fit is the "identification problem." The identification problem is encountered when one has more unknowns to explain than can be independently estimated from the data. In the particular case of change believed to be caused by some combination of life cycle, period, and generational effects, this means that knowing an individual's (or group's) location on two of these characteristics fully determines his or her location on the third, making an independent estimate of the latter's impact impossible. For example, if we know that an individual is 30 years old, and that the data was collected in 1972, then we know with certainty which generation (and even which subgeneration) that individual is a member of. Similarly, if we know the generation and year, we must know

Data and Methods

the age group, or if we know the generation and age, we must know what year the data was collected in. This problem is made more complicated when interaction effects are included, since the number of unknowns is increased without increasing the ability of the data to provide information.

The solution to this problem, assuming one is working with cross-sectional data gathered over a number of years, depends upon the nature of the substantive issue under consideration and the theoretical assumptions one is willing to make in order to provide information that otherwise cannot be obtained directly. The most common approach to avoiding the identification problem is to provide additional information (side information) that allows the researcher to assume one or more of the hypothesized effects (life cycle, period, generational, or the interaction effects) to be either zero or of some independently estimable magnitude. If one assumes an effect to be zero, then that term can be eliminated from the model, making the remaining two terms identifiable. Suppose, for example, that we are interested in the changing racial composition of the United States. Such a change could be due to generational differences (different birth rates could lead to one generation having a larger or smaller percentage of blacks for instance), or to period differences (blacks might immigrate to the United States during a particular period at unusual rates because of changing immigration laws or because of conditions abroad). It is a safe assumption, however, that changes are not due to the life cycle. One does not change race with age. Thus, one can use cross-sectional data over time to estimate the effects of generational replacement and period differences without encountering the identification problem.

If it is unrealistic to assume away one of the effects, it is still possible to avoid the identification problem by using side information. With this approach one attempts to independently estimate one or more of the effects, and then use this estimate in a more complicated model, using other data. Claggett (1981), for example, estimated generational effects on partisanship for the period from 1952 to 1964, and then used this estimate in a more complicated model for the 1964 to 1976 period. In short, this approach involves changing one of the unknowns to a known, and then estimating the model with this information included.

Kritzer (1983) suggests a way of estimating multiple effects that, rather than being based upon assumptions concerning the *impact* of some of those effects, is based upon assumptions concerning the *structure* of such impacts. He argues that the identification problem arises only when the independent variables involved are linear combinations of each other. If only one of the variables is assumed to be linear, while the others are assumed to be categorical (or dummy variables), the model is identified. In his example concerning partisanship, Kritzer argues that the life cycle effect is largely linear, while generational and period effects are categorical, leading to an identified model.

Consider the example involving age, generation, and period used above to introduce the identification problem and the solutions offered to get around such a problem. What Kritzer's approach suggests is that the use of dummy variables in the model combines the simplifying notions underlying (1) setting certain effects to zero and (2) providing independent estimates of those effects. That is, either an effect is zero (someone is not a member of a particular generation, or the year is not 1972), or the effect is constant for all members of the category. Put another way, data set up in this fashion does not determine with certainty in which generation or period all individuals or responses should be placed. Instead the data determine only those in which they should not be placed. One knows, for example, that an individual

Data and Methods

is not part of a particular generation if his score is zero, but this information cannot be combined with the age variable to determine the time period. Nor can it be combined with the period variable to determine the respondent's age. This element of independence, when considered in the data as a whole, results in an identified model.

The particular problems we have chosen to examine in this research and the particular way in which we have conceptualized generational change allow us to borrow from the methodological approaches of other researchers, but also suggests the need to modify or adapt those approaches. In some ways we were at an advantage, in that, unlike other attempts to examine generational change, we were concerned only with the impact of a single generation, and a particular period. This allowed us not only to simplify parts of the model, but also to use information about the population prior to the 1960s as side information. However, our somewhat rigorous definition of generation and our expectation of not only all three main effects but also interaction effects makes our particular methodological needs unique.

In the previous chapters we argued that the way in which the world imprints different generations is unique and that, as a result, any examination that attempts to uncover generational differences must be sensitive to such idiosyncratic configurations. Does this mean that in order to understand the 1960s and the generation that grew up in that decade we must first document the distinct impact of all prior generations and all prior periods? While such documentation may in fact be desirable, it would be a task of overwhelming proportions. The usual solution is to assume away much of the uniqueness of what one might call "generational crystallization" and to use equally proportioned age cohorts as surrogates for the more complex notion of generation. While in many cases this may be acceptable, given the arguments presented in Chapter One, such a solution would be inappropriate for this analysis. How then does one simplify the reality of political change in a way that is consistent with this notion of generational change?

The solution reached in this analysis is based loosely on Kritzer's observation concerning linear and nonlinear change. Political change brought about by the life cycle is assumed to be essentially linear. That is, the process of aging, and the incremental experiencing and learning about the world that is a part of the process, is conceptualized as affecting one's political orientations at a relatively constant rate. This does not imply that the life cycle must affect all political orientations, nor that it must be the same for different types of attitudes and actions. It only says that such an effect, when it does exist and when separated from other effects, is essentially linear.

The effects of the generation one is born into and the period one reacts to are, on the other hand, nonlinear. Knowing the attitudes, opinions, and behaviors of one generation need not tell us much about the attitudes, opinions, and behaviors of earlier or subsequent generations, once the effects of the life cycle have been accounted for. This is due to the fact that each generation develops its identity from a unique combination of historical, cultural, social, economic, political, and even biological circumstances. Similarly, periodic events and the reaction to those events by different generations are discrete and nonlinear.

How does distinguishing linear from nonlinear effects help us to overcome the problem of developing a context for the introduction of the 1960s and the sixties generation? The answer lies in the essentially random nature of period and generational effects when considered on a wide array of people and events. While the characteristics of each generation, each event or period, and the reaction of generations to events are

Data and Methods

clearly not random, there is no reason to expect a consistent, linear pattern of characteristics, events, or reactions to be developed across a number of generations. For example, while there are clear reasons to expect those socialized in the Depression to develop a similar political character that is attributable (in part) to that experience, nothing about the development of that generation allows one to say much about the character of the preceding or following generation. This becomes more true when one considers not two or three generations, but many.

Similarly, while one can offer explanations for the reaction of individuals and groups to specific events, the occurrence of a particular event provides little for anyone to predict the details of the next period or event. It is difficult, for example, to argue a linear progression in the Eisenhower, Kennedy, Johnson, Nixon, Ford, Carter, and Reagan years and even more difficult to argue for such a progression in the specific events that constitute the substance of those periods. What is the linear link between the Depression of the 1930s and JFK's assassination? Between World War II and Watergate?

If we accept that there is this nonlinear element to the effects of generation and period, especially when examining individuals who represent a large number of generations and who have experienced the events of many different periods, then we can assume that the linear relationship that does exist between age and political orientations in the population that grew up before the 1960s is due primarily to the life cycle. While this assumption is of little use if one is interested in determining the political effects of generation and period prior to the 1960s, it is invaluable for a study such as this, which is interested in the effects of a new generation and particular periods.

Because the measurement of life cycle effects described above is different from (though related to) previous ones, we use the term "ecological life cycle" to describe it. We chose this term because the concept it describes is really the life cycle as it applies not to specific generations or periods, but to the whole. It is the life cycle as it actually exists in the context of a complex and varied environment. Its weakness compared to other measures of the life cycle is that, to the extent to which it also picks up systematic patterns that are unique to particular generations and periods, it measures a somewhat different concept than the term usually implies. Rather than measuring the effects of the life cycle in some absolute sense, it is measuring the particular effects present at the time when the sixties and the sixties generation became a factor in politics in the United States.

The strength of the measure is that it distinguishes life cycle effects from those of generation and period without requiring unacceptably artificial definitions of the latter two concepts. In addition, as we shall see, it allows us to estimate a more realistic model of the effects of the 1960s by allowing us to include a greater number of hypothesized effects without encountering the identification problem.

We leave it to the reader to decide whether the concept of the ecological life cycle, as measured here, represents the effects of the life cycle in some absolute sense, or instead captures the particular life-cycle pattern that ended as the United States entered the 1960s. While we prefer to think of it in the former terms, its utility as a guide for understanding changes introduced by new generations and new events is preserved in both cases.

The notion of an ecological life cycle (and the assumptions underlying it) allows us to estimate the effects of the life cycle, generation, periods, and interactions without encountering the identification problem. More formally, the basic model to be used in the analysis to follow is

$$P = b_0 + b_1 LC + b_2 G + b_3 P50 + b_4 P60 + b_5 P70 + b_6 LC \times$$

Data and Methods

$$G + b_7 LC \times P50 + b_8 LC \times P60 + b_9 LC \times P70 + b_{10} G \times P60 + b_{11} G \times P70$$

where
- P = particular political orientation being examined
- b_0 = constant term
- LC = age (in years after 18)
- G = sixties generation (1 = member; 0 = nonmember)
- $P50$ = 1956 or 1960 Survey (1 = yes; 0 = no)
- $P60$ = 1964, 1968, or 1972 Survey (1 = yes; 0 = no)
- $P70$ = 1976 or 1980 Survey (1 = yes; 0 = no)
- $LC \times G$ = age × sixties generation
- $LC \times P50$ = age × P50
- $LC \times P60$ = age x P60
- $LC \times P70$ = age x P70
- $G \times P60$ = sixties generation x P60
- $G \times P70$ = sixties generation x P70 and
- b_1 through b_{11} = estimates of effects of the variables

In order to estimate this model, each of the eight surveys is divided into six-year age cohorts, resulting in a total aggregated N of 88. Following Converse (1976) and Claggett (1981), the model is estimated using ordinary least squares, and weighting each age cohort by its respective sample size.[1] Each aggregated observation is coded for its mean age, the year in which the survey was conducted, and whether or not it is part of the sixties generation. This process is repeated for each of the political orientations under observation. Threeway interactions are assumed to be zero both to avoid the identification problem and because of the difficulty in theorizing about and interpreting such interactions.

In the previous chapters it was suggested that even within generations there may be different subgroups that form because of the interaction of age and the experiences and events that characterize different periods. In order to test for this it is necessary to perform a somewhat more-detailed analysis, this time distinguishing among subgenerations within the sixties generation. For this analysis the model above is replicated except that the main effect of generation and the interaction of generation and both the life cycle and periods are replaced with the following variables:

Amb = percent of each cohort which was between the ages of 25 and 36 during the sixties

Exp = percent of each cohort which was between the ages of 13 and 24 during the sixties

Soc = percent of each cohort which was between the ages of one and 12 during the sixties

where each *individual* is coded for the fraction of his or her life cycle between the ages of one and 36 which fell into each of the three subgenerational categories.

Each age cohort is, therefore, also coded for the percent of its members which fall into each subgenerational category. Interaction effects are estimated by substituting the subgenerational measures for the generational one (SOC × P70 is not calculated, due to the relatively short period of time this cohort has been in the electorate and the resultant difficulty in distinguishing its interaction with the life cycle from that with period).

INTERPRETING THE ESTIMATES OF EFFECTS

The method of analysis described above allows us to distinguish generational, period, life cycle and interaction effects on a host of political attitudes, opinions, and behaviors, with a particular focus on the impact of the 1960s and the 1960s generation. In addition it allows for a more detailed exploration of the effects of more finely specified segments of that generation. In the chapters to follow, all results are presented as unstandardized regression coefficients in order to avoid

Data and Methods

the confounding effects of sample variability and to focus more clearly on the theoretical importance of each independent variable relative to the others (Achen, 1982). To allow comparability across the dependent variables, all of the measures of political orientations are recoded to vary from zero to one.

The presentation of results as regression coefficients rather than as simple percentages makes interpreting them slightly more difficult, especially to the nonspecialist. This problem is easily overcome if the reader keeps the following in mind. Since all the dependent variables are coded to run from zero to one, and since the coefficients are unstandardized, the estimates as presented represent the relative "theoretical importance" of each variable (Achen, 1982). If, for example, the estimated effect of being a member of the sixties generation on a particular measure of participation is $-.15$, this means that this generation will average .15 less on this measure than preceding generations do, when age, the period, and all two-way interactions are controlled for. A life-cycle effect of .01 would mean that older cohorts out-participate younger ones by an average increment of .01 for each year older it is (twenty year olds out-participate nineteen year olds by .01; twenty-one-year-old people out-participate twenty-year-olds by .01, etc.), again controlling for other effects. A period effect for the 1960s of .10 would mean that during those years, when other effects are controlled for, people were likely to score .10 higher than in the base year of 1952. If the interaction of being a member of the sixties generation during the 1970s results in an estimate of $-.12$, this means that members of this generation, in addition to whatever general period effect there was, reacted uniquely to the period by a lowered participation rate of .12, and so on. Since all measures run from zero to one, these coefficients can be interpreted as the percentage of the absolute scale by which the measure is affected (for example, a coefficient of .20 means an increase of 20 percent on a scale which runs from zero to one).

In addition to this interpretation of a variable's theoretical importance, the coefficients can easily be used to make more clearly substantive interpretations. If one is interested, for example, in determining how important a generational effect of .05 is, relative to the average score of the population as a whole, one need only look at the mean scores over time (which are provided in each chapter). If the population as a whole averages .10 on a particular item (participation in political organizations, for example), then a generational effect of .05 would seem quite important, in that it is a 50 percent increase over the norm. If the average score were .85, however, then a generational effect of .05 would appear less dramatic. Similarly, one can simply compare the size of estimates to the constant terms for each model (provided in Appendix C) in order to judge their relative significance.

While our analysis is generally limited to the unstandardized regression coefficients, by using in addition the constant term for each model, the mean age of various cohorts, and/or the percentage of the electorate that is a member of the sixties generation (provided in Table 2.1) one can perform numerous real and hypothetical reconstructions. One can, for example, estimate the average turnout of the 18-year-old cohort of the sixties generation in the 1970s by simply adding together the constant term and the estimated effects of generation, of the 1970s, and of the interaction of the two. Similarly, one can estimate hypothetical situations such as the turnout rate of the sixties generation had it been around in the 1950s, or its turnout rate when it reaches an average age of 60. By multiplying generational effects by the percentage of the electorate which is part of the sixties generation one can also estimate the generation's impact on (again for ex-

Data and Methods

ample) the overall turnout rate. In short, while we will on occasion go beyond a discussion of theoretical effects, one can use the information provided in this analysis to make numerous additional comparisons and estimates.

A final point to be considered is the issue of statistical versus substantive significance. Because of the relatively few cases that were examined in the aggregate analysis (88 cases at most), because of the relatively large number of independent variables (at least 11) and because of the relatively limited variance in some of the political variables examined, not all relationships to be discussed attained statistical significance at the normally accepted levels. While we will present both significance levels and indications concerning the size of the standard errors, we will not use these as absolute arbitors of the substantive significance of the findings. Rather, since we consider many individual measures of the political concepts under examination in each chapter, we will concentrate on the overall tendencies of the findings. Occasionally we had to be content with findings that were substantively significant, though statistically ambiguous (Achen). This is a limitation of this kind of cohort analysis that one must live with, but one that we feel does not outweigh the benefits to be derived from it.

SUMMARY AND CONCLUSION

In this chapter we focused on a brief description of the data to be used, reviewing the costs and benefits of our choice. The National Election Studies from 1952 to 1980 were selected because they provided a national sample, appropriate survey items, comparability over time, and a times series that not only covers the sixties, but also periods before and after that decade. While our ability to deal with some aspects of the sixties and the sixties generation is limited by this choice, it is the best alternative available.

Most of this chapter was devoted to an examination of the way in which the effects of the life cycle, periods, generation, and interactions were estimated. If one assumes, as we do, that generational and period effects are both nonlinear within generations and random between generations, then the ecological life cycle can be interpreted as a measure of the pure effects of the life cycle. If one is uncomfortable with such an assumption, then the ecological life cycle is better interpreted as a measure of the effect of age on political orientations for a particular set of generations over a particular historical period: the generations comprised of individuals born between 1894 and 1931, and the period ending in 1960. Regardless of which definition one chooses, however, two points remain unaltered. First, the concept remains a useful baseline against which to measure the effects of generation, periods, and interactions that began in the mid-1960s. Second, because we concentrated on a single generation, and because our definition of generation is sensitive to the combined effects of age and historical, political, social, economic, and cultural conditions, this approach is considered superior to any in which a mechanical or arbitrary division of presixties generations was made.

In the following eight chapters we apply this method in order to demonstrate the unique effects of generation, periods, and the life cycle, as well as their interactions, on political orientations in the United States. We begin the next chapter with the most basic set of attitudes to be examined: diffuse support for the political system.

NOTE

1. Since age is so critical to the analysis to follow, and since we will

Data and Methods

want to be able to relate findings to the larger population, the original surveys were also weighted by age groups so as to more accurately reflect the age distribution of the population. These weights were determined from the 1950 through 1980 census surveys.

REFERENCES

Abramson, Paul. "Developing Party Identification: A Further Examination of Life Cycle, Generational, and Period Effects." *American Journal of Political Science*, 23 (February, 1979), pp. 78–96.

Achen, Christopher H. *Interpreting and Using Regression*. Beverly Hills: Sage Publications, 1982.

Campbell, Angus, Philip E. Converse, Warren E. Miller, and Donald E. Stokes. *The American Voter*. New York: John Wiley and Sons, 1960.

Claggett, William. "Partisan Acquisition v. Partisan Intensity: Life Cycle, Generation, and Period Effects." *American Journal of Political Science*, 25 (1981), pp. 193–214.

Converse, Philip E. *The Dynamics of Party Support: Cohort-Analyzing Party Identification*. Beverly Hills: Sage Publications, 1976.

Cutler, Neil, and Vern L. Bengston. "Age and Political Alienation." *Annals of the American Academy of Political and Social Science*, 415 (1974), pp. 160–175.

Cutler, Neil. "Political Socialization Research as Generational Analysis: Cohort Approach versus the Lineage Approach." In Stanley A. Renshon (ed.), *The Handbook of Political Socialization*. New York: The Free Press, 1977, pp. 294–326.

Glenn, Norval D., and Ted Hefner. "Further Evidence on Aging and Party Identification." *Public Opinion Quarterly*, 36 (1972), pp. 31–47.

Glenn, Norval D. *Cohort Analysis*. Beverly Hills: Sage Publications, 1977.

Jennings, M. Kent, and Richard G. Niemi. *Generations and Politics*. Princeton: Princeton University Press, 1981.

Kritzer, Herbert M. "The Identification Problem in Cohort Analysis." *Political Methodology*, 9 (1983), pp. 35–50.

Markus, Gregory B. "Dynamic Modelling of Cohort Change: The Case of Political Partisanship." *American Journal of Political Science*, 27 (November, 1983), pp. 717–739.

PART TWO

The Effects of Generation, Periods, and the Life Cycle on Mass Political Orientations

CHAPTER 4

Diffuse Political Support

In Chapters One and Two we defined generation, the specific profile of the sixties generation (and subgenerations), and how, in general terms, that profile leads one to expect an impact on politics. In this chapter we examine the first of several specific aspects of mass politics, and how it is affected by generational, life cycle, and period-based change. The chapters in this part of the book are organized to reflect the range of mass political orientations, from deep-seated attitudes, to more specific opinions, to decision-making resources, and ultimately to actual political behavior. Below we discuss the concept of diffuse support, its importance to mass politics, and the reasons one might expect a connection between this kind of support and the life cycle, the sixties, and the generation that grew up in the period. Section three presents the specific items to be used in measuring diffuse support, and shows the overall trends in such support over time. The fourth section presents findings concerning the effects of the life cycle, periods, generation, and their interactions, and the final section is a summary, discussion, and some concluding remarks. This format is repeated in each of the chapters in Part Two.

DIFFUSE SUPPORT AND THE GENERATIONAL PROCESS

"I am the law." When Frank Hague, machine boss of Jersey City in the early twentieth century, uttered those words, he was dissolving a distinction between rulers and rules that is critical, perhaps to any political system, but certainly to democratic ones. The shock value of the statement comes from a violation of the notion, embedded at least in the mythology of democratic politics, that there are clear differences between the structure of a political system, the rules of the game that should be adhered to, and the individual leaders who fill particular roles in that system.

To the extent that people's perceptions of leaders and of the political system itself differ, so also can their opinions of and support for each. Support for particular political leaders, or particular policies has become known as "specific support" (Easton, 1965). Support for the underlying system itself is known as "diffuse support." The distinction between the two is critical to maintaining the balance between a dynamic, responsive system where change is possible, and a stable, responsible system that does not collapse with each change in leadership. A working democracy is one in which specific support varies with time and between groups in the society but where diffuse support remains steady and strong. A weakening of specific support suggests the possibility of a change in the leadership or political agenda. The weakening of diffuse support portends a more-fundamental restructuring of the rules of the game.

The literature on political socialization suggests that diffuse support develops early in childhood, well before the development of more specific opinions or even the acquisition of specific political information (Schwartz, 1975; Dennis, 1973; Easton and Dennis, 1965, 1967, 1969). By the time individuals are ready to fulfill their roles as citizens, these feelings of support are well ingrained into their political psyche.

Diffuse Political Support

How resistant is diffuse support to change? Primacy theorists argue that those attitudes learned earliest are most resistant to change, and so, while experiences as adults may erode some of the more naïve beliefs underlying this support, by and large the reservoir of good feelings should survive all but the most severe crises of faith. From this perspective, the most-serious threat to diffuse support lies in the socialization experiences of future generations. If children and adolescents are raised in an environment that does not instill diffuse support, then as adults, this generation will be less inclined to show the same allegiance to the system as their predecessors.

Not all socialization theorists accept the primacy argument as it applies to political development, however (Sigel and Hoskin, 1977). Adult experiences can lead to fundamental changes in any kinds of attitudes and opinions, including diffuse political support (Pollock, et al., 1975). Unfortunately, research on adult socialization has lagged behind that of children, and little evidence is available concerning the effects of aging and of adult experiences on levels of diffuse support. It seems reasonable to expect, however, that both childhood socialization and adult political experiences are important in determining the level of diffuse support in the political system at any particular time. When both forces work in conjunction, the levels of support move more rapidly in a single direction, while when they are in contention (positive support instilled in childhood being overcome by negative adult experiences, for instance), the outcome depends upon the strength of each.

The pertinence of this general discussion of diffuse support to the period and generational effects of the sixties should be readily apparent. The 1960s represent both a period of intense adult political experiences (direct or indirect) as well as a unique incubator for the political development of a generation of children and adolescents. The specific effects of these adult experiences and adolescent development on politics, however, are complex.

Whether the period from 1963 to 1974 saw a threat to the level of diffuse support in the United States or saw some encouragement for the growth and maintenance of such support depends upon what element of that era is emphasized and what group within the population is referred to. As mentioned in Chapter Two, the sixties were characterized by unprecedented economic prosperity and growth. Because of increases in income, in the number of people in white-collar occupations, in consumption, and in education, it is difficult to think that this period would result in anything but support for the political system. And at the center of this growth was the government. With post-Keynsian manipulation of the economy, the growth in services provided first to the very needy and then to middle and upper America, and the consequent growth in the size of government and the rate of its expenditures, the connection between the daily lives of citizens and government action was never clearer. From this perspective, therefore, one might expect diffuse support, both as the result of socialization and through adult reinforcement, to be high and stable, and perhaps even increasing.

Unprecedented economic prosperity for middle-class America and continued prosperity for upper-class America was only part of the story, however. At the same time, certain individuals and groups were raising their voices in protest over the escalating war in Vietnam, racial prejudice in the South and in urban America, and the inequities of an economic system that were leaving a sizable minority further and further behind. In addition, social "issues of discontent" (Nie, Verba, and Petrocik, 1979) such as crime, student unrest, and urban violence for the established generations, and restrictive life styles and mores for the young, came increasingly to dominate the political agenda. Here, as with economic issues, the government stood, either symbolically or substantively, at the center of these controversies. To the extent that citizens grew dissatisfied with the state of the nation or of society, the level of diffuse support seems sure to have dissipated.

Several interactions complicate the determination of which subgroups were most affected by the positive or negative aspects of this period. First, issues that revolved around students and the young tended to cut across economic issues. For example, it was often individuals from families who had most benefited from the economic prosperity who protested restrictive social norms and the war in Vietnam. Second, the expansion of the mass media meant that issues and controversies that would at one time have caught the attention of only particular individuals and groups became issues of concern to the *entire* population. Finally, the cross-cutting nature of class and race issues led to unusual alliances (middle-class white students from elite educational institutions and poor Southern blacks, for example) and to unfortunate barriers between groups with common grievances (white ethnic working-class groups and urban blacks, for instance).

In summary then, the sixties was a period of change with clear implications for the level of diffuse support, but the effects are muddied by diverse, often contradictory, currents. The established generations had to weigh economic prosperity against social and political upheaval that threatened the values and structures that had led to prosperity in the first place. For the new generation, economic prosperity was less an end than a beginning, a given. It afforded both the opportunity to concentrate on other issues and the freedom to consider the personal and social price of such prosperity. And for the disadvantaged members of both the old and the new generations, it offered either a vision of their (or their

The Effects of Generation, Periods, and the Life Cycle

children's) future, or of a promised land from which they had been permanently barred.

AGGREGATE TRENDS IN DIFFUSE SUPPORT

Measuring so deep-seated and complex a notion as diffuse support is a difficult task. The levels of such support can only be approximated. Fortunately, the election surveys do include several items over the period from 1952 to 1980 that allow us to make such approximations. Eight items were selected that measure various aspects of an individual's feelings about whether the political system is responsive to him or her or to people like him or her, and whether involvement in the system as it is currently structured is a worthwhile or meaningful experience. Table 4.1 presents the eight measures along with a brief description of the underlying attitude each attempts to tap (for the actual wording of the questions, see Appendix B). All variables are coded so that higher scores

TABLE 4.1
Description of Measures of Diffuse Support

Variable	Description
Vote care	Should vote even if you don't care about the outcome (1 = agree strongly)
Officials	Public officials care about people like you (1 = agree strongly)
Vote only	The vote is one's only political influence (1 = agree strongly)
Local	Voting in local elections is important (1 = agree strongly)
Vote matters	One's vote matters (1 = agree strongly)
Have say	People like you have a say in government (1 = agree strongly)
Vote win	One should vote even if your candidate party cannot win (1 = agree strongly)
Complex	Politics is not too complicated to understand (1 = agree strongly)

Diffuse Political Support

FIGURE 4.1
Patterns of Change in Diffuse Support, 1952–1980

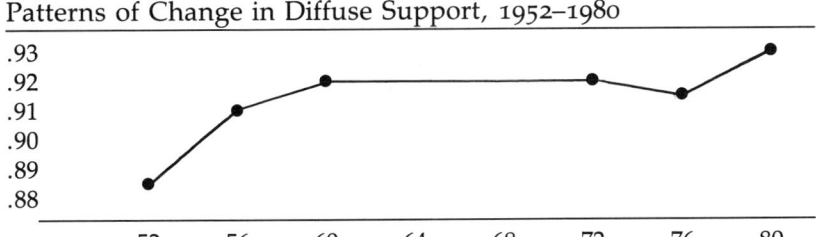

FIGURE 4.1A
Vote care

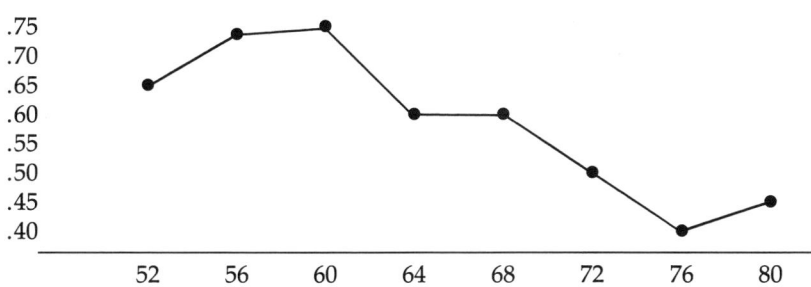

FIGURE 4.1B
Officials

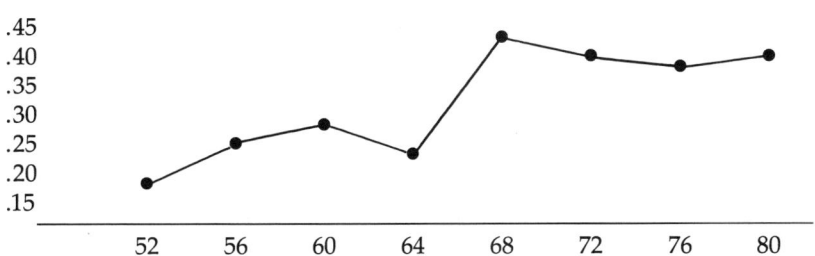

FIGURE 4.1C
Vote only

The Effects of Generation, Periods, and the Life Cycle

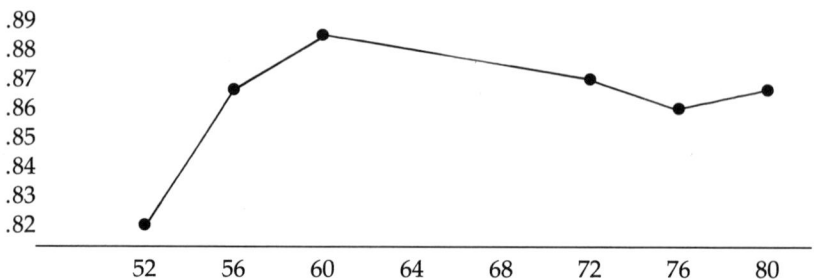

FIGURE 4.1D
Local

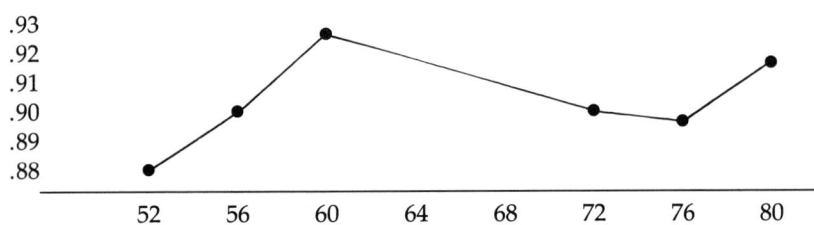

FIGURE 4.1E
Vote matters

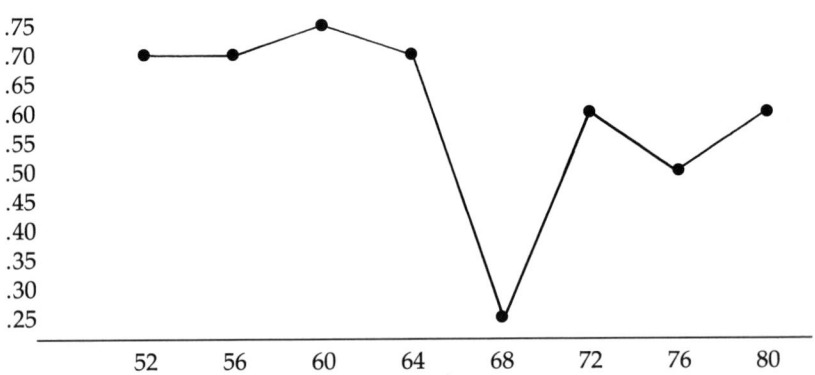

FIGURE 4.1F
Have say

Diffuse Political Support

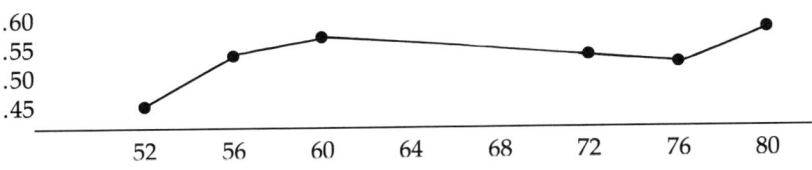

FIGURE 4.1G
Vote win

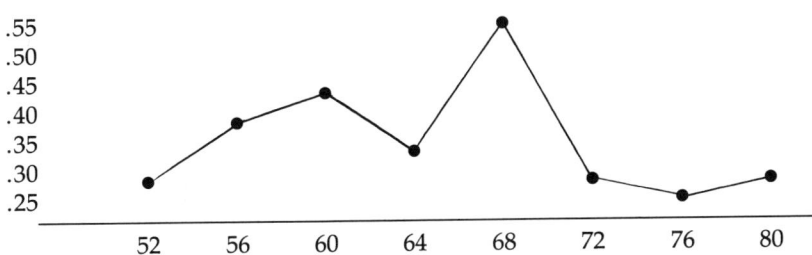

FIGURE 4.1H
Complex

indicate greater support.[1] While some of these measure roles rather than structures, all of them presented the choices to respondents in terms general enough that we were confident that they are tapping underlying attitudes concerning the system as a whole and not simply reactions to particular leaders.

The first issue addressed concerns the overall levels of support for the political system between 1952 and 1980. Figure 4.1 presents the aggregate level of support as demonstrated by each of the eight items (the numbers represent the mean response for the population in each year). Several points concerning the level of support should be noted. First, while some measures demonstrated less change than others, overall the level of diffuse support did change, often radically, from year to year during the three decades examined. The pattern for the population as a whole reflects the cross pressures described above. Several measures indicate a general loss of support (Figures B, F, and H), while others show increased support (Figures A, C, and G). In addition, attitudes towards the importance of local elections (D) and the importance of one's vote (E) demonstrate more volatile patterns. In short, the period under study is clearly not easily characterized in terms of the overall level of diffuse support. It is our contention, however, that these aggregate trends mask more consistent patterns of change.

THE EFFECTS OF LIFE CYCLE, GENERATION, AND PERIODS

The central question for us is, of course, to what extent are variations in the level of diffuse support across time and across measures the result of periods, generation, and the life cycle? To determine the answer, we employed the technique detailed in Chapter Three. Some results of this analysis are presented in Table 4.2, which shows the main effects of life cycle, generation, and periods on diffuse support. The inconsistent patterns displayed by the overall trends in Figure 4.1 become clearer when they are broken down into more basic components. With the exception of voting even if one is unconcerned about the outcome (Vote Care), all the measures of diffuse support show a negative relationship with life cycle (recall that the numbers, which are unstandardized regression coefficients, represent the change in diffuse support for each year of aging once an individual enters the electorate). It would seem, as suggested at the beginning of this chapter, that experiences gained from politics over time do significantly erode the foundation of support that is built up in childhood and adolescence. This suggests that when the entire life cycle from birth to death is considered, its effect on diffuse support is curvilinear, peaking before an individual's actual entrance into the political arena.

When we turn to the effects of the sixties generation, the

Diffuse Political Support

TABLE 4.2
Effects of Life Cycle, Generation, and Period on Diffuse Support[a]

Variable	Life Cycle	Generation	Period		
			Fifties	Sixties	Seventies
Vote care	.002**	−.104**	.163**	.214**	.235**
Officials	−.004**	−.154**	.128**	.039	−.049
Vote only	−.002**	−.207**	.170**	.268**	.403**
Local	−.003**	−.007	.056**	.061*	.083**
Vote matters	−.001**	−.046**	.040**	.085**	.115**
Have say	−.002*	−.045	.058	−.074*	−.084*
Vote win	−.002**	−.016	.038**	.091**	.116**
Complex	−.001	−.086	.092*	.260**	.099

[a] Entries are unstandardized regression coefficients.
* = standard error ≤ B.
** = $p \le .05$.

pattern is equally consistent and equally negative. On every measure, the effect of being a member of this generation is to weaken diffuse support for the political system. That is, members of this generation entered the electorate with considerably lower levels of support for the political system than did previous cohorts. This supports their popular characterization as a generation alienated from "the system" but also indicates that this view of politics survived beyond adolescence and beyond the tumult of the 1960s.

How is it possible that the aggregate trends in diffuse support could show such varied patterns of change when both the life cycle and the effects of generation are so consistently negative in their impact? The answer lies in the overwhelming positive effects of period during the fifties, sixties, and seventies. With the exception of trust in public officials, which shows a negative relationship with the 1970s (partly a reaction to Watergate), and the feeling that one has a say in government, which is negatively associated with both the sixties and seventies, all of the period effects on diffuse support were positive, and most were quite strong. Indeed, five of the measures showed a consistent increase in the size of

TABLE 4.3
Interaction Effects on Diffuse Support[a]

Variable	Life cycle				Generation	
	Generation	Fifties	Sixties	Seventies	Sixties	Seventies
Vote care	.013**	−.003**	−.002*	−.002*	−.175**	−.210**
Officials	.007**	−.001	−.003**	−.003**	−.037	−.128**
Vote only	.009**	−.003**	−.003**	−.005**	.131**	−.021
Local	.003**	.000	.000	.000	−.071**	−.094**
Vote matters	.006**	.000	−.001*	−.002**	−.076**	−.141**
Have say	.006*	−.001	−.002	−.001	−.117	−.104
Vote win	.004*	−.001	−.001	−.001	−.086*	−.127*
Complex	.006*	.000	−.004*	−.003	−.072	−.081

[a] Entries are unstandardized regression coefficients.
* = standard error ≤ B.
** = $p \leq .05$.

the relationships from the fifties through the sixties and into the seventies. The tension between competing pressures for support and alienation described earlier appear in part to be the result of the entrance of an alienated generation into the electorate during a time of generally increasing political support.

Our model allowed us to also examine the interaction effects among the main independent variables. Table 4.3 presents these interaction effects as they pertain to diffuse support. Of particular interest is the interaction between generation and life cycle. Recall that the main effects of these two variables were both negative: Both led to a loss of diffuse support. Taking these two effects alone into account would suggest that a growing segment of the population (the sixties generation) not only entered the electorate with less support for political institutions than has been typical of earlier generations, but also that they are becoming increasingly disenchanted as they grow older. The interaction effect of generation and life cycle, however, suggests that this erosion is counteracted. The positive interaction of life cycle and generation is strong enough so that it matches or overwhelms the negative main effects of aging for every measure of dif-

Diffuse Political Support

fuse support. The sixties generation, while starting out with more negative feelings towards the system than their predecessors, are becoming less rather than more cynical with age. Whatever threat to the political structure a nonsupportive population might introduce is being partly curtailed by this process. But this interaction is not strong enough to eliminate the rather large main negative effects of generation on most of the measures of support for quite some time. It would take eight or nine years in the electorate for the negative effects of generation on the level of "Vote Care," "Vote Matters," or "Vote Win" to be counteracted, 11 years for "Have Say," 17 for "Complex," 30 for "Vote Only," and 51 years for cynicism concerning "Officials" to converge with that of the general population (attitudes towards voting in local elections will never converge due to aging, though the differences were small to begin with).

The interaction between generation and periods also demonstrates some interesting consistencies. With the exception of "Vote Only" in the sixties, the interactions are negative, and most are quite large. Being a member of the sixties generation and being exposed to the events of the midsixties to late seventies combined to further increase the loss of support already evident in that generation. This is particularly illuminating since the main period effects demonstrated in Table 4.2 were largely positive in their impact. Taken together, these two pieces of information suggest that while the preceding generations were becoming more supportive of the system during these times, the sixties generation was consistently losing support for the system. Equally interesting, this negative interaction appeared not to be fading as we move further from the trauma of the 1960s and early 1970s. To the contrary, the negative interaction is greatest in 1976 and 1980, the period that showed the most positive effects overall.

The determination of the interaction between life cycle and

TABLE 4.4
Subgenerational Effects on Diffuse Support[a]

Variable	Ambivalent	Experienced	Socialized
Vote care	−.057	−.312**	−.999**
Officials	−.218**	−.287**	−.135
Vote only	−.402**	.015	−.265
Local	.039	−.059*	−.262*
Vote matters	−.004	−.156**	−.396**
Have say	−.053	−.218*	−.585
Vote win	.040	−.075**	−.300**
Complex	−.081	−.220**	−.653*

[a] Entries are unstandardized regression coefficients.
* = standard error ≤ B.
** = p ≤ .05.

periods helps to complete the picture. In every case in which there is an interaction (20 of the 24 relationships) it is negative. Older cohorts reacted to the events and changes of the last three decades with an additional loss of support. Not surprisingly, the magnitude of this loss was greater in the sixties and seventies than in the fifties. While we cannot say definitively, it is no doubt the case that older cohorts were becoming alienated for very different reasons than was the sixties generation, though both were reacting to the same general environment. The net result is that support for the system during the years under study was eroding from both ends of the life cycle, though at a greater rate for the young than for the old.

To this point we have treated the sixties generation as a unified whole that would react to events and processes in homogeneous ways. While we expected (and indeed found) such similarities, we have also argued that different segments of this generation might react differently depending on their age during the 1960s. Table 4.4 presents the effects of generation presented in Table 4.2, but here the sixties generation is broken down into its smaller subgenerations. The consistency demonstrated by the generation as a whole (Ta-

TABLE 4.5
Interaction Effects between Subgenerations, Life Cycle, and Periods on Diffuse Support[a]

Variable	Life Cycle			Seventies	
	Ambivalent	Experienced	Socialized	Ambivalent	Experienced
Vote care	.005	.028**	.217**	−.158**	−.202**
Officials	.002	.025**	.002	−.039	−.230**
Vote only	.015**	.027**	.000	−.047	−.438**
Local	−.002	.005	.055*	−.070	−.124**
Vote matters	−.001	.005*	.060**	−.047	−.036
Have say	.006	.009	.179	−.092	−.011
Vote win	−.002	.006*	.044*	−.069	−.116**
Complex	−.001	.011	.158*	.040	−.033

[a]Entries are unstandardized regression coefficients.
* = standard error ≤ B.
** = $p \leq .05$.

ble 4.2) is still present when it is disaggregated. The conclusion remains that the effects of generation weaken diffuse support. The magnitude of this erosion varies strongly between the three cohorts, however. The ambivalent cohort, true to its "split loyalties," showed the least loss of support. The experienced cohort, socialized as children prior to the sixties but directly involved in the events of that period, showed a greater loss of support. And the cohort, socialized as preteens during the sixties, entered the electorate with the least support of all for the political system. In sum, all three cohorts demonstrated a common pattern of alienation, but the youngest cohorts, having had less of an opportunity to experience the normal socialization of support, showed the most dissipated support.

As a final look at the relationship between the subgenerations and the individual measures of diffuse support, we present a partial examination of their interaction with periods and with the life cycle (Table 4.5). The interaction of subgeneration and life cycle provides further evidence that this process is working to achieve some level of stability by counteracting the negative main effects of generation. The stronger the negative main effects of subgeneration, the stronger the positive interaction effects. The ambivalent cohort showed the smallest loss of support, and therefore, also shows the fewest positive interactions. However, the socialized cohort, having moved furthest from the norm of diffuse support, showed the strongest tendency to become supportive with age. What we appear to be witnessing is the ability (or at least the attempt) of an established social and political system to recover from an unanticipated erosion in its attitudinal foundation. These conclusions are tentative, however, especially given the short time the youngest cohort has been in the electorate.

The final interaction to be examined is between the events of the seventies and the two older cohorts within the sixties generation. The cohort that experienced most directly the events of the sixties remained most negative towards the system in the following decade. Again we are led to conclude that one's point in the life cycle during the 1960s is critical in determining the period's effect on diffuse support and that this distinction remains important long after those events have passed.

SUMMARY, DISCUSSION, AND CONCLUDING REMARKS

We began this chapter by discussing the nature of diffuse support and its perceived importance to the stability of a political system. Diffuse support represents the "margin for error" or the "benefit of the doubt" built into a system, allowing it to survive change and conflict at the level of issues, agendas and personnel, without necessitating parallel changes in the basic rules of the game. It also keeps individuals and groups who lose political battles committed to the system and abiding by the decisions of the winners. Such

Diffuse Political Support

support develops early in an individual's life, and though it may erode with age and experience, it is generally considered to maintain itself at a "safe level" throughout the life cycle (when the system is operating efficiently).

The 1960s was a period in the history of the United States of diverse, even contradictory, events, some of which increased the level of support and others which decreased it. The analysis in this chapter suggests that the overall level of support reflected these diverse forces, changing as events and predispositions came together in different combinations over time. Underlying this volatility were some clear and consistent patterns, however. The sixties generation showed significant and sizable losses of support relative to the age of its members and to the times. It demonstrated a greater likelihood to react to the events of the sixties and seventies with a further loss of support than the presixties population and to show no indication of slowing this tendency in more recent times. Within that generation, those who were of an age to have directly experienced the events of the 1960s, and to a greater extent those who were socialized by them, were the most likely to demonstrate this alienation from the established system, with the oldest cohorts within this generation demonstrating less-dramatic losses. The only evidence of slowing in this general trend is the interaction of age and generation, which apparently is working to revitalize some of the lost support in those segments of the sixties generation which most strongly rejected the status quo in their youth. Even with this "regression to the mean," however, in 1980 the sixties generation as a whole remained less supportive of the rules and norms of the electoral system than their age and the times alone would have dictated.

Once the effects of aging and of the presence of the sixties generation are taken into account, the last three decades demonstrate consistently positive effects on support. The answer to the riddle of declining support in an era of prosperity lies in uncovering this generation gap. It was the young who rejected the system most directly. We would further argue that the loss of support demonstrated in the interaction between age and period was the result of a reaction to this new generation's protest and not to the status quo.

The trends discussed here need to be considered in light of two more general issues. First, are these findings reason for concern? The answer depends largely on one's perspective concerning the line between stability and stagnation, and on one's own satisfaction with the current political structure. While constant change and disputed, contradictory rules would most certainly make governing impossible, blind acceptance of procedures and norms that do not work (or worse, that work only for some) could result in a more intolerable state of affairs. To the extent that a loss of diffuse support is a necessary prerequisite for procedural and structural change that adapts a political system to new times and demands, such loss may be beneficial on occasion. Whether the loss of support noted in the sixties generation represents this kind of constructive rejection of the past depends ultimately on one's own satisfaction with the current state of affairs, one's sense that the system as currently designed and executed can satisfactorily deal with that state of affairs, and one's personal analyses of the tradeoffs involved in a period of turmoil, which would most certainly accompany any attempt to restructure the basic rules of the game.

The second issue concerns what these findings mean, regardless of one's personal preferences, for the future stability of the current system. As of 1980, the sixties generation represented over 60 percent of the entire population, with the experienced and the socialized subgenerations, which showed the greatest loss of support, representing about 40 percent. In addition, these latter two cohorts will continue to grow in both relative and absolute size, as older cohorts continue to be replaced with the many members of the socialized cohorts who have yet to enter the electorate. Since the interaction of aging and generation seems unable to completely counteract this loss of support, it seems safe to assume that this generation will remain less committed to the system than its predecessors. Two points then become critical. First, future period effects may well determine the way in which this lessened support translates into direct political ramifications. Second, and perhaps more importantly, is the level of support that future generations bring with them to adulthood. Should these generations return to a pre-sixties level, then the generation examined here may represent an historical aberration that will have its effect in the short run, but that will remain isolated from the attitudes of those that preceded and that succeed them. And, with time, they will be replaced just as they replaced generations before them. We have no data that allow us to answer this question, precisely because it is our contention that generational change is not by its nature linear. We can say, however, that the answer to this question is being decided by the events of the seventies and eighties and by the children and adolescents who are being shaped by those events.

NOTE

1. The variable "Vote Only" is problematic in that it is not easy to say with assurance whether greater support is indicated by feeling that one has numerous ways to participate, or that voting is the main form. While it is tempting from the perspective of democratic theory to argue for the former, our concern in this chapter is with the impact of support on political stability. As such, it is arguable that the system is most stable when participation is channelled into the periodic ritual of elections (Berelson, et al., 1954; Prezeworski, 1975; Ginsberg, 1982). For this reason, greater support is coded as dependency on voting for political expression.

REFERENCES

Berelson, Bernard R., and Paul F. Lazarsfeld. *Voting: A Study of Opinion Formation in a Presidential Campaign.* Chicago: University of Chicago Press, 1954.

Dennis, Jack (ed.). *Socialization to Politics.* New York: John Wiley, 1973.

Easton, David. *A Systems Analysis of Political Life.* New York: John Wiley, 1965.

Easton, David, and Jack Dennis. *Children in the Political System: Origins of Political Legitimacy.* New York: McGraw-Hill, 1969.

———. "The Child's Image of Government." *The Annals of the American Academy of Political and Social Science,* 361 (1965), pp. 40–57.

———. "The Child's Acquisition of Regime Norms: Political Efficacy." *The American Political Science Review,* 61 (1967), pp. 25–38.

Ginsberg, Benjamin. *The Consequences of Consent: Elections, Citizen Control and Popular Acquiescence.* Reading, Mass.: Addison-Wesley, 1982.

Pollock, John C., Dan White, and Frank Gold. "When Soldiers Return: Combat and Political Alienation among White Vietnam Veterans." In David C. Schwartz and Sandra Kenyon Schwartz (eds.). *New Directions in Political Socialization.* New York: Free Press, 1975, pp. 317–333.

Prezeworski, Adam. "Institutionalization of Voting Patterns, or is Mobilization the Source of Decay." *The American Political Science Review,* 69 (1975), pp. 49–67.

Sigel, Roberta, and Marilyn Brookes Hoskin. "Perspectives on Adult Political Socialization—Areas of Research." In Stanley Allen Renshon (ed.). *The Handbook of Political Socialization.* New York: Free Press, 1977, pp. 259–293.

Schwartz, Sandra Kenyon. "Preschoolers and Politics." In David C. Schwartz and Sandra Kenyon Schwartz (eds.). *New Directions in Political Socialization.* New York: Free Press, 1975, pp. 229–253.

CHAPTER 5

The Political Agenda

Before deciding how to solve a problem or how to deal with an issue, that problem or issue must be perceived as important enough to be considered at all. The issues a nation considers to be important are known as its political agenda. In this chapter the relationship between the political agenda and the effects of generation, periods, and the life cycle on it is explored.

AGENDA-BUILDING AND THE SIXTIES

Even in the age of large bureaucratic governments and extensive entitlement programs, not all issues people consider important become part of a nation's priority list. This imbalance between demands and the government's ability to satisfy those demands leads to competition among advocates of different issues to have their concerns included on the national agenda. This can be attempted in a number of ways. A case can be placed on a court's docket. A bill can be introduced or hearings held in Congress. It might be included in the president's State of the Union address. It can be touted as a campaign issue or made part of a party platform. It can be presented in such a way that it gains a lot of media attention. Whatever the means, the issue must attain a legitimacy that will result in some action being taken on it.

An issue can become part of a nation's political agenda in several ways. The simplest is for people in positions of power to consider it important. Political leaders, economic and social elites, and the national media have easy access to the means by which issues become part of the agenda (Mills, 1956; Edleman, 1967). When, for example, a president becomes personally concerned with human rights issues, when the communications industry lobbies for changes in the laws that regulate them, or when the media focuses national attention on a political scandal like Watergate, these issues usually become part of the political agenda. Getting an issue on the agenda does not necessarily mean it will be resolved, but it is a necessary step in the process of having it dealt with.

Some issues can also become part of the agenda as a result of events (Burnham, 1970; Sundquist, 1973). The outbreak of war, an economic depression, or the assassination of a political leader, for example, are so important or dramatic that they demand action of some kind. They literally force themselves onto the political agenda. The depression of the early 1930s, or the attack on Pearl Harbor are obvious examples of this type of agenda setting.

National priorities can also be set from the "bottom up" (Cobb and Elder, 1972). That is, issues can reach prominence because intense public interest in them forces elites such as the media or government officials to address them. The civil-rights movement of the fifties, the ERA movement of the seventies, and the nuclear-freeze movement of the eighties are examples of issues that have been forced onto the political agenda by grassroots activism. Again, becoming part of the agenda does not guarantee success, but is a necessary prerequisite if success is ever to be achieved.

Finally, issues can become part of the political agenda

through a more passive, evolutionary process of change. Changes in the makeup of a population can slowly lead to shifts in its priorities. Many such shifts (though not all of them) eventually lead to changes in the type of leaders selected and the types of issues dealt with. Consider the role of population shifts in the New Deal realignment (Andersen, 1979A; 1979B), and in the rise of post-materialist issues during the 1970s (Inglehart, 1971, 1977). Similarly, increases in spending for public education paralleled the "baby boom" generation's reaching school age, and the spread of federal entitlements to the middle class occurred as large segments of the population became part of that class.

Most issues that find their way onto the political agenda do so by combining elements from several or all of the approaches outlined above. In this chapter we are interested in the part of this process requiring some change in the public's political priorities. That is, in order for agendas to develop as the result of gradual change in the public, the mobilization of public interest by intense minorities, reaction to sudden events, or (though less often) the changing priorities of elites, there must, at some point, be a change in the political focus of the citizenry. This change can signal the beginning of the process (as in gradual agenda change), the middle of the process (as in change through social movements), or the end of the process (as in some instances of elite-based agenda change), but it is a prerequisite for most lasting forms of agenda setting (Ginsberg and Weissberg, 1978; Ginsberg, 1982).

In particular, how did some of the developments of the sixties come to play a part in this critical stage of agenda setting? First, the sixties witnessed many "events" that affected the political priorities of the public. These included the assassinations of several political leaders, the war in Vietnam, urban violence, student unrest, and racial tensions. All were significant enough to force rather abrupt agenda changes. What was politically important to people in the fifties was not necessarily what was politically important to them in the sixties.

A second aspect of the sixties that undoubtedly affected agenda setting was the rise to prominence of several social movements, and the favorable public reception accorded to them. We discussed in Chapter Two the willingness of the dominant culture to respond to subcultural forces during this decade. This tendency resulted in movements such as the civil-rights movement, the antiwar movement, and the youth movement having access to the political agenda of the larger public in unprecedented ways during this era.

Finally, there were changes in the makeup of the population itself during this time that affected the national agenda. Generational replacement, the aging of both the sixties generation and the presixties cohorts, and the interaction of these processes suggests the possibility that the population's political agenda would come to reflect these changes. To the extent that the links between mass political attitudes and opinions and the cultural, economic and political environments discussed in Chapter Two are real, they should be apparent in the political priorities of the sixties generation and in the changing priorities of the presixties cohorts.

PATTERNS OF AGGREGATE CHANGE

To determine changes in the political priorities of the American public from the fifties through the seventies, we selected from the National Election Studies a survey item that was asked from 1960 through 1980 and that tapped people's personal political agendas.[1] The item is an open-ended question that asked respondents to give their opinions of the most important issue currently facing the nation. It serves, there-

The Political Agenda

fore, as a measure of the political priorities of individual citizens, and when aggregated can be used as a measure of the public's political agenda.

Responses were coded by the Center for Political Studies according to the general issue-areas listed in Table 5.1.[2] In the analysis to follow, each of these categories was treated as a separate item by the use of dummy variables (if an issue is mentioned, it is coded as one; if not, it is coded as zero).

As can be seen, many different issues were mentioned as matters of political concern during the three decades examined. These issues ranged from domestic to international and from political to social and economic. Not all issues were mentioned with equal frequency from one year to the next,

TABLE 5.1
Description of Measures of the Public's Political Agenda[a]

Variable	Description
Social welfare	Social welfare problems (unemployment, education, health care, aid to minorities, etc.)
Agriculture	Problems relating to agriculture, etc.
Environment	Problems relating to environment, wildlife, etc.
Labor	Problems relating to labor or management relations, unions, wage guideline, etc.
Race	Problems relating to civil rights, etc.
Public order	Problems relating to racial, student unrest, civil disorder, crime, etc.
Economy	Problems relating to inflation, taxes, state of the economy, etc.
Consumer	Problems relating to consumer protection, etc.
Vietnam	Problems relating to the war in Vietnam
Foreign affairs	Problems relating to U.S. relations with other countries, world tension, communism, etc.
Defense	Problems of defense spending, national security, etc.
Arms race	Problems relating specifically to the arms race
Government	Problems related to the running of government (honesty, size of government, federalism, etc.)
Other	General category (other responses, issues, etc.)

[a] All variables coded as 1 = mentioned; 0 = not mentioned.

however. Figure 5.1 presents the aggregate patterns of change in the political agenda of the U.S. population. The entries can be interpreted as the percentage of the electorate which mentioned that issue area as one of the most important problems facing the nation. As can be seen, there is a fair

FIGURE 5.1
Patterns of Change in the Political Agenda, 1960–1980

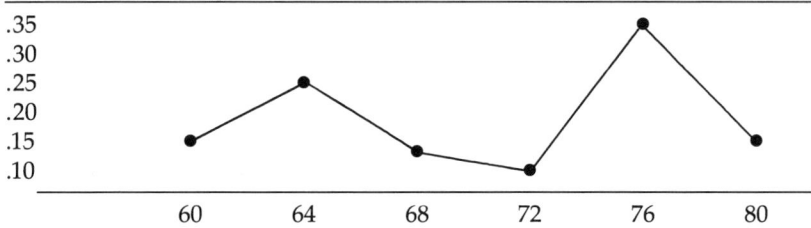

FIGURE 5.1A
Social welfare

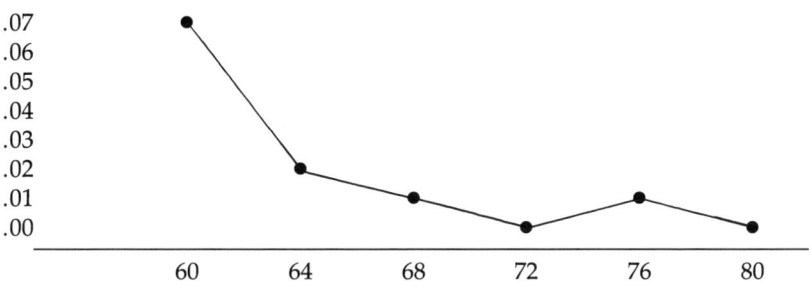

FIGURE 5.1B
Agriculture

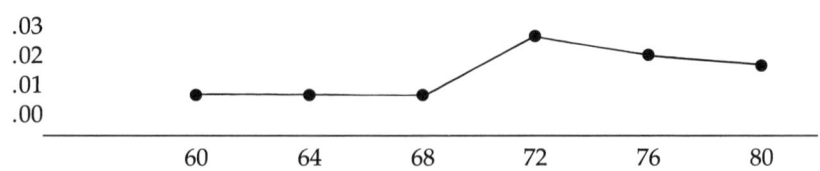

FIGURE 5.1C
Environment

The Political Agenda

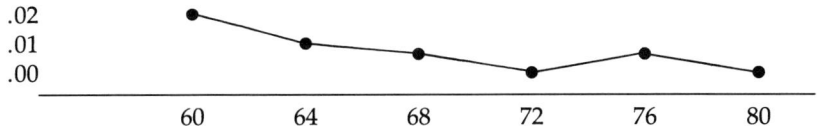

FIGURE 5.1D
Labor

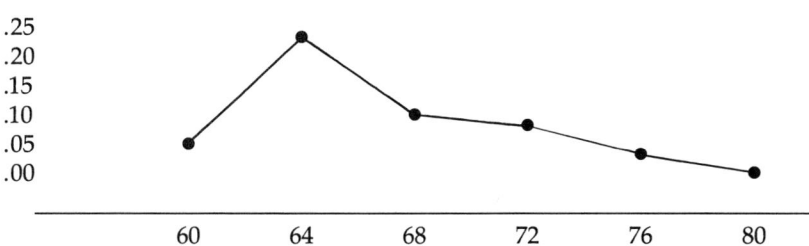

FIGURE 5.1E
Race

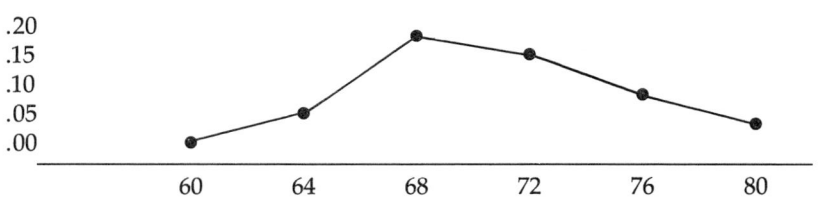

FIGURE 5.1F
Public Order

The Effects of Generation, Periods, and the Life Cycle

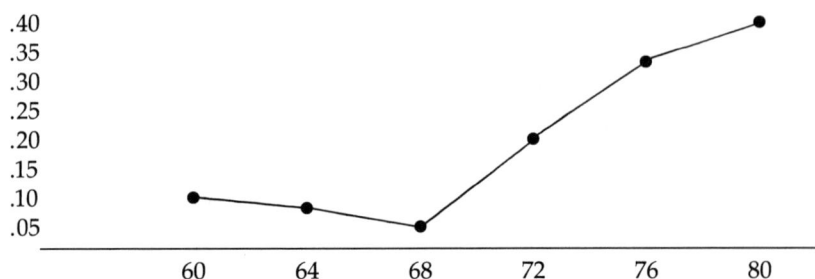

FIGURE 5.1G
Economy

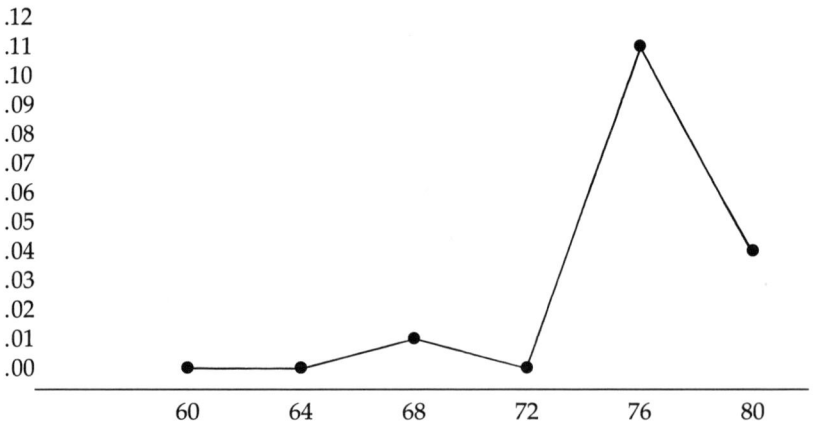

FIGURE 5.1H
Consumer

The Political Agenda

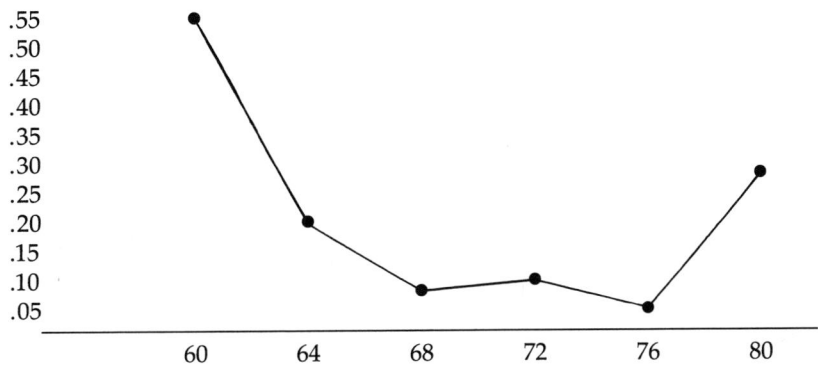

FIGURE 5.1I
Foreign Affairs

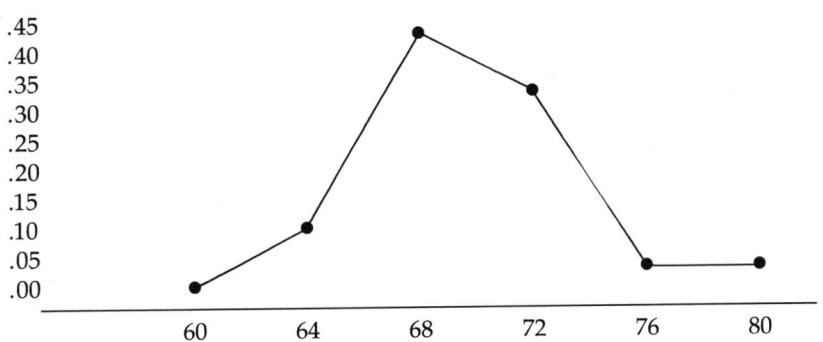

FIGURE 5.1J
Vietnam

The Effects of Generation, Periods, and the Life Cycle

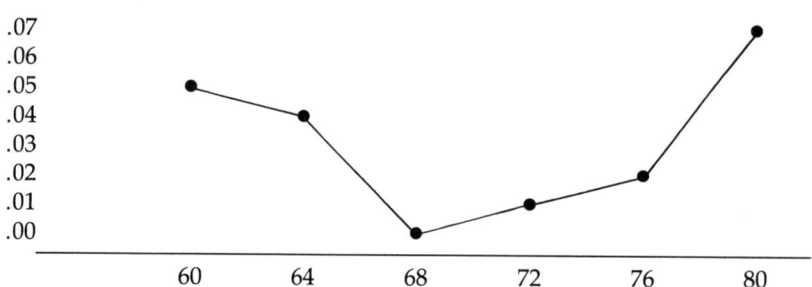

FIGURE 5.1K
Defense

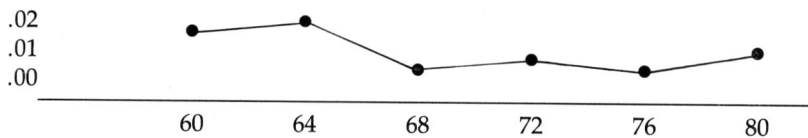

FIGURE 5.1L
Arms Race

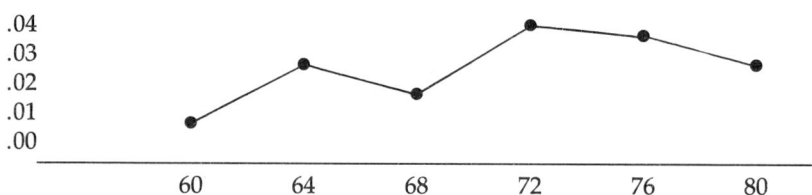

FIGURE 5.1M
Government

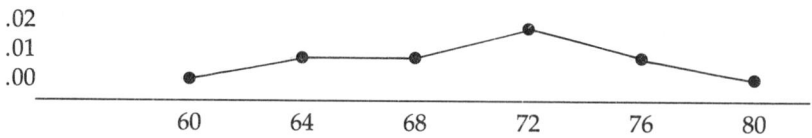

FIGURE 5.1N
Other

The Political Agenda

amount of volatility in the choice of issues over time. Social welfare, for example, was mentioned by almost 25 percent of the population in 1964, but less than 10 percent in 1972, and by 36 percent in 1976. Certain issues, such as foreign affairs and national defense, were considered to be important prior to and following the sixties, but were thought to be relatively unimportant during that period. Others (public order and, of course, Vietnam) demonstrate exactly the reverse trend. Issues revolving around agricultural concerns and race relations were considered less and less important from 1960 on, while environmental issues and concern over the economy became of increased concern in the late sixties and remained relatively important thereafter. Consumer affairs became an important issue in 1976, but seems unable to maintain momentum beyond that point. Finally, issues relating to labor, the arms race, and the running of government show some fluctuation, but generally remained "undercurrents," never really becoming of great concern.

LIFE CYCLE, GENERATION, PERIODS, AND AGENDA CHANGE

To what extent are the patterns of change and stability in the political agenda of the public the result of life cycle, periods, and generation? To answer this question we again performed the cohort analysis described in Chapter Three, this time with the 14 measures of the political agenda as the dependent variables. Table 5.2 presents the main effects of our three independent variables. The effects of the life cycle suggest that some priorities in the agenda are related to age, though seven of the 14 measures show no relationship in this regard. The relationships that do exist hint at a movement as one grows older away from public concerns (as demonstrated by the negative effects on race, foreign affairs, and defense matters) and toward private, personal concerns such as social

TABLE 5.2
Life Cycle, Generation, and Period Effects on the Political Agenda

Variable	Life Cycle	Generation	Period	
			Sixties	Seventies
Social welfare	.002	.036	.084	.271**
Agriculture	.001**	.026**	−.021**	−.058**
Environment	.000	.000	−.001	.040**
Labor	−.001**	−.024**	−.038**	−.040**
Race	−.001	.028	.174**	−.090*
Public order	.000	−.003	.067*	.061
Economy	.001	−.014	.028	.323**
Consumer	.000	−.006	.002	.123**
Foreign affairs	−.001	−.049	−.464**	−.614**
Vietnam	.000	.010	.141**	−.024
Defense	−.001	−.024	−.027	−.042*
Arms race	.000	.012*	.003	−.010
Government	.000	−.006	.039**	.028*
Other	.000	.015**	.012**	.028**

* = standard error ≤ B.
** = p ≤ .05.

welfare and the state of the economy. The decreasing interest in labor issues does not obviously fit this pattern, though undoubtedly part of this negative association is due to retirement. Similarly, the positive relationship with agriculture issues might reflect a concern over food prices (which are included in this measure). We do not want to make too much of age-related differences between concern over public and private issues, however, since the tendency is a weak one at best, and because these relationships could easily be interpreted in some other way. The safer conclusion is to note simply that age does have some small effect on the choice of an agenda.

What impact did the entrance of the sixties generation into the electorate have on the political agenda? Several patterns suggest themselves. First, consistent with Inglehart's notion of postmaterialist change, this generation demonstrates less concern than its predecessors with material issues such as

The Political Agenda

the economy and consumer affairs and with security issues such as public order, foreign affairs and defense.[3] In addition, the generation also appeared, as Inglehart has argued, to be less involved with the hierarchical, traditional institutions that characterize industrial democracies (evidenced by the negative relationships with concern over the running of government and labor issues). Surprisingly, however, they were not any more concerned with environmental issues than other generations, though such issues are typical of the "quality of life" concerns that Inglehart argues should have disproportionately attracted this generation.[4] More consistent with the traditional image of this generation is its emphasis on the issues of the sixties: social welfare, racial matters, Vietnam, and the arms race. The sizes of the three latter coefficients are surprisingly small, however. Finally, the positive association with "other" issue stands suggests that this generation was interested in issues that were not part of the mainstream agenda.

It is the effects of distinct political periods that had the greatest impact on the choice of issues for the agenda. During the sixties concern lessened for issues centering on agriculture, labor, foreign affairs, and defense. In their place came issues that characterize this decade: social welfare, race, public order, Vietnam, and the running of government. In addition, one can see the beginnings of interest in the economy and in consumer affairs, two issues that would become much more important in the following decade. Again, concern over the environment, an issue usually associated with the sixties, fails to materialize as important. Finally, the small but positive association with "other" issues again suggests that this was a period of an expanding agenda (Bell, 1975; Nie, et al., 1979).

Shifting attention from the sixties to the seventies, one can note some continuity between the two periods—the legacy of the sixties, if you will. Declining interest in agriculture, labor, foreign affairs, and defense which began in the sixties continued through the seventies. Concern with social welfare, public order, and the running of government as well as with "other" issues also persisted. Despite this continuity, however, there were important differences. The seeds of interest in the economy and in consumer affairs, planted in the sixties, reach maturity in the seventies. Issues of race, Vietnam, and, to a lesser extent, the arms race, salient in the sixties, were of less importance in the seventies.[5] And finally, the environment begins to stand out as a matter of at least some small concern. In sum, it is change and continuity in the social, political, cultural and economic environment that is the mainspring of the agenda process.

The relatively small impact of the sixties generation on the agenda of the nation is somewhat surprising given its perceived role as the public's conscience during the 1960s and early seventies. Perhaps the effects of generation are more indirect. To test for this possibility the interaction effects among generation, life cycle, and periods are examined (see Table 5.3). The results of this examination give little indication that the sixties generation contributed much to the formation of the public agenda. To the contrary, the interaction effects suggest that what little distinctiveness existed was being masked. The interaction between life cycle and generation shows that, as the sixties generation grew older, it "returned to the fold": seven of the eight measures of priorities in which there was any interaction are in the opposite direction of the main generational effects (only declining interest in foreign affairs is accentuated with age). This tendency towards conformity as members of this generation grew older is similar to that found for diffuse support (Chapter Four). As with diffuse support, however, the interaction of age and generation is not strong enough to eliminate com-

The Political Agenda

TABLE 5.3
Interaction Effects on the Political Agenda

Variable	Life Cycle			Generation	
	Generation	Sixties	Seventies	Sixties	Seventies
Social welfare	−.003*	−.001	−.003	−.046	−.092
Agriculture	−.001**	−.001**	.000	−.032**	−.001
Environment	.000	.000	−.001**	.007	−.010
Labor	.000	.001**	.001**	.028**	.025**
Race	−.001	−.002*	.001	−.092*	−.006
Public order	.000	.001	.000	.027	−.012
Economy	.007**	.000	−.002	−.037	−.081
Consumer	.001	.000	−.001*	−.002	−.021
Foreign affairs	−.004*	.001	.004*	.028	.197**
Vietnam	−.001	.002	.001	.171*	.021
Defense	.001	.000	.001	.001	.024
Arms race	.000	.000	.000	−.019**	−.010
Government	.000	.000	.000	−.019*	.000
Other	.000	.000	−.001**	−.016**	−.033**

* = standard error ≤ B.
** = p ≤ .05.

pletely the unique character of this generation for quite some time (with concern over the economy the one notable exception).

The interaction of generation and particular political periods further masks the distinctiveness of the sixties generation, with over two-thirds of these interactions working in the opposite direction of the main effects of generation. In the sixties, only four of the generational effects are reinforced by this interaction: a lack of interest in the economy, consumer issues, and the running of government, and a heightened interest in Vietnam. In the seventies only concern over the public order, the economy, consumer affairs, and Vietnam showed reinforcing main and interaction effects. When the interactions of generation and period are considered along with the interaction of generation and life cycle, one is left with little choice but to conclude that what distinctiveness this generation may actually have in its political agenda has been substantially masked by its interaction with period effects, and is eroding with the passage of time. Only in its concern over Vietnam does this generation consistently stand apart from the times and from its predecessors, and here only in the degree of concern. The only other distinctiveness this generation shows is an odd tendency to react to the sixties and seventies in a rather contrary if unsystematic way (compare the interactions of generation and period in Table 5.3 to the main effects of period in Table 5.2). In light of our other findings, we seem to have uncovered empirical evidence for the characterization of members of this generation as "rebels without a cause," who moved against the mainstream without a clear direction. These findings also suggest the existence of a "generation gap," though not one that was firmly anchored in substantive or even consistent areas of disagreement.

The final set of interactions are those between the life cycle and periods. As with the main effects of life cycle, the interaction effects, where they exist, are relatively small. However, as noted in the chapter on diffuse support, older cohorts tend to resist the effects of distinct periods, with 14 of the 17 interactions that show any relationship working counter to the main effects of both periods. We again attribute this to the conservatizing effects of age which lead to a resistance to change.

When generations are broken down into more specific subgenerations (Table 5.4), we can see one reason why the sixties generation as a whole had so little impact on the political agenda. The three cohorts demonstrated relatively different agendas, with each selecting different issue areas to emphasize. There were some areas of agreement. All three subgenerations showed concern for social welfare issues (though the ambivalent cohort did so to a much greater degree); all three deemphasized foreign affairs to a great degree

TABLE 5.4
Effects of Subgenerations on the Political Agenda

Variable	Ambivalent	Experienced	Socialized
Social welfare	.217**	.006	.049
Agriculture	.057**	−.017*	.044
Environment	−.017	.036**	−.021
Labor	−.046**	−.003	−.047*
Race	.167**	−.183**	−.199
Public order	−.045	.075*	.359*
Economy	−.050	.077**	−.613**
Consumer	−.024	.034**	.080
Foreign affairs	−.208*	−.228**	−.152
Vietnam	−.091	.294**	.246
Defense	−.051	−.092**	.299**
Arms race	.030**	−.018**	−.156**
Government	−.011	.012	.105**
Other	.220**	.005	.032

* = standard error ≤ B.
** = p ≤ .05.

and labor issues to a slight degree; and all three showed a greater than normal interest in "other," less common issue areas, though again this is particularly true of the ambivalent cohort. Beyond these similarities, however, few issues were consistently emphasized or ignored by all three subgenerations. Thus, the ambivalent cohort was particularly concerned with agriculture, race, and the arms race, and less interested in the environment, public order, consumerism, the economy, defense, the running of government, and, somewhat surprisingly, Vietnam. The experienced cohort was more concerned with the environment, public order, consumer affairs, the economy, Vietnam, and the running of government; less emphasis was placed on agriculture, race, defense, and the arms race. Finally, the socialized cohort was primarily concerned with agricultural, public order, consumer affairs, Vietnam, defense, and government issues, and relatively unconcerned with the environment, race, the economy, and the arms race.

Clearly then, the three cohorts that comprise the sixties generation have distinctive agendas that are hidden when combined into a single group. But why have these agendas developed as they have? The areas that show common agreement are not particularly surprising. The common concern over social welfare is consistent with both the purported liberalism of this generation and of the times in which its members came of political age. The particularly strong support by the ambivalent cohort no doubt reflects its closer ties to the Great Society programs of the Johnson administration (it being the oldest of the sixties cohorts). The relative lack of concern over labor issues and foreign affairs (beyond the war in Vietnam) also reflects the nature of the times in which these cohorts entered the electorate: a time free of the world wars which dominated the first half of the century and a highpoint for domestic labor successes. Finally, as was noted for the whole generation, the positive association with "other" issues is consistent first with this generation's focusing on alternative agendas and, second, with the increased number and types of issues that came to be considered relevant to government more generally.

The distinctive elements within each cohort's agenda also have more method than madness to them. Each subgeneration emphasized issues that were most visible or attractive when it was entering the electorate. The ambivalent cohort, entering the electorate when the civil-rights movement was at its peak and when the cold war was chilling relations between the United States and the Soviet Union, places special emphasis on issues of both race and the arms race. However, this cohort entered the electorate before environmental issues, student and urban unrest, consumer affairs, the war in Vietnam, or political corruption and the crises of leadership had come fully onto the scene. Consequently, such issues are less critical to this cohort.

The Political Agenda

The experienced generation's agenda also reflects the times in which it came of age. Environmental issues, public order, consumer affairs, the running of government, and, in particular, Vietnam had all become part of the political environment by the late sixties and early seventies, the time when most of this cohort joined the electorate. The civil-rights movement and the cold war were less visible by this time as well, and, as a result, both had low priorities for this subgeneration. In addition, the economy had begun its downturn as younger members of this cohort entered the electorate, a fact reflected in the interest they pay to this issue area.

Finally, the socialized cohort, which began to enter the electorate in the midseventies, formed an agenda that reflects a mixture of the sixties and seventies. It demonstrates a strong concern over issues of public order, consumer affairs, Vietnam, and the running of government, along with a rising concern over issues of defense as the cold war again heated up. Concern over the environment, an issue of import to the experienced cohort, and concern over race and the arms race, issues focused on by the ambivalent cohort, are downplayed by the socialized subgeneration.

In sum, the analysis of the agendas of the subgenerations suggests that the distinctiveness of the sixties generation lies largely within its specific cohorts rather than across them. All the issues of the sixties are reflected in the agendas of one or another of these cohorts but in distinct ways that result from the juncture of events and age. Not all the patterns are consistent with this argument (in particular, the very strong negative relationship with economic issues for the socialized subgeneration), but taken as a whole they do point out both the logic and the complexity of the agenda-setting process as it applies to this generation. Entering the electorate during a time of tremendous change, each cohort

TABLE 5.5
Interaction Effects between Subgenerations, Life Cycle,
and Periods on the Political Agenda

Variable	Life Cycle			Seventies	
	Ambivalent	Experienced	Socialized	Ambivalent	Experienced
Social welfare	−.021**	−.034**	−.142**	.111	.226**
Agriculture	−.002**	−.002	−.005	−.008	.047**
Environment	.001**	−.003**	.000	−.011	−.003
Labor	.000	−.001*	.011*	.050**	.013*
Race	−.014**	−.010**	.040	.102	.237**
Public order	.004*	−.004	−.108**	−.025	.006
Economy	.017**	.017**	.148**	−.258**	−.305**
Consumer	.003**	−.008**	−.068**	.008	−.001
Foreign affairs	.004	.024**	.222**	.183	.136
Vietnam	.009*	.010	−.056	−.102	−.344**
Defense	.002	.011**	−.046**	.022	.004
Arms race	.000	−.001	.042**	−.012	.033**
Government	.001	.001	−.031**	.000	−.032**
Other	.001**	.001	−.012**	−.061**	−.014*

* = standard error ≤ B.
** = p ≤ .05.

was influenced by events in a way different enough to lead to quite distinctive agendas, yet all with the clear markings of the sixties.

Our final look at the complexities of the sixties generation and the agenda-setting process involves the interactions of subgenerations, life cycle, and periods (Table 5.5). Both the ambivalent and the socialized cohorts reveal the now familiar pattern of becoming less distinctive with age, with 11 of the 12 interactions for the former and all 13 for the latter tending in the opposite direction of the main effect of subgeneration. The experienced cohort, in contrast, does not conform to this pattern; 6 of the 14 interactions actually reinforced the main generational effect. This reinforcement does not increase the emphasis on issues of the sixties, however. Rather, it speeds the deemphasis on race, agriculture, labor, and the arms race, while increasing the emphasis on economic issues.

The Political Agenda

Only the increased emphasis on issues related to the war in Vietnam reflect some continuity that is based on the issues of the sixties, and since even the vestiges of the war are fading in importance, this too will undoubtedly be of little relevance as we move into the end of the eighties.

The interaction of the ambivalent and the experienced cohorts with the seventies reflects the more general pattern found for the generation as a whole: the main effects of subgeneration are masked, and the subgenerations tend to resist the main period effects with little coherence or logic. The subgenerational analysis also suggests that the experienced cohort is more likely than the ambivalent one to demonstrate both of these tendencies, adding to the image of the former cohort as most typical of the sixties generation as a whole.

SUMMARY AND CONCLUDING REMARKS

In this chapter we have examined the relationship between the life cycle, the sixties generation, and specific periods, and the selection of a political agenda by the mass public. The political agenda of a nation can be formed in several different ways, but in most cases public support is a necessary part of the agenda-building process. Public opinion can catalyze that process, be a weapon in the arsenal of competing interest groups, or simply legitimize an agenda after the fact, but in the long run the connection between popular support and political success is both theoretically and substantively important in mass politics. The agenda of a population can change for many reasons. The process of aging acts to change both one's personal priorities and perspectives and one's sense of the nation's needs. Events of the day are also critical in this process, as economic, political and social conditions often force certain issues into positions of priority. Finally, the political concerns of a nation can change because the population itself changes. New generations with unique histories and experiences bring new concerns into the electorate with them.

Our analysis of these forces as they pertain to the sixties suggests that the agenda-setting process is indeed affected by environmental and population changes. Period effects demonstrated the most consistent and interpretable impact on the mass political agenda, with issue areas rising or falling in prominence in response to changes in the social, economic and political environments. The effects of the life cycle were relatively small. At best they hinted at movement away from public concerns and towards personal ones as one ages. Generational differences showed more and slightly larger effects on the agenda. They also provided some evidence that the agenda of the sixties generation was directly affected by the unique times in which it was shaped. This underlying distinctiveness was masked by the interactive effects of both aging and the changing times, however, with the net result that the generation as a whole contributed little to the changes in the national agenda.

A look at the subgenerations helps to explain the relative lack of distinctiveness found in the generation as a whole. While several issue areas were consistently emphasized or deemphasized by all three cohorts, it was the unique pattern of priorities that each adopted that was most notable. This distinctiveness appears to result from the combination of the rapid change in the political environment throughout the sixties and seventies and the different times at which the three cohorts entered the electorate. Issues that were prominent as each cohort came of age hold places of particular emphasis, while others are downplayed. As a result, all the issues of the sixties are emphasized by at least one of the cohorts, but few are emphasized by all three. This subgenerational pattern is also partially obscured by its interaction with aging and with period. The experienced cohort appears most resistant to both these trends. This resistance appears to reflect a lack of clear direction rather than commitment to a specific alternate agenda, however.

What conclusions should be drawn from the analysis presented in this chapter? First, the driving force behind the significant changes in the agenda over the years examined was clearly period-based. By and large the agenda was shaped by the nature and the events of the times. The impact of generational replacement, while present, was mitigated by the effects of its unique interaction with age and period, by the lack of consistent support for or rejection of the more general period effects, and by a lack of agreement among the three cohorts comprising the generation. As the sixties generation ages, therefore, and becomes a still larger percentage of the adult population, there is little reason to anticipate major changes in the dominant priorities of the nation beyond those attributable to the changing environment. In times of economic prosperity and national security it is possible that different segments of this generation would become more responsive to appeals focusing on issues of race, the environment, public order, and the running of government, but for each of these issues, segments of the generation will also remain unmoved. On the other hand, interest in labor issues and in foreign affairs that do not involve direct U.S. intervention may be more difficult to stimulate than in past times. Overall, however, there is little reason to anticipate any systematic restructuring of the political agenda as a result of generational replacement.

NOTES

1. Since the Survey Research Center did not start asking this question

until 1960, the time span being considered in this chapter is shorter than in others. For the analysis which follows, 1960 rather than 1952 serves as the presixties baseline. In addition, period effects for the fifties, based in other chapters on the years 1956 and 1960, are not included here.

2. The general categories provided by the Survey Research Center can be broken down into finer distinctions. In this analysis we include several of them when there was reason to anticipate that they might be relevant to life cycle, period or generational differences. In particular, environmental issues are separated from more general issues concerning agriculture. Race and public order are separated; consumer affairs and economic issues are separated; Vietnam and more general foreign affairs are separated; and the arms race and issues of defense are separated. For more details, see Appendix B.

3. The negative association of generation with foreign affairs could be interpreted as contradicting Inglehart's thesis since he argues that the postmaterialist generation should be more internationalist in its perspective. It is our feeling that this measure captures more of the issues of foreign intervention and concerns of the United States and the Soviet Union than supranationalism however, and so interpret this as supportive of Inglehart's argument concerning security.

4. It is possible, however, that interest in environmental issues is indirectly the driving force behind the positive association between generation and an interest in agricultural issues.

5. The idea of Vietnam remaining an issue into the seventies may seem implausible. The reason it still appears as important in some instances is that citizens continued to raise issues such as the POWs, veterans of the war, relations between the United States and Vietnam, compensation to Vietnam, etc., after the military involvement of the United States was over.

REFERENCES

Andersen, Kristi. "Generation, Partisan Shift, and Realignment: A Glance Back to the New Deal." In Norman Nie, et al., *The Changing American Voter.* Cambridge, Mass.: Harvard University Press, 1979, pp. 74–95.

——. *The Creation of a Democratic Majority.* Chicago: The University of Chicago Press, 1979.

Bell, Daniel. "The Revolution of Rising Entitlements." *Fortune* 91 (April 1975), pp. 98–103.

Burnham, Walter Dean. *Critical Elections and the Mainspring of American Politics.* New York: Norton, 1970.

Cobb, Roger W., and Charles D. Elder. *Participation in American Politics: The Dynamics of Agenda-Building.* Boston: Allyn and Bacon, 1972.

The Political Agenda

Edelman, Murray. *The Symbolic Uses of Politics*. Urbana: The University of Illinois Press, 1967.

Ginsberg, Benjamin. "Polling and the Transformation of Public Opinion," paper presented at the American Political Science Association Meeting, Denver, 1982.

Ginsberg, Benjamin, and Robert Weissberg. "Elections and the Mobilization of Popular Support." *American Journal of Political Science*, 22 (February, 1978), pp. 31–55.

Inglehart, Ronald. "The Silent Revolution: Intergenerational Change in Post-Industrial Societies." *The American Political Science Review*, 65 (1971), pp. 991–1017.

———. *The Silent Revolution*. Princeton: Princeton University Press, 1977.

Mills, C. Wright. *The Power Elite*. New York: Oxford University Press, 1956.

Nie, Norman H., Sidney Verba, and John R. Petrocik. *The Changing American Voter*. Cambridge, Mass.: Harvard University Press, 1979.

Sundquist, James L. *The Dynamics of the Party System*. Washington, D.C.: Brookings, 1973.

CHAPTER 6

Issue Stands

In the last chapter we discussed the effects of the sixties and the sixties generation on the public's political agenda. One of the significant findings concerning the formation of this agenda was that current events are critical in directing the attention of the public to different issues at different times. Determining that an issue is important, however, and deciding specifically what should be done concerning it involve two very different processes. Two individuals or groups may agree, for example, that unemployment is an important problem, but one might feel that the government should do more to increase employment, while the other might be equally certain that the private sector should take the lead. In this chapter we explore the impact of life cycle, generation, and periods on the stands that the American public took on various issues during the fifties, sixties, and seventies. Again, the focus will be on how the events of the sixties and the coming of age of the sixties generation have changed what means the public selects to solve the social and political problems facing the nation.

STANDS ON ISSUES, AGING, AND THE SIXTIES

If there is any agreement in the popular wisdom about the 1960s, it is that it was a period of social, cultural, and political

Issue Stands

liberalism, a shift to the left of dramatic proportions. Discussions of the supposed "shift to the right" in the late seventies and early eighties implicitly or explicitly work from a baseline that assumes a liberal public opinion in the sixties (Steinfels, 1979; Viguerie, 1980). Analyses based on generations also show that the youth of the eighties is becoming conservative compared (again both implicitly and explicitly) to the youth of the sixties (Yankelovich, 1984; Shogan, 1984; Ladd, 1984; Hagstrom, 1984). (Similar conclusions are reached when the fifties are compared to the sixties) (Jones, 1980; Reich, 1970).

A cursory examination of the sixties supports this characterization. The popularity of political figures such as Robert Kennedy, George McGovern, and Eugene McCarthy, the expansion of social programs, the increase in civil-rights legislation, the liberal decisions of the Supreme Court, etc., all indicate a political environment that was shifting to the left. Research on this period reaches similar conclusions, with evidence found for increases in liberal opinions, postmaterialist values, and tolerance for a wider variety of political views (Renshon, 1974; Knutson, 1972; Inglehart, 1977; Nie, et al., 1979). This shift to the left is directly connected to two of the factors under study in this research: generational change and period effects.

The rise of a new and more liberal generation underpins much of the research on opinion change in the 1960s. Conditions of economic growth, political security, and rising educational opportunities combined to offer both the opportunity to consider providing more for the public good and the luxury of paying the costs of this policy without undue hardship. The development of a more liberal perspective was also due to the prior development of a more socially concerned set of values (Renshon, 1974; Knutson, 1972; Inglehart, 1977), as well as to greater receptivity within the young middle class to the norms and needs of various subcultures (discussed in Chapter Two).

The Effects of Generation, Periods, and the Life Cycle

In addition to a more-liberal orientation, it has also been argued that the rise of a new generation in the sixties changed the focus of liberalism away from the economic issues of the New Deal and towards a more-social orientation. This "new left," as it has been called, emphasized civil liberties, education, and social issues over the more-traditional issues of the economy and the workplace (Inglehart, 1977; Miller and Levitan, 1976).

Not all of the ideological changes were brought about by the rise of a new generation of Americans. The sixties also had an impact on the larger population's political stances. The economic conditions that encouraged the young to be more public-oriented in their opinions also influenced members of older cohorts, suggesting the possibility of increased liberalism among the latter as well. The plight of disadvantaged members of the society such as blacks, the poor, and native Americans were made more visible than ever before, in part because they became more vocal, in part because mass media made their demands more visible, and in part because the children of the middle class were bringing some of these demands into their homes. In addition, the increased entitlements stressed by the political programs of the period (Johnson's Great Society) provided an environment that emphasized liberal approaches to political problems (Bell, 1975; Beck and Jennings, 1979).

Despite the liberal tendencies of the sixties, however, one is not compelled to expect liberal opinions to be the norm. As discussed in Chapter Two, economic success is often tied to political conservatism, especially in a society that stresses individual self-determination and a Calvinistic work ethic (Weber, 1958). The demands of vocal minorities could be considered threats to one's personal position as easily as they could be considered reasonable. In addition, the social and cultural heterogeneity of the period could underpin a reac-

Issue Stands

tionary set of opinions if the new values and norms seemed to challenge the ethics that led to the current success of American society in the first place. Finally, the old left might easily perceive the rise of a new left as a new rival for government and public attention rather than as an ally in a struggle between the left and right. In short, both within the middle-class segment of the youth movement (which constituted most of that generation) and between generations, the period contained cross pressures that could bring about changing stands, but not necessarily in a consistently liberal direction.

If the formation of stands on issues is considered a dynamic process taking place over time, the process is complicated by the effects of the life cycle. Research suggests that with age, one's political views become more conservative (Jennings and Niemi, 1974, 1981; Nie, et al., 1979). To the extent that shifts in the aggregate opinions of the population of the United States in the sixties result from a large and vocal young cohort entering the electorate (with sympathetic or reactionary changes occurring among older cohorts) rather than from change based on the entrance of a new generation or from the changing political environment, the long-term stability of such shifts is in doubt. Recent suggestions that public sentiment has moved to the right may indicate either new period effects or the aging of the public. The key to documenting the extent of changes in the issue stands of the American public, determining the sources of those changes, and interpolating their stability over time, lies in untangling their life cycle, generational and period-based roots.

AGGREGATE PATTERNS OF ISSUE STANDS

Between 1952 and 1980 the National Election Surveys asked questions concerning several important and wide-ranging is-

The Effects of Generation, Periods, and the Life Cycle

sues.[1] These are described in Table 6.1. They include social issues (spending on education, health care), civil-rights issues (black welfare, integration), economic issues (employment), and issues of international scope (foreign aid, interventionism). These measures tap the extent to which the public preferred to see more or less government involvement in the particular areas under consideration, and so provide not only a look at stands on specific issues, but also a more general sense of movement on a liberal-conservative continuum.[2] It is these issues that will be used to determine the effects of generation, life cycle, and periods on the stands taken by the American public.

Our first task is to examine the aggregate levels of change in the issue stands during the periods in question. Figure 6.1 presents the mean scores for the population over time. The scales upon which these scores are based run from zero to one, with one indicating a desire for more federal government involvement and zero indicating a desire for less federal

TABLE 6.1
Description of the Measures of Issue Stands[a]

Variable	Description
Education	Should the government do more to aid public education?
Health	Should the government provide national health care/insurance?
Jobs	Should the government actively work towards guaranteeing work for all?
Integration	Should the government work towards aiding racial integration?
Black welfare	Should the government help to insure jobs and housing for blacks?
Interventionism	Should the U.S. stay out of world affairs?
Foreign aid	Should the U.S. provide financial aid to foreign countries?

[a]All variables are coded as follows: 1 = greater government involvement; 0 = less government involvement.

Issue Stands

involvement. To the extent that federal involvement in the domestic issues listed here is a measure of a liberal political strategy, increases in the mean scores indicate a move to the left. (The isolationist and foreign-aid issues are more complicated to interpret in simple left-right terms, an issue we deal with later in this chapter.)

As can be seen in Figures 6.1A to 6.1G, the trend from the fifties through the sixties was an increasing desire for less government involvement in domestic issues, a tendency that by contemporary use of the term indicates movement in a conservative direction. While some researchers would not be surprised by this trend (Bishop, et al., 1978; Podhoretz, 1981; Scammon and Wattenberg, 1970), most students of the sixties would have anticipated a growing liberalism compared to the prior decade. Less surprising is the increasing conservatism that developed (for the measures that are available in 1976 and/or 1980) in the years following the sixties, though there is disagreement on the substance of this trend as well (Frankovic, 1980; Paletz and Entman, 1982).

The changes in issue stands concerning isolationism and

Figure 6.1
Trends in Selected Issue Stands, 1952–1980
(entries are the mean score on a scale running from zero to one)

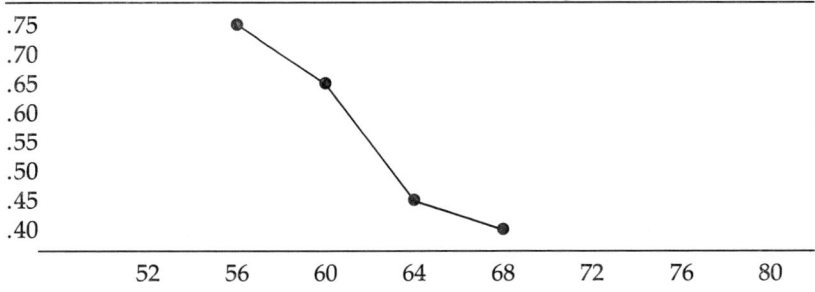

FIGURE 6.1A
Education

The Effects of Generation, Periods, and the Life Cycle

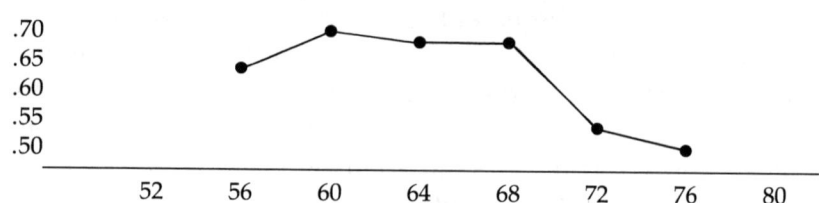

FIGURE 6.1B
Health Care

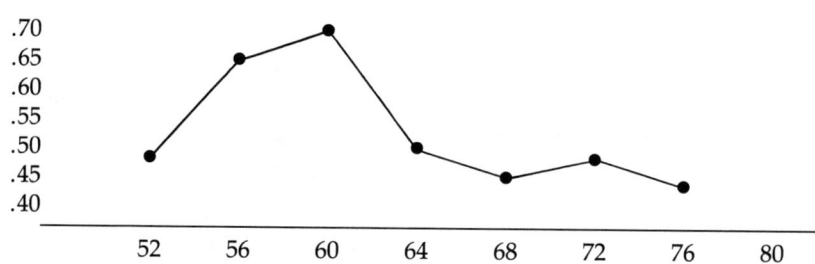

FIGURE 6.1C
Jobs

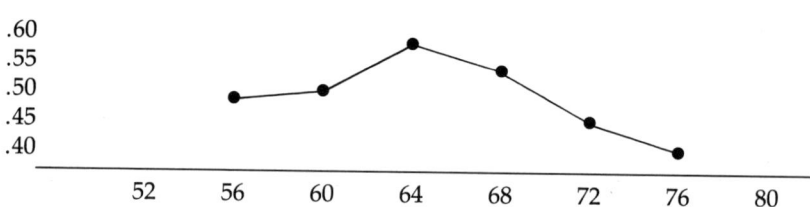

FIGURE 6.1D
Integration

Issue Stands

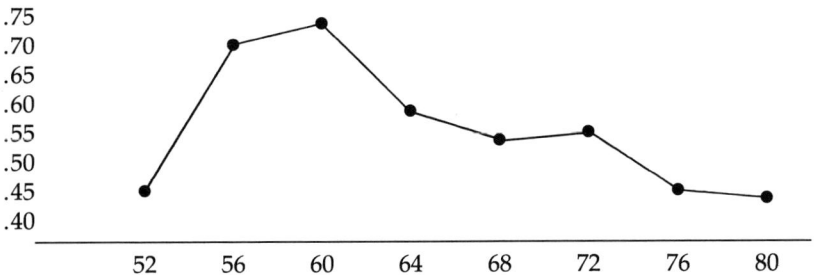

FIGURE 6.1E
Black welfare

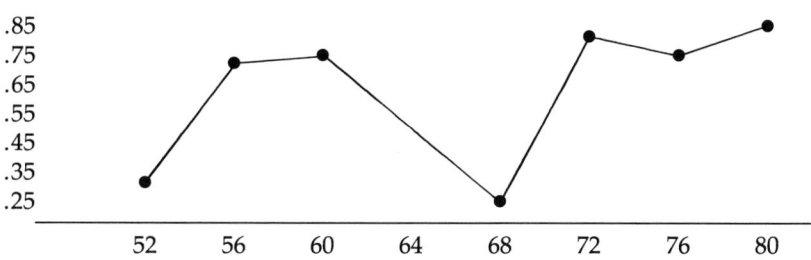

FIGURE 6.1F
Interventionism

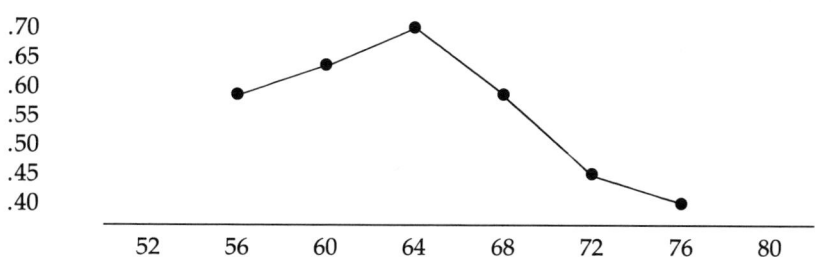

FIGURE 6.1G
Foreign Aid

foreign aid were more difficult to interpret in part because of the nature of the patterns over time and in part because of the difficulty in determining what represents a liberal or conservative stand. The trend in support for government involvement in world affairs ("interventionism") shows very low support in 1952 and 1968, with the other years demonstrating a very slight increase. No doubt the two low points represent a reaction to the Korean and Vietnam wars, and so it is tempting to argue that decreased support for government involvement indicates a more liberal stand. On the other hand, isolationism is often linked to more conservative philosophies, especially during times of peace (McCloskey, 1958). In this case, rising support might indicate greater liberalism of a sort.

Opinions on aid to foreign countries show yet a different pattern, with support growing until 1964, but then decreasing markedly until 1976. Again the decline could represent a rising distrust of the motives of the United States, or an increasing isolationist attitude. We will, therefore, delay interpreting these trends as being liberal or conservative until the more specific analyses are discussed. Overall, however, there was a good deal of change in opinions over the three decades examined, and where these changes can be interpreted as being liberal or conservative, the evidence points to growing conservatism in the sixties and seventies. Why there should be growing conservatism in a period noted for its liberal policies is a question we attempt to answer in the next section.

EFFECTS OF THE LIFE CYCLE, PERIODS, AND GENERATION ON ISSUE STANDS

To what extent are the effects of the life cycle, generation and periods responsible for the aggregate patterns of issue stands discussed above? Table 6.2 provides the first clue, showing

Issue Stands

TABLE 6.2
Effects of Life Cycle, Generation, and Period on Issue Stands

Variable	Life cycle	Generation	Period		
			Fifties	Sixties	Seventies
Education	−.003**	.003	−.106**	−.240**	***
Health	.003**	.151**	.035	.043	−.180**
Jobs	−.002**	.123**	−.003	−.122**	−.165**
Integration	−.004**	.054*	.053	.030	−.091
Black welfare	−.001	.010	.217**	.110**	−.002
Interventionism	−.003*	−.064	.363**	−.193*	.426**
Foreign aid	.001	−.015	.063	.264**	−.107

* = standard error ≤ B.
** = $p \leq .05$.
*** = not calculated.

the main effects of these three processes. A positive coefficient indicates that greater government involvement was favored; a negative coefficient indicates the reverse. As can be seen, the process of aging does indeed generally lead to more conservative stands, with older cohorts more likely to favor less government involvement in education, employment, integration, black welfare, and world affairs. Not surprisingly, this growing conservatism with age is *not* found in the area of health care, an issue of increasing relevance as one grows older. Only the slight positive relationship between the life cycle and support for aid to foreign countries is inexplicable either by growing conservatism or self-interest. As was discussed earlier, it is possible that such support represents a different dimension of conservatism than the one tapped by the other measures.

When we turn to the effects of being a member of the sixties generation, the reverse pattern is uncovered. In all five domestic issue areas, the sixties generation consistently supported government involvement. These liberal leanings cut across issues of race, civil liberties, economics, and social concerns. The tendency towards isolationism and less foreign

The Effects of Generation, Periods, and the Life Cycle

aid is also understandable in light of the resistance to the Vietnam war and the suspicion the war engendered concerning the intentions of the United States abroad. But again we can only speculate on the motives underlying these trends (though we look at this in greater detail later in this chapter).

The period effects demonstrate somewhat less consistent patterns, though even here the overall trends are still revealing. For domestic policies the movement is clearly conservative, as can be seen by both the relative change in the size of the coefficients and, especially in the seventies, the direction of those coefficients. By the seventies all four of the domestic policies for which we have measures show negative relationships, indicating a desire for less government involvement in these policy areas. Opinions concerning the issues of foreign aid and interventionism show a more volatile pattern. The fifties was a period of great support for government involvement on both measures. The sixties and seventies were periods of mixed support. The sentiment in the sixties was undoubtedly due to a reaction to the war in Vietnam, with support declining for interventionism but increasing for foreign aid more generally. The pattern found in the seventies may indicate a conservative "backlash" of sorts, with strong support for interventionism, but a lack of support for aid to foreign nations. It is particularly revealing to note how quickly period-based support for government involvement in world affairs "rebounded" after the end of the war to even greater levels than those demonstrated during the fifties.

In Table 6.3 the effects of interactions among the three main variables are presented. Of particular interest is the interaction between life cycle and generation. As the sixties generation aged, almost all its stands began to erode, with some of the main effects reversing rather quickly. The somewhat liberal stand of this generation on educational policy

Issue Stands

TABLE 6.3
Interaction Effects on Issue Stands

Variable	Life cycle				Generation	
	Generation	Fifties	Sixties	Seventies	Sixties	Seventies
Education	−.003*	.003**	***	***	.009	***
Health	−.007**	.001	−.002*	.000	−.059	.037
Jobs	−.005**	.005**	.002**	.003**	−.044*	−.056
Integration	−.005**	.000	.001	.001	−.038	−.039
Black welfare	−.002**	.002**	−.001*	−.001	.019	.031
Interventionism	.006*	−.001	.008**	−.001	.157	−.058
Foreign aid	.000	.000	−.007**	−.002	−.151**	−.033

* = standard error ≤ B.
** = p ≤ .05.
*** = not calculated.

was overwhelmed by the interaction of age and generation in a single year, while support for government aid for blacks was lowered to the consensus of the rest of society after members of the generation had been in the electorate for five years. Liberal stands on integration (11 years), health care (22 years) and employment (25 years) were more resistant to erosion over time, however.

Support for government involvement in world affairs is also increasing among members of the sixties generation, with their opinions in this regard matching those of their predecessors (when they were the same age) after ten or 11 years in the electorate. Opinions concerning foreign aid, which were slightly less supportive among members of the sixties generation, showed no interaction with age. Overall, however, one again is struck with the "pull" towards the status quo or norm that aging exerts (or more accurately, that society exerts through the life-cycle process).

The interaction of generation and distinct periods produced some interesting but complex patterns that are not easily interpreted. The tendency towards liberal stands demonstrated by the sixties generation was reinforced for edu-

The Effects of Generation, Periods, and the Life Cycle

cation policy and aid to blacks in the sixties, but was weakened for issues concerning health care, employment, and integration. With the exception of education policy, all of these interactions are consistent with the relative changes in period effects from the fifties to the sixties. As such, they probably reflect the additional influence of the sixties environment on the generation then reaching political maturity (the failure of educational policy to reflect this conservative interaction no doubt results from the relevance of this issue to members of the sixties generation, many of whom were students during that period). The interaction of generation and the seventies indicates slightly greater resistance to the main effects of period, however, with opinions on health care and black welfare showing positive (liberal) interactions in the face of the more conservative environment. In addition, the interaction terms for both foreign aid and interventionism are consistent with the main effects of generation and run counter to the period effects of the sixties, adding to the image of resistance in the sixties generation (the coefficients for these two interactions in the seventies are less consistent).

The final set of interactions (between age and periods) again demonstrate the tendency of older cohorts to resist changes in the political environment, with 11 of the 16 interactions that show any relationship working in the opposite direction of the main effects of the period. Finding this pattern even when the period effect is conservative adds further evidence to the interpretation that we are capturing a distinct dimension of conservatism, representing resistance to sudden change rather than the ideological conservatism tapped by the measures themselves.

Are the subgenerations within the sixties generation homogeneous in their issue stands? The relationships demonstrated in Table 6.4 indicate that by and large they are not,

Issue Stands

TABLE 6.4
Effects of Subgenerations on Issue Stands

Variable	Ambivalent	Experienced	Socialized
Education	−.030	.886**	***
Health	.323**	.170**	−.445**
Jobs	.211**	.124**	.117
Integration	.117*	−.020	−.095
Black welfare	.003	.088**	.187
Interventionism	−.439**	.467**	.768**
Foreign aid	.128*	−.199**	−.461*

* = standard error ≤ B.
** = $p \leq .05$.
*** = not calculated.

the three cohorts being consistently liberal concerning employment policy and black welfare only. Concerning domestic policy the experienced cohort is most supportive of government involvement in education, the ambivalent cohort of government involvement in health care, employment, and integration, and the socialized cohort of government involvement in economic aid to blacks. Overall the greatest contrast is between the ambivalent and experienced cohorts, which are more liberal in their stands on domestic policy, and the socialized cohort, which is less liberal as a rule. This perhaps reflects the fact that the socialized generation came of age in the seventies, the most conservative of the three periods examined.

The subgenerations also had different opinions concerning foreign policy. The ambivalent cohort was opposed to the involvement of the United States in world affairs, though supportive of foreign aid, while the experienced and socialized cohorts demonstrated the reverse views. We are at a loss to explain either why each cohort held its particular stands on the two issues, or why the ambivalent cohort differed from the others. The stands of the ambivalent cohort were most consistent with a reasoned rejection of military

TABLE 6.5
Interaction Effects between Subgenerations, Life Cycle, and Periods on Issue Stands

Variable	Life cycle			Seventies	
	Ambivalent	Experienced	Socialized	Ambivalent	Experienced
Education	−.001	−.260**	***	***	***
Health	−.016**	−.043**	***	.044	.338**
Jobs	−.005**	−.019**	***	−.097*	.111*
Integration	−.010**	−.012	***	.009	.184*
Black welfare	−.002	−.014**	−.049*	.070	.068*
Interventionism	.056**	.055**	−.169	−.732**	−.932**
Foreign aid	−.022**	−.029*	***	.213*	.324**

* = standard error ≤ B.
** = p ≤ .05.
*** = not calculated.

expansionism coupled with support for economic aid to foreign countries; as such it appears the most liberal, but again the measures are too general to draw a compelling conclusion from this.

The interaction effects of subgeneration, life cycle, and periods presented in Table 6.5 demonstrate much greater consistency across the cohorts.[3] For both the ambivalent and the experienced subgenerations (and for the one interaction for the socialized cohort) aging clearly leads to increased conservatism on domestic issues, with the experienced cohort losing its liberalism at a greater rate. Both older cohorts are also consistent in their becoming more supportive of the involvement of the United States in world affairs and less supportive of foreign aid, trends also that can be interpreted as conservative. Interestingly the socialized cohort, initially the most supportive of interventionism, is becoming less so with age, indicating that the interaction results in a pull back to the status quo and not to ideological conservatism in and of itself.

The ambivalent and experienced cohorts are also consis-

Issue Stands

tent (with each other and, to a slightly lesser degree, with the interaction of generation and the seventies) in their reaction to the seventies, with both demonstrating increasingly liberal stands in the face of a more conservative trend in domestic and in foreign policy. This pattern is more pronounced for the experienced cohort than for the ambivalent one.

The inconsistency among the subgenerations concerning foreign affairs (Table 6.4, above) is the one part of this analysis that is the most difficult to interpret. Clearly the war in Vietnam is at least partly responsible for the variations, and yet the measures did not allow us to address this issue directly. In 1952, however, two questions were asked concerning the Korean conflict, and these questions were asked again in 1968 and 1972 concerning the war in Vietnam. Acknowledging that the two wars were dissimilar in many ways, there were enough parallels between the two to use these measures as imperfect gauges of opinions concerning such military interventionism. The first ("Involvement") measures the extent of support for involvement by the United States in these southeast Asian nations, with complete support coded as one and complete opposition coded as zero. The second item ("Solution") measures the strategy preferred to end the conflicts, with one indicating support for a military solution and zero for an immediate withdrawal.

Table 6.6 presents the main and interaction effects for the generation as a whole. Older cohorts were more opposed to both the involvement and to a miliary solution. In addition, opposition to the involvement of the United States in Vietnam was greater than to its involvement in Korea (as demonstrated by the period effects of the sixties), as was opposition to a military solution. The sixties generation was considerably more opposed to involvement by the United States in southeast Asia than preceding generations, but sur-

TABLE 6.6
Main and Interaction Effects for Life Cycle, Generation, and Period on Opinions towards Korea and Vietnam[a]

Variables	Life Cycle	Generation	Sixties
Involvement	−.005**	−.164**	−.048*
Solution	−.001**	.059*	−.069**

Variables	Life cycle	
	Generation	Sixties
Involvement	.007**	−.002**
Solution	−.006**	−.001

[a]Positive relationship indicates greater support for involvement by the United States and a desire for military solution.
* = standard error ≤ B.
** = $p \leq .05$.

prisingly, less supportive of immediate withdrawal. Again, the interaction of age and generation caused this generation to conform to the norm on both measures, but the interaction of age and the sixties did not show its usual resistance to period effects, with older cohorts even more opposed to the war and a military solution during this time. This set of findings is consistent with the analysis of Erikson, et al. (1980). They found that aside from students in the elite educational institutions, the young were more supportive of the war than were older generations, though our findings suggested a distinction between opinions about being involved and those concerning ending the conflict.

An examination of subgenerational differences (Table 6.7) indicates that the distinction between involvement and solution existed for both of the sixties cohorts that were part of the electorate in 1968 and 1972. The experienced cohort, however, was both more opposed to the initial involvement of the United States in Vietnam and less supportive of a military solution than the ambivalent one. In addition, unlike the am-

Issue Stands

TABLE 6.7
Effects of Subgenerations on Opinions Concerning
Korea and Vietnam

Variables	Ambivalent	Experienced
Involvement	−.074	−.108*
Solution	.124**	.050

Variables	Life Cycle	
	Ambivalent	Experienced
Involvement	.001	−.011
Solution	−.010**	−.005

* = standard error ≤ B.
** = $p \leq .05$.

bivalent cohort, those who directly experienced the sixties became more opposed to the war as they aged (both cohorts increasingly favored immediate withdrawal). Overall, the sixties generation, while more opposed to the involvement of the United States in southeast Asia, was not convinced that, once involved, withdrawal was the best solution. This distinction may be the reason why opinions by different cohorts concerning more-general foreign policy appear to be erratic over time. It also suggests that the sixties generation itself was not totally nor accurately represented by its more vocal representatives.

SUMMARY AND CONCLUDING REMARKS

In this chapter we have examined the effects of aging, period and the sixties generation on the stands taken by the American public on various issues. The complexities of the time might lead one to believe that movement in either a conservative or a liberal direction was plausible, with the very real possibility of polarization by age groups and across particular types of issues. The analysis in this chapter indicates several things about these speculations. First, the aggregate sentiment during the period studied was for less government involvement in most issues, implying that whatever the mix of competing opinions, the net result was generally conservative. Second, the strongest inducement to assume conservative stands was due to the effects of period and from the aging process (and the presence of older cohorts in individual years), while the greatest support for liberal stands came from the sixties generation. The pattern of interaction effects indicates that cross pressures existed, leading to some liberalization among older cohorts during particular periods, and to some conservative trends among the sixties generation as it aged. On the whole, however, these cross pressures did not include a distinction between new left and old left issues either within the sixties generation or across the population as a whole.

As in prior chapters the analysis of subgenerations revealed that the sixties generation consisted of distinctive cohorts, which differed on the stands they took on issues, though liberal stands remained the norm for the two older cohorts. Opinions concerning foreign affairs showed the most inconsistent and least interpretable patterns, resulting in part from an ambiguity between a general opposition to the involvement of the United States in Vietnam and a lack of support for immediate withdrawal. The interaction effects with aging again, with a few notable exceptions, worked to limit the distinctiveness of subgenerations over time, with unusually liberal stands slowly being replaced by a return to the general consensus of society.

What, then, is the relationship between issue stands and the influence of the 1960s? First, the sixties generation appeared to have been liberally inclined beyond the effects of its relative youth. This liberalism was somewhat reduced, however, by the conservatizing process of aging and by period effects. In addition, members of the youngest cohort within this generation were less liberal than their older brothers and sisters on most of the measures examined. As a result, it appears that the views of the sixties generation have been integrated with those of the mainstream without much more than a slight reduction in the larger conservative trends. As this generation becomes a larger percentage of the population, the effects of aging will reduce the potential for any liberal shift, so that at best it appears that although the rate of growing conservatism may be reduced, it will not be eliminated.

NOTES

1. Not all measures were included in every survey from 1952 to 1980, meaning that some effects (in particular some interaction effects and period effects) could not be calculated.

2. The reader is no doubt aware that the extent of government involvement in the issue areas examined is only one aspect of liberalism or conservatism out of several that are possible. We do not argue that this is the best or only dimension, but only that it is an important one, given the use of this term in the late twentieth century.

3. So few interactions between life cycle and the socialized cohort are presented because the shortened time span for which most of these measures are available limits our ability to make these finer distinctions (see Chapter Three for a discussion of the identification problem).

REFERENCES

Bell, Daniel. "The Revolution in Rising Entitlements." *Fortune* 91 (April, 1975), pp. 98–103.

Beck, Paul Allen, and M. Kent Jennings. "Political Periods and Political Participation." *American Political Science Review* 73 (September, 1979), pp. 737–750.

Bishop, George, Alfred J. Tuchfarber, Robert W. Oldendick, and Stephen E. Bennett. "Change in the Structure of American Political Attitudes." *American Journal of Political Science*, 22 (May, 1978), pp. 250–269.

Erikson, Robert S., Norman R. Luttbeg, and Kent L. Tedin. *American Public Opinion*. New York: John Wiley, 1980.

Frankovic, Kathleen A. "Public Opinion Trends." In Gerald M. Pomper (ed.). *The Election of 1980*. Chatham, N.J.: Chatham House, 1980.

Hagstrom, Jerry. "The Baby Boom Generation: Coming of Age Politically?" *National Journal*, 17 (April 28, 1984), pp. 804–810.

Inglehart, Ronald. *The Silent Revolution*. Princeton: Princeton University Press, 1977.

Jennings, M. Kent, and Richard C. Niemi. *The Political Character of Adolescence*. Princeton: Princeton University Press, 1974.

———. *Generations and Politics*. Princeton: Princeton University Press, 1981.

Jones, Landon Y. *Great Expectations: America and the Baby Boom Generation*. New York: Ballantine Books, 1980.

Knutson, Jeanne. *The Human Basis of Polity*. New York: Aldine Atherton, 1972.

Ladd, Everett Carl. "Opinions Roundup: Values." *Public Opinion* 6 (Fall, 1984), pp. 21–40.

McCloskey, Herbert. "Conservatism and Personality." *American Political Science Review* 52 (1958), pp. 27–45.

Miller, Warren E., and Teresa E. Levitan. *Leadership and Change: The New Politics and the American Electorate*. Cambridge, Mass.: Winthrop Publishers, 1976.

Nie, Norman H., Sidney Verba, and John R. Petrocik. *The Changing American Voter*. Cambridge, Mass.: Harvard University Press, 1979.

Paletz, David L., and Robert M. Entman. *Media Power Politics*. New York: The Free Press, 1981.

Podhoretz, Norman. "The New American Majority." In Seymour Martin Lipset (ed.). *Party Coalitions in the 1980s*. San Francisco: Institute for Contemporary Studies, 1981.

Renshon, Stanley A. *Psychological Needs and Political Behavior*. New York: The Free Press, 1974.

Reich, Charles A. *The Greening of America*. New York: Random House, 1970.

Scammon, Richard M., and Ben J. Wattenberg. *The Real Majority*. New York: Coward-McCann, 1970.

Shogan, Robert. "The Upright Stuff: Our Values and Our Politics." *Public Opinion* 6 (Fall, 1984), pp. 9–10.

Steinfels, Peter. *The Neo Conservatives*. New York: Simon and Schuster, 1979.

Viguerie, Richard A. *The New Right: We're Ready to Lead*. Falls Church, Va.: The Viguerie Company, 1980.

Weber, Max. *The Protestant Ethic and the Spirit of Capitalism*. New York: Scribner's, 1958.

Yankelovich, Daniel. "American Values: Change and Stability." *Public Opinion* 6 (Fall, 1984), pp. 2–8.

CHAPTER 7

Political Involvement

In the study of American political behavior, the level of political involvement (interest in and information about politics) has been important theoretically and empirically. Theoretically, mass involvement in politics has been considered a necessary prerequisite for a meaningful democracy, that is, one in which government is based upon the reasoned participation of the citizenry. Empirically, various conceptualizations of involvement have been found to serve as both a stimulus for active participation in the political system and as a correlate to such critical elements of rational participation as issue constraint, ideological conceptualization, and political information (Verba and Nie, 1972; Nie, et al., 1979; Campbell, et al., 1960; Patterson, 1980). In this chapter we explore the links between changes in political involvement in the United States and changes brought about by aging, by events, and by the influx of the sixties generation into the electorate.

POLITICAL INVOLVEMENT AND THE 1960S

A political system that is based upon the direct or indirect expression of will by a population is not easy to maintain at an even keel. On the one hand, it is important that enough people participate in the political process to ensure that the allocation of goods, services, and values accurately reflects the priorities of the public and to ensure that the acts of government are based upon a mandate that the public bestows. Participation by a select (or self-selected) few opens the door for decisions that are both inequitable and that lack legitimacy for many citizens. On the other hand, political writers since Aristotle have feared the spectre of a system in which the public participates en masse, but without the appropriate skills and resources to do so properly. Such a system is susceptible to erratic, intemperate decisions and mob rule, as well as to manipulation by better prepared but self-serving groups or individuals.

Key to a democracy's navigation of this political Scylla and Charybdis is the ability of the citizenry to maintain a healthy level of participation, while insuring that such participation is based on reasoned decision making. This combination of political interest or concern, and political information is what we mean by political involvement. It is a concept that refers to the immediacy of politics to the mass public. An involved public is one that follows politics and which makes an effort to inform itself about the details of the process. Such involvement helps to insure both greater participation and more thoughtful, consistent participation. Politically involved citizens are more likely to know how different parties, candidates, and issues relate to each other, to the public, and to themselves. They are more likely to act upon that knowledge. And, they are more likely to stay alert both to changing conditions that might require modified agendas and to modifications that result from leaders straying unnecessarily from their promises. While personal involvement is only one of the requirements, and variables such as the availability of appropriate information and meaningful links between participation and policy are often beyond the control of the pub-

Political Involvement

lic, it is nonetheless a critical component of democratic politics.

Is there reason to anticipate a connection between the level of political involvement in the United States and changes in the population brought about by aging, generational replacement, or the social, political, and economic environment? As with the other areas of mass politics examined, it is much easier to argue for the likelihood of change than to describe the particular direction in which that change will move because the sources of change are varied and because within sources the pressures are often contradictory. Consider the effects of the environment of the sixties. Rising income and education levels, as well as the increased availability and use of the mass media for political reasons appear to have brought about greater political involvement on the part of the public (Inglehart, 1977; Bell, 1973). The relatively extreme choices offered in the 1964 and 1972 presidential elections, as well as the visible and salient issues of race, war, crime, and domestic unrest that characterized the period also piqued the interest and attention of the public (Pomper, 1975; Nie, et al., 1979; Beck and Jennings, 1979). In addition, the meshing of politics and culture, the growing expectation of finding political solutions to social problems, and the increasing pervasiveness of government made politics more immediate (Cantril and Roll, 1971; Bell, 1975; Benjamin, 1980). Finally, the political dormancy of the fifties increased the likelihood that citizens would turn to the public arena in search of personal and social satisfaction (Hirschman, 1983).

Another interpretation is plausible, however, and leads to quite a different view of the sixties. If involvement results from dissatisfaction with current conditions (Schumpeter, 1950; Berelson, 1952; Hirshman, 1983), the economic growth of the period may have engendered less concern with politics on the part of some people (middle- and upper-class America at least). As information about the government (and as the government itself) became more pervasive, some citizens undoubtedly turned away from politics, having become "over saturated." The conflictual nature of elections and issues of the day as well as the violent edge to politics in the sixties also repulsed part of a public used to a more consensual, peaceful environment (Gilmour and Lamb, 1975). Their alienation was certainly exacerbated by the political betrayals of Johnson and Nixon (Converse, 1976). Finally, the merger of culture and politics turned some people away from mainstream involvement rather than towards it: the substitution of pop politics for more traditional forms (Marsh, 1977; Barnes and Kasse, et al., 1979).

To the extent that the sixties generation was socialized by or directly experienced the competing period effects described above, generational effects on political involvement are also subject to conflicting expectations (Inglehart, 1977; Marsh, 1977). If the forces pushing towards greater involvement outweigh those pushing towards a rejection of mainstream politics, then the sixties generation should reflect this involvement with added vigor. If the reverse is true for this generation, then they would enter the electorate with less political involvement than prior cohorts.

Finally, the process of aging plays a role in the extent of political involvement. Previous studies suggest that older citizens are more politically involved than younger ones, though the specific reasons for this pattern are unclear (Berelson, et al., 1954; Lazarsfeld, et al., 1944; Milbrath and Goel, 1977). Generally it is assumed that commitment to the system increases as one's stake (job, income, family, and property) in political outcomes increases. How this relationship interacts with the effects of period and generation is uncertain, however, in part because the main effects of the latter two are unclear, and in part because the strength of each relative

Political Involvement

to the other is unknown. Does one's stake in the system still result in greater involvement when such involvement seems ineffective? Is there a point at which the effects of the life cycle outweigh generational ones? These questions need empirical evidence to be answered, and it is that evidence we turn to now.

CHANGE AND STABILITY IN POLITICAL INVOLVEMENT

Table 7.1 presents the measures of political involvement used in the analyses to follow. These tap various dimensions of involvement, from interest (in campaigns specifically and politics more generally) to political exposure (through newspapers, magazines, radio, and TV) to information (about partisan control of congress), to opinionatedness (number of opinions offered about the political parties). Taken as a

TABLE 7.1
Description of the Measures of Political Involvement

Variables	Description
Papers	Do you read about the campaign much in the newspapers? (0 = never; 1 = often)
TV	Do you follow the campaign on TV? (0 = never; 1 = often)
Radio	Do you follow the campaign on radio? (0 = never; 1 = often)
Magazines	Do you read about the campaign much in magazines? (0 = never; 1 = often)
Campaign	Are you very interested in the campaign? (0 = not very; 1 = very)
Politics	Are you very interested in politics? (0 = not very; 1 = very)
Majority I	Who controlled the House before the election (0 = don't know; 1 = know)
Majority II	Who controls the House after the election (0 = don't know; 1 = know)
Totals	Number of opinions offered about the political parties (0 = 1–4) (1 = 9–12)

The Effects of Generation, Periods, and the Life Cycle

whole, they are meant to represent one's psychological involvement in mainstream politics.

In Figure 7.1 the aggregate trends in involvement from 1952 to 1980 are presented. The four measures of following politics through the media show similar patterns, with involvement having declined steadily through 1972, and then increased somewhat thereafter (though not to the extent of the fifties). The number of opinions concerning parties also declined over the years examined, though the specific pattern differed from that found with the media measures. Fi-

FIGURE 7.1
Trends in Political Involvement, 1952–1980
(numbers are the mean score for each year)

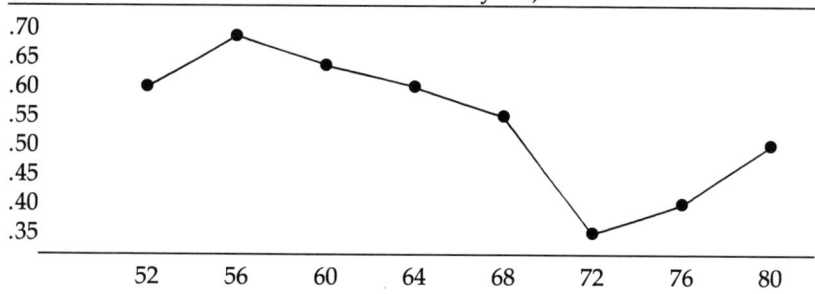

FIGURE 7.1A
Papers

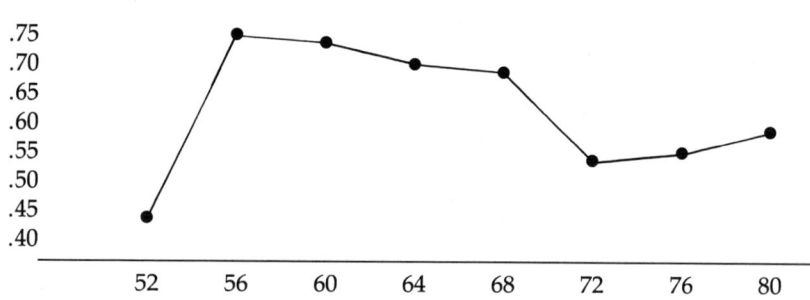

FIGURE 7.1B
TV

146

Political Involvement

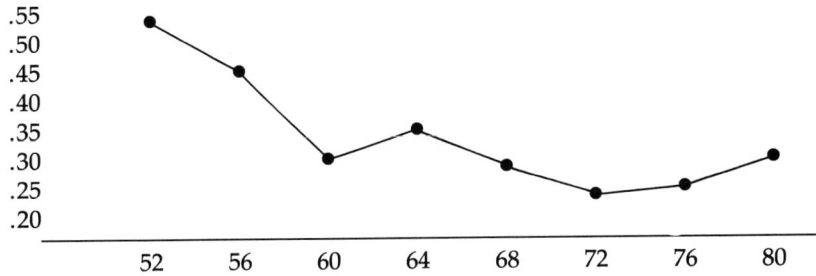

FIGURE 7.1C
Radio

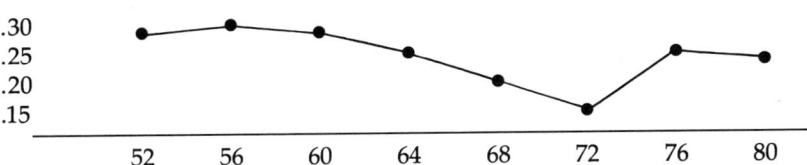

FIGURE 7.1D
Magazines

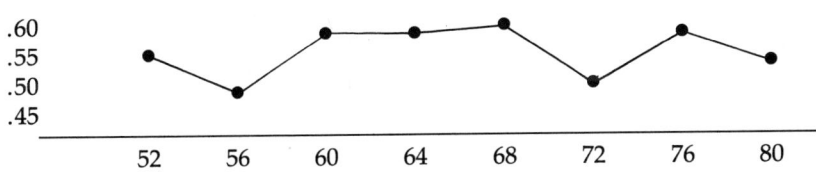

FIGURE 7.1E
Campaigns

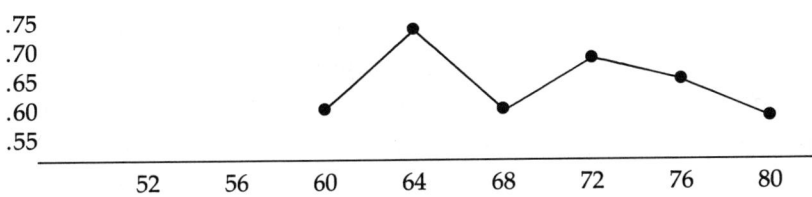

FIGURE 7.1F
Politics

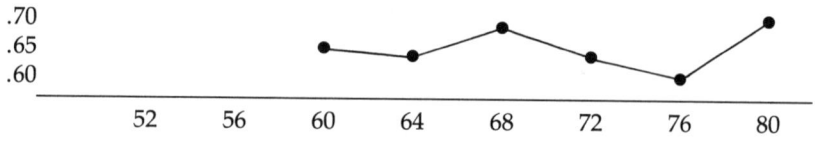

FIGURE 7.1G
Majority I

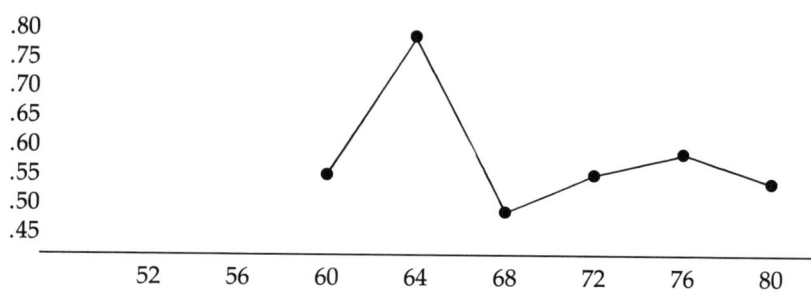

FIGURE 7.1H
Majority II

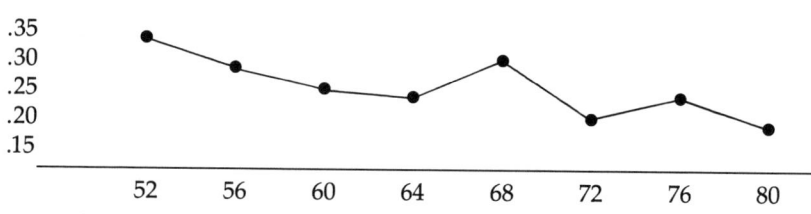

FIGURE 7.1I
Totals

nally, the interest measures ("Campaigns" and "Politics") and the information measures ("Majority I" and "Majority II") were more volatile, though again overall they indicate declining involvement. This pattern of decline suggests, first, that something about the sixties did affect the level of political involvement and, second, that on balance the forces discouraging participation in mainstream politics were stronger than those that would encourage it.

Political Involvement

TABLE 7.2
Effects of Life Cycle, Generation, and Period on Political Involvement

Variables	Life Cycle	Generation	Period		
			Fifties	Sixties	Seventies
Papers	.002**	−.202**	.145**	.110**	−.081
TV	−.003**	−.178**	.328**	.237**	.029
Radio	.003**	.037	−.161**	−.154**	−.239**
Magazines	.000	−.145**	.071**	.033	.086*
Campaign	.000	−.135**	−.029	.103**	.133**
Politics	.000	−.188**	***	.159**	.161**
Majority I	−.001	−.256**	***	.089*	.039
Majority II	−.005**	−.260**	***	.136*	.164*
Totals	.001	−.107**	−.100**	−.035*	.021

* = standard error ≤ B.
** = $p \leq .05$.
*** = not calculated.

EFFECTS OF LIFE CYCLE, GENERATION, AND PERIODS ON POLITICAL INVOLVEMENT

To what extent are life cycle, periods, generation, and their interactions responsible for the decline in political involvement? Table 7.2 presents a partial answer to this question. The life cycle does have an effect on political involvement, but this effect is neither pervasive nor is it consistent. Three measures ("Magazines," "Campaign" and "Politics") show no change with age, and the remaining measures split equally between increased involvement ("Papers," "Radio" and "Totals") and decreased involvement ("TV," "Majority I" and "Majority II"). Taken together, a certain pattern suggests itself. The use of the media and the formation of opinions increases with age, but accurate political information decreases and basic interest is largely unaffected. The patterns for the use of television and magazines do not conform with this generalization, however. The declining reliance on TV as one grows older is probably more a reflection on the

The Effects of Generation, Periods, and the Life Cycle

medium than on the level of involvement. The more-general conclusion, however, is that aging does not ensure increasing attention to politics.

The impact of being a member of the sixties generation on political involvement is more uniform. Eight of the nine measures show sizable negative coefficients. Only the use of radios runs counter to this trend and no doubt reflects the central role music plays in the culture of this generation. That TV would show a negative relationship is somewhat surprising, given that this cohort really grew up as the television generation. However, when one considers that only political television is being measured and that TV news broadcasts are much longer and less frequent than are those on the radio, this finding becomes less surprising. Instead, it indicates the extent of this generation's lack of political interest.[1] The dominant conclusion to be drawn from these interrelationships is that the sixties generation is less psychologically involved in mainstream politics than its predecessors. They are less likely to be interested in politics, less likely to follow politics with any regularity, less likely to express a political opinion, and less likely to have accurate information relevant to politics.

The period effects reflect the competing pressures of the times, though by and large it is here that impetus for greater political involvement was most apparent. In the sixties only the use of radios and the presence of opinions concerning the parties are reduced by period effects. The remaining seven measures indicate that the environment increased involvement. This general pattern is carried over to the seventies, where again seven of the nine measures show positive period effects. The fact that the positive effects of period are found in both the sixties and the seventies suggests either that it is the more structural aspects of change that are responsible (the media, increased resources, the

Political Involvement

changing responsibilities of government, etc.) or that specific events and campaigns sensitized the public to politics beyond the event or campaign itself (Converse, 1976).

Despite the pattern of increased political involvement due to period effects, there is still some indication of the competing forces alluded to in the beginning of this chapter. The effects of period on media use were positive, for instance, but the trend from the fifties through the seventies was for the size of these positive relationships to decline (or in the case of radio, for the negative effect to increase). On the other hand, the interest, opinion, and information measures show relative increases in involvement over the decades. In summary, overall change in the amount of political involvement came from the distinction between the sixties generation, which entered the electorate with greatly reduced involvement, and events of the sixties and seventies, which, while demonstrating competing influences, mainly led to greater attention to politics.

When we turn from main effects to the effects of interactions some very interesting additional information is uncovered (Table 7.3). First, the interaction of aging and generation indicates that all of the main effects of generation are being reversed over time. That is, members of the sixties generation have become more involved in politics as they aged. However, the main effects will not easily be cancelled out. It takes about 22 years in the electorate before a member of the sixties generation reaches the level of involvement shown by his or her parents' generation.

The interaction of generation and different political periods showed relatively sizable effects. Most of these interactions were negative; that is, the sixties generation reacted to the events of the sixties and seventies by becoming less involved than the rest of the population. In addition, there is little indication that this negative interaction has declined in any

TABLE 7.3
Interaction Effects on Political Involvement

	Life Cycle				Generation	
Variables	Generation	Fifties	Sixties	Seventies	Sixties	Seventies
Papers	.011**	−.002*	−.005**	−.001	−.107*	.007
TV	.005**	.000	.002*	.005**	−.024	.055
Radio	−.001	.001	−.001	.000	−.119**	−.028
Magazines	.005**	−.001*	−.003*	−.003*	.004	−.007
Campaign	.007**	.001	−.002**	−.001	−.035	−.121**
Politics	.009**	***	−.002*	−.002	−.027	−.100
Majority I	.013**	***	−.003*	−.001	−.021	.011
Majority II	.014**	***	−.001	−.002	−.085	−.154
Totals	.008**	.000	−.002**	−.003**	−.056**	−.127**

* = standard error ≤ B.
** = $p \leq .05$.
*** = not calculated.

consistent manner in the seventies, suggesting that as the sixties ended this generation did not become more involved in mainstream politics to any great extent.

Finally, the interaction of life cycle and events again suggests a pattern of "contrariness" or suspicion towards change that should now be familiar to the reader. That is, older cohorts reacted to the pressure for increasing involvement by resisting much (though not all) of it.

To what extent did the three cohorts that make up the sixties generation become involved in politics? A partial answer to this question is presented in Table 7.4. More than in the other substantive areas examined, there is general uniformity in the direction of effects, with only radio use by the ambivalent cohort showing a unique (and positive) effect. Beyond this, however, there is a strong indication that, from the ambivalent to the experienced to the socialized cohorts, the drop in political involvement becomes more pronounced. Put another way, being socialized during the sixties seems to have resulted in the greatest loss of political involvement.

When we turn to the interaction of the subgenerational

Political Involvement

TABLE 7.4
Effects of Subgenerations on Political Involvement

Variables	Ambivalent	Experienced	Socialized
Papers	−.230**	−.450**	−.708**
TV	−.245**	−.257**	−.593**
Radio	.131*	−.131**	−.431*
Magazines	−.182**	−.129**	−.293*
Campaign	−.151**	−.180**	−.481**
Politics	−.187*	−.161**	−.618**
Majority I	−.358**	−.342**	−.999**
Majority II	−.218	−.517**	−.664**
Totals	−.137**	−.152**	−.396**

* = standard error ≤ B.
** = p ≤ .05.

TABLE 7.5
Interaction Effects between Subgenerations, Periods, and Life Cycle on Political Involvement

Variables	Life Cycle			Seventies	
	Ambivalent	Experienced	Socialized	Ambivalent	Experienced
Papers	−.003	.008	.129*	.265**	.185**
TV	−.006*	.001	.097*	.304**	.117*
Radio	−.011**	.001	.108*	.026	.030
Magazines	−.005**	−.004	−.011	.216**	−.010
Campaign	−.003	.002	.033	.073	−.050
Politics	−.001	−.003	.017	.092	−.057
Majority I	.010**	.037**	.237**	.091	−.228**
Majority II	−.004	.015	.052	.114	.062
Totals	.004**	.006*	.028	−.047	−.082**

* = standard error ≤ B.
** = p ≤ .05.
*** = not calculated.

effects of the life cycle and of periods, the similarity among cohorts begins to disappear (Table 7.5). Both the experienced and socialized cohorts showed the typical pattern of approaching the norm with age, with the most uninvolved cohort (the socialized one) doing so more quickly. The ambivalent cohort, however, actually became less involved as it aged, despite the fact that it entered the electorate already less involved than preceding cohorts. As the rest of the sixties

The Effects of Generation, Periods, and the Life Cycle

generation became more involved in politics, this cohort increasingly stood out from both its predecessors and its successors in this regard.

The interaction of the two oldest cohorts of the sixties generation with the 1970s adds further evidence of the distinct character of subgenerations. In both the size and the direction of the coefficients, the ambivalent cohort reacted to the seventies by becoming more politically involved than the experienced cohort. Considered in light of the previous interaction effects, these patterns suggest a reason for the former cohort's lack of involvement over time. The ambivalent cohort, less directly a part of the sixties environment, may very well have become less politically involved because of the conflictual, countercultural aspects of that period. With the return to normalcy during the seventies, members of this cohort reacted with the greatest increase in involvement. The experienced cohort, on the other hand, still entering the electorate during the seventies, was unattracted to the more stable (and more conservative) times. While highly speculative, this interpretation adds to the notion that even when they appear to be reacting in similar ways overall, the subgenerations were in fact responding in slightly different ways to the events of the sixties and seventies, resulting in subtle variations. In turn, these subtle variations lead to lasting distinctions in political involvement over time.

SUMMARY AND CONCLUDING REMARKS

Political involvement, or the psychological investment one makes to politics, is critical for the success of democratic societies because it provides a proper balance between the quantity and quality of mass participation. In this chapter we have explored the relationship between political involvement and aging, the sixties generation, and the effects of

Political Involvement

social and political changes since 1952. Our expectation was that aging would show a fairly consistent positive effect on involvement, due largely to the stake in the system one develops with age. The effects of generation and periods were much more difficult to determine, encouraging *both* more and less political involvement.

Our analysis revealed several points. First, political involvement generally declined from the early fifties to the midseventies, with some increase in 1976. Second, while the life cycle had slightly more positive than negative effects, overall the results were mixed. Third, members of the sixties generation were much less involved in mainstream politics than their elders. Fourth, period effects reflected the diverse currents of the time, though overall the most consistent impact was to increase the level of political involvement. This impact clearly resulted from changes that occurred in the environment of the sixties, though most of the effects survived into the seventies. Fifth, the rejection of political involvement by the sixties generation was counteracted over time by an interaction between generation and the life cycle, though at a slow rate relative to the main effects of generation. In addition, while all three cohorts within the sixties generation were not much involved with politics, several distinctions among them exist. Members of the ambivalent subgeneration entered the electorate as the least uninvolved, but became less involved with age. However, this cohort also reacted most positively to the return to "normal" politics in the seventies. The socialized cohort was the least involved at first, but also showed the largest increase in involvement with age.

The key findings in this chapter centered on two sets of competing forces: the main effects of generation and their interaction with aging; and the tension between the effects of generation and period. Overall the sixties generation is less involved with politics than one would expect from simply considering its age or the times they live in. Over time, however, the generation has become more involved. If this trend continues, it is possible that the sixties generation will emerge in middle age as more politically involved than their predecessors. This assumption does not consider the separate patterns now underlying the sixties generation as a whole, however, which could lead instead to even greater distinctions among cohorts (especially the ambivalent cohort) over time.

The competing effects of period and generation on political involvement are informative because they help us understand the paradox of an era in which expanding resources have gone hand in hand with decreasing political involvement. That is, were it not for the entrance of the sixties generation into the electorate (and its growing percentage of that electorate), the sixties and seventies may very well have been years of unprecedented political involvement. The sixties generation, bringing its mistrust of the political system (Chapter Four), its distinctive agenda (Chapter Five), and its liberal stands on issues (Chapter Six) into a political system with an agenda and an ideological environment that was not consistent with it, reacted by turning away from mainstream politics. The result was a separation of this generation from the larger population—a generation gap—which not only counteracted the positive effects of the events of the sixties and seventies, but which actually led to a reduction in the aggregate level of involvement over the past two decades—a reduction which even the interactive effects of aging and generation have not yet been able to overcome.

NOTE

1. The positive association with radio and the negative association with

Political Involvement

TV is also the result of this generation's love affair with the car. Much of their recreation often involved "cruising" for hours with no particular destination in mind and listening to the radio. The slight positive relationship is an almost passive byproduct of this activity. That this positive association is exclusively the result of the ambivalent cohort (Table 7.4) adds further credence to this interpretation, in that this pastime was more prevalent during a time of cheap gas prices.

REFERENCES

Barnes, Samuel H., et al. *Political Action: Mass Participation in Five Western Democracies.* Beverly Hills: Sage, 1979.

Beck, Paul Allen, and M. Kent Jennings. "Political Periods and Political Participation." *American Political Science Review* 73 (September, 1979), pp. 737–750.

Bell, Daniel. *The Coming of Post-Industrial Society.* New York: Basic Books, 1973.

———. "The Revolution of Rising Entitlements." *Fortune* 91 (April 1975), pp. 98–103.

Benjamin, Roger W. *The Limits to Politics.* Chicago: University of Chicago Press, 1980.

Berelson, Bernard. "Democratic Theory and Public Opinion." *Public Opinion Quarterly* 16 (Fall, 1952), pp. 313–330.

Berelson, Bernard R., Paul F. Lazarsfeld, and William N. McPhee. *Voting.* Chicago: University of Chicago Press, 1954.

Campbell, Angus, Philip E. Converse, Warren E. Miller, and Donald E. Stokes. *The American Voter.* New York: John Wiley, 1960.

Cantril, Albert H., and Charles W. Roll, Jr. *The Hopes and Fears of the American People.* New York: University Books, 1971.

Converse, Philip E. *The Dynamics of Partisan Support.* Beverly Hills: Sage, 1976.

Gilmour, Richard, and Richard Lamb. *Political Alienation in Contemporary America.* New York: St. Martin's, 1975.

Hirschman, Albert O. *Shifting Involvements.* Princeton: Princeton University Press, 1983.

Inglehart, Ronald. *The Silent Revolution.* Princeton: Princeton University Press, 1977.

Lazarsfeld, Paul, Bernard Berelson, and Hazel Gaudet. *The People's Choice.* New York: Columbia University Press, 1944.

Marsh, Alan. *Protest and Political Consciousness.* Beverly Hills: Sage, 1977.

Milbrath, Lester W. and M. L. Goel. *Political Participation.* Chicago: Rand McNally, 1977.

Nie, Norman H., Sidney Verba, and John R. Petrocik. *The Changing American Voter*. Cambridge, Mass.: Harvard University Press, 1979.
Patterson, Thomas. *The Mass Media Election*. New York: Praeger, 1980.
Pomper, Gerald M. *Voters' Choice: Varieties of American Electoral Behavior*. New York: Dodd, Mead, 1975.
Schumpeter, Joseph A. *Capitalism, Socialism and Democracy*. New York: Harper & Row, 1950.
Verba, Sidney, and Norman H. Nie. *Participation in America*. New York: Harper and Row, 1972.

CHAPTER 8

Political Decision Making

The process by which one reaches a political decision, such as whom to vote for or what stand to take on a particular issue, is a complicated one, involving a myriad of psychological, informational, social, and political considerations. In this chapter we explore one facet of this process: decision-making cues or the referents an individual uses to evaluate various political alternatives. While our study is limited to the evaluation of presidential candidates, the process is assumed to apply to other political decisions as well.

THE SIXTIES AND POLITICAL DECISION MAKING

The political decisions that citizens make most often involve choosing among clearly established alternatives: Should I vote for candidate A or candidate B? Should I vote yes or no on this referendum? Do I support the Democrats' Central American policy or the Republicans'? Underlying each choice, however, is a more complex set of alternatives. Each decision involves an explicit or implicit weighing of political options against personal notions of what criteria are important. The decision of whom to vote for, for instance, depends not only on the candidates' qualities but also on what particular standards are used by the individual in judging those candidates (Fiorina, 1977). Are personal qualities such as the candidate's family life or integrity most important? Are party affiliations the key factor? Does the candidate's stand on a particular issue make any difference? It is the combination of one's personal standards, how well a candidate or issue meets those standards, and how willing or able one is to weigh the latter against the former that underlies the decision-making process.

Political cues, though they take many different forms, all serve as a means of determining what political decisions will best lead to a desired end. One may, for instance, have a vision of how society would be were it operating properly. This "world view," no matter what its specific characteristics and no matter how well articulated, underlies one's political decision making: Which choice will help make the real world more closely approximate the world view? Given, first, that people rarely articulate their world views in fine detail (even to themselves), and second, that it is extremely difficult to know how any particular decision will actually affect society, one must depend on certain cues which, it is hoped, will lead to satisfactory decisions.

Two dimensions are of particular importance when considering this process at a systemic (as opposed to a purely individual) level: the sophistication of the decision-making cue and the scope of the world view underlying it. Different cues are more or less likely to produce satisfactory outcomes and the success of a cue is usually inversely related to the ease with which it can be applied to reach a decision. For instance, party labels might be used as a relatively easy way to reach a decision (Shively, 1979). I support policy A because the Democrats support it; you vote for candidate B because she is Republican. Underlying this choice is some notion of what kind of world Democrats and Republicans will try to

Political Decision Making

build and which world is more appealing. Of course the cost of using such an easy rule is that the underlying premise is often wrong. The Republican candidate you voted for might be more liberal than the Democrat you rejected. One might base decisions on specific policy stands instead, but at the cost of more time and energy, in order to delineate clearly among one's own policy views, the aims of a particular piece of legislation, and/or the views of the candidates themselves (Delli Carpini, 1983).

The process of making political decisions also depends on the scope of each person's world view. Are your political concerns focused exclusively around yourself? (How will I benefit from a Democratic victory?) Are they concerned with the well-being of a particular group or class of people (the middle class, blacks, Pennsylvanians, etc.)? Or are they concerned with more general notions of the public good? Different cues are more or less likely to achieve different ends. Thus, if one is most concerned with how political decisions will affect blacks, the candidates' stands on issues relevant to blacks become paramount. If a more-general sense of the public good is important, then a general ideological decision rule may be more appropriate.

From the perspective of the individual, efficiency is critical to making a political decision. The goal is finding cues that provide acceptable decisions at acceptable costs. From the point of view of society, however, what is considered an acceptable decision can be quite different. Whereas the public good is one of many goals individuals may seek to pursue, it is *the* goal for society as a whole. Individuals with little concern for politics or with a low expected pay off may consider potentially less successful but less expensive cues acceptable. The political system as a whole, however, requires (at least in democratic theory) greater and more consistent involvement from its citizens than this. In short, decision-making cues form a hierarchy ranging from unsophisticated and myopic to highly sophisticated and far-sighted. The cues any individual chooses to use depend upon personal abilities and desire and can, therefore, legitimately be selected from any part of the hierarchy. From the perspective of the political system as a whole, however, the costs of poor decisions and the benefits of good ones are great enough to limit the range of what is considered acceptable.

To what extent has the process of generational change, the period effects of the 1960s, and the aging of the entire population affected political decision making? As with the other areas examined, the influence of the times can be expected to have various results. At the level of individual decision making, one can argue that increased educational opportunities, rising income levels, and greater availability of information through the mass media all suggest the likelihood of a more sophisticated use of decision-making cues, with the sixties generation being the most likely to use them (Nie, et al., 1979; Shively, 1979; Inglehart, 1977). In addition, the heightened political drama of the period increased the involvement of the public (Chapter Seven), resulting in an increased willingness to pay extra costs to reach more successful decisions (Pomper, 1975). However, the more conflictual, violent, and alienating aspects of the period also led some of the public to doubt the utility of political solutions and to avoid costly political decision making that held no promise of effecting change (Gilmour and Lamb, 1975). For others, the same economic prosperity that improved people's ability to pay the costs of making decisions carefully could also lead to complacency concerning the need to become involved in the details of a system that seemed to work well enough as it was (Berelson, et al., 1954).

The goals of one's political decisions are also subject to complex generational and period effects. The communitarian

Political Decision Making

aspects of the times and the rhetoric concerning social justice and equality moved political aims away from individualistic concerns (especially for the sixties generation itself), but the extent to which the new focus was group-oriented (blacks, the poor, students) or more generally ideologically-oriented is unclear. While groups like the SDS did push for more comprehensive, ideologically based programs early in their existence, overall the period is more notable for its eclectic, events-driven politics (Gitlin, 1980).

In addition to the complexities of generation and period, the process of aging comes into play in diverse ways. The costs to be incurred from using more sophisticated decision-making cues should become more affordable with the increase in knowledge and affluence associated with the life cycle. Yet there is no compelling reason to assume that older cohorts will devote these additional resources to this process. The loss of political support as one ages, demonstrated in Chapter Four, could just as easily lead to less interest in careful decision making. Similarly, aging might expand one's world view from the specific to the general as the interconnectedness of people and events becomes more obvious, but it is equally plausible that with the loss of youthful idealism, the movement will be exactly the reverse. We are again entering into largely uncharted ground, and while what we know suggests the likelihood that age-related change will occur, the direction of that change is unclear.

AGGREGATE PATTERNS OF CHANGE IN DECISION-MAKING CUES

The National Election Studies have, since 1952, included a series of questions asking respondents to express their likes and dislikes concerning the candidates for president. These open-ended responses were then coded into specific categories based upon the underlying standards the public uses in its evaluations. Nie, Verba, and Petrocik (1979), in a coding scheme based on the work of Campbell, et al. (1960), have further categorized the responses into a seven-part scheme that reflects broad categories of decision making.[1] The categories, along with a brief description of each, are presented in Table 8.1. Underlying this scheme is an implicit ranking of decision-making cues along dimensions similar to those discussed in the previous section. While the specific placement of each category is subjective, taken as a whole they run from those that were low cost, inefficient, and relatively narrow cues (such as personality traits of the candidates or responses such as "I like him") to more costly, sophisticated, and encompassing cues (such as the ideological stands of the candidate). The assumption underlying the work of both Campbell, et al. and of Nie, Verba, and Petrocik is that the larger the percentage of the population that engages in ideological decision making (and the smaller that depends upon nonpolitical cues), the higher the quality of political decision

TABLE 8.1
Description of Measures of Decision-making Cues[a]

Variables	Description
Ideology I	Explicit use of ideological terminology.
Ideology II	Implicit or indirect use of ideological evaluations.
Groups	Evaluation based upon policies towards or treatment of specific groups or classes of people.
Policy	Evaluation based upon position on a specific issue or category of issues.
Times	Evaluation based upon perceived effect on the nature of the times.
Party	Evaluation based upon party loyalties and support.
Nonpolitical	Personal characteristics, nonpolitical responses, "Don't know."

[a]All variables were coded 1 if all responses fall into a selected category and zero if none fall into the selected category (12 possible responses).

Political Decision Making

making by the mass public, and, therefore, the better off the political system.

Beyond this loose hierarchy of cues, the pattern of decision making indicated by the individual cues themselves is also revealing. Changes in the importance of political referents tell us a great deal about the nature of decisions. Are parties less important to the public now than in the past (Nie, et al., 1979)? Do people focus on issues more now than in the past (Pomper, 1975)? Are evaluations more likely to depend on cues that arise from heightened group consciousness (Verba and Nie, 1972; Shingles, 1981) or from the growth in the number of political organizations (Boyte, 1980)? To what extent are decisions based on general reactions to the goodness or badness of the times (Tufte, 1975, 1978) or to more careful calculations that connect government actions with political outcomes by means of a broader political philosophy (Nie and Andersen, 1974)? The answers to these questions are important for understanding how the public translates agendas and issue stands into action.

Each respondent was allowed up to three positive and three negative evaluations for each of the two major candidates, leading to a maximum of twelve statements each.[2] As in other chapters, responses were recoded so that one indicated that all 12 responses fell into the category under consideration, and zero indicated that none of them did. In Figure 8.1 we present the mean scores for each category for the years between 1952 and 1980. Several points concerning these patterns are noteworthy. First, very few people gave the full number of possible responses (recall that the nonpolitical category includes the "Don't Knows"). Citizens averaged less than three of a possible 12 political answers. Also, there was a great disparity in the selection of decision-making cues both across categories and at different times. Concerning the former, party and policy were the political cues

The Effects of Generation, Periods, and the Life Cycle

FIGURE 8.1
Trends in Decision Making, 1952–1980
(entries are mean scores for each year)

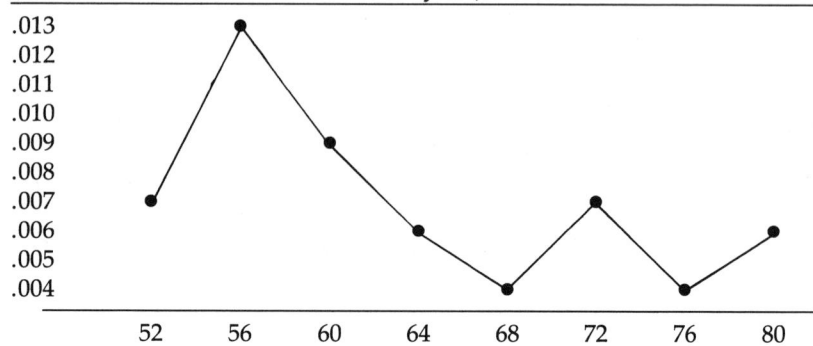

FIGURE 8.1A
Ideology I

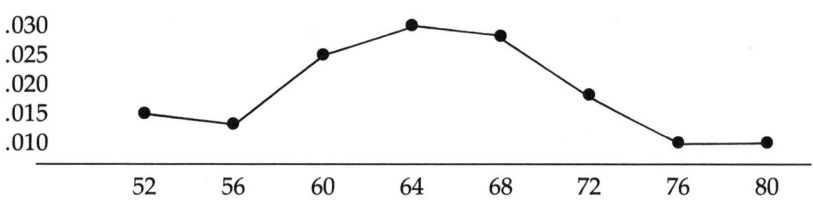

FIGURE 8.1B
Ideology II

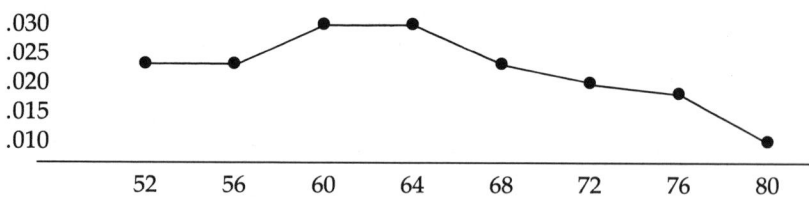

FIGURE 8.1C
Groups

Political Decision Making

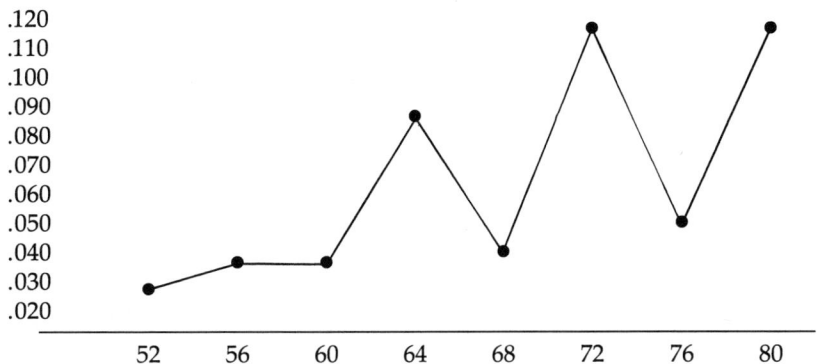

FIGURE 8.1D
Policy

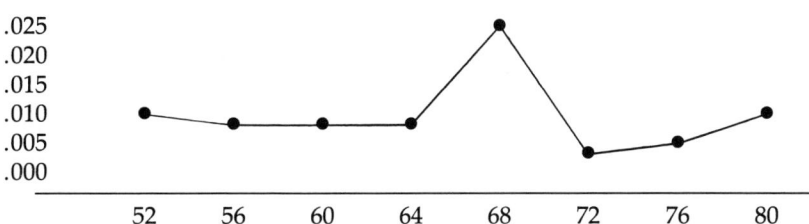

FIGURE 8.1E
Times

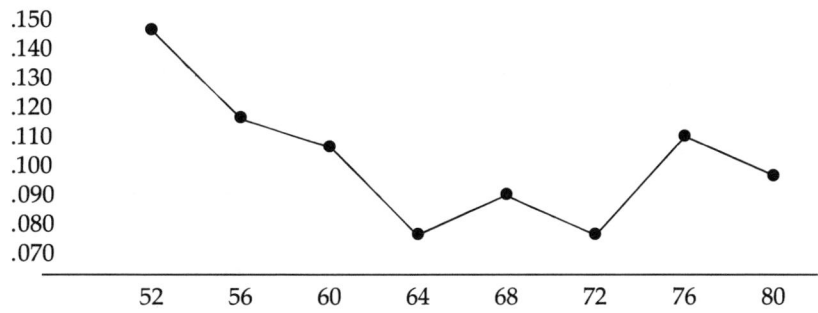

FIGURE 8.1F
Party

The Effects of Generation, Periods, and the Life Cycle

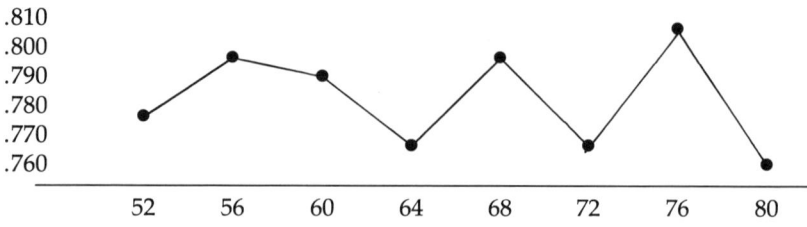

FIGURE 8.1G
Nonpolitical

most frequently chosen, followed, in decreasing order, by group-based cues, implicit ideological cues, the nature of the times, and, finally, explicit ideology. As regards the latter, the choices over time were erratic, but certain trends are evident. Policy mentions have generally increased, though in a stepwise fashion, while party mentions have decreased over time. Dependence on group-based cues peaked in 1960 and 1964, and have been declining in importance since. The nature of the times was chosen at a stable rate as a cue, except in 1968 when it was chosen two and a half times more often than usual. Nonpolitical responses (or no responses) remained the most common "cue" throughout the years examined, though it shows a great deal of volatility since 1960.

The patterns demonstrated by the choice of the two ideological cues are particularly interesting because they generally run counter to the normal characterization of this era as one of increased ideological sophistication. Explicit ideological responses generally declined since 1956, while implicitly ideological cues were used more in the 1960s, but then steadily declined from 1968. The coding and conceptual differences between these measures and those used by Nie, et al. lead to opposing interpretations of change in this regard. When considered together they suggest that increases in the number of "ideologues" and "near ideologues" in the sixties and seventies was due to an increase in policy referents, not to an increase in ideological concerns.[3]

Political Decision Making

TABLE 8.2
Effects of Life Cycle, Generation, and Period on Political Decision Making

Variables	Life Cycle	Generation	Period		
			Fifties	Sixties	Seventies
Ideology I	.0001**	−.0039**	.0056**	.0011	.0006
Ideology II	−.0002**	−.0084**	−.0018	.0177**	−.0022
Groups	−.0002**	−.0038	.0018	.0023	−.0108*
Policy	−.0002	−.0189	.0167	.0671**	.0533*
Times	−.0001	−.0044	−.0019	−.0019	−.0073
Party	.0000	−.0296**	−.0355**	−.0738**	−.0077
Nonpolitical	.0006**	.0689**	.0145	−.0143	−.0262

* = standard error ≤ B.
** = $p \leq .05$.

In terms of the patterns as a whole, there is little evidence of a systematic movement toward more sophisticated or more coherent decision making. While the period from 1964 to 1972 does show great volatility in the cues selected, it is not consistent change of any kind. Again we are led to the conclusion that the greatest political effect of the sixties was in its unmooring of established norms rather than its coherent charting of new courses. Perhaps this seemingly random motion hides more systematic change due to the effects of generation, periods, and the life cycle.

THE EFFECTS OF GENERATION, PERIODS, AND THE LIFE CYCLE ON DECISION MAKING

Table 8.2 presents the main effects of life cycle, generation, and period.[4] The relationship between aging and decision making shows a "splitting up" of the evaluation process, with movement towards the extremes of explicitly ideological cues and of nonpolitical referents, and away from four of the remaining five categories (age shows no relationship to party-based cues). This behavior is consistent with the notion that aging combines elements of *both* increasing sophistication

The Effects of Generation, Periods, and the Life Cycle

and growing disillusionment with politics. (Whether this is a conflict within individuals or across segments of the population through the life cycle is an issue dealt with in Part III.)

The relationship between the sixties generation and the selection of decision-making cues is both more surprising and more consistent. Being a member of that generation decreased the likelihood of using every one of the political cues and increased the likelihood of either not having an opinion, or of basing one's opinion on very subjective, non-political evaluations. Recall that since age is controlled for, these effects are beyond those resulting from the relative youth of this cohort. The failure to consider party-based cues might have been anticipated from the work of Inglehart, who suggested that this generation was less likely to be tied to organizations that were formed during the era of industrial development. The failure to rely upon ideological cues is more surprising given the increased education of this generation, but is consistent with our argument that changes during the sixties lacked an ideological basis (Chapter Two). The overall pattern of rejecting political cues is unanticipated in the literature, however, and suggests further evidence of this generation's lack of involvement in and concern for mainstream electoral politics.

Again, it is in the period effects that the progressive forces of the last few decades become evident. There is movement away from the narrower and simpler cues (apolitical, party, and the nature of the times) and towards those of a "higher order" (explicit and implicit ideology, policy, and group consciousness). This trend peaked in the sixties and, while it partially persists into the seventies, both the size and the direction of several coefficients suggest that much of the change was time bound.

In Table 8.3 we present the interaction effects of the peri-

Political Decision Making

TABLE 8.3
Interaction Effects on Political Decision Making

Variables	Life Cycle				Generation	
	Generation	Fifties	Sixties	Seventies	Sixties	Seventies
Ideology I	.0002**	.0000	−.0001**	−.0001**	−.0001	.0014
Ideology II	.0004**	.0001	−.0002**	−.0001	−.0050	−.0039
Groups	−.0001	.0001	.0001	.0002	−.0022	.0004
Policy	.0010*	−.0002	−.0005	−.0005	.0067	.0217
Times	.0001	.0000	.0001	.0000	.0024	.0043
Party	.0016**	−.0002	.0000	−.0010**	.0101	−.0266**
Nonpolitical	−.0032**	.0003	.0006*	.0014**	−.0114	−.0014

* = standard error ≤ B.
** = $p \leq .05$.

ods, the life cycle, and generation. The interaction of generation and life cycle demonstrates the consistent erosion of the main effects of generation, which, by now, we have come to expect. As the sixties generation aged, it turned to all of the cues it once had ignored, with the exception of group-based decisions. In addition, it became less likely to turn to nonpolitical cues. Again, however, the initial distinctiveness of this generation has been slow to fade. On average it takes 24 years in the electorate before its decision-making process becomes consistent with that of prior generations.

The interaction of period and generation provides further evidence of tension between the politics of the time and the politics of the sixties generation. In the sixties, the population as a whole was moving toward more complex decision making, while the sixties generation resisted this tendency: Only the interactions between generation and the sixties on the choice of policy cues and nonpolitical cues are consistent with the main period effects. By the seventies, much of this aspect of the generation gap had disappeared, however, and the sixties generation fell much more in step with the times.

Finally, the interaction of life cycle and the events of the times again demonstrated the tendency for older cohorts to

TABLE 8.4
Effects of Subgenerations on Political Decision Making

	Ambivalent	Experienced	Socialized
Ideology I	−.0085**	−.0022	−.0024
Ideology II	−.0100**	−.0163**	−.0268**
Groups	−.0027	−.0039	−.0019
Policy	−.0749**	−.0025	−.2279**
Times	−.0066	−.0083*	−.0558*
Party	−.0321**	−.0192**	−.1558**
Nonpolitical	.1350**	.0540**	.4664**

* = standard error ≤ B.
** = $p \leq .05$.

resist period-based change. This was most evident in the sixties (the period of greatest change) and least evident in the fifties.

As a final analysis, we again examine the behavior of subgenerations of the sixties to see if different combinations of socialization and experience lead to different decision-making rules. While the sizes of the relationships are fairly distinct, the overwhelming conclusion to be drawn is that all three cohorts are remarkably similar in their political decision making. All three groups rejected the standard cues used by the larger population, turning to nonpolitical cues (or no identifiable cues) instead. This pattern of behavior is strongest for the socialized cohort (Table 8.4).

When we turn to interaction effects (Table 8.5) between life cycle and subgenerations, we see that the homogeneity of the cohorts breaks down. Returning to the norm, which occurred as the whole generation aged, was most evident in the socialized cohort, but none of the cohorts consistently replicated the pattern. While all three cohorts turned away from nonpolitical cues as they aged, the ambivalent cohort was as likely to reinforce its rejection of the standard cues as to weaken it, while the experienced cohort was more likely to consistently reject these cues. The only consistency among

TABLE 8.5
Interaction Effects Between Subgenerations, Life Cycle, and Period on Political Decision Making

	Life Cycle			Seventies	
	Ambivalent	Experienced	Socialized	Ambivalent	Experienced
Idelogy I	.0005**	.0008**	−.0002	−.0024	−.0069**
Ideology II	−.0001	−.0001	.0048	.0100	.0071
Groups	−.0008**	−.0012**	−.0081*	.0130*	.0160*
Policy	.0073**	.0107**	.0940**	−.0560*	−.0708**
Times	.0000	−.0002	.0165**	.0108	.0102
Party	−.0008	−.0006	.0095	.0184	−.0199*
Nonpolitical	−.0060**	−.0096**	−.1162**	.0060	.0643**

* = standard error ≤ B.
** = $p \leq .05$.

these political cues across all three cohorts is the increasing rejection of group-based politics in favor of policy-based decisions. This is the only evidence of changing decision making that is consistent with the notions of increased sophistication and an orientation towards the public good within the sixties generation. And even here its effects are lost when the generation is considered as a whole (Tables 8.2 and 8.3).

Finally, the interaction of the two older cohorts of the sixties generation with the 1970s indicates that both of these subgenerations were still very much resisting changes in decision-making into the seventies. It also implies that it was the entrance of the socialized cohort into the electorate and not changes within the two older cohorts that led to the diminution of the generation gap found in Table 8.3.

SUMMARY AND CONCLUDING REMARKS

In this chapter we examined the links among generation, life cycle, and periods and the cues used to evaluate candidates and make political decisions. The test of an appropriate cue for an individual is whether it achieves an acceptable balance of personal cost and personal benefit. For the system as a whole, however, the goal is less idiosyncratic. Democratic politics strive for an involved and sophisticated electorate and decisions that are comprehensive, consistent with other decisions, and concerned for the public good.

Our analysis suggests that the forces during the sixties that led to rejection of or indifference to mainstream electoral politics had the strongest influence on the decision-making patterns of the sixties generation. This generation was less likely to use ideological cues of any kind; less likely to emphasize group politics, policy implications, or the nature of the times; and less likely to depend on party-based cues. In fact, the only type of cue more likely to be relied on by members of this generation were nonpolitical ones, which often meant there was no basis of evaluation at all. Where the sixties did lead to more sophisticated political decision making was in its period effects, though even these are eroding with time. Aging appears to offer little relief from this negative pattern of decision making, for while the interaction of age and generation slowed the rejection of political cues, this interaction seldom counteracted the negative main effects of either. More than in other substantive areas examined thus far in the book, this rejection of politics cuts across all of the subgenerations, adding to the likelihood that it will remain a part of electoral politics in the years to come.

Since it is ideological decision making that most captures the ideals of sophistication, consistency, and the public good, the negative relationship between it and the sixties generation is most significant. It suggests that to the extent that this generation does become involved in electoral politics, such involvement will not be ideologically-based and, therefore, the generation will be fluid in its support for a wide range of politically distinct ideas and individuals. Indeed, the six-

Political Decision Making

ties, a politically contradictory period, has spawned a politically contradictory generation. Ironically this occurred when environmental changes were increasing ideological decision making among the rest of the population. When these competing effects of generation and period are considered along with the effects of aging and the other, more volatile effects of certain interactions, the recent instability in political leadership and the conflicting currents of liberalism and conservatism that have characterized recent politics in the United States seem less surprising, and perhaps even expected.

NOTES

1. The measures formulated by Nie, et al. differ from the ones used here in several important respects. First, since our interest is in decision making as opposed to levels of conceptualization, we use the original seven categories presented in Appendix 2C of *The Changing American Voter* and do not recombine them into types of respondents. Second, our measures are based on the number of responses as a percentage of the total possible responses (12), while Nie, et al. categorize individuals by the single most "sophisticated" answer given.

2. In fact, in most years up to five responses were allowed per question, or a total of 20. Since 1972 included only three, we, following Nie, et al. and for the sake of comparability over time, used only the first three in each year.

3. This is not an issue of one interpretation being right and the other wrong. Instead, it demonstrates the complexities of change in the mass public and the difficulties in characterizing that change.

4. Given the extremely rigorous nature of our conceptualization and operationalization of cues (a respondent would have to give 12 explicitly ideological responses to receive a score of one on "Ideology I" for example), relatively small changes are both substantively and statistically significant. As a result, the entries in the tables are carried out to four figures rather than the usual three. The reader is asked to keep this in mind and not be deceived by the absolute sizes of the unstandardized coefficients.

REFERENCES

Berelson, Bernard R., and Paul F. Lazarsfeld. *Voting: A Study of Opinion*

Formation in a Presidential Campaign. Chicago: University of Chicago Press, 1954.

Boyte, Harry C. *The Backyard Revolution.* Philadelphia: Temple University Press, 1980.

Campbell, Angus, Philip E. Converse, Warren E. Miller, and Donald E. Stokes. *The American Voter.* New York: John Wiley, 1960.

Delli Carpini, Michael X. "Political Distillation: The Changing Impact of Partisanship on Electoral Behavior." *American Politics Quarterly,* 11 (April, 1983), pp. 163–180.

Fiorina, Morris. "An Outline for a Model of Party Choice." *American Journal of Political Science,* 21 (1977), pp. 601–626.

———. *Retrospective Voting in American National Elections.* New Haven: Yale University Press, 1981.

Gilmour, Richard, and Richard Lamb. *Political Alienation in Contemporary America.* New York: St. Martin's Press, 1975.

Gitlin, Todd. *The Whole World is Watching.* Berkeley: University of California Press, 1980.

Inglehart, Ronald. *The Silent Revolution.* Princeton: Princeton University Press, 1977.

Nie, Norman H., and Kristi Andersen. "Mass Belief Systems Revisited: Political Change and Attitude Structure." *Journal of Politics,* 36 (August, 1974), pp. 540–591.

Nie, Norman H., Sidney Verba, and John R. Petrocik. *The Changing American Voter.* Cambridge, Mass.: Harvard University Press, 1979.

Pomper, Gerald. *Voters' Choice: Varities of American Electoral Behavior.* New York: Dodd, Mead, 1975.

Shingles, Richard. "Black Consciousness and Political Participation." *American Political Science Review,* 75 (March, 1981), pp. 76–91.

Shively, W. Phillips. "The Development of Party Identification Among Adults." *American Political Science Review,* 73 (1979), pp. 1039–1054.

Tufte, Edward R. "Determinants of the Outcomes of Midterm Congressional Elections." *American Political Science Review,* 69 (September, 1975), pp. 812–826.

———. *Political Control of the Economy.* Princeton: Princeton University Press, 1978.

Verba, Sidney, and Norman H. Nie. *Participation in America.* New York: Harper and Row, 1972.

CHAPTER 9

Political Participation

Participation is the linchpin of democratic politics. With it there is at least the possibility of citizen control; without it the will of the citizenry is at the mercy of the good graces of political leaders. In mass democracies such as that in the United States, participation in politics centers around the electoral system. Voting is the only form of political behavior engaged in regularly by more than half the population (Verba and Nie, 1972), and it is the real and symbolic importance placed on elections that draws most citizens into the political process more generally (Ginsberg, 1982). In this chapter we explore trends in various forms of mass participation in electoral politics and examine the extent to which changes in the level of such participation can be traced to the effects of life cycle, generation, or period.

LIFE CYCLE, GENERATION, PERIODS AND POLITICAL PARTICIPATION

The period from the 1950s to the 1980s is something of an enigma in American politics. While personal and societal resources that correlate positively with political participation have increased (consider the trends in education, income, and mass media discussed in Chapter Two), participation in elections, at least as measured by voting statistics, has declined rather steadily. This curious relationship has been explained by various observers in different ways. Some have put the blame on the demise of parties and the party system (Burnham, 1965, 1970). Some have cited the poor quality of candidates and office holders (Broder, 1971) or the limited scope of issues addressed (Schattschneider, 1960). And others have sought explanations in the elements of campaigns themselves: media coverage (Graber, 1980), registration laws (Rusk, 1970; Converse, 1972), the primary system (Ranney, 1975), and the length and number of campaigns (Flanigan and Zingale, 1983).

Besides these "top down" explanations, attention has also been paid to causes that emanate, at least indirectly, from the mass population itself. The expansion of the electorate to include new groups less used to, less willing and/or less able to participate is often cited as a source of the declining participation in politics (Converse, 1972; Flanigan and Zingale, 1983). Growing political alienation and declining trust, efficacy and partisan attachments are also often mentioned (Gilmour and Lamb, 1975; Abramson and Aldrich, 1982). Brody (1978), in a comprehensive analysis of competing explanations for the decline in electoral participation, finds some evidence that decreasing political involvement and increasing indifference towards candidates and outcomes may be responsible, though by his own admission the data raise more questions than they answer. Finally, in an interesting twist, Inglehart (1977) has argued that the rise of a new and more capable generation has meant that simple and nonfulfilling participation in politics such as voting, which is dominated by archaic structures and old values, no longer appeals to a growing segment of the population.

To what extent did the events of the sixties and the generation shaped by those events contribute to aggregate trends in electoral participation? We have already suggested that much of the social and economic change of the sixties would lead one to expect greater levels of participation. The intense political climate of that era has also been pointed to as a galvanizer of a political consciousness in the public (Cantrill and Roll, 1971; Nie, et al., 1979). The links in both cases are not as straightforward as they initially appear, however. Greater personal resources provide the potential for more participation, but not necessarily the incentives to do so. Increased media attention to politics such as that found in the sixties can serve, either through a saturation effect or through negative coverage (Robinson, 1976; Graber, 1980) to decrease political participation just as easily as it might increase it. And, again, the conflictual, often violent, and inconsistent nature of political events during the sixties could have tipped the balance against rather than for joining the fray (Converse, 1976). In addition, the fact that much of the politics of the day were nonelectoral could have brought about greater involvement, but not in mainstream politics. As with the other aspects of politics discussed, in the sixties it was hard to determine what political avenues (if any) would be the most rewarding.

The same contradictions evident in the sixties generally apply to the sixties generation in particular. The tendency toward political action that characterized the generation did not include electoral participation. The extent to which this non-electoral propensity "spilt over" into electoral politics, had no impact on electoral politics, or resulted in a rejection of it is difficult to say, though the anti-establishment edge to the rhetoric and role models of the time would suggest the latter. Both the generation's lack of support for the political system (Chapter Four) and its general lack of psychological involvement in mainstream politics (Chapter Seven) would

The Effects of Generation, Periods, and the Life Cycle

add to this expectation. Finally, there is the issue of whether the process of aging, generally considered to have a positive effect on participation rates (Campbell, et al., 1960; Milbrath and Goel, 1977; Wolfinger and Rosenstone, 1980; Nie, et al., 1974; Hudson and Binstock, 1976), is interacting with the potential for participation in this generation to move them into the forefront of electoral politics as they grow older. The question again becomes, how do these diverse forces ultimately shape the rates of participation in the United States?

TRENDS IN ELECTORAL PARTICIPATION

Before attempting to answer the question posed at the end of the last section, let us look at what those trends actually show. Table 9.1 describes the ten measures of participation examined in this chapter. They range from long term voting patterns ("Always") to more immediate vote-related acts (registering to vote and actually voting for president and congress), to more costly forms of participation, such as working for a candidate, attending meetings, etc. In Figure 9.1 the mean scores over time for these various forms of participation

TABLE 9.1
Description of the Measures of Political Participation[a]

Variables	Description
Always vote	Do you always vote in presidential elections?
Register	Are you registered to vote in this election?
President	Did you vote for president this year?
Congress	Did you vote for congress this year?
Meetings	Have you attended any political rallies or meetings?
Organization	Do you belong to a political organization?
Display	Did you display a campaign slogan?
Work	Did you work for a party or candidate?
Influence	Did you try to influence anyone's vote?
Contribute	Did you contribute any money to a party or candidate?

[a] All variables are coded as one = yes; zero = no.

Political Participation

are presented. Several points should be noted about these trends. First, there is a clear distinction, both within each year and across elections, between the vote-related acts and the other forms of participation. All four vote-related measures have relatively high mean scores, but all show a similar

FIGURE 9.1
Trends in Political Participation, 1952–1980
(entries are mean scores in each year)

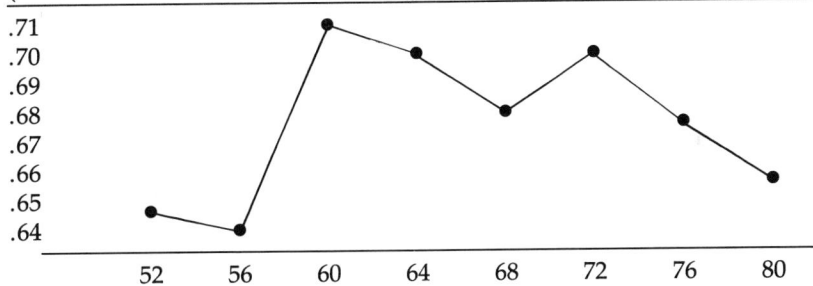

FIGURE 9.1A
Always vote

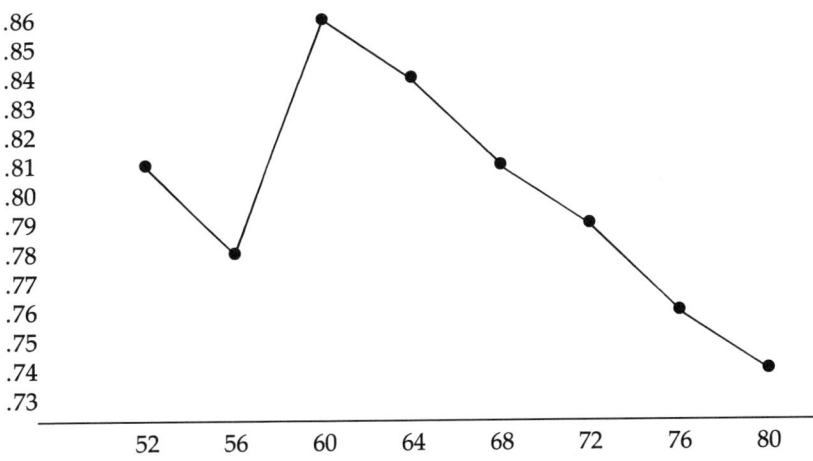

FIGURE 9.1B
Register

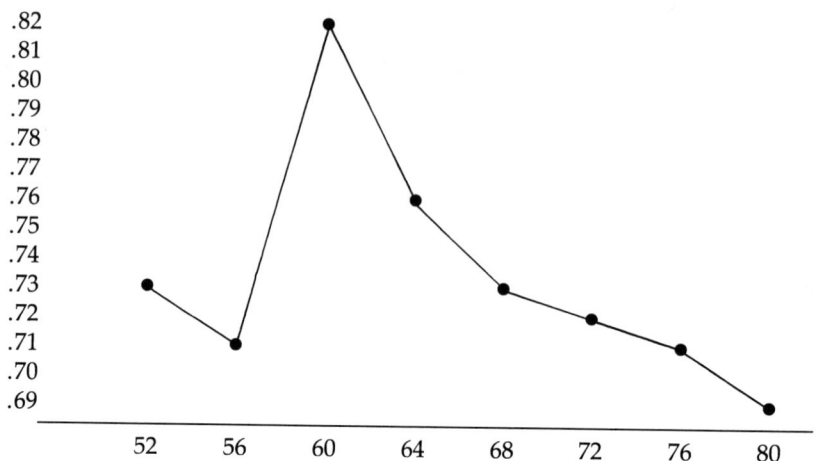

FIGURE 9.1C
President

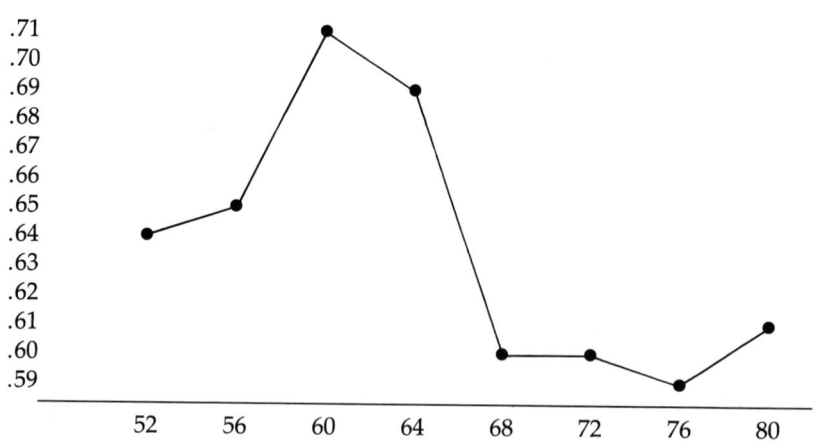

FIGURE 9.1D
Congress

Political Participation

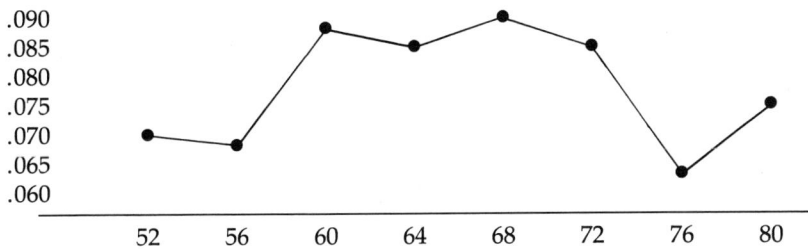

FIGURE 9.1E
Meetings

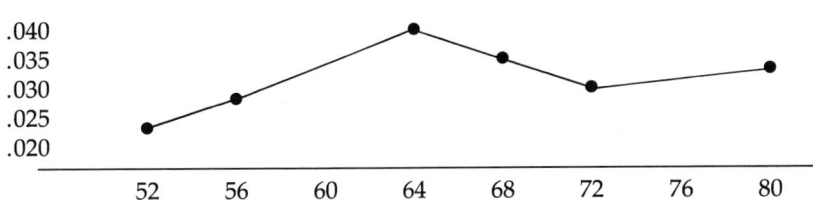

FIGURE 9.1F
Organizations

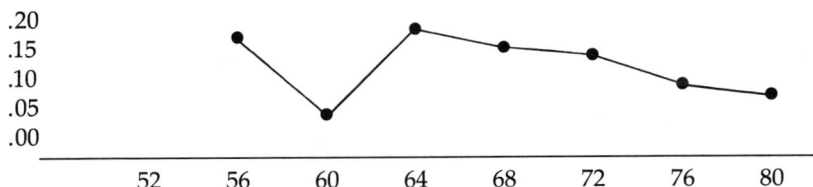

FIGURE 9.1G
Display

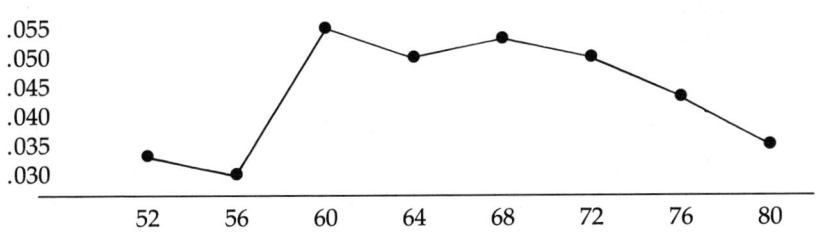

FIGURE 9.1H
Work

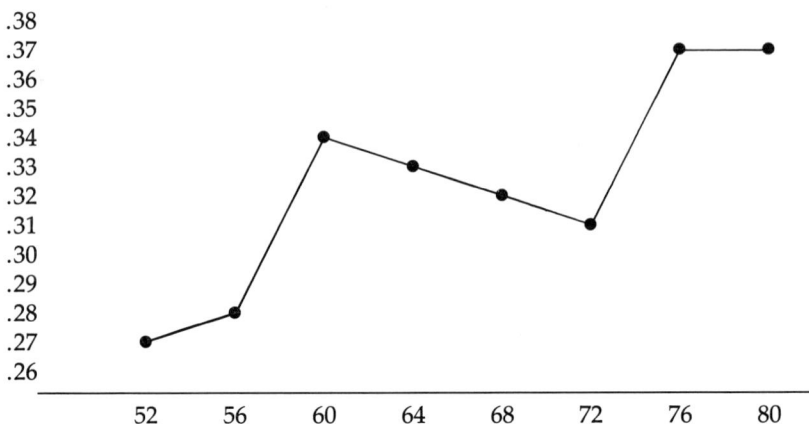

FIGURE 9.1I
Influence

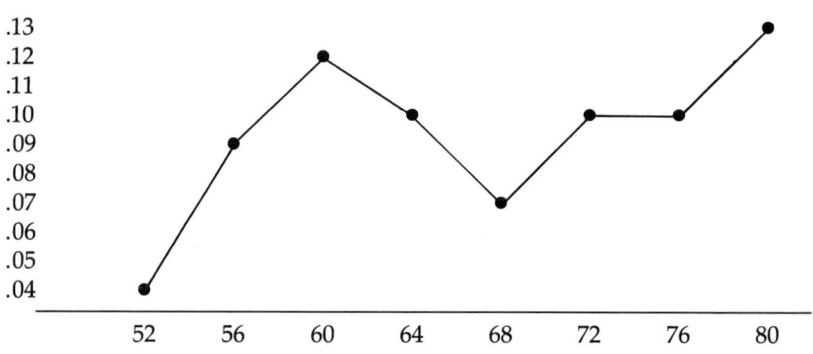

FIGURE 9.1J
Contribute

pattern of peaking in 1960 followed by a gradual but relatively steady decline through the seventies (though voting for congress did increase slightly in 1980). The other forms of participation are, of course, much less common, but evi-

Political Participation

denced a slight increase during the sixties, followed by either a decline more recently ("Meetings," "Organizations," "Display," and "Work") or continued expansion ("Influence," "Contribute"). Were it not for the more recent decline in some of these latter measures this juxtaposition of voting and nonvoting behavior would provide some indirect evidence for Inglehart's thesis. The recent declines suggest that a more complex process is at work, however. In any event, it is not the case that electoral participation uniformly declined over the three decades considered.

The jagged pattern that underlies the more dramatic peaks and valleys also suggests that short term as well as long term forces were affecting the level of participation. For example, 1960 appears to be a watershed year for a number of the participation measures. Clearly, some combination of factors were at work in producing these changes, factors that are both episodic and incremental, and that are to some extent pulling in opposite directions.

LIFE CYCLE, PERIODS AND THE SIXTIES GENERATION: THEIR IMPACT ON PARTICIPATION IN ELECTORAL POLITICS

In Table 9.2 the main effects of life cycle, period and generation on political participation are presented. The impact of aging on voting and nonvoting forms of participation is distinctly different. Participation through all four vote-related acts increased with age, a finding consistent with the literature cited earlier in this chapter. The other, more direct, costly, or self-involving forms of participation show either no relationship with age, or, in the case of displaying campaign literature and trying to influence someone else's political views, a slightly negative relationship. It appears that it is the rate of voting that increases with age, and not participation in politics more generally.

TABLE 9.2
Effects of Life Cycle, Generation, and Period
on Political Participation

Variables	Life cycle	Generation	Periods		
			Fifties	Sixties	Seventies
Always vote	.004**	−.348**	.078**	.190**	.260**
Register	.003**	−.313**	.063**	.201**	.258**
President	.002**	−.318**	.037	.240**	.237**
Congress	.002**	−.354**	.057*	.273**	.211**
Meetings	.000	−.025	.004	.070**	.071**
Organization	.000	−.009	−.002	.040**	−.007
Display	−.001	−.028	−.144*	.095	.093
Work	.000	−.068**	.023**	.055**	.089**
Influence	−.001**	−.081**	.017	.147**	.229**
Contribute	.000	−.095**	.079**	.117**	.191**

* = standard error ≤ B.
** $p \leq .05$.

The impact of being a member of the sixties generation on participation demonstrates no such split between vote and non-vote modes of participation: every measure shows a negative association with generation, with almost all of the effects being sizable. Members of this generation were much less likely to engage in electoral politics of any kind than their predecessors, and their "dropping out" was due much less to their relative age than to the predispositions that are part of the character of their generation. This finding is particularly interesting when compared to the period effects of the fifties, sixties and seventies. In almost every case (except for displaying literature in the fifties and organizational involvement in the fifties and seventies), the period effects were positive. In addition, the size of these relationships generally increased as one moved from the fifties through the sixties and into the seventies. That is, when generational and life cycle effects are removed, the increases in political participation that the changes in personal and societal resources during these years would lead one to expect become appar-

Political Participation

TABLE 9.3
Interaction Effects on Political Participation

Variables	Life cycle				Generation	
	Generation	Fifties	Sixties	Seventies	Sixties	Seventies
Always vote	.012**	−.001	−.004**	−.005**	.090**	.015
Register	.016**	−.001*	−.005**	−.006**	−.029	−.124**
President	.017**	.000	−.006**	−.005**	−.083**	−.121**
Congress	.018**	.000	−.007**	−.005**	−.128**	−.113**
Meetings	.003**	.000	−.001**	−.001**	−.046**	−.077**
Organization	.001**	.000	−.001**	.000	−.032**	−.005
Display	.000	.001	−.003	−.003	−.039	.005
Work	.004**	.000	−.001**	−.001**	−.009	−.053**
Influence	.005**	.001	−.003**	−.003**	−.038	−.078*
Contribute	.007**	.000	−.002**	−.003**	−.030	−.085**

* = standard error ≤ B.
** = p ≤ .05.

ent. Were it not for generational replacement, participation in all forms of electoral politics during the 1960s and 1970s might very well have shown aggregate increases in voting (and registration) and even greater, more consistent increases in other forms of electoral participation than actually occurred.

The negative impact of the sixties generation on participation becomes more apparent when interaction effects are considered (Table 9.3). While the main period effects were almost exclusively positive, the interaction of generation and period shows a consistently negative pattern, adding to the already non-participatory leanings of this cohort. In short, members of the sixties generation were decreasingly politically engaged during an era that was politically charged. The one set of relationships countering this overall rejection of electoral politics by the sixties generation was its interaction with the life cycle. Here there is evidence of movement towards greater participation of all kinds as they aged, though, again, not at a particularly fast rate. It takes, on average, 22 years in the electorate before the main generational effects

TABLE 9.4
Effects of Subgenerations on Political Participation

Variables	Ambivalent	Experienced	Socialized
Always vote	−.575**	−.264**	−.471*
Register	−.487**	−.387**	−.111
President	−.502**	−.433**	−.183
Congress	−.526**	−.530**	−.814**
Meetings	−.045	−.131**	.432**
Organization	−.008	−.040**	.279*
Display	−.026	−.183**	.540
Work	−.107**	−.096**	.051
Influence	−.104**	−.136**	−.331**
Contribute	−.167**	−.146**	.103

* = standard error ≤ B.
** = $p \leq .05$.

are counteracted for the vote-related acts, and about thirteen years for the other types. Finally, the interaction of life cycle and periods indicated that not only the sixties generation was shunning electoral involvement. Older cohorts were also reacting to the sixties and seventies by participating less than younger ones. This not only adds to the overall drop in participation (or to a slowed rate of increase in some cases) but also again demonstrates the tendency of older cohorts to resist period-based change of any kind.

When we turn to a more detailed examination of the sixties generation we can see a distinction between voting and other forms of participation (Table 9.4). All three cohorts were dramatically less likely to register or to vote, with the ambivalent cohort somewhat more "disengaged" than the other two on three of the four measures. For the other forms of participation, however, there is a clear break between the two oldest cohorts and the youngest, socialized one. The former two demonstrated the rejection of electoral politics that was evident in the main effects, with the experienced cohort slightly more negative than the ambivalent one. The socialized cohort, in contrast, showed positive and sizable relationships

TABLE 9.5
Interaction Effects between Subgenerations, Life Cycle, and Period on Political Participation

Variables	Life Cycle			Seventies	
	Ambivalent	Experienced	Socialized	Ambivalent	Experienced
Always vote	.012**	.016**	***	.245**	−.103**
Register	.012**	.027**	−.110**	.077	−.124**
President	.015**	.032**	−.065	.071	−.146**
Congress	.011**	.034**	.097*	.163*	−.148**
Meeting	.006**	.017**	−.090**	−.110**	−.063**
Organization	.001	.001	−.076*	.004	.070*
Display	−.005	.011	−.313**	−.049	.339**
Work	.003**	.006**	−.039**	−.008	−.030
Influence	.002	.018**	.038	−.058	−.211**
Contribute	.010**	.020**	−.038	−.106**	−.170**

* = standard error ≤ B.
** = $p \leq .05$.
*** = not calculated.

on five of the six measures, indicating a willingness to get involved in these more elaborate types of participation. This is the only indication of the sixties generation's having been made more politically active as a result of its particular set of experiences.

The interaction of subgenerations and aging (Table 9.5) again demonstrates that the effect of the life cycle is to pull people back to the norm, and not to push in a consistent substantive direction. Both the ambivalent and socialized cohorts, having entered the electorate less involved in all forms of electoral politics, are slowly becoming more involved with age. Interestingly, however, the ambivalent cohort did so at a slower rate than the experienced cohort, regardless of the size of the main relationship, suggesting that the former cohort was more resistant to society's "gravitational pull." The socialized cohort, however, having entered the electorate more involved in nonvoting forms of participation, quickly becomes less involved in these activities with age. This pattern of regressing to the mean does not hold for this cohort for either vote registration or voting for the president, however. In both cases the socialized cohort was less likely to participate despite an already reduced inclination as it entered the electorate. This could be an artifact of the short time span in which this subgeneration was in the electorate and may, therefore, reverse itself with time.

Finally, the interaction of the older two cohorts with the influences of the seventies indicates that while both reacted to that period by becoming even less involved in most forms of nonvoting political participation, the ambivalent cohort actually became more likely to register and vote during this period. Overall then, it was the experienced cohort that reacted most negatively to the seventies in terms of "dropping out" of the system.

SUMMARY AND CONCLUSION

Political participation is the *sine qua non* of mass democratic politics, and for better or worse, in large societies participation is essentially equivalent to electoral politics. In this chapter we have examined the effects of generation, period, and the life cycle on the changing levels of a variety of election-related activities. In particular, we were interested in trying to explain the dilemma of decreasing or erratically changing participation during an era of increasing resources for such participation. The answer, it seems, lies in the distinction between the period effects of these environmental changes and their effects on the generation that entered the electorate at this time.

It was found that aging, while having a slightly positive effect on vote-related behavior, was relatively unimportant as an influence on other forms of participation. Generation, in contrast, had a substantively strong and consistent effect of decreasing participation in electoral politics, especially turnout. The rejection of electoral involvement by the sixties generation was largely responsible for declines in registration and voting since 1960, and in more recent declines in other forms of political activity, reducing or reversing the more positive effects of period. The interaction of period and generation added to this negative trend in many instances and suggests an even greater distinction between this generation and its predecessors. While aging appeared to reduce this distinctiveness over time, it did so at a relatively slow rate. Finally, all three of the subgenerations demonstrated this withdrawal from mainstream politics in terms of voting. However, the socialized cohort was more rather than less involved in other forms of political behavior. As these cohorts age, the distinctiveness of each (no matter what the substance of that distinctiveness) is slowly disappearing.

When combined with the findings of Chapters Four and Seven, we begin to get a picture of the sixties generation that is consistent in its relative disengagement from mainstream politics. These findings mesh quite nicely with research that stresses the role of psychological motivations in the recent declines in electoral participation (Brody, 1978; Abramson and Aldrich, 1982). The findings presented in these chapters demonstrate that such motivations are less prevalent in the sixties generation. In addition, when considered in light of prior research, they also raise the possibility that the link between motivations and behavior is stronger for this generation than for previous ones. Ironically, in terms of electoral involvement and participation at least, the impact of being raised in the 1960s may very well have been to heighten one's political consciousness enough to strengthen the link between attitudes and behavior, but at the same time to sow the seeds of discontent and disinterest that would then lead to decreased participation. This is, however, speculation that is suggested but not demonstrated by our analysis.

The extent to which these trends should be viewed with

TABLE 9.6
Generational and Subgenerational Differences in
Alternative Forms of Participation[a]

Variables	Predecessors	Sixties	Ambivalent	Experienced	Socialized
National Issues					
Letter to editor	3.6%	4.1%	5.0%	3.7%	1.9%
Write to congress	16.9%	17.1%	20.3%	14.1%	9.7%
Work with others	8.3%	8.5%	9.8%	7.6%	4.9%
Sign a petition	8.6%	14.8%	15.0%	18.3%	13.6%
Protest	0.5%	2.7%	2.1%	3.1%	1.9%
Local Issues					
Letter to editor	4.1%	5.6%	6.5%	5.1%	2.0%
Write to congress	18.9%	20.1%	23.5%	16.5%	12.9%
Work with others	19.2%	23.9%	27.6%	21.3%	15.8%
Sign a petition	17.2%	25.9%	28.1%	24.2%	14.9%
Protest	0.8%	2.8%	1.8%	3.6%	5.0%
School board	15.8%	22.3%	29.2%	18.3%	10.9%

[a]Entries are given as a percent of each cohort that has performed a particular activity.

alarm depends largely on whether or not one agrees that high levels of participation are important to the success of democracy, on whether or not these trends are irreversible, and on whether or not they represent a decline in all forms of participation or only a substitution of one form of activity for others. The first question is beyond the scope of this study, though from the point of view of either the stability and legitimacy of the political system or a commitment to democratic politics it does give pause. The second question, while substantively of import to this research, cannot be answered because of the potential effects of future periods or events as of yet unforeseen. We can say that short of such effects, however, the negative impacts of generation and the current pattern of interactions with periods are stronger than any gains made due to aging. This suggests low levels of participation in the years to come.

The last question is also difficult to answer, because we

Political Participation

do not have data on nonelectoral behavior over time, but we can hint at an answer here as well. The 1976 survey included items concerning several forms of participation beyond those discussed here. While we cannot break the relationship between age and participation down into its generational, life cycle, and period subcomponents, we can at least look at the simple pattern that exists. Table 9.6 presents these patterns. As can be seen, for every form of participation the sixties generation was more involved than preceding cohorts. While these differences are often not large, when they are considered in light of both age differences and the patterns presented above concerning electoral politics, they do indicate that we are witnessing a partial shifting of energies rather than a complete rejection of politics. When the behaviors of the specific subgenerations are considered, the ambivalent cohort was often the most politically involved, though we cannot say whether this results from the interaction of generation and age or from a more direct subgenerational difference. If it is the former, then we can expect increased participation in these areas as the generation as a whole ages and as it becomes a larger percentage of the electorate. Interestingly, the only activities in which the ambivalent cohort did not participate to a greater extent than the others were those most directly associated with the sixties—petition signing and protest. In both cases, it is the cohort most directly a part of those experiences that was most likely to engage in such activities in the seventies.

REFERENCES

Abramson, Paul R., and John H. Aldrich. "The Decline of Electoral Participation in America." *American Political Science Review,* 76 (September, 1982), pp. 502–521.

Broder, David. *The Party's Over.* New York: Harper and Row, 1971.

Brody, Richard A. "The Puzzle of Political Participation in America." In

Anthony King (ed.). *The New American Political System.* Washington, D.C.: The American Enterprise Institute, 1978, pp. 287–324.

Burnham, Walter Dean. "The Changing Shape of the American Political Universe." *American Political Science Review,* 59 (1965), pp. 7–28.

———. *Critical Elections and the Mainspring of American Politics.* New York: Norton, 1970.

Campbell, Angus, Philip E. Converse, Warren E. Miller, and Donald E. Stokes. *The American Voter.* New York: John Wiley, 1960.

Cantril, Albert H., and Charles W. Roll. *The Hopes and Fears of the American Public.* New York: University Books, 1971.

Converse, Philip E. "Change in the American Electorate." In Angus Campbell and Philip E. Converse (eds.). *The Human Meaning of Social Change.* New York: Sage Publications, 1972.

———. *The Dynamics of Party Support: Cohort-Analyzing Party Identification.* Beverly Hills: Sage Publications, 1976.

Flanigan, William, and Nancy Zingale. *The Political Behavior of the American Electorate.* Boston: Allyn and Bacon, 1983.

Gilmour, Richard, and Richard Lamb. *Political Alienation in Contemporary America.* New York: St. Martin's Press, 1975.

Ginsberg, Benjamin. *The Consequences of Consent: Elections, Citizen Control and Popular Acquiescence.* Reading, Mass.: Addison-Wesley, 1982.

Graber, Doris. *Mass Media in American Politics.* Washington, D.C.: Congressional Quarterly Press, 1980.

Hudson, Robert H., and Robert H. Binstock. "Political Systems and Aging." In Robert H. Binstock and Ethel Shanas (eds.). *Handbook of Aging and the Social Sciences.* New York: Van Nostrand, 1976.

Inglehart, Ronald. *The Silent Revolution.* Princeton: Princeton University Press, 1977.

Milbrath, Lester W., and M. L. Goel. *Political Participation.* Chicago: Rand McNally, 1977.

Nie, Norman H., Sidney Verba, and John R. Petrocik. *The Changing American Voter.* Cambridge, Mass.: Harvard University Press, 1979.

Nie, Norman H., Sidney Verba, and Jae-On Kim. "Political Participation and the Life Cycle." *Comparative Politics,* 6 (1974), pp. 319–340.

Ranney, Austin. *Curing the Mischiefs of Faction.* Berkeley: University of California Press, 1975.

Robinson, Michael. "Public Affairs Television and the Growth of Political Malaise." *American Political Science Review,* 70 (June, 1976), pp. 409–432.

Rusk, Jerrold G. "The Effect of the Australian Ballot Reform on Split Ticket Voting, 1876–1908." *American Political Science Review,* 64 (December, 1970), pp. 1220–1238.

Schattschneider, E. E. *The Semi-Sovereign People.* New York: Holt, Rinehart and Winston, 1960.

Political Participation

Verba, Sidney, and Norman H. Nie. *Participation in America*. New York: Harper and Row, 1972.

Wolfinger, Raymond E., and Steven J. Rosenstone. *Who Votes*. New Haven: Yale University Press, 1980.

CHAPTER 10

Partisan Support

In the previous chapter we found that the sixties generation demonstrated a consistent tendency to refrain from participating in electoral politics, relative to preceding generations. But what of the nature of the electoral participation they do engage in? In this chapter we explore the partisan leanings of the sixties generation, focusing on both the level of support for the party system generally and the specific partisan direction of that support. In the following chapter we examine the stability of that support.

THE LOGIC OF PARTISAN SUPPORT

The relationship between democracy and political parties has long been both intricate and contradictory. Early political theorists and practitioners saw in parties the seeds of destruction for democratic politics (Hofstadter, 1969). Parties, or factions, were seen as overly narrow and ideological, inevitably ripping apart the systems in which they existed (Bolingbroke, 1965, 1973). Other observers believed parties were driven by blatant self-interest, with rhetoric appealing to the public good masking the desire for personal gain (Trenchard and Gordon, 1969). To the extent that parties were seen as inevitable, they were viewed as unavoidable evils to be controlled (Hume, 1953). Of the early political writers, only Burke saw political parties as being potentially beneficial to the system, but he expressed his conclusion with obvious reluctance (1897, 1956).

The founders of the American democratic experiment were very much influenced by this negative view of parties, with Hamilton and Madison leading the early attempts to curb the mischiefs of faction. The political system of the United States was specifically designed to limit both the likelihood that competing parties would develop and to insure that any parties that did evolve would find the accumulation of power an elusive task. As late as Washington's farewell address (1799), parties were considered the major threat to the stability of this infant democracy.

As is always the case, the juncture of theory and practice led to changing theory. By the midnineteenth century a new generation of politicians, led by Jackson and Van Buren, had come to view parties not only as unavoidable elements of democratic politics but as integral parts of the system (Hofstadter, 1969). So firmly entrenched has this revisionist view of parties become that by the midtwentieth century a leading theorist of American politics stated that democratic politics was unthinkable save in terms of political parties (Schattschneider, 1942).

What lay behind this apparent change of heart? In part it was simply a matter of nothing succeeding like success. Parties proved to be a useful mechanism for the peaceful transfer of power among competing elites and a rallying point for the loyal opposition. More important, rather than dividing the population into many vocal, intense and competing factions, the party system in the United States, based as it is on two dominant parties, served to concentrate the diverse opinions and interests of a heterogeneous population into two options that have, with few exceptions, stood consistently near the center of the ideological spectrum. In short, parties helped to ensure that the views of the citizenry could be heard and that political change could occur, but that both would be contained in a way that did not threaten the basic structure of the system nor the interests that most benefited from that system. Parties in general, and the two-party system in particular, therefore, have come to be seen not only as the sail that keeps democracy in the United States moving, but also as the rudder that keeps it on a charted, predictable course.

Key to the success of such a system is the level of support granted by the mass public. This support must be given at both a general, diffuse level to the party system as a whole, and at a more party-specific level. The former gives legitimacy to the system, helps assure that participation is channeled through the accepted institutions, and increases the likelihood that opposition will remain loyal. The latter is necessary if participation is to provide a meaningful link between the issue stands and agendas preferred by the public, the issue stands and agendas offered by the parties, and, ultimately, the actual policy outputs of government.

The historical rejection of political parties noted above, as well as the recent acceptance of them as critical to stable democratic politics are reflected both in the support given to parties by the mass public, and the importance placed on that support by modern-day theorists and practitioners. Citizens of the United States consistently demonstrate an ambivalence towards parties and the party system that borders on a love-hate relationship (Ranney, 1975). On the one hand, attachment to political parties is remarkably high in the United States, with as much as ninety percent of the population having claimed loyalty to one of the major parties in this century (Nie, et al., 1979). The inability of third party or independent candidates to win major political offices in the

Partisan Support

United States further attests to the importance placed on the party label by the public (Rosenstone, et al., 1984). On the other hand, opinion surveys demonstrate suspicion towards parties and the party system. Parties consistently appear among the least-trusted of institutions; often they are rated lower than the much-maligned "special interest groups" (Dennis, 1976). Majorities or near majorities of the American public believe parties care more about one's vote than one's opinion, feel parties cater to the interests of a few, and would support the elimination of party labels from the ballot and the introduction of a national primary system (Ranney, 1975; Dennis, 1976). The ambivalence towards parties is perhaps best evidenced by the fact that large percentages of the population agree that parties *both* confuse issues by not taking distinct stands *and* that they add to the conflictual nature of politics by taking opposing stands on issues (Ranney, 1975). Apparently while writers on political parties have resolved their competing views on the importance of parties, the public has not.

In contrast to the ambivalent support generally provided to parties and the party system is the consistent support for individual parties over time. As noted above, a sizable majority of Americans claim to identify with one or the other of the two major parties. That identification is the greatest single predictor of the vote choices of the electorate (Schulman and Pomper, 1975; Nie, et al., 1979). Finally, the combination of partisan stability and the usually low salience of politics to Americans has resulted in a pattern of relatively stable electoral coalitions, political leadership, and political agendas, marked by periodic shifts or realignments (Burnham, 1970; Sundquist, 1973). However, recent evidence suggests that this predictable pattern of stability and change is beginning to unravel as partisan attachments weaken and as the links between attachment and actual behavior become more tenuous (Nie, et al., 1979; Pomper, 1975; Schulman and Pomper, 1975).

The negative current that runs through attitudes and opinions toward political parties has been a subject of some concern for students of American politics. For parties to provide a combination of coherent choices and relative stability in the political system, citizens must support both the idea of a party system and the policies and leaders of particular parties. Whether recent trends are the beginnings of another realignment in allegiance to parties (Phillips, 1969) or represent a more deep-seated rejection of the system altogether (Burnham, 1975) is unclear. One can begin to answer this question, however, by examining in more detail the sources of changing general and specific partisan support.

LIFE CYCLES, PERIODS, GENERATIONS, AND CHANGING PARTY SUPPORT

Changes in the level of support for particular parties and in the level of support for the party system more generally can result from a changing political and social environment, a changing population, or some combination of the two. In the years from the early 1950s to 1980, several such changes occurred that are relevant to this issue. In terms of specific party support, these years were filled with important events and trends. The entire period under study falls into what Hbrenner and Scott have called the "tideless era" of the fifth party system (1979). The party system that was formed with the realignment of 1932 and that brought together the now-familiar Democratic coalition which has dominated politics in the United States since then, has been characterized as lethargic since the early fifties, with no clear policy direction, muted differences between the parties, and little enthusiasm among the electorate. In addition, cyclical theories of realign-

Partisan Support

ment pointed to the late sixties as a time ripe for a major restructuring of party coalitions. Finally, the years from 1960 on have been filled with events that bear directly on the choice of which party to support: the JFK administration and its abrupt end; Johnson's "Great Society" and the escalation of the war in Vietnam; the rise in what Nie et al. have called the "issues of discontent" (crime, urban and student unrest, the war, civil rights, poverty, etc.); Nixon's political triumphs and disasters; the rise of ideological candidates such as Goldwater, McGovern, and Reagan; the economic and foreign policy crises of the seventies; and the decisive Republican victories of 1980. One gets the sense throughout the period that the system has become loose from the moorings established in 1932, yet has been unable to find a suitable place to redock.

In addition to these issue, candidate and party-specific factors, larger systemic factors were at work to effect not only which party one supported, but one's support for the party system itself. The growth of the mass media and its importance both as a tool used by candidates and as an independent source of information had a devastating effect on parties. First, it allowed candidates to go directly to the public, usurping one of the major functions of the party organization (Sorauf, 1984). Second, it increased the emphasis on marketing candidates through image and on personality rather than issues (McGinnis, 1969). Third, it provided an independent source of information, taking away yet another function once dominated by the parties (Hbrenner and Scott, 1979). Finally, the media's emphasis on the game over the substance of campaigns (Patterson, 1980; Keeter and Zukin, 1983) and the generally negative, cynical coverage of politics and campaigns (Graber, 1980) added to the already high levels of public distrust and low levels of interest and information.

The Effects of Generation, Periods, and the Life Cycle

Along with the new role for the media, changes, such as the rise of the direct primary, the opening up of party organization, and the greater reliance on public-opinion polls to choose issue stands and agenda emphases all added to the blurring of distinctions (in people's minds, if not in reality) between the major parties. Finally, control of political events seemed to be beyond the reach of the representatives of either party. Leaders ranged from well-meaning and well-liked people who were perceived as outmatched by the problems they faced (Carter, Ford) to individuals who took the trust of huge majorities and, for different reasons, betrayed it (Johnson, Nixon).

In addition to these changes in the political environment, changes in the population (which should now be familiar) were also relevant. The relationship between age and partisan support is well established, though the root causes of that relationship are subject to much debate (Converse, 1976, 1979; Abramson, 1979). There is evidence that the tendency to become more conservative with age increases the attractiveness of the Republican party, though this tendency appears rather weak (see Chapter Six). In addition, aging seems to strengthen the bond felt towards whichever party one identifies with (Claggett, 1981; Converse, 1976). As we have seen in Chapter Four, however, aging also brings a decrease in general support for the system, which could carry over to support for the party system more specifically.

Generational differences are also important in understanding the level of partisan support. The sixties generation entered the electorate with unmatched levels of education, making the need for shortcuts to decision making (such as party labels) less crucial (Shively, 1979; Fiorina, 1977). However, as was discussed in Chapter Seven, this generation was less likely to follow electoral politics than preceding cohorts, making independent decisions more difficult. We have also

Partisan Support

found that the sixties generation was much less supportive of the system generally (Chapter Four) and somewhat more liberal on a number of issues (Chapter Six), both of which bear on the selection of a party and the likelihood of supporting the party system. In short, there is reason to expect both life-cycle and generational change to affect the partisan support found in the system, though the specific factors involved are cross cutting rather than uniform.

TRENDS IN PARTISAN SUPPORT

As usual, let us begin our examination of the effects of generation, period and life cycle by first looking at the aggregate patterns of change. The specific dimensions of partisan support discussed in this chapter are described in Table 10.1.

TABLE 10.1
Description of the Measures of Partisan Support

Variables	Description
ID strength	Strength of party identification (1 = strong identifier)
Care win	Do you care which party wins? (1 = care very much)
Party difference	Are there real differences between the political parties? (1 = important differences)
Intentions	Planned choice for president (1 = Democrat)
President	Vote choice for president (1 = Democrat)
Congress	Vote choice for congress (1 = Democrat)
Local	Vote choice in state and local elections (1 = Democrat)
Last time	Vote in last presidential election (1 = Democrat)
Usual vote	General voting pattern in presidential elections (1 = always Democratic)
Party ID	Direction of party identification (1 = strongly Democratic)
Party evaluation	Net direction of evaluations of the political parties (1 = net Democratic advantage)

The Effects of Generation, Periods, and the Life Cycle

Three of the measures ("Party Differences," "Care Win," and "ID Strength") tap diffuse support for the party system; five ("Intentions," "President," "Congress," "Local" and "Last Time") measure behavioral, short-term support for specific parties; and three ("Party Evaluations," "Usual Vote" and "Party ID") reveal more long-term support for particular parties. All the variables are coded so that a higher score indicates either a response in favor of parties (for the diffuse support measures) or a response in favor of the Democratic Party and its candidate.

In Figure 10.1 the trends in partisan support as measured by the eleven items described above are presented. The three measures of diffuse partisan support (10.1A, B and C) show different patterns, with ID Strength demonstrating a precipitous decline, care over which party wins showing a slightly less dramatic decline, and a sense that there are important differences between the parties showing a sawtoothed pattern, with evidence of an increase since 1968. The ambivalence described earlier in this chapter is clearly reflected in the pattern of aggregate diffuse support for parties from 1952 to 1980.

When we turn to the measures of specific, short-term partisan choice (Figures 10.1D through H), a different pattern emerges. All five measures demonstrate a similar pattern of low to moderate Democratic support in the fifties, followed

FIGURE 10.1
Trends in Partisan Support, 1952–1980

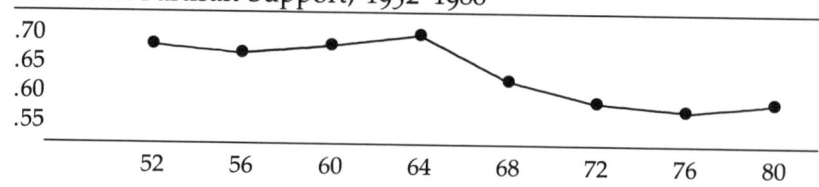

FIGURE 10.1A
ID strength

Partisan Support

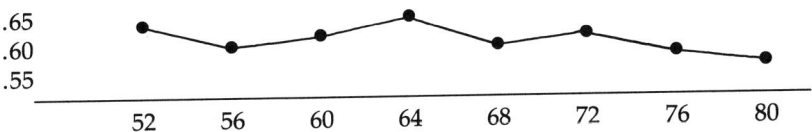

FIGURE 10.1B
Care win

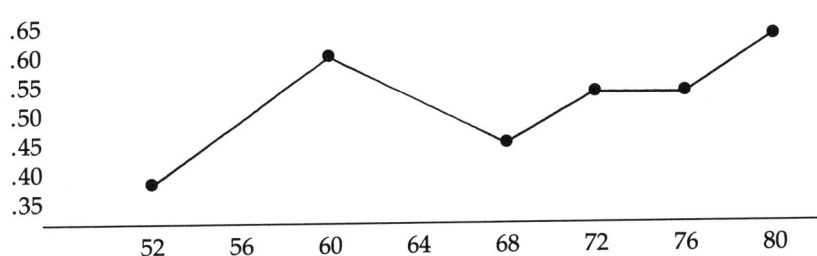

FIGURE 10.1C
Party differences

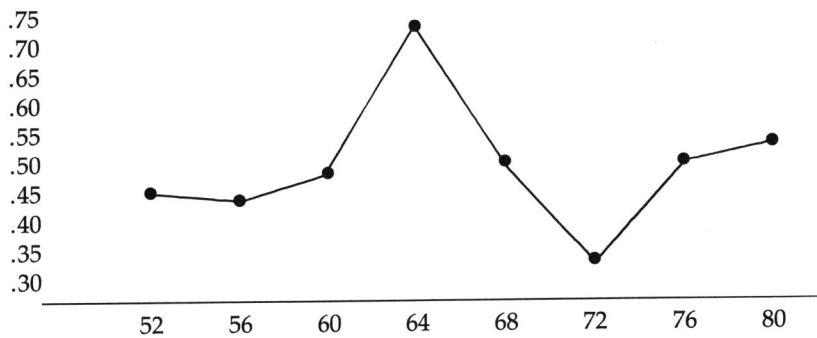

FIGURE 10.1D
Intention

The Effects of Generation, Periods, and the Life Cycle

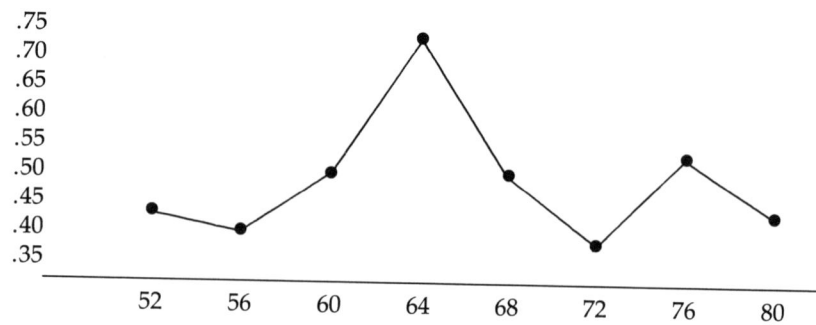

FIGURE 10.1E
President

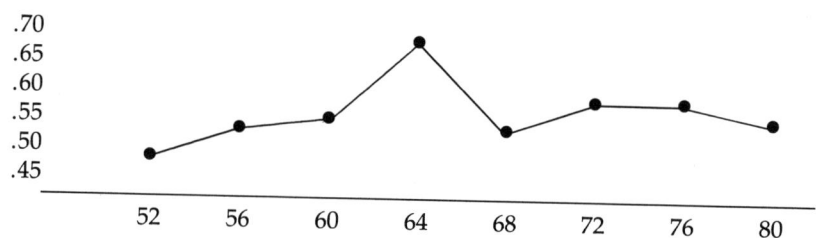

FIGURE 10.1F
Congress

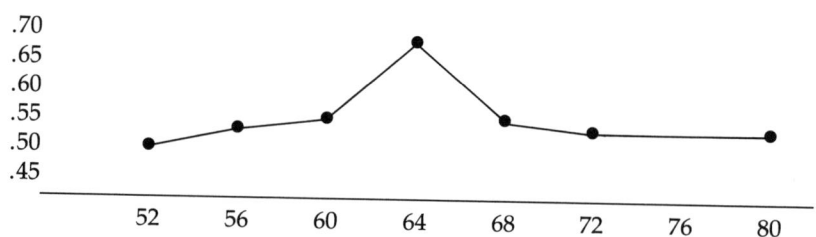

FIGURE 10.1G
Local

Partisan Support

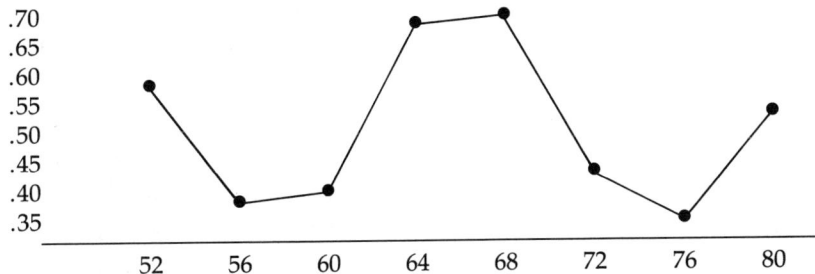

FIGURE 10.1H
Last time

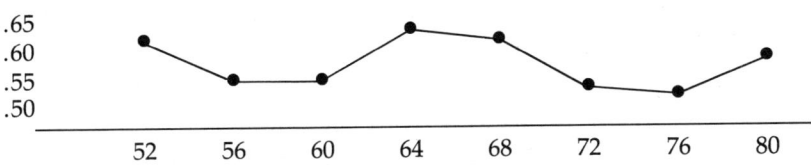

FIGURE 10.1I
Usual vote

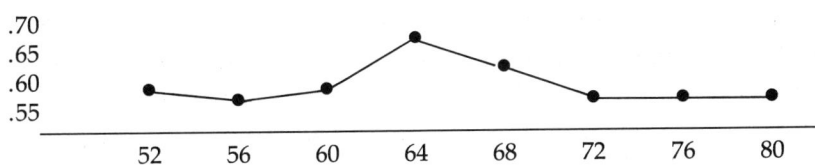

FIGURE 10.1J
Party ID

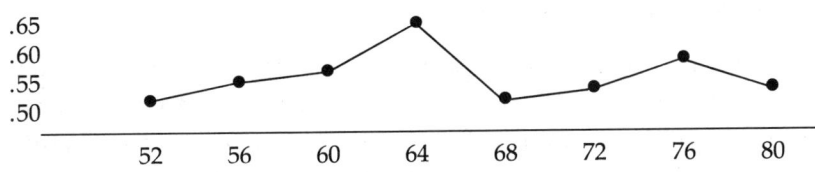

FIGURE 10.1K
Party evaluations

by increased support in the early sixties, and then a reduction of Democratic support from the late sixties on (with a slight increase in 1976). The pattern is accentuated in the presidential measures, with lower valleys and higher peaks, and more restricted for the congressional and local measures, a finding which is not surprising since the presidential race is much more affected by short-term forces and personality. Note also that all the measures demonstrate a pro-Democratic bias, with few years dipping very far below the 50 percent mark.

The final three measures (Figure 10.1I through K) tap a longer-term element of party choice. They are interesting in that all three parallel the short-term trends, except that they are more resistant to change. That is, while Democratic support ebbed in the fifties and from the late sixties on, it never dropped below the 50 percent mark on any of these measures.

In sum, we can characterize the years from 1952 to 1980 as a time of erratic diffuse support with some evidence of a general decline; erratic short-term specific party support, with movement back and forth from Republican to Democrat to Republican; and relatively stable long-term support that demonstrates a moderate but steady advantage for the Democratic party throughout the years examined.

THE EFFECTS OF LIFE CYCLE, PERIOD AND GENERATION ON PARTY SUPPORT

To what extent are these patterns of party support attributable to the effects of the life cycle, periods and generation? In Table 10.2 the main effects of each are presented. While as usual the results are not completely uniform, there are some clear patterns. The measures of diffuse support show little consistent relationship with the life cycle. While the

Partisan Support

TABLE 10.2
Effects of Life Cycle, Generation, and Period on Partisan Support

Variables	Life Cycle	Generation	Period		
			Fifties	Sixties	Seventies
ID strength	.002**	−.004	−.036*	−.035*	−.129**
Care win	.000	−.095**	−.013	.053**	.005
Party differences	.000	−.038	.244**	.134**	.233**
Intentions	−.002	.058	−.052	.210**	.027
President	−.002*	.091*	−.036	.230**	.051
Congress	−.003**	.043	.013	.145**	.104
Local	−.002*	.040	.051	.153**	−.012
Last time	−.003**	.046	−.289**	.120**	−.314**
Usual vote	−.003**	−.058*	−.168**	−.025	−.189**
Party ID	−.002**	−.016	−.037*	.064**	−.026
Party evaluations	−.003**	−.031	−.016	.058*	.028

* = standard error ≤ B.
** = p ≤ .05.

strength of one's partisan attachments, in agreement with Claggett and Converse, increases with age, the remaining two measures show no relationship at all. All eight of the measures of party choice show a pro-Republican tendency with aging, however, suggesting that there may be some truth to the argument that aging leads to a more-conservative political outlook. This was the trend for all kinds of elections and for both the short and the long term measures.

Effects of generation show a more intricate, but equally consistent pattern. Members of the sixties generation entered the electorate with relatively low diffuse partisan support; this cohort was less likely to develop a partisan attachment, less likely to perceive important differences between the parties, and less likely to care which party won. The pattern of political alienation from mainstream politics demonstrated in Chapter Four carries over to party politics as well.

Particularly interesting is the juxtaposition of patterns between short and long-term party choices for the sixties generation. All five short-term measures indicate a pro-

The Effects of Generation, Periods, and the Life Cycle

Democratic leaning for this generation, a finding consistent with their liberal tendencies (Chapter Six) and the era in which they were socialized. This short-term support masks an underlying anti-Democratic Party tendency which is demonstrated in the long-term measures, however. Members of this generation are less Democratic in their partisan leanings, less likely to usually vote Democratic over time, and less positive in their evaluations of the Democratic party than one would expect, given their age and the time in which they live.

Period effects are the least uniform of the main effects, though overall there are still some clear patterns. Short-term vote choices in the fifties were generally more Republican (or, more accurately, less Democratic), while the sixties was a pro-Democratic era, and the seventies a mixed, unstable time. The presidential-based measures show this pattern to a greater degree than the others, again due to the resistance of lower, less visible offices to such short-term forces.

The measures of long-term trends reveal that the fluctuations in short-term party preferences are a reflection of a more deep-seated struggle over partisan leadership. The fifties show consistent pro-Republican leanings, the sixties demonstrate some return to the Democratic party, and the seventies swing back to the Republican party. The one long-term behavioral measure—one's usual vote—shows a consistent anti-Democratic trend across all three periods, though it was smallest in the sixties. In short, the sixties stand out as a brief and partial respite from a more long-term erosion of the Democratic coalition.

The period effects concerning diffuse partisan support showed the least consistent results. ID strength decreases steadily from the fifties through the seventies, but concern over which party wins peaked in the sixties at the same time that a perception of party differences was at a low point

Partisan Support

TABLE 10.3
Interaction Effects on Partisan Support

Variables	Life Cycle				Generation	
	Generation	Fifties	Sixties	Seventies	Sixties	Seventies
ID strength	.001*	.001*	.000	.001*	−.086**	−.035
Care win	.004**	.000	−.001*	.000	−.035*	−.049*
Party difference	.003**	−.002	.000	−.001	−.037	−.046
Intentions	−.005**	.002	−.004**	.001	−.178**	−.006
President	−.003*	.002	−.004*	.002	−.202**	−.108
Congress	−.001	.001	−.001	.000	−.125**	−.110*
Local	−.001	.000	−.002*	.001	−.114**	−.032
Last time	−.001	.002	−.002	.004*	−.212**	.039
Usual vote	−.001	.003**	.001	.004**	.009	.085*
Party ID	.000	.001	−.001	.001	−.077**	−.040
Party evaluation	.001	.002*	.000	.001	−.056*	−.043

* = standard error ≤ B.
** = $p \le .05$.

(relative to the fifties and seventies). This apparent inconsistency may very well reflect the ambivalent, often contradictory attitudes held by the public towards parties. That the period effects for concern over outcomes and a sense of the differences between parties were somewhat inversely related quite possibly indicates the public's aversion to the politics of conflict (Ranney, 1975). That is, the public was most interested in party politics when differences between the parties existed (note that the period effect in the sixties is still positive) but when these differences are also *not too* great.[1]

In Table 10.3 the interaction effects of age, generation, and periods are presented. The interaction of generation and life cycle reveals that as the sixties generation ages, its voting behavior (across all offices and including long-term patterns) is becoming less Democratic, a finding consistent with the main effects of both life cycle and the long-term tendencies of that generation (Table 10.2). In addition, while there is a slight counteracting of anti-Democratic evaluations due to aging, it would take an average of over 30 years before this

The Effects of Generation, Periods, and the Life Cycle

generation's view of the party converged with that of older citizens. Finally, as with other measures of diffuse support (Chapter Four), aging has seemed to soften the sixties generation's negative view of the party system, though again at a slow rate relative to the size of the negative main effects.

The interaction of periods and generation provides further evidence that the sixties generation has been less supportive of the Democratic party than one might expect as well as unsupportive of the party system more generally. With the exception of one's usual (professed) vote, all measures of support, and of short-term and long-term vote choices in the sixties show very strong interactions with generation. These interactions are all anti-party generally and anti-Democratic party in particular. This pattern persists into the seventies, though the magnitude of most of the interactions decreases. Apparently the main effects of the sixties and of the voting behavior of the sixties generation masked evidence that the support of this generation for the Democratic party is "soft" at several levels.

Finally, the interaction of age and periods reveals the tendency of older cohorts to resist change more than younger cohorts have. The general pattern is for the interaction to be in the opposite direction of the main effect of period. Thus, when the nation moved towards the Republican party in the fifties and seventies, older cohorts resisted; when it moved to support the Democrats in the sixties they resisted as well (though, not surprisingly, to a slightly greater degree). It would again seem that as we age we do, in fact, become "set in our ways."

As a final consideration of the effects of generation on party support we again explored the differences among the ambivalent, experienced, and socialized cohorts that make up the sixties generation. Table 10.4 presents the main effects of these subgenerations. Several patterns become immedi-

Partisan Support

TABLE 10.4
Subgenerational Effects on Partisan Support

Variables	Ambivalent	Experienced	Socialized
ID strength	.049	−.131**	−.343**
Care win	−.131**	−.159**	−.251*
Party differences	−.185**	−.110**	.236*
Intentions	.248*	−.244**	−.122
President	.333**	−.167**	−.211*
Congress	.103*	−.074	−.262*
Local	.144*	−.074	.339*
Last time	.171*	−.811**	.541*
Usual vote	−.051	−.456**	.670**
Party ID	.019	−.112**	−.032
Party evaluations	−.019	−.078**	.276*

* = standard error ≤ B.
** = $p \leq .05$.

ately evident. First, all three subgenerations showed lowered levels of diffuse partisan support, though this pattern is most consistent for the experienced cohort. Second, the ambivalent cohort was most likely to demonstrate pro-Democratic voting patterns, the experienced cohort least likely, and the socialized cohort demonstrated an erratic pattern. Finally, in terms of long-term party choice, the experienced cohort was again the least Democratic, with the ambivalent and socialized cohorts again showing erratic patterns that lean generally in a pro-Democratic direction. Overall then, it is the cohort that directly experienced the events of the sixties that was most negative towards the Democratic party, while the two cohorts which were less directly a product of that era were most unstable in their stands.

In Table 10.5 the interactions of subgenerations and life cycle, and their partial interaction with the seventies are presented. The former interactions reveal little systematic change in support for the party system within any of the subgenerations as they age. Support for a particular party showed a more uniform pattern across all three subgenera-

TABLE 10.5
Interaction Effects between Subgenerations, Life Cycle, and Period on Partisan Support

Variables	Life Cycle			Seventies	
	Ambivalent	Experienced	Socialized	Ambivalent	Experienced
ID strength	−.006*	−.008**	.072**	.061	.164**
Care win	−.001	.002	.022*	.065*	.032*
Party differences	.018**	.033**	−.025*	−.224*	−.173**
Intentions	−.029**	−.021*	.007	.266*	.394**
President	−.029**	−.025**	−.010	.156*	.253**
Congress	−.005*	−.004*	.013*	−.132*	.082
Local	−.011**	−.014*	−.128*	.038	.232*
Last time	−.010*	−.021*	***	.017	.638**
Usual vote	−.009**	.008*	***	.208**	.342**
Party ID	−.007**	−.006*	−.024*	.073	.135**
Party evaluations	−.004	−.008*	−.129**	.057	.127**

* = standard error ≤ B.
** = p ≤ .05.
*** = not calculated.

tions as they aged, with a general tendency to become less supportive of the Democratic party. This holds true for both short- and long-term measures of party choice, and is less true of the youngest subgeneration than the other two (keep in mind that, given the short period of time this cohort was part of the electorate when the study was made, these estimates are the least reliable). Last, the interactions of the seventies with the ambivalent and the experienced cohorts reveal the only consistent pro-Democratic tendencies for the latter subgeneration, and slightly less support for the Democrats by the former. The large size of many of these relationships suggests it is this interaction that has given the appearance of a pro-Democratic bias to the sixties generation, masking (temporarily?) its less-Democratic leanings.

SUMMARY AND CONCLUSIONS: REALIGNMENT OR DISARRAY?

In this chapter we have examined the effects of life cycle, period and generation on the level of partisan support in the

Partisan Support

United States. Parties are perhaps the most paradoxical institutions in the political system in the United States. In a system designed to keep them from forming or at least limit their power, they have become the "mainspring" of American politics. Once regarded as the nemesis of democracy by political theorists, they are now considered its *sine qua non*. The attitudes and opinions of the American public reflect this history of ambivalence.

Even the role of parties is a compromise of opposites. At their "best," parties combine an ability to bring about real, sometimes dramatic, policy and leadership change with a stabilizing impact that has essentially eliminated extremists of both the left and right from mounting a serious challenge to the status quo. In the United States, the competitive left and right is defined respectively by McGovern and Reagan, both representative of relatively moderate extremes when compared to political leaders in the history of the rest of the world. This compromise of responsiveness and responsibility is not automatic, however. It requires stable support among the population both for the system itself and for particular parties over time. Recent trends suggest that support for the system has declined, and support for the most recently dominant party—the Democrats—has also declined, without a clear move to the Republicans. Instead, we have been in a thirty-year doldrum in which instability, shifting coalitions, and short-term majorities have become the norm.

The results of the analysis presented here suggest that the shifts in support from one party to another we have seen over the past three decades are the responses of the public to period effects, with short-term forces swinging public sentiment and behavior back and forth like a pendulum. Beneath this instability lie several more uniform patterns that in many ways result from this directionless movement. Support for the party system shows evidence of erosion across periods, though it does increase as individuals have a greater opportunity to witness and participate in the system. In addition, there is a new generation of Americans, raised during the peak of this unstable era, who are even less supportive of that system. Raised in a Democratic era, and liberal as a result of their experiences and their age, they tend to vote (when they vote) Democratic, and to support the party in other ways, but this support masks a systematic decay in long-term measures of responsiveness to Democratic appeals. This is not a Republican cohort by any stretch of the imagination, but neither is it a Democratic one. It is a generation without a party, and uncertain that it wants one.

What are the implications of these findings? If the indicators used in our study are accurate, the passage of time (and the aging and generational replacement that takes place) will find a growing segment of the population becoming alienated from the party system in general and that is becoming especially alienated from the Democratic party in particular. The full extent of this trend will, of course, depend on future "period effects," and on the extent to which the socialized subgeneration follows the lead of its experienced brothers and sisters, but all three subgenerations have demonstrated a fair amount of anti-party, anti-Democratic sentiment. The options then seem to be between a realignment of some kind, in which one of the major parties (or a new one) is able to restore both the general and specific support of this generation, or a continued pattern of split government, of short-term coalitions, and of erratic swings in the governing philosophy. It is to evidence of such electoral instability that we now turn.

NOTE

1. That parties should be seen as having been least dissimilar in the sixties may seem odd, since it was this period that was the most conflictual

of the three examined. Four points should be considered in this regard. First, the sixties do show a positive effect, indicating that the public did see sizable differences between the parties in this period. Second, the conflict in the sixties was generally outside of the party system. Third, the public's *perception* of party differences (as with other things) need not be anchored to any real difference between party platforms. Finally, as a methodological point, the absence of this item in the 1964 election survey undoubtedly lowered the mean score during this period.

REFERENCES

Abramson, Paul R. "Developing Party Identification: A Further Examination of Life-Cycle, Generational, and Period Effects." *American Journal of Political Science*, 23 (February, 1979), pp. 78–96.

Bolingbroke, Henry Saint-John. In Sidney W. Jackman (ed.). *The Idea of a Patriot King*. Indianapolis: Bobbs-Merrill, 1965.

———. In Isaac Kramnick (ed.). *Political Writings*. New York: Appleton-Century-Crofts, 1970.

Burke, Edmund. In Albert F. Pollard (ed.). *Thoughts on the Causes of the Present Discontent*. New York: Holt, 1897.

———. In B. W. Hill (ed.). *Edmund Burke on Government, Politics and Society*. New York: International Publication Service, 1956.

Burnham, Walter Dean. *Critical Elections and the Mainspring of American Politics*. New York: Norton, 1970.

———. "American Politics in the 1970s: Beyond Party?" In Louis Maisel and Paul M. Sacks (eds.). *The Future of Political Parties*. Beverly Hills: Sage Publications, 1975.

Claggett, William. "Partisan Acquisition vs. Party Intensity: Life-Cycle, Generation, and Period Effects." *American Journal of Political Science*, 25 (1981), pp. 193–214.

Converse, Philip E. *The Dynamics of Party Support: Cohort-analyzing Party Identification*. Beverly Hills: Sage Publications, 1976.

———. "Rejoinder to Abramson." *American Journal of Political Science*, 23 (February, 1979), pp. 97–100.

Dennis, Jack. "Trends in Public Support for the American Party System." *British Journal of Political Science*, 5(1976), pp. 187–230.

Fiorina, Morris P. "An Outline for a Model of Party Choice." *American Journal of Political Science*, 21 (1977), pp. 601–626.

Graber, Doris. *Mass Media and American Politics*. Washington, D.C.: Congressional Quarterly Press, 1980.

Hbrenner, Ronald J., and Ruth K. Scott. *Parties in Crises: Party Politics in America*. New York: John Wiley, 1979.

Hofstadter, Richard. *The Idea of a Party System*. Berkeley: University of California Press, 1969.

Hume, David. In Charles W. Hendel (ed.). *Political Essays*. New York: Liberal Arts Press, 1953.

Keeter, Scott, and Cliff Zukin. *Uninformed Choice: The Citizen in the Presidential Nominating Process*. New York: Praeger, 1983.

McGinnis, Joe. *The Selling of the President*. New York: Pocket Books, 1969.

Nie, Norman H., Sidney Verba, and John R. Petrocik. *The Changing American Voter*. Cambridge, Mass.: Harvard University Press, 1979.

Patterson, Thomas. *The Mass Media Election*. New York: Praeger, 1980.

Phillips, Kevin P. *The Emerging Republican Majority*. New Rochelle, New York: Arlington House, 1969.

Pomper, Gerald M. *The Voters' Choice: Varieties of American Electoral Behavior*. New York: Dodd, Mead, 1975.

Ranney, Austin. *Curing the Mischiefs of Faction*. Berkeley: University of California Press, 1975.

Rosenstone, Steven J., Roy L. Behr, and Edward H. Lazarus. *Third Parties in America*. Princeton: Princeton University Press, 1984.

Schattschneider, E. E. *Party Government*. New York: Rinehart, 1942.

Schulman, Mark A., and Gerald M. Pomper. "Variability in Electoral Behavior: Perspectives from Causal Modeling." *American Journal of Political Science*, 19 (1975), pp. 1–18.

Shively, W. Phillips. "The Development of Party Identification Among Adults." *American Political Science Review*, 73 (1979), pp. 193–214.

Sorauf, Frank J. *Party Politics in America*. Boston: Little, Brown, 1984.

Sundquist, James L. *Dynamics of the Party System*. Washington, D.C.: Brookings, 1973.

Trenchard, John, and Thomas Gordon. *Cato's Letters*. New York: Russell and Russell, 1969.

CHAPTER 11

Political Stability

In the last two chapters we have examined both the extent of political participation and party loyalty. In those chapters we found that members of the sixties generation were much less likely to participate in electoral politics than their predecessors and that, despite their liberal leanings, they were less supportive of the Democratic party on a number of key measures. In addition, they were quite unsupportive of the idea of parties more generally. Despite this deep-seated aversion towards parties generally and the Democratic party in particular, the full impact of this attitude has been diminished by effects of period, the distinction between ambivalent and experienced subgenerations on behavioral measures of short-term choice, and the apparent lag between long-term erosion and the short-term consequences of that erosion.

The lack of support for political parties (and the decline in participation) has resulted in the development of neither a new governing coalition nor of a consistently unique voting pattern for the sixties generation. It is possible, however, that the cross-cutting pressures of issue stands, participation rates, and partisan leanings have led to greater instability in electoral behavior. This issue is explored in this chapter.

The Effects of Generation, Periods, and the Life Cycle

ELECTORAL INSTABILITY AND SYSTEM INSTABILITY

In Chapter Ten it was argued that parties and the party system provide a generally accepted level of compromise between change and stability, and add to the political legitimacy provided by the real and symbolic importance of elections. However, this compromise requires that people participate in the system, that they see the system as effective and worthwhile, and that they participate in consistent ways over time. In the preceding chapters we have seen evidence to suggest that, in part due to the sixties and to the generation spawned by that period, participation in the system is seriously declining, and sentiment is growing that the system, and in particular the party system, is ineffective and illegitimate. While these patterns have not led to an instability that resulted in extreme, system-challenging factions of the right or left taking over the reins of government, there is another sort of instability for which there is evidence and which may be a precursor to the more obvious type of system collapse.

The patterns of change uncovered in the areas of issue stands, involvement, participation rates, and partisan support are all consistent with the initial discussions concerning the nature of the sixties and the sixties generation in at least one important way. They demonstrate a rejection of the politics of the past, but without a clear substitute to take its place. It is a rejection of some of the rules but not enough to design a new game. The results of this behavior are likely to be the destabilizing of a system whose greatest virtue was its stability, rather than the restabilizing of the system around some new political equilibrium. Because the basic parts of the political system remained unaltered (electoral politics remains the keystone, the Democratic and Republican parties remain the alternatives), stability of a sort survived; the underlying tenets of representative democracy and welfare cap-

Political Stability

italism remained unscathed. Underlying this stability is a frenetic pattern of shifting loyalties and short-term coalitions that make purposive change difficult. The system has always succeeded because it could adapt to new conditions sufficiently to avoid major restructuring, while at the same time providing real satisfaction of some kind to those pressuring for change (Burnham, 1970; Ginsberg, 1982). As it currently operates, the American political system seems more and more locked into a situation in which it is stable enough to prevent major changes in modes of participation, agenda choices, or leadership but not stable enough to hold together the coalitions which do form within the status quo. The result is one-term presidents, split governments, and short-term solutions to long-term problems.

At the heart of this double bind is the behavior of the electorate. In a system designed to limit change under the best of circumstances, shifting support between and across elections for candidates and parties with different, often opposing agendas and philosophies results in almost certain paralysis. Since Eisenhower, the presidency has been split almost equally between the Democrats and the Republicans. No president since Eisenhower has held office for a full two terms. We have witnessed a president win a stunning landslide only to be forced by public opinion not to seek reelection four years later. Another president, in the midst of one of the greatest political scandals in American history, was forced to resign three years after a major victory in which he failed to carry only one state. We have seen both a Democratic and a Republican incumbent barely survive primary challenges within their own party, and then go on to lose in the general election. In the period from 1952 to 1980 the country has been led by moderates, liberals, and conservatives, and we have witnessed three landslides that were the result of shifting support from one end of the accepted ideological spectrum to the other. There have been almost twice as many years of split government as unified government at the national level. In short, partisan stability has become increasingly rare.

We are not arguing that all of this instability is the result of the electoral instability of citizens alone. To the contrary, unusual circumstances, party behavior, the behavior of office holders, the mass media, and the incredible complexity of both government and the problems it faces also are part of the cause. That is, we are arguing that the behavior of the electorate, driven by both the changing environment and by internal changes, lies at the center of this new dynamic. The electorate reacts to the environment and the environment reacts to the electorate in a type of downward spiral that shows little evidence of breaking.

While there are numerous causes for the pattern of political instability outlined above, we are, of course, interested primarily in the "contribution" of the life cycle, generation, and periods effects. The evidence on aging and political stability suggests that older cohorts should be more consistent in both their level of participation and in their partisan choices (Campbell, et al., 1960; Converse, 1976; Verba and Nie, 1972; Claggett, 1981). This stability is the result of the reinforcing effects of repetitive behavior, the greater political involvement that comes with age, and the decreased likelihood that new information will be enough to disrupt set opinions concerning alternative behaviors.

Period effects depend, of course, on the nature of the times themselves, though longer-term trends that cut across distinct political periods are also relevant. In terms of the specific periods defined here, we would anticipate relative stability in the fifties, given the general tenor of the times and the desire of most people to retreat from the tumult of the thirties and forties. The sixties, however, were a period

Political Stability

of great disarray, and we would expect this to be reflected in the stability of the electorate's behavior. Many new issues cut across traditional party lines, forcing the population to reconsider many of its more traditional preconceptions. The Vietnam War, race, student and urban unrest, and the candidacy of relative extremists such as McGovern, McCarthy, Wallace, and Goldwater all complicated what often had been an automatic decision-making process. Finally, the seventies offered some return to normalcy, though the aftermath of Watergate, the rise of economic and foreign-policy crises, and the candidacy of the strong, ideological, and popular Ronald Reagan on the heels of the low-keyed Ford and Carter complicates even this period.

Underlying all three periods is the steady trend, identified at different levels by Bell (1973), Broder (1971), Burnham (1970), Nie, et al. (1979), and discussed throughout the preceding chapters. This trend points towards a general decline in stability that resulted from the interaction of circumstance, questionable party leadership, changing party rules, the rise of the media, and the complexity of a political, social, and economic environment that overwhelmed the archaic structure of American political institutions.

Generational change, our central concern in this study, is also relevant to the issue of political stability. We have already seen evidence of political alienation, lowered participation rates, and a loss of underlying support for the Democratic party within the sixties generation. Given the lack of a clear alternative around which to coalesce, this loss of commitment is likely to have resulted in a greater susceptibility to short-term influences, a greater willingness to change opinions and behaviors, and a lack of commitment to choices made four years ago. This tendency was enhanced both by the greater relevance of the sixties' issues to the members of this generation and to the lessened stabilizing effect of aging

The Effects of Generation, Periods, and the Life Cycle

for them because of the absence of consistent repetitive behaviors. In short, the forces that have led to instability in the electorate as a whole should have had a greater effect on the generation that came of political age during this era of instability.

TRENDS IN ELECTORAL INSTABILITY

In Table 11.1 the ten measures of stability to be used in this chapter are listed and described. Two of the measures focus on stability in the level of participation, with "Rolloff" measuring participation across electoral races in a single year and "Regularity" measuring voting in a single race (for the presidency) across consecutive contests. The remaining measures

TABLE 11.1
Description of Measures of Political Stability

Variables	Description
Rolloff	Voting in one race, but not another on the same ballot (president, congress, senate) (1 = vote in all races)
Regularity	Voting in current and prior presidential election (1 = voted in both)
ID different	Considering yourself once attached to a different party than now (1 = no)
Loyalty	Voting for same party as party ID (presidential, congressional and state and local) (1 = loyal)
Always	Always voting for the same party for president (1 = always do)
Local split	Voting for candidates of different parties at the state and local level (1 = vote same way)
National split	Voting for candidates of different parties at the national level (president, congress, senate) (1 = vote same way)
Other	Voting for candidate for president other than a Democrat or Republican (1 = never do)
Timing	When one decided who to vote for for president (1 = knew all along)
Suredness	Actually voting for presidential candidate one supported earlier in campaign (1 = voted as planned)

Political Stability

are aimed at uncovering the level of partisan stability, with three measures ("ID Different," "Loyalty," and "Always") showing the extent of deep-seated predispositions and/or their relationship to actual behavior, two measures ("Local Split" and "National Split") the extent of the behavioral stability of partisan choice within and across elections, one measure ("Other") focusing on the willingness to choose a candidate from a third political party, and the final two measures ("Timing," and "Suredness") concerned with the stability of individual choices within a particular campaign period. Taken as a whole they are used to try to determine the attitudinal and behavioral stability of the electorate's choice of partisan leadership.

In Figure 11.1 we present the aggregate patterns of change in the ten measures of stability. While each individual measure shows a unique configuration over time, some generalizations can be made. The low point for every measure (that is, the point of greatest instability) occurred after 1964, with five measures "bottoming out" in the sixties and five in the seventies. The two measures of stability in the level of participation showed similar patterns, with increased stability to 1960, a steady decrease through 1972, and then a slight rise to 1980. The two measures of the relationship between predispositions and behaviors ("Loyalty" and "Always")

FIGURE 11.1

Trends in Political Stability, 1952–1980
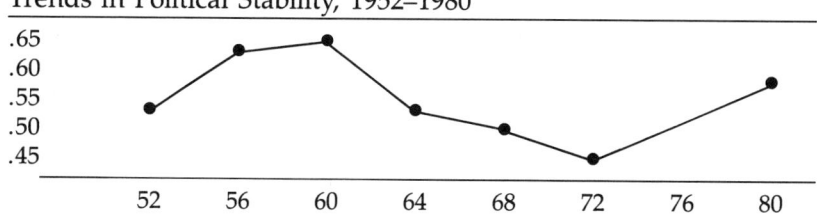
FIGURE 11.1A
Rolloff

The Effects of Generation, Periods, and the Life Cycle

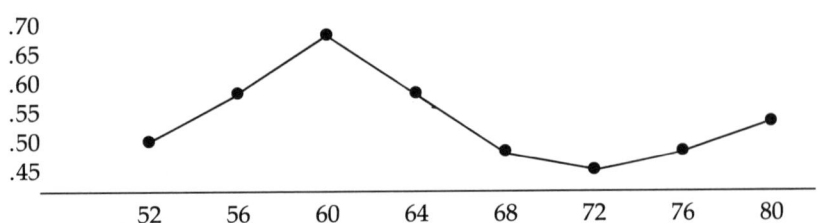

FIGURE 11.1B
Regularity

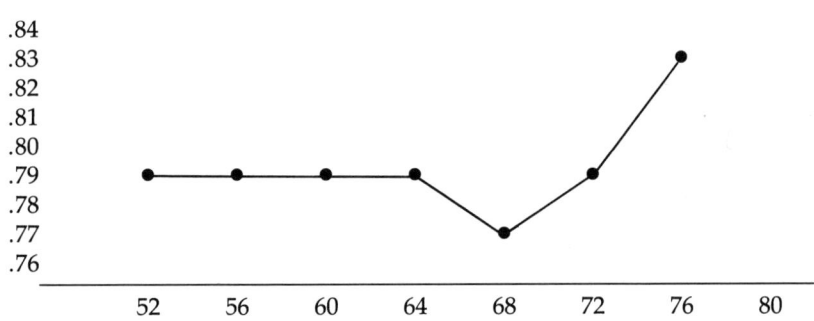

FIGURE 11.1C
ID Different

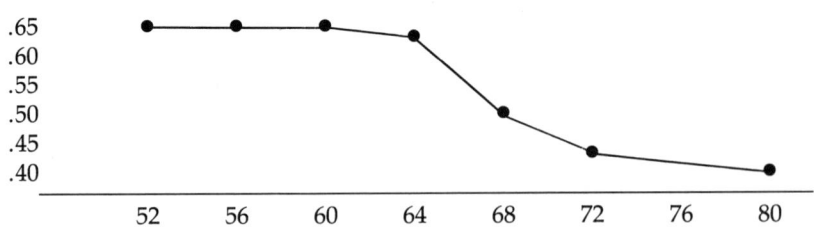

FIGURE 11.1D
Loyalty

Political Stability

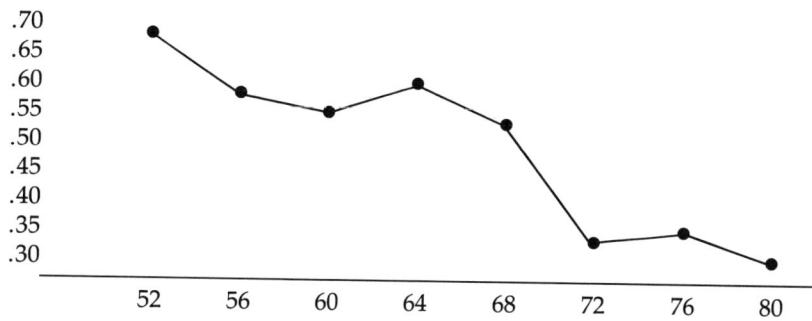

FIGURE 11.1E
Always

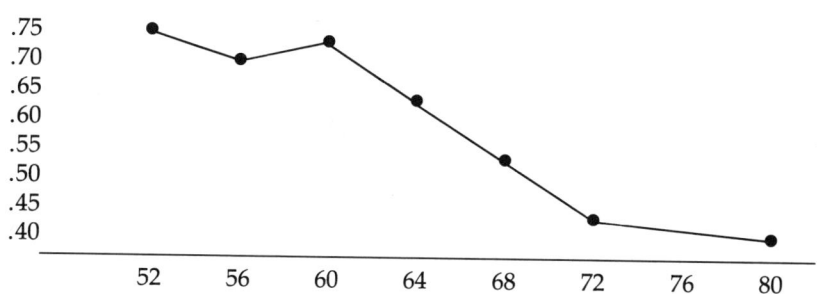

FIGURE 11.1F
Local Split

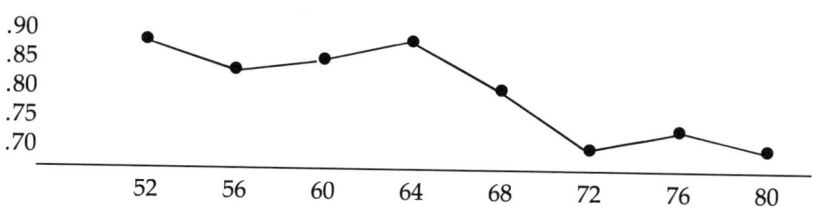

FIGURE 11.1G
National Split

The Effects of Generation, Periods, and the Life Cycle

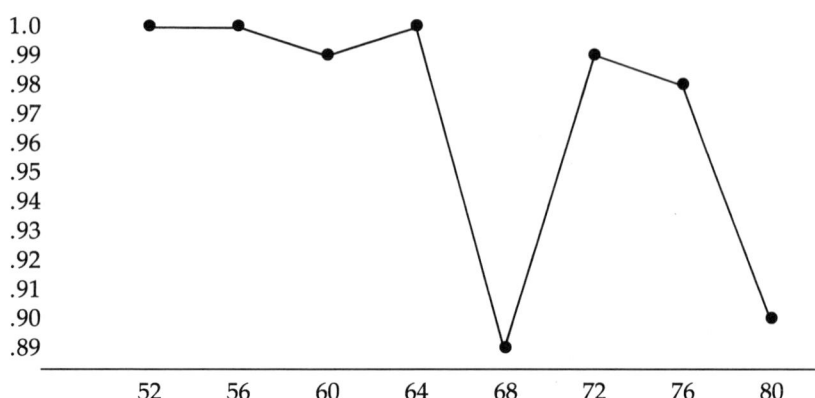

FIGURE 11.1H
Other

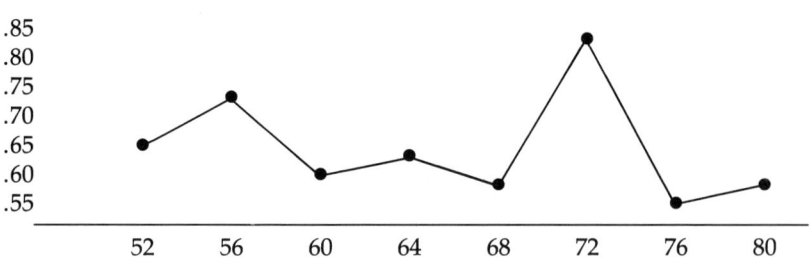

FIGURE 11.1I
Timing

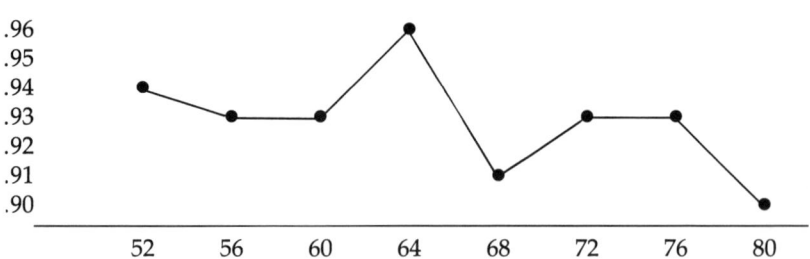

FIGURE 11.1J
Suredness

Political Stability

showed steady and dramatic declines in the sixties and seventies, though the purely attitudinal measure ("ID Different") actually became more stable after 1968. Both measures of purely behavioral partisan stability demonstrate declines over the period examined, with the most dramatic drop in straight-ticket voting in local elections and the least consistent pattern found at the national level. Voting for third-party candidates showed an idiosyncratic pattern, though the two years of greatest third-party voting occurred in the sixties (1968) and the seventies (1980). Finally, the two measures of stability within a single campaign indicate an overall decline in stability over time, though these patterns are not as clear nor as consistent as those found in other measures. In general, then, declining stability is the most common trend uncovered by all ten measures, though the specific pattern of decline varies within the type of stability being measured, and, ultimately within each individual measure. A finding of increased instability is consistent with the work of other writers in this area (Burnham, 1970; Nie, et al., 1979). More important to our study is the connection between shifts in stability and the effects of life cycle, period and generation.

THE EFFECTS OF LIFE CYCLE, GENERATION, AND PERIODS

Table 11.2 presents the main effects of life cycle, generation and periods on the ten measures of electoral stability. The effects of the life cycle are by far the most consistent, with seven of the ten measures demonstrating an increasing stability with age. This finding is in line with our initial expectations. That stability in one's party ID and in one's long-term choice of party should decrease with age is not particularly surprising, since the longer one is in the electorate the greater the opportunity one has to stray occasionally from one's normal predispositions and patterns of behavior. The

TABLE 11.2
Effects of Life Cycle, Generation, and Period on Political Stability

Variables	Life Cycle	Generation	Period		
			Fifties	Sixties	Seventies
Rolloff	.002**	−.312**	.152**	.187**	.264**
Regularity	.004**	−.491**	.160**	.307**	.314**
ID different	−.002**	.104**	−.054**	−.153**	.002
Loyalty	.003**	.167**	−.039	−.117**	−.306*
Always	−.006**	.367**	−.230**	−.322**	−.764**
Local split	.002*	.092*	−.010	−.271**	−.378**
National split	.001	.024	−.045	−.065*	−.235*
Other	.000	.006	−.005	−.042*	−.070*
Timing	.004**	−.014	.115*	−.002	−.128
Suredness	.001**	−.027*	−.001	.017	−.064*

* = standard error ≤ B.
** = $p \leq .05$.

only other exception to the positive effect of age on stability is voting for third-party candidates, which shows no relationship with the life cycle at all.

The relationship between stability and the sixties generation is much more inconsistent and difficult to interpret. Recall that we expected the previous patterns of political involvement, participation, and partisan support would indicate great instability in the behavior of this cohort. In the case of stability in the level of participation this appears to be true, with both "Rolloff" and "Regularity" showing sizable negative relationships with the sixties generation. The two measures of stability within the single campaign ("Timing" and "Suredness") also show negative relationships with generation. The measures of predispositions and behavior do not conform to our expectations, however. The sixties generation demonstrated greater partisan stability, a greater likelihood to vote in conformity with party identification, and a greater tendency to vote consistently for the same party for president over time. These findings, taken in conjunction with the conclusion made in Chapter Ten, that this genera-

Political Stability

tion was less likely to form party affiliations, and that made in Chapter Nine, that it was less likely to vote, suggest that while fewer members of the sixties generation participated in politics or identified with parties, those that did took that loyalty seriously and used it in deciding whom to support.

The relationship between generation and political stability is further complicated when we examine the purely behavioral measures. Contrary to our expectations, the sixties generation was less likely to split its vote at either the state and local or at the national level than older cohorts. In addition, members of this generation were less likely to vote for third-party candidates. In sum, while the level of participation demonstrated the instability among members of the sixties generation that we anticipated, and while they also demonstrated a good deal of waffling and indecision during political campaigns, their actual vote choices and overall partisanship demonstrated greater stability than one would expect, given their age and the times in which they live.

Period effects also demonstrate a complex pattern of political behavior, but one that is more readily interpretable. Both measures of stability in the level of participation showed positive effects for all three periods, with the size of the relationship increasing over time. This suggests that for those who do vote, there has been a steadily increasing likelihood that they vote regularly and in all the elections open to them. The choice of whom to vote for showed increasing instability, however, and this instability cuts across predispositions and behaviors, short as well as long term. Loyalty to one's party ID, long-term voting patterns for president, ticket-voting at the national and the local level, voting for one of the two major parties, and the timing of one's vote decision all showed increasing instability from the fifties to the sixties to the seventies. Even the remaining two measures ("ID Different" and "Suredness") were generally consistent with this

TABLE 11.3
Interaction Effects on Political Stability

	Generation	Life Cycle			Generation	
		Fifties	Sixties	Seventies	Sixties	Seventies
Rolloff	.013**	−.001	−.006**	−.004**	−.039	−.052
Regularity	.017**	−.002*	−.008**	−.007**	.012	.022
ID different	−.004**	.002**	.004**	.002*	.004	−.081*
Loyalty	−.003	.001	−.001	.002	−.207**	−.096
Always	−.013**	.004**	.005**	.012**	−.155*	.026
Local split	−.005**	.000	.002	.002	−.047	.002
National split	.002*	.001	.000	.002	−.085*	.014
Other	.000	.000	.000	.001	−.008*	−.020
Timing	−.006**	−.002	.000	.001	.235**	.123
Suredness	.000	.000	−.001	.001	.010	.054*

* = standard error ≤ B.
** = $p \leq .05$.

pattern, though not so clearly as the other six. Overall, then, it would seem that generational politics are responsible for the instability in the level of participation over the past few decades, while short- and long-term period effects are most responsible for the instability in partisan choice.

Do the interaction effects among the three main variables shed any more light on the stability of political activity? Table 11.3 presents these interactions. As the sixties generation aged, it appeared to grow more stable in its level of participation but less stable in its vote choice. In short, it began to conform to the behavior of the population as a whole (as demonstrated by the trends in the period effects). This convergence happens slowly relative to the main effects, however, and was not present for all measures of stability ("Suredness" and "Other" showed no interactions and "National Split" showed increasing stability).

The interactions of life cycle and periods show patterns that are essentially the inverse of those demonstrated by the main effects of period. This pattern, perhaps the most common we have uncovered in the previous chapters, suggests

Political Stability

TABLE 11.4
Effects of Subgenerations on Political Stability

	Ambivalent	Experienced	Socialized
Rolloff	−.501**	−.395**	−.431*
Regularity	−.817**	−.512**	−.247
ID different	.196**	.182**	−.129
Loyalty	.358**	−.305**	−.557
Always	.899**	−.544**	.679
Local split	.193*	−.069	.652
National split	.086	−.098**	−.267
Other	.020	.076**	.374**
Timing	−.270**	.303**	.703**
Suredness	−.028	.016	.012

* = standard error ≤ B.
** = $p \le .05$.

that older cohorts are more resistant to the changes in voting patterns brought about by the events and conditions of the last three decades, and is consistent with a type of non-ideological conservatism described earlier.

The final set of interactions—between generation and period—add to the baffling pattern of behavior already described for the sixties generation in this chapter. The interaction of generation with the 1960s tends to reinforce the main period effect, with seven of the ten former relationships consistent with the latter. In the seventies, however, the generation began to react quite differently. Seven of the ten interactions are in the opposite direction of the main effects of the seventies. This again implies a resistance to the pattern of growing partisan instability: a resistance that was unanticipated by findings in other chapters.

Perhaps we can shed some light on the behavior of the sixties generation by examining the subgenerations comprising it. Table 11.4 presents the main effects of these three subgenerations. As can be seen, all three subgenerations showed strong tendencies towards instability in the level of participation ("Rolloff" and "Regularity"); the ambivalent cohort was the most unstable in this regard. In terms of partisan predispositions, the ambivalent cohort was the most stable, showing positive relationships with all three of the relevant measures. The experienced and socialized cohorts, in contrast, demonstrated a greater tendency towards instability; both showed negative relationships on two of the three measures. This pattern was largely repeated for the more directly behavioral measures of local and national voting, where the ambivalent subgeneration again was consistently stable, but the experienced group was consistently less stable (negative relationships), and the socialized one was split.

When we turn to the measures of stability within a campaign, we find a very different pattern. Now it is the ambivalent cohort that shows a negative relationship, while both the experienced and socialized cohorts demonstrate positive coefficients on both measures. Finally, all three cohorts were less likely to vote for third-party candidates than those who had not been directly touched by the sixties, with the socialized subgeneration having showed the greatest stability.

The results uncovered above begin to help clarify the relationship between the sixties generation and electoral stability. It is the ambivalent cohort that most closely reflects the rather inconsistent political behavior demonstrated by the generation as a whole. Both the socialized and to a slightly greater extent the experienced cohorts are more likely to reflect the instability initially anticipated. This is especially true of the five variables that most directly measure partisan stability: "ID Different," "Loyalty," "Always," "Local Split," and "National Split." The ambivalent segment of the generation demonstrated increased stability on all five of these measures, while the socialized cohort showed decreased stability on three of the five. The experienced cohort, however, showed decreased stability on all but one of them. Again, we find that, when subgenerations are examined, it is the

Political Stability

TABLE 11.5
Interaction Effects between Subgenerations, Life Cycle, and Period on Political Stability

Variables	Life Cycle			Seventies	
	Ambivalent	Experienced	Socialized	Ambivalent	Experienced
Rolloff	.008**	.024**	.023	.250**	−.062
Regularity	.018**	.029**	***	.330**	−.043
ID different	−.007**	−.035**	***	−.041	.165**
Loyalty	−.010*	.035*	.303	−.057	−.070
Always	−.043**	−.027*	***	.055	.795**
Local split	−.012**	−.005	−.012	.222	.315
National split	−.001	−.006	.089	.026	.155**
Other	−.001	−.014**	−.162**	.008	.041
Timing	.023**	.038**	−.189**	−.271*	−.509**
Suredness	−.004**	−.002	−.035	.124**	.001

* = standard error ≤ B.
** = $p \leq .05$.
*** = not calculated.

cohort that directly experienced the 1960s that most clearly reflects the effects of that era.

When we turn to the interaction effects for subgenerations, the uniqueness of the experienced cohort again emerges. Recall that the overall interactions of generation and life cycle indicated that there was a gradual convergence of the level of stability of the sixties generation and the rest of the population (Table 11.3). In Table 11.5 we can see, however, that while every one of the interactions for the ambivalent and the socialized cohorts demonstrates a reversing of the main effect of subgeneration, four of the ten interactions between the experienced cohort and aging act to reinforce the main effect. In addition, three of these four reinforcing relationships involve the variables that most directly measure behavioral stability in party support (local and national voting and long-term presidential voting). All three of these interactions increase the level of instability with age. To sum up, the experienced cohort again demonstrates its uniqueness

The Effects of Generation, Periods, and the Life Cycle

and again does so in a way that fits closest to our original expectations for the sixties generation as a whole. (The final interactions—those between the seventies and the subgenerations—are not particularly informative in distinguishing the various cohorts in this case.)

SUMMARY AND CONCLUSIONS

In this chapter we have continued to explore the relationships between life cycle, generation, and periods and the party system that was begun in the previous chapter. Given earlier findings that the sixties generation was less involved in mainstream politics, less likely to participate in electoral politics, less supportive of the party system, and less committed to the Democratic party (though unattached as well to the Republican party) than the greater population, it was our expectation that this cohort would demonstrate relatively changeable patterns of behavior both in terms of the level of participation and the partisan direction of that support. In addition, we anticipated greater stability with age for the population as a whole, and greater instability with time as the nation moved from the fifties to the sixties to the seventies.

The latter two expectations, above, were born out fairly well, though there did seem to be a tendency for greater stability in participation over time that was unanticipated. The relationship between stability and generation proved to be complex, however. We found instability in the level of participation for the sixties generation as a whole and for all three subgenerations, although partisan instability (in terms of predispositions and/or behaviors and in terms of short- and long-term indicators) was less clearly related to generation. The ambivalent cohort showed tendencies towards greater rather than lesser stability on most measures. The

Political Stability

experienced cohort, and to a lesser extent the socialized cohort, most closely paralleled the unstable partisan we had anticipated, though even here the results were not completely consistent with expectations. In addition, the experienced cohort appeared to be the most resistant to greater stability with age.

What is to be made of these findings? First and foremost, there is a clear trend towards greater instability in partisan choice over time. It was a trend that affected all age groups and seemed to result from the cultural, political, social, and economic environments of the past three decades. This instability also appeared to grow stronger with the passage of each period. Second, the sixties generation has demonstrated a greater instability in the level of participation, but a resistance to the trend towards partisan instability. Third, this resistance appears in large part to be due to the behavior of the ambivalent cohort, with the experienced and, to a lesser extent, the socialized cohorts showing signs of greater instability relative both to the ambivalent cohort and the population as a whole. Since the experienced and the socialized cohorts will gradually become a larger and larger percentage not only of the sixties generation in the electorate but also of the electorate as a whole, we can expect even greater partisan instability in the future (barring a radical shift in the effects of future periods). Such behavior should indicate a continued pattern of shifting electoral coalitions, split governments, and single-term presidents, with the inability to govern coherently that this implies.

The distinction between the ambivalent cohort and the experienced cohort is worth a final comment. This distinctiveness does not pit a stable, ideal type of partisan against an unstable, unattached voter as one might be tempted to argue. Recall that in Chapter Ten it was shown that while members of the ambivalent cohort supported the Democratic party with great vigor, their underlying concern about outcomes, their evaluations of the parties, and their perceptions of party differences all indicated relatively weak support for the system. In other chapters we have indicated similar signs of unconcern. Instead of identifying one positive type of partisan and one negative type within the sixties generation, we seem to have found two different forms of apathy. The ambivalent cohort behaved very much like the apolitical citizen of Berelson's initial studies of the American electorate: uninterested, uninvolved, participating in marginal ways, but guided by a relatively blind attachment to party. The findings in this chapter, which show this cohort as unstable in both its rate of participation and in its deliberation, but not in its final choice, adds to this view. In fact, Berelson's description of the apolitical citizen of the 1940s and 1950s (1952, 1954) could easily have been written to describe the ambivalent cohort uncovered in the last few chapters.

Members of the experienced cohort are a new kind of citizen. They are no more active or supportive (in many ways less so), but they demonstrate a rebellious, cynical, unpredictable edge that lacks the conformity of its slightly older cohort. If, in fact, Berelson was correct that the American democratic system traded off a highly active mass citizenry for greater stability, the rise of this portion of the sixties generation may signal the end of the latter without the rise of the former.

REFERENCES

Bell, Daniel. *The Coming of Post-Industrial Society.* New York: Basic Books, 1973.

Berelson, Bernard R. "Democratic Theory and Public Opinion." *Public Opinion Quarterly,* 16 (1952), pp. 313–330.

Berelson, Bernard R., Paul F. Lazarsfeld, and William N. McPhee. *Voting: A Study of Opinion Formation in a Presidential Campaign.* Chicago: University of Chicago Press, 1954.

Political Stability

Broder, David. *The Party's Over*. New York: Harper and Row, 1971.

Burnham, Walter Dean. *Critical Elections and the Mainspring of American Politics*. New York: Norton, 1970.

Campbell, Angus, Philip E. Converse, Warren E. Miller, and Donald E. Stokes. *The American Voter*. New York: John Wiley, 1960.

Claggett, William. "Partisan Acquisition vs. Partisan Intensity: Life Cycle, Generation and Period Effects." *American Journal of Political Science*, 25 (1981), pp. 193–214.

Converse, Philip E. *The Dynamics of Party Support: Cohort-Analyzing Party Identification*. Beverly Hills: Sage Publications, 1976.

Ginsberg, Benjamin. *The Consequences of Consent: Elections, Citizen Control, and Popular Acquiescence*. Reading, Mass.: Addison-Wesley, 1982.

Nie, Norman H., Sidney Verba, and John R. Petrocik. *The Changing American Voter*. Cambridge, Mass.: Harvard University Press, 1979.

Verba, Sidney, and Norman H. Nie. *Participation in America*. New York: Harper and Row, 1972.

PART THREE

Situations and Structures: The Impact of the Social, Cultural, and Economic Environments on Generational Change

CHAPTER 12

Demographic Change

INTRODUCTION

Through the last eight chapters we have described the political character of the sixties generation, and the political impact of short- and long-term environmental changes in the fifties, sixties, and seventies. Our analysis has uncovered a complex, often bewildering mix of attitudes, opinions, and behaviors that reflected the conflicting forces under which political development generally and the development of the sixties generation in particular took place.

Underlying this kaleidescope of political orientations are some common images that, when considered together, reveal a more consistent and disturbing pattern. The sixties generation is relatively unsupportive of the political system in the United States. It has a political agenda that distinguishes it from the rest of the population, but not in any coherent ideological manner. It is somewhat more likely to take liberal stands on certain issues, though this tendency is not true of all issues and appears to weaken with age. In addition, what distinctiveness there is in the sixties generation's agenda and in stands on issues is lost because of a decided avoidance of mainstream politics. Members of this generation are uninterested in following politics. They do not depend upon the

Situations and Structures

same decision-making cues as prior generations, and yet they do not seem to have alternative cues to take their place. They are much less likely to participate in electoral politics, either by voting or through more self-involving or costly activities. Though they vote Democratic at a greater rate than average, they support the Democratic party more generally with less vigor than one would expect. Deep-seated support for this party, and for the party system in general, show the strongest signs of decay. Yet, they still do not appear to have shifted to the Republicans or to another party, but remain instead in a permanent (to this point) state of political limbo. Finally, their behavior across time and within elections demonstrates erratic levels of participation involving either blind "loyalty" to a system they feel little allegiance to or frenetic shifting from party to party.

In the first two chapters we outlined the kinds of forces that arose out of the 1960s and speculated on the types of impact they were to have on both the generation coming of age and on the larger population. The logic of that argument was, first, that structural and situational change can lead to individual change, and second, that certain kinds of change were occurring in a way that uniquely affected a whole generation. Useful as these assumptions have been, three more specific corollaries now need to be considered in an effort to more finely pinpoint both the nature of the political change that occurred and the subgroups in which that change was most evident. In addition, it is time to consider the reverse pattern of change: To what extent can political change in the ideas of individuals and groups lead to more structural change? Or, put another way, can changing political orientations survive without institutional and structural change to support them?

In this chapter we describe some structural and situational characteristics of the population of the United States over the

Demographic Change

period from 1952 to 1980 and consider the extent to which there have been changes in the population as a whole and in the sixties generation in particular. In the next two chapters we examine the relationship between these changes and the development and maintenance of new political orientations.

SITUATION, STRUCTURE, AND CHANGE

The origins of the political change under examination in this study are not easily pinpointed. In Chapters One and Two it was suggested that a unique intersection of economic, cultural, social, and political circumstances together produced the environment that shaped the political character of the sixties and of the sixties generation. And yet one must note the individual and group consciousness that must be, in part, responsible for the environmental changes as well. In short, the relationship between the environment within which individual ideas and patterns of behavior are developed and those ideas and behaviors themselves is interactive; each affects the development of the other. The actual point at which particular change began, or the true cause of that change, cannot, therefore, ever really be determined. At best one can cut into this spiral of change and hope to uncover some portion of the underlying dynamic.

To say that individual and structural change interact is not to argue that they are equal partners in this transaction. Once established, certain structures may be more or less able to shape the development of opinions and behaviors so as to guarantee the future stability of those structures. Political socialization is the process by which political and social institutions, subsystems and systems encourage the development of the attitudes, opinions, and behaviors necessary for that continued stability.

In a perfectly controlled environment, a system, once established, would continue unchanged and unchallenged ad infinitum. That institutions change and that new ideas develop is testimony to the difficulty of controlling all aspects of the relevant environment. That fundamental change (in either individual opinion and behavior or in institutions) is rare, however, is as much testimony to the power of the socialization process as to the inherent desirability of the status quo.

The maintenance of a particular political system beyond the lifetime of the individuals originally responsible for it requires institutions that serve as socializing agents. Such institutions are often not directly political: The basic attitudes and behaviors that complement a liberal democratic capitalist system such as that in the United States arise from places like the family, schools, the media and the workplace (Dawson, et al., 1977). Often institutional change at this level sows the seeds for the attitudinal and behavioral change that can threaten the larger system. Not all change is challenging to the system, however, nor is all change equally likely to survive.

Individuals find themselves in many different situations as they develop, both in terms of the particular institutions they interact with and in terms of the particular role they fill within those institutions. Children interact most directly with family, friends, and school, and do so (in the former and latter case at least) from positions of relatively little power. For adults, the workplace becomes an institution of importance, while previously central institutions such as school lose their immediacy. Others, such as family, take on new meaning as the individual's position within it changes. Such changes are expected during the normal process of socialization (indeed they are important stages in that process). They are based not upon structural change of any kind, but instead upon one's particular situation within the structures of society. This distinction between structurally based change and situationally based change is important in understanding their long-term implications.

In addition to distinguishing between situational and structural sources of change, it is important to distinguish between system-maintaining, system-adjusting, and system-challenging types of change. Change that maintains the system is the normal process of individual development through a successful socialization process. The development of diffuse support, the learning of accepted bounds to ideologies, and the preferred forms of political expression all require change, but change that results in a particular type of citizen. Change that adjusts the system results in a modified set of opinions and behaviors that are necessary for the system to contend with changes in the environment without a fundamental restructuring of power relationships. The shift from laissez-faire capitalism in the nineteenth century to social-welfare capitalism in the twentieth century is an example of such an adjustment as are, on a smaller scale, changes in support for particular parties or in attitudes towards other nations. Finally, change that threatens the system is that which results in attitudes, opinions, and behaviors that run counter to maintaining the dominant set of power relationships. That is, it is the development of ideologies outside the defined boundaries of liberalism and conservatism for example, or participating in politics through ways considered illegitimate by the mainstream.

A final dimension of change to consider is what we call its "constructiveness." "Restructive" change is that which leads to the development of new or altered institutions that both reflect the new ordering of the allocation of goods, services, and values, and that serve to reproduce this order in future generations. "Instructive" change is that which replicates existing relationships. "Destructive" change is that which de-

Situations and Structures

stabilizes existing relationships without replacing them with coherent new ones. Finally, "astructive" change is that which does not affect the basic ordering of existing relationships: it is sound and fury signifying nothing.

Where do the changes resulting from the events and the environment of the 1960s and occurring most strongly in the sixties generation fit into this taxonomy? To answer this we must examine changes in some of the basic institutions of American society, in the characteristics of the American public, and in the sixties generation's relationship to them.

TRENDS IN SITUATIONAL AND STRUCTURAL CONDITIONS

Table 12.1 describes several measures that are meant to tap, as well as possible given the limitations of the data, various aspects of the population's cultural and social characteristics. These characteristics are usually considered important transmitters of the values of our system. Measures of early socialization experiences ("Childhood Class" and "Father"), economic status ("Class," "Income," "Ownership," etc.), culture (the regional measures, "Marital," "Attendance," etc.), as well as more general status ("Professional," "Education," "Houseperson," etc.) are included. The measures also include both situational ("Student" for example) and structural emphases. While we do not pretend to hit upon all, or even the most important measures of the social fabric of twentieth-century America, these items do provide a glimpse into the nature of its weave and texture.[1]

In Figure 12.1 the trends in these measures from 1952 to 1980 are presented. It is immediately evident that these decades were a time of real change at this fundamental level. Trends in perceived class, home ownership, and real income demonstrate the relative prosperity of this era. The decline in church attendance, marriage, and the structure of the fam-

Demographic Change

TABLE 12.1
Description of the Measures of Demographic Characteristics

Variables	Description
Childhood class	What class were you as a child (1 = upper class)
Father	Was your father a professional or manager (1 = yes)
Class	Self-selected class (1 = upper class)
Income	Annual family income (adjusted for inflation) (1 = 50,000+)
Ownership	Do you own or rent home (1 = own)
Education	Level of education attained (1 = college degree+)
Professional	Are you employed in a professional or managerial position (1 = yes)
Service	Are you currently employed in the service sector (1 = yes)
Union	Member of a union (1 = yes)
Race	Racial heritage (1 = white)
Head	Are you currently a head of the household (1 = yes)
Dependent	Are you currently a dependent (1 = yes)
Student	Are you currently a student (1 = yes)
Houseperson	Are you currently a houseperson (1 = yes)
Marital	Are you single or married (1 = married)
Children	Do you have children living in your family (1 = yes)
Attendance	Do you attend religious services (1 = regularly)
Northeast	Do you live in the northeastern United States (1 = yes)
Midwest	Do you live in the midwestern United States (1 = yes)
South	Do you live in the southern United States (1 = yes)
West	Do you live in the western United States (1 = yes)

ily show the deterioration of social institutions considered by many as important underpinnings to the American ethic. The steady rise in education levels has numerous political, social, and cultural implications that have been well documented in the literature. Population movements imply both changes in the aggregate mix of cultural perceptions and changes within each regional culture. The decline in the number of people (almost exclusively women) who are predominantly housepersons and the rise in the number of professional, white collar workers indicates fundamental changes in the occu-

Situations and Structures

pational structure of society, as does the move towards a more service-oriented society. All of the patterns suggest a society in flux. As usual, however, our interests lie in understanding the extent to which these patterns are the result of changes within certain parts of the population (aging and/or

FIGURE 12.1
Trends in Demographic Characteristics, 1952–1980

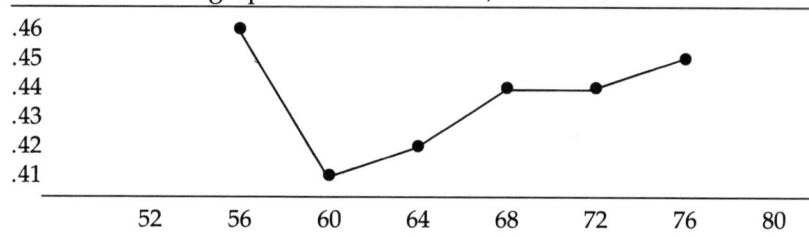

FIGURE 12.1A
Childhood class

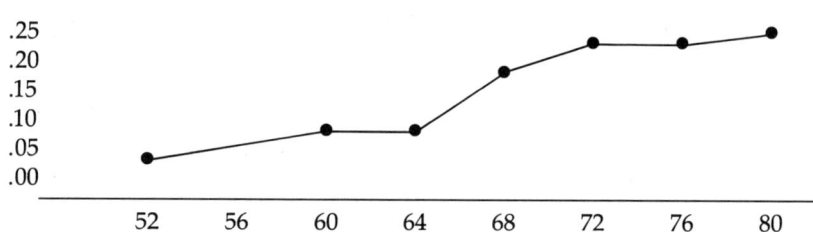

FIGURE 12.1B
Father professional

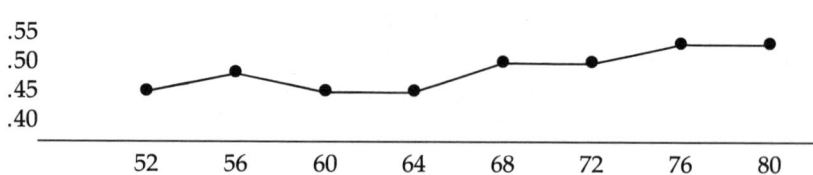

FIGURE 12.1C
Class

Demographic Change

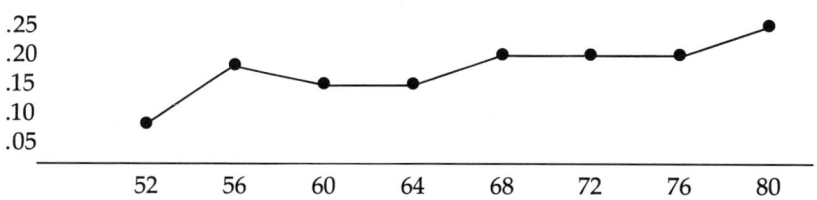

FIGURE 12.1D
Income

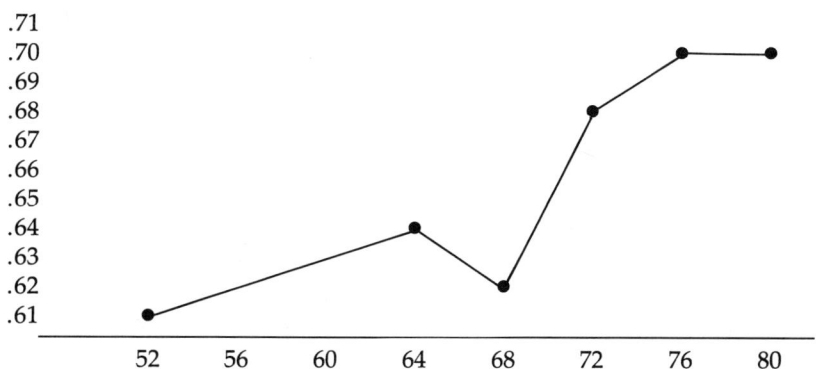

FIGURE 12.1E
Ownership

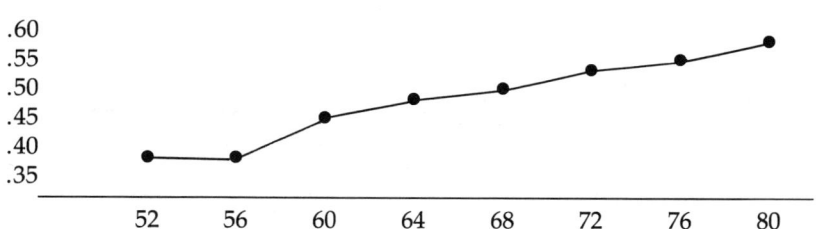

FIGURE 21.1F
Education

Situations and Structures

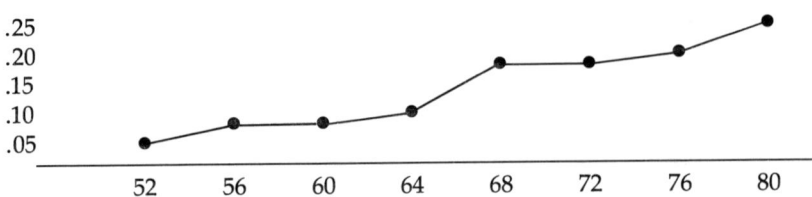

FIGURE 12.1G
Professional

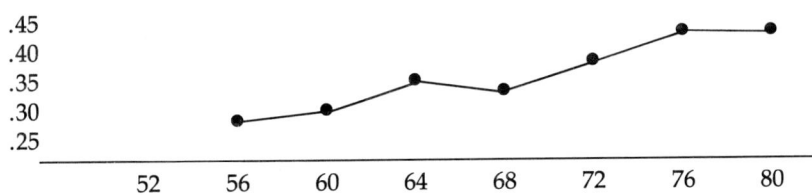

FIGURE 12.1H
Service

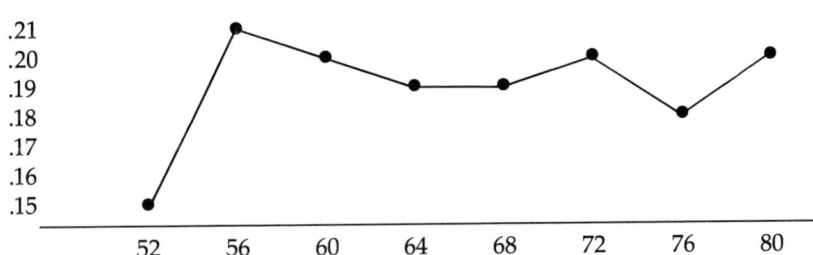

FIGURE 12.1I
Union

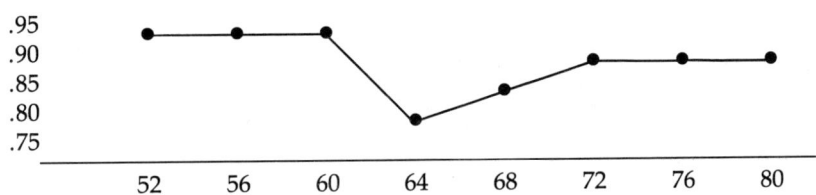

FIGURE 12.1J
Race

Demographic Change

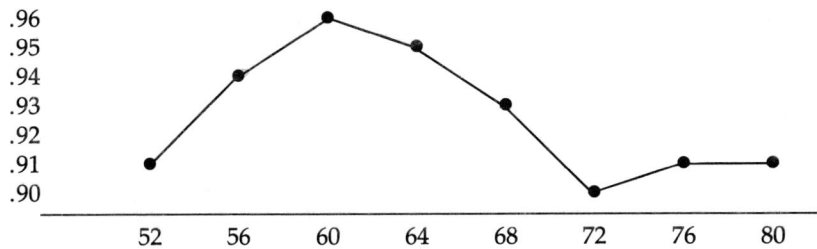

FIGURE 12.1K
Head

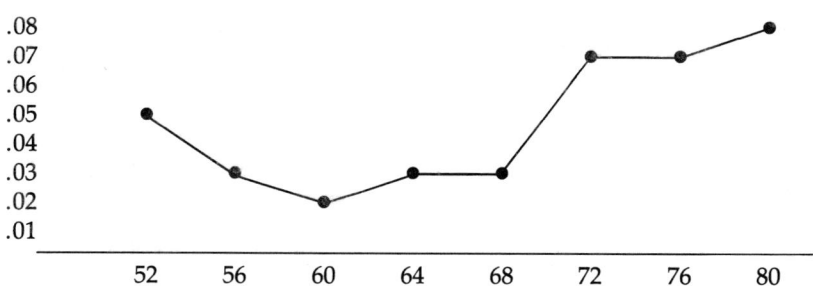

FIGURE 12.1L
Dependent

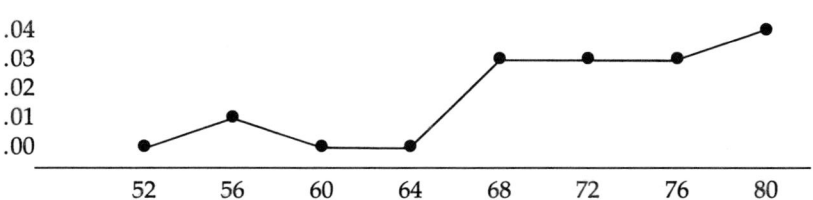

FIGURE 12.1M
Student

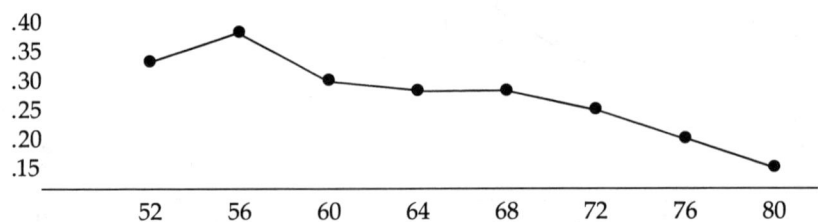

FIGURE 12.1N
Houseperson

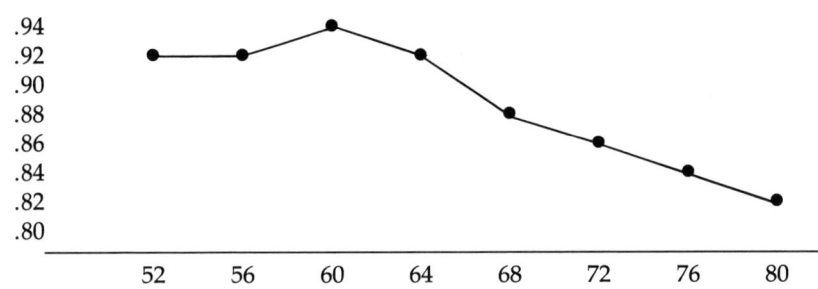

FIGURE 12.1O
Marital

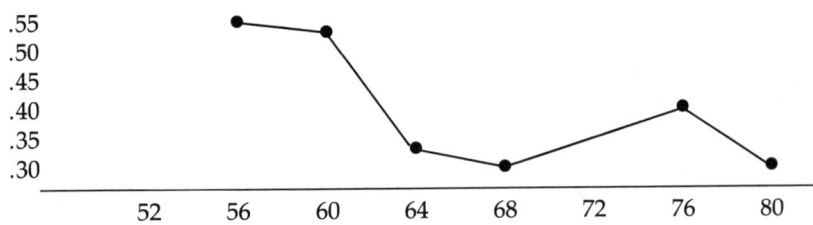

FIGURE 12.1P
Children

Demographic Change

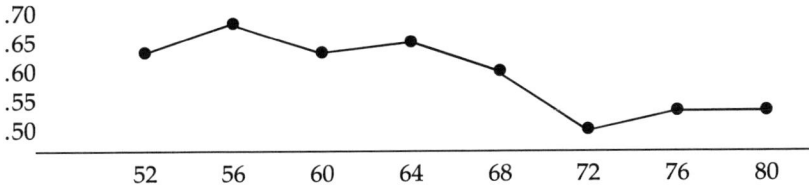

FIGURE 12.1Q
Attendance

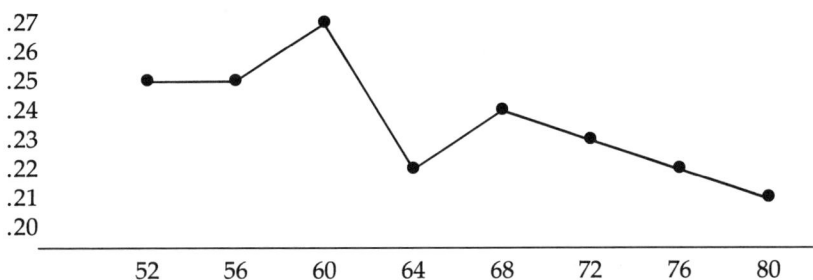

FIGURE 12.1R
Northeast

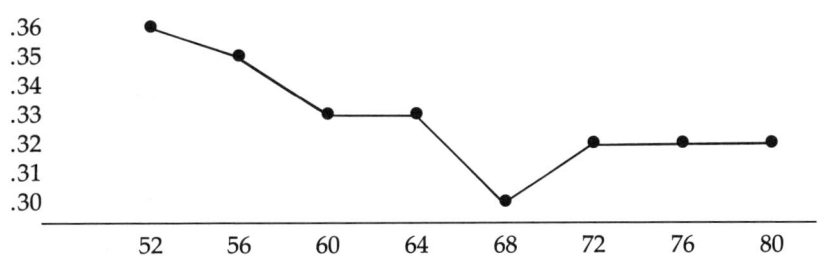

FIGURE 12.1S
Midwest

Situations and Structures

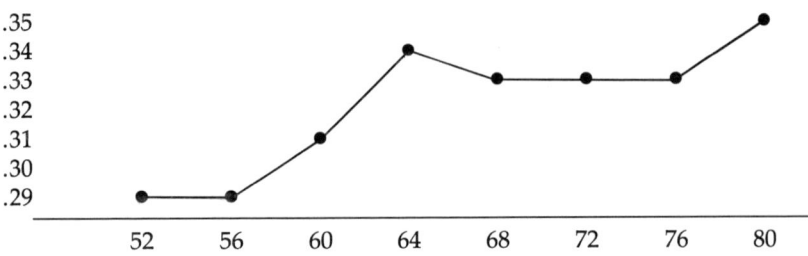

FIGURE 12.1T
South

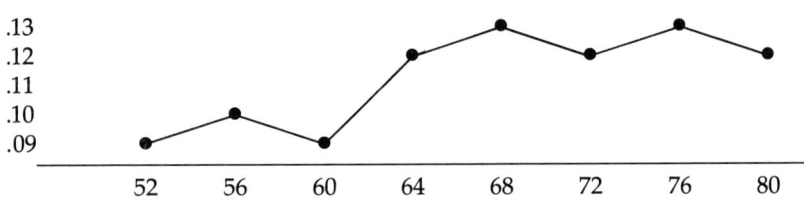

FIGURE 12.1U
West

generational replacement) or changes that cut across the population (period effects).

LIFE CYCLE, GENERATION, AND PERIODS

What dynamics are driving the changes seen in Figure 12.1? Table 12.2 presents a partial answer to this question by showing the main effects of life cycle, generation, and periods. The process of aging, and the advantanges and disadvantages that go along with it, is partly responsible, though not for all aspects of change, nor always in predictable ways. The improvement in class, the greater likelihood of owning a home, and the pattern of decreased dependency (and of becoming a family head) are to be expected. Seven measures show no relationship with age, however, suggesting that other forces are more directly responsible for the aggregate

Demographic Change

TABLE 12.2
Effects of Life Cycle, Generation, and Period on Demographic Characteristics

Variables	Life Cycle	Generation	Period		
			Fifties	Sixties	Seventies
Childhood class	***	.000	***	−.035**	−.036*
Father	***	.011	.016	.101**	.169**
Class	.001**	−.080**	.074**	.083**	.140**
Income	.000	−.252**	.158**	.269**	.512**
Ownership	.008**	−.394**	***	.309**	.580**
Education	−.003**	−.119**	.030	.114**	.224**
Professional	.000	−.154**	.079**	.138**	.259**
Service	−.001*	−.127**	***	.119**	.175**
Union	−.003**	−.119**	.070**	.137**	.168**
Race	***	−.040*	−.010	−.084**	−.037**
Head	.002**	−.203**	.101**	.122**	.126*
Dependent	−.003**	.130**	−.076**	−.093**	−.052
Student	.000	.086**	−.001	.002	.001
Houseperson	.001	.151**	−.006	−.173**	−.254**
Marital	−.007**	−.250**	−.013	−.010	−.069
Children	−.020**	−.525**	***	−.412**	−.574**
Attendance	.000	−.128**	.118**	−.003	−.061
Northeast	.000	−.074**	.018	.038*	.067*
Midwest	.000	−.018	−.047**	−.037*	.056
South	−.001	.080**	−.007	−.055**	−.131**
West	.000	.026*	.022*	.053**	.010

* = standard error ≤ B.
** = $p \leq .05$.
*** = not calculated.

change. The positive relationship with houseperson no doubt reflects the tendency in our society for women to leave occupations after marriage to take responsibility for raising a family. The negative relationships of the life cycle with both unionization and service occupations may result from changes in occupation from lower level jobs to management or professions, but could also be an artifact of generational differences not tapped in our design. No doubt the negative correlation with education is also an artifact of this kind, since the oldest cohorts were raised prior to the initial expansions of the public education system. Finally, the negative relationship of the life cycle with having children is due to the curvilinear nature of having children in the household. Overall, it can be concluded that aging did play a role in changing the social and economic environment, though not a particularly strong one.

Changes in the economic environment attributable directly to the sixties generation are much more pervasive and substantively more interesting. Despite the prosperity of the times, they indicate that at this point the generation was characterized more by its lowered status than by its improved position. Measures of perceived class, home ownership, income, and occupation all indicate sizable decreases in SES for this group. This is particularly interesting because there is a slight tendency for this generation to have come from professional or white collar families. Most surprisingly, there is a sizable negative relationship with educational attainment even though educational opportunity was being increased. In part this results from the fact that for many in this cohort the educational process is not complete (consider the positive relationship with "Student"). In part it also suggests that the educational opportunities available reflect a more general benefit, and not one exclusively the domain of this generation (as demonstrated by the sizable and increasing period effects).[2]

When we turn to social and cultural indicators, we again see that the sixties generation is distinctive. They are less likely to marry, less likely to participate in organized religion, and less likely to have children or live in households with children present. They are less likely to populate the Northeast and Midwest and more likely to be part of the nation's migration to the West and South. The racial composition of this generation is also distinctive, with a smaller percentage of whites than the preceding cohorts. This generation was

Demographic Change

also more likely to remain dependent rather than to head the household in which they were a part. Finally, despite their characterization as postmaterialists and children of the post-industrial era, once period and age effects are removed, they were more likely to become housepersons and less likely to be occupied in the service sector.[3]

It is in the period effects that the signs of prosperity are reflected. All the measures of SES show positive relationships, with the size of these relationships increasing as we move from the fifties to the seventies. Signs of decay in traditional institutions are also evident here, though generally to a lesser degree than is demonstrated specifically by the sixties generation. Overall, period effects appear to be following the lead of the sixties generation in terms of social and cultural decay, but moving at odds with it in terms of economic prosperity. Finally, certain situational and structural factors such as student status, being part of the professional occupations or the service sector, and one's relationship in the family also show a divergence between general trends and the tendencies of those raised in the sixties.

When we observe the interaction among the three variables (Table 12.3), the tendency for society to demand conformity can be seen. All of the measures of status on which the sixties generation showed signs of downward mobility and of movements in the opposite direction than the larger society, show signs of reversing with age. In addition there was a movement back to the traditional relationships of family, marriage, and organized religion. Even migration patterns show a reversal of the main generational effects on mobility. Some of these interactions overwhelmed the main generational effects rather quickly (educational levels converged within seven years, for instance), while others will never compensate for the main effects of generation (housepersons). Overall, the distinctiveness of the sixties genera-

TABLE 12.3
Interaction Effects on Demographics

Variables	Life Cycle				Generation	
	Generation	Fifties	Sixties	Seventies	Sixties	Seventies
Childhood class	***	***	***	***	.064**	.076**
Father	***	***	***	***	.051	.025
Class	.002**	−.002**	−.002**	−.002**	.074**	.022
Income	.017**	−.003**	−.005**	−.009**	−.072**	−.219**
Ownership	.018**	***	−.007**	−.012**	−.155**	−.124**
Education	.006**	.000	−.002**	−.002**	.051*	.022
Professional	.011**	−.002**	−.001*	−.003**	.031	−.033
Service	.004**	.000	−.001	−.001	.045	.051
Union	.007**	.000	−.002**	−.002**	−.075**	−.109**
Race	***	***	***	***	.026	.022
Head	.019**	−.002*	−.002**	−.002	−.111**	−.151**
Dependent	−.015**	.002*	.002**	.001	.102**	.116**
Student	−.009**	.000	.000	.000	.054**	.072**
Houseperson	−.001	−.001	.003**	.003*	−.081*	−.107*
Marital	.024**	.007**	.007**	.008**	−.169**	−.210**
Children	.021**	−.003	.008**	.017**	.041	.052
Attendance	.003**	−.003**	.000	.000	.005	.027
Northeast	.005**	.000	−.002**	−.002**	−.013	−.060
Midwest	.001	.001	.000	−.002**	−.019	−.074**
South	−.005**	.001	.003**	.005**	.038	.091**
West	−.001	−.001**	−.001**	.000	−.021	.028

* = standard erorr ≤ B.
** = p ≤ .05.
*** = not calculated.

tion will remain for quite a while, however, with economic, social, cultural, and status differences taking an average of over 20 years to disappear.

The result of this tension between the main effects of generation and the pull of more systemic trends is most evident in the interaction of the two (Generation × Periods). Here we can see these counter trends resulted in a tremendous inconsistency in status during the sixties and seventies. Some indicators of economic status show positive relationships while others show negative ones. Similar tensions are

Demographic Change

evident in the social and cultural indicators. These interactions, along with the patterns demonstrated in the main effects (Table 12.2) provide empirical evidence for the incongruities during this time and within this generation that were postulated in Chapter Two.

Finally, the interactions of age and periods reaffirm the pattern established in other chapters that older cohorts remain the most resistant to (or in this case, perhaps excluded from) the main effects of changing times. Nearly every interaction between life cycle and period shows the opposite relationship to that demonstrated by the main period effects. Once they are socialized and established within a set of institutions, values, and behaviors, members of society are less likely to change.

Are the subgenerational categories, which have proven useful in making fine distinctions among political orientations within the sixties generation, useful in the case of situational and structural factors? Table 12.4 presents the main effects of the three subgenerations. While there are some notable differences, it is the similarity of the patterns that stands out. Two thirds of the relationships are in the same direction across any two cohorts. The socialized cohort does appear to be somewhat less downwardly mobile, more likely to come from middle-class, professional families, and more supportive of organized religion than the ambivalent cohort but these patterns are far from clear. Other relationships (such as being a head of the household or a student) also show large differences in the magnitude of the relationships, but these were undoubtedly partly the result of age differences that, due to the short time the youngest cohort had been in the electorate, were not completely controlled for. Nevertheless, it is the similarity in the situations across subgenerations that is most striking.

With the interaction effects we begin to see greater dis-

TABLE 12.4
Effects of Subgenerations on Demographic Characteristics

Variables	Ambivalent	Experienced	Socialized
Childhood class	−.048**	.067**	.084**
Father	−.009	.118**	.028
Class	−.161**	.013	.138
Income	−.430**	−.342**	−.269*
Ownership	−.656**	−.377**	.682**
Education	−.233**	−.089**	−.278**
Professional	−.277**	−.152**	−.537**
Service	−.241**	−.062*	−.218*
Union	−.191**	−.170**	−.154
Race	−.080*	.049**	−.006
Head	−.187**	−.560**	−.999**
Dependent	.061**	.417**	.999**
Student	.079**	.247**	.499**
Houseperson	.360**	−.056	.223
Marital	−.199**	−.690**	−.999**
Children	−.791**	−.783**	−.999**
Attend	−.198**	−.168**	.193
Northeast	−.101*	−.063*	−.260*
Midwest	−.032	−.048*	−.030
South	.090*	.081**	.402**
West	.073**	.030*	−.118

* = standard error ≤ B.
** = $p \leq .05$.

tinctions among the subgenerations (Table 12.5), though again there are still marked similarities. As the ambivalent and experienced cohorts aged, they tended to change in very similar ways and in ways consistent with the overall interaction effects shown in Table 12.3. The socialized cohort (which showed some SES advantages in the main effects) demonstrated less of a tendency to improve its status, however. Having started from a position of advantage (relative to the other two cohorts), aging appears to bring fewer advantages for the youngest subgeneration. For the other social and cultural indicators, the socialized cohort generally made the greatest move back to the more typical patterns of the

Demographic Change

TABLE 12.5
Interaction Effects between Subgenerations, Life Cycle, and Period on Demographic Characteristics

Variables	Life Cycle			Seventies	
	Ambivalent	Experienced	Socialized	Ambivalent	Experienced
Childhood class	***	***	***	.049**	−.009
Father	***	***	***	.004	−.052
Class	.004**	.007**	−.040*	.054	−.144**
Income	.023**	.037**	.012	−.203**	−.347**
Ownership	.027**	.030**	−.234**	−.125**	−.160**
Education	.011**	.021**	.039	−.017	−.112**
Professional	.018**	.024**	.091*	−.064	−.102*
Service	.006**	.002	.047	.148*	.012
Union	.007**	.010**	−.033	−.071	−.065*
Race	***	***	***	.060	−.064**
Head	.007**	.038**	.181**	−.016	.072*
Dependent	−.001	−.027**	−.165**	.010	−.059**
Student	−.004**	−.015**	−.071**	.009	−.069**
Houseperson	−.010**	.001	−.069	−.146*	.089
Marital	.006**	.043**	.065*	.002	.066*
Children	.004	.011	.154	.721**	.376*
Attendance	−.002	−.006	−.060	.248**	.194**
Northeast	.003	.001	.009	.021	−.001
Midwest	.002	.001	.004	−.073	−.027
South	.000	.003	−.027	−.021	.018
West	−.004**	−.005*	.015	.042	.105

* = standard error ≤ B.
** = p ≤ .05.
*** = not calculated.

society, a finding consistent with our argument concerning the pressure that society exerts for conformity to its hegemonic center (recall that this cohort was the most extreme on these measures in the main effects).

Finally, the interaction of the two former cohorts with the seventies shows the greatest distinctions among the subgenerations. Of these two, the experienced cohort most resisted the main period effects, both in terms of the magnitude and the direction of these relationships. Again the subgeneration that most directly experienced the events of the 1960s stood out as most distinctive in the 1970s.

SUMMARY AND CONCLUSION

In this chapter we have begun to explore the extent to which society in the United States has undergone changes in some of its basic institutional relationships, and the impact of life cycle, generation, and the events of different periods on those changes. For lasting and meaningful change in the political orientations of the public to occur, it must either arise out of or result in changes in institutional structures. The most fundamental change is structurally based, challenges the system, and offers alternative institutions to those it would overcome. Periods of such change are rare and seldom occur without tremendous disruption. Even dramatic changes such as those that occurred in the United States in the 1930s were made more to adjust the system than to fundamentally alter it; as likely to replicate existing economic and social relations as to restructure them.

How do the changes that have arisen out of the juncture of the events, situations, and the generation of the 1960s fit into this definition of social change? We began to answer this question by looking for evidence of "disturbances" in some of the basic institutional arrangements in society in the United States. Clearly the last three decades have been periods of change in this regard. Economic indicators point to years of relatively steady growth. Levels of education have also risen steadily during these years. The growth of the white-collar professional class and of the service sector has meant changes in the occupational structure in the United States as well. There have also been changes in the social and cultural structure of the nation: a changing ethnic and racial composition; regional shifts in the population; a decline

Demographic Change

in marriage and a changing family structure; and a decline in organized religion. Again, while these indicators capture only a fraction of the important situational and structural relationships in a complex society such as that of the United States, they serve as a useful barometer of the larger change that has been taking place.

While we have found evidence of rather consistent change over the periods examined, there is also evidence that this change is not uniform across generations. The decay of traditional social patterns and changes in the racial mix of the population was greatest for the sixties generation, though the direction of change in these areas is consistent with the more inclusive effects of period. The characterization of this generation as rejecting many of the traditions and institutions of the past appears to stand up to more rigorous scrutiny. Less expected, however, is the SES profile of this generation. In the midst of a period of growth, they demonstrated relatively low income, less home ownership, and lowered class. They also run counter to the trend of increased white collar and service employment, though they are also less likely to be associated with unions. This was true of all three subgenerations, though social and cultural change was strongest for the experienced cohort and downward mobility was most prevalent among the ambivalent. As they aged, members of the sixties generation appeared to be conforming to the more-general trends evident during the years examined, though these changes are occurring slowly. In addition, the interaction effects with the seventies suggests that the experienced cohort is still resistant to this societal pull.

The rise of "Yuppies" or "Yumpies"—young upwardly mobile members of the "baby boom" generation—seems to contradict the profile of the sixties generation presented in this chapter. While the interaction effects do indicate slow movement in this direction, the image of downward mobility (relative to both general trends and the situations in which much of this generation was raised) remains the most accurate. Two points on this seeming contradiction are in order. First, in this chapter we have characterized the generation as a whole. It may very well be (in fact, it is probable) that it is the upwardly mobile segment of the generation which is most visible and most likely to catch the eyes and the imaginations of the press and the politicians of mainstream politics. Second and more importantly, students of generational politics are becoming aware that while Yumpies may exist, they are not typical of this generation. As the editors of *The New Republic* noted in reflecting on this phenomenon: "If anything, yuppy culture is permeated with a sense of 'downward' mobility, of couples struggling with two incomes to achieve a middle-class life that their parents enjoyed with one [July 9, 1984]." Landon Jones writes of this generation: "In the 70s, millions of baby boomers who had been promised everything from their education were being delivered nothing . . . for the first time in recent American history, the relative earnings of college graduates declined [Jones, 1980; pp. 179–182]." In addition, college graduates represent only a portion of the generation as a whole. As Jones said in a recent interview "I see them splitting. In my book, I thought what they had in common was bigger than the socioeconomic differences between them. . . . I really wonder whether that is still true [*National Journal*, 1984, pp. 804–805]." For both these reasons then, the findings of this chapter become less surprising. Perhaps the editor of *The New Republic* captured it best:

When my family made the big leap to the suburbs twenty-two years ago, my father worried that his children did not fully appreciate this achievement. I remember vividly that he sat me down in our new home and said pointedly: "You know, this is the nicest house I've ever lived in." I'm sure it never occurred to him, and it cer-

Demographic Change

tainly never occurred to me until much later, that it might be the nicest house I'd ever live in as well [July 9, 1984, p. 41].

A final point to note about the kinds of change uncovered in this chapter concerns some of the situational factors that apply to the sixties generation. As a group they were more likely to be students, more likely to be dependents, less likely to own homes, and less likely to have family responsibilities. They were, quite simply, free from many of the responsibilities that pressure both for conformity and for the privatization of interests. They were also in a situation where the likelihood of interaction with others in similar circumstances was increased. This combination may prove important for understanding both the development of a unique political profile and changes in that profile that result from changing situations. It is this connection between changing situations, changing social structures, and political orientations that is explored in the next two chapters.

NOTES

1. Using survey data to trace demographic changes can be somewhat problematic, since samples are not designed to be representative on all of the characteristics of interest. While the margin of error should not be any greater than for the attitudinal items, normally one would depend on census data to document change of this kind. Since we are using the survey data in both the analysis in this chapter and in the next, however, it seemed more appropriate to present trends as found in this data. In addition, the patterns found very closely parallel those documented in census data and in surveys designed more specifically to determine these characteristics.

2. It should also be remembered that despite generally increasing educational levels, by the time the sixties generation was entering the electorate in large numbers the rate of high school diplomas among 17-year-olds was on the decline (Chapter Two).

3. The positive association of the sixties generation with housepersons is in part due to the fact that women represent a slightly greater percentage of this cohort than of the total population, and in part due to the fact that men in this generation are slightly more likely to take on this role.

REFERENCES

"Arise Ye Yuppies." *The New Republic* (July 9, 1984), pp. 4, 41.

Dawson, Richard E., Kenneth Prewitt, and Karen S. Dawson. *Political Socialization*. Boston: Little, Brown, 1977.

Hagstrom, Jerry. "Baby Boom Generation May Have to Wait A While to Show Its Political Clout." *National Review,* 17 (April, 1984), pp. 804–810.

Jones, Landon Y. *Great Expectations: America and the Baby Boom Generation.* New York: Ballantine Books, 1980.

CHAPTER 13

The Political Impact of the Socioeconomic Environment

In the last chapter we argued that developing and maintaining political orientations in a population is critically linked to the social, economic, and cultural environments in which they are formed. We also examined the degree of stability and change in some of the basic situations, structures, and institutions of those environments, focusing on the extent to which such patterns were related to the 1960s and the sixties generation. That analysis uncovered evidence of both systematic period-based change and of change specific to the sixties generation itself. In addition, much of the generational change conflicted with the changes due to period. In this chapter the relationship between the socioeconomic environment and the political orientations of the sixties generation is examined in order to distinguish different subgroups within the generation and to document the interaction between individual and structural-based political change. Chapter Fourteen provides a similar analysis of the sociocultural environment.

SUMMARIZING THE MAIN EFFECTS OF LIFE CYCLE, GENERATION, AND PERIODS

The first step in examining the relationship between the socioeconomic environment and the development of political orientations is to simplify the measures of political attitudes, opinions, and behaviors. In this study over 75 different measures have been examined. While this approach has been useful in pointing out the richness and the complexity of the relationships between the life cycle, generations, events, and politics, the addition of demographic measures to this calculus requires a reduction in the number of dependent variables. As a result, we have combined the individual items into 20 summary measures. These measures are based upon the general divisions presented in Chapters Four through Eleven and are described in Table 13.1. All scales are simple additive indices, rescaled to run from zero to 1 (for greater detail on scale construction, see appendices B and D). As can be seen, the measures maintain the basic divisions in attitudes, opinions, and behaviors that were proposed in the theory and supported throughout the findings of this re-

TABLE 13.1
Description of Summary Measures of Political Orientations

Variables	Description
Support	Summary scale of measures of diffuse support (1 = complete support)
Sixties agenda	Summary of agenda areas of particular relevance to the 1960s (1 = only sixties agenda is mentioned)
Economic agenda	Summary of agenda areas focusing on economic issues (1 = only economic agenda is mentioned)
Social-welfare agenda	Summary of agenda areas focusing on social welfare (1 = only social welfare agenda is mentioned)

The Political Impact of the Socioeconomic Environment

Foreign agenda	Summary of agenda areas focusing on foreign policy (1 = only foreign policy agenda is mentioned)
Domestic issues	Summary of stands on domestic issues (1 = complete support for greater government involvement)
Foreign issues	Summary of stands on foreign policy issues (1 = complete support for greater government involvement)
Political involvement	Summary of measures of political involvement (1 = complete involvement)
Ideological DM	Summary of use of ideological decision-making cues (1 = use of only ideological cues)
Cue-specific DM	Summary of group, issue or nature of the times based decision making (1 = use of only these cues)
Party-based DM	Summary of use of party-based decision-making cues (1 = use of only party-based cues)
Nonpolitical DM	Summary of use of nonpolitical decision-making cues (1 = use of only nonpolitical cues)
Electoral participation	Summary of measures of electoral participation (1 = complete participation)
Diffuse party support	Summary of measures of support for the party system (1 = complete support)
Long-term party choice	Summary of measures of long-term party choice (1 = complete Democratic party support)
Short-term party support	Summary of measures of election-specific party choice (1 = complete Democratic party support)
Behavioral stability	Summary of measures of stability in the amount of participation (1 = complete stability)
Long-term stability	Summary of measures of long-term stability in party choice (1 = complete stability)
Short-term stability	Summary of measures of short-term stability in party choice (1 = complete stability)
Campaign stability	Summary of measures of stability in party choice during a single campaign (1 = complete stability)

Situations and Structures

TABLE 13.2
Summary of Effects of Life Cycle, Generation, and Period

Variables	Life Cycle	Generation	Periods		
			Fifties	Sixties	Seventies
Support	−.002**	−.090**	.093**	.150**	.136**
Sixties agenda	−.001	.022	***	.420**	.138
Economic agenda	.001	−.012	***	−.033	.225**
Foreign affairs agenda	−.003	−.061	***	−.489**	−.666**
Social-welfare agenda	.002	.036	***	.084	.271**
Domestic issues	−.001**	.082**	.041*	−.034*	−.154**
Foreign issues	−.003**	−.064	.363**	−.193*	.426**
Political involvement	−.001	−.158**	***	.063**	.012
Ideological DM	.000	−.012**	.004	.108**	−.002
Cue-specific DM	−.001*	−.030*	.018	.069**	.036
Party-based DM	.000	−.030**	−.036**	−.074**	−.008
Nonpolitical DM	.001**	.069**	.015	−.014	−.026
Electoral participation	.001**	−.179**	.040**	.158**	.184**
Diffuse party support	.001**	−.033**	.067**	.028*	.038*
Short-term party choice	−.002**	.112*	−.073*	.165**	−.135
Long-term party choice	−.003**	−.038*	−.074**	.030	−.049
Behavioral stability	.003**	−.402**	.143**	.234**	.319**
Campaign stability	.002**	−.021	.057	.079*	−.096
Short-term stability	.001*	.041	−.020	−.126**	−.280**
Long-term stability	−.002*	.305**	−.109**	−.194**	***

* = standard error ≤ B.
** = $p \leq .05$.
*** = not calculated.

search. These measures allow us to examine the relationship between social structures and political orientations in a way that helps simplify what is still a complex task.

Table 13.2 presents the main effects of the life cycle, generation, and periods on these measures. The procedure used here is identical to that described in Chapter Three.[1] The results of this analysis conform, not surprisingly, to the general conclusions drawn from the more item-specific analyses of previous chapters and, therefore, suggest that these summary measures will serve adequately as "representatives" of the various orientations under examination.

The Political Impact of the Socioeconomic Environment

SOCIOECONOMIC STRUCTURES, POLITICAL ORIENTATIONS, AND THE SIXTIES GENERATION

The next step in this study was to "remove" the effects of period, life cycle, and the interactions of the three main variables from our measures so that we can focus exclusively on the generational impact. Since we have estimates of these effects (from the analysis partly presented in Table 13.2) it is relatively simple to subtract them from the summary variables (Claggett, 1981). The resulting measures are estimates of each cohort's level of support, agenda choice, etc., when effects of period, life cycle, and interaction are set at zero. (See Appendix D for a detailed discussion of this method). With these effects removed we can attend exclusively to the relationship among generational change, political orientations, and social situations and structures.[2] This is done by running regression analyses with the measure of political orientation in question as the dependent variable and a social measure, the generational measure, and a measure of the interaction between the two as the independent variables.[3]

Table 13.3 presents the results of this analysis for the level of political support. The demographic variables have been divided into "socioeconomic factors" and "sociocultural factors" to help in the interpretation of results. The socioeconomic variables are the subject of this chapter.[4] The results, which, as usual, are unstandardized regression coefficients, are presented in five different categories. "Main" refers to the main effect of the demographic variable in question and measures the general effect of that variable on the level of political support. "X Generation" refers to the interaction effect of being a member of the sixties generation and having the social characteristic in question, and thereby measures the unique reaction of certain segments of the sixties generation in terms of their political support: in effect it measures

273

Situations and Structures

change in orientations that are occurring *within* certain segments of society as a result of generational replacement. The "Δ Structure" column measures the change in political orientations attributable to the different situations members of the sixties generation find themselves in relative to prior generations (and documented in the previous chapter). It is calculated by multiplying the main effect of the social factor in question by the generational change in that factor estimated in Chapter Twelve. For example, if greater income is positively associated with political support, and if members of the sixties generation find themselves, on average, in a position of relatively low incomes, then this will result in a certain loss of political support relative to the rest of the population. This measure captures the extent to which change in orientations is due to changing structures and situations in which the sixties generation found itself.

The measure we have labeled "Hegemony" in Table 13.3 allows us to estimate the effect of the social structure in question on the development of unique political orientations by members of the sixties generation. It is derived by subtracting the main effect of being a member of this generation when the social factor is not controlled for from that same main effect when it is controlled for. It is a measure of the tendency of social structures to exaggerate or constrain the unique political profile of the sixties generation (the initial assumption, based on the arguments in Chapter Twelve, was that social structures would work to increase conformity: hence the label "Hegemony"). Finally, "Total" in Table 13.3 measures the overall or net effect of the socioeconomic environment on the aggregate level of support, etc., found in the population as a whole. It is determined by multiplying each of the four specific effects by the mean of that variable and then summing those four products (Achen, 1982). It is simply a summary of the more-specific effects of the particular social situation, structure or institution under examination.

TABLE 13.3
Effects of Socioeconomic Factors on Political Support within the Sixties Generation

Variables	Main	× Generation	Δ Structure	Hegemony	Total
Childhood class	−.167*	−.225	.000	.003	−.182*
Father	.081**	.125*	.001	.049*	.048*
Class	.213**	−.150	−.017	−.068	.026
Income	.030	.196**	−.008	.047**	.035
Ownership	.071**	−.026	−.028	−.017	.005
Education	.133**	−.014	−.016	.017	.056*
Professional	.140**	−.007	−.022	.015*	.007
Service	.176**	−.217**	−.022	−.068**	−.024
Union	−.061	.187*	.007	.039*	.029

* = standard error ≤ B.
** = p ≤ .05.

Since differences among cohorts on many of the structural and situational variables to be used in this and the next chapter are often small (relative to individual-level variances), and since other relevant demographic and individual factors cannot be controlled for in each model, item-specific estimates are occasionally counterintuitive and undoubtedly the result of the estimation process. Again it is important to keep in mind that we are interested in observing the *general patterns* that are uncovered across the numerous measures of the socioeconomic and sociocultural environment rather than what any single item reveals. By presenting the relationships for separate items, however, the limits of and exceptions to these general patterns (and to the estimation procedures themselves) remain visible.

As is evident from Table 13.3, the main effects demonstrate increases in the level of political support in the population as socioeconomic status (SES) increases. Only perceived social class directly counters this relationship (the negative association with unionization is less easily characterized in terms of status). The interaction of the socioeconomic variables with generation (column 2) is not easily generalized, but it seems to suggest that higher socioeconomic status leads to decreased support beyond that evident in the generation as a whole. Upper-status members of the generation are more alienated from the system than their less-affluent contemporaries (although income and being socialized in a professional or managerial class do not conform to this characterization). The fact that members of the sixties generation are lower on the SES ladder than their parents adds to this negative political outlook, demonstrated by the "Δ Structure" column.

Both the interaction of the sixties generation with the socioeconomic factors, and the changes in this generation's position in that structure point to a movement away from the more positive association demonstrated in the main effects. The final two measures tell us the extent to which this movement was enough to lead to a more-general lack of support in either the sixties generation or the population as a whole. Hegemony, which focuses on the effect that the social factor in question has on the level of support in the sixties generation, suggests that the overall socioeconomic position of the generation actually increased its level of support relative to what it would have been if such factors were eliminated. This finding is consistent with the notions of hegemony and society's pressure to conform with the status quo that we have developed throughout this book. When all the dimensions of SES are combined (the "Total" column), we see that, despite the tendency towards weakened support demonstrated by the generation as a whole (Chapter 4 and Table 13.2), and by the upper-status members of the generation in particular, the net effect of the socioeconomic environment is to increase the overall level of support found in the population slightly (relative to what it would be were SES effects eliminated). Put another way, it demonstrates that the main effects of SES and the hegemonic pull of the generation's overall socioeconomic position outweigh the negative tendencies of interaction and changing structure.

TABLE 13.4
Effects of Socioeconomic Factors on Selection of a
Sixties Agenda within the Sixties Generation

Variables	Main	× Generation	Δ Structure	Hegemony	Total
Childhood class	−.207	1.73	.000	.732	.538
Father	.474**	.837**	.005	−.138*	−.053
Class	.641	.179	−.052	.104	.351
Income	.438*	−.977**	−.110	−.319**	−.256
Ownership	−1.06**	.330	.419*	.432*	−.011
Education	−.184	−.985**	.022	−.653*	−.606*
Professional	.872**	−.960**	−.134	−.258**	−.182
Service	−.175	−1.48**	.022	−.584**	−.546*
Union	.327	−.791	−.040	−.149	−.112

* = standard error ≤ B.
** = p ≤ .05.

TABLE 13.5
Effects of Socioeconomic Factors on Selection of an
Economic Agenda within the Sixties Generation

Variables	Main	× Generation	Δ Structure	Hegemony	Total
Childhood class	−.190	−.117	.000	−.067	−.132
Father	.549**	.105	.006	.012	.114*
Class	.891**	.208	−.071	.061	.444*
Income	.075	.917**	−.019	.128**	.132*
Ownership	1.13**	−.612**	−.444**	−.620**	−.126
Education	.280**	.915**	−.033	.519**	.569**
Professional	.432**	.342**	−.066	.030	.047
Service	.461**	.737**	−.058	.251**	.344**
Union	−.063	.345	.007	.011	.030

* = standard error ≤ B.
** = p ≤ .05.

In Tables 13.4 through 13.7 we find the effects of the socioeconomic environment on the selection of a political agenda. The main effects of socioeconomic advantage are generally consistent in involving the population with economic issues at the expense of social welfare or foreign policy, suggesting a type of rational and individualistic self-interest was at work. The impact of SES on the selection of the sixties agenda, however, was much less consistent.

Situations and Structures

Within the sixties generation itself (× Generation), we find a different pattern. Upper-status individuals within this generation are more likely than their older counterparts to be concerned with an economic agenda, but they are less consistent in their rejection of social welfare concerns. In addition, they are generally likely to demonstrate greater concern over foreign-policy issues than either their less-affluent sixties counterparts or older cohorts of the same status. Finally, they are more consistent than those in upper socioeconomic brackets as a whole or less-affluent members of the sixties generation in their lack of concern over the issues of the sixties. The changing economic structure of this generation also contributes to its distinctiveness, having increased its emphasis on social welfare and foreign policy agendas. This relative change in SES also works to mute the emphasis on economics, however, and again produces an apparent inconsistency concerning the attention paid to issues of the sixties.

When the effect of the economic structure of the generation as a whole on agendas is considered, we again see a pattern consistent with the influence of hegemony: clear movement away from agendas opposed to the social and economic mainstream (the sixties agenda and the social-welfare agenda) and toward traditional concerns for the economy and foreign policy. Finally, when all these forces are combined, the net result of the socioeconomic structure of the population was a decreased interest in the sixties agenda, increased interest in the economic agenda, and mixed effects on both social welfare and foreign policy agendas. These were trends that again ran counter to the main effects of generation presented in Table 13.2.

When we move from general agendas to specific issue stands (Tables 13.8 and 13.9), we again find that the socioeconomic environment is relatively consistent in both its

The Political Impact of the Socioeconomic Environment

TABLE 13.6
Effects of Socioeconomic Factors on Selection of a
Social Welfare Agenda within the Sixties Generation

Variables	Main	× Generation	Δ Structure	Hegemony	Total
Childhood class	.105	−.459	.000	−.243	−.142
Father	−.405**	−.164	−.004	−.087**	−.126*
Class	−.457**	−.132	.036	−.090	−.259*
Income	−.121	−.367**	.030	−.095*	−.067
Ownership	−.105	.092**	.041	.053	.019
Education	−.214*	−.227	.025	−.180*	−.221*
Professional	−.436**	.294**	.067	.017	.027
Service	.135	.004	−.017	−.009	.029
Union	−.159	.207	.019	.022	.016

* = standard error ≤ B.
** = p ≤ .05.

TABLE 13.7
Effects of Socioeconomic Factors on Selection of a
Foreign Agenda within the Sixties Generation

Variables	Main	× Generation	Δ Structure	Hegemony	Total
Childhood class	.629	−1.22*	.000	−.796	−.466
Father	−.996**	.805	−.011	.120**	−.052
Class	−1.95**	.347	.156	.175	−.661*
Income	−.419**	.855**	.106	.182**	.185
Ownership	−.795**	.857**	.313*	.614**	.282
Education	−.060	−.185**	.071	−.327*	−.149
Professional	−1.20**	1.06**	.185	.170**	.149
Service	−.676**	.250	.088	.098	−.075
Union	.086	.354	−.010	.103	.082

* = standard error ≤ B.
** = p ≤ .05.

main effects and in its impact on the sixties generation. Higher-status cohorts are opposed to government involvement in domestic affairs and support government involvement in foreign affairs.

Despite this conservative main effect, however, the upper-status groups of the sixties generation are the most liberal on domestic stands. This liberalism is accentuated by the

TABLE 13.8
Effects of Socioeconomic Factors on Domestic-issue Stands within the Sixties Generation

Variables	Main	× Generation	Δ Structure	Hegemony	Total
Childhood class	−.146	−.163	.000	−.082	−.128
Father	−.282**	.111	−.003	−.001	−.041
Class	−.314**	.012	−.025	−.001	−.179*
Income	−.154**	.121	.039	.018	.030
Ownership	−.544**	.523**	.214**	.401**	.167*
Education	−.100*	.033	.012	.004	−.029
Professional	−.204**	.127*	.031	.009	.012
Service	−.009	−.113	.001	−.045*	−.041
Union	−.103**	.367**	.012	.070**	.055

* = standard error ≤ B.
** = $p \leq .05$.

TABLE 13.9
Effects of Socioeconomic Factors on Foreign-issue Stands within the Sixties Generation

Variables	Main	× Generation	Δ Structure	Hegemony	Total
Childhood class	−.532	−.169	.000	−.094	−.301
Father	.244	.231	.003	.083	.102
Class	.100	−.255	−.008	−.134	−.072
Income	.183	.037	−.046	.008	−.006
Ownership	.156	.146	−.061	.056	.107
Education	.376*	−.303	−.045	−.127	.015
Professional	.230	−.209	−.035	−.033	−.029
Service	.435*	.067	−.055	.043	.134
Union	.218	.261	−.026	.047	.059

* = standard error ≤ B.
** = $p \leq .05$.

changing economic structure within the generation. The effects of the interaction of economic status and generation on foreign-policy stands are less consistent. Some socioeconomic advantages led to a desire for greater involvement by the United States, while others led to a desire for less involvement. The *changing* economic structure within the generation, however, does seem to have led to a desire for less interventionism.

The Political Impact of the Socioeconomic Environment

The influence of the socioeconomic composition of the sixties generation was less effective in counteracting its liberal tendencies than it was for the other political orientations examined (this may be due in part to the general acceptance of liberalism in the contemporary system of welfare capitalism). The desire for greater government involvement in domestic issues and less in foreign affairs is characteristic of the sixties generation even when economic constraints are not considered (Chapter 6 and Table 13.2 in this chapter). Both traits generally survive when economic constraints are added, although support for government involvement in domestic affairs is less emphatic. These preferences are obscured, however, once all four dimensions of socioeconomic status and generation are evaluated together. Total effects demonstrate an unusually inconsistent pattern. The inability of these tendencies to survive when combined into the total effects is due largely to the strong counterpressures of the main effects of SES which naturally affect upper-class members of the sixties generation as well.

Perhaps the most surprising findings uncovered regarding the relationship between socioeconomic status and political orientations are in the area of political involvement (Table 13.10). The main effects of status indicate overwhelmingly that higher-status cohorts are less likely to follow politics. It is important to remember that the effects of age, of events of the times, and of all the interactions have been controlled for at this point, suggesting that perhaps the positive association with involvement in politics normally found for upper-class individuals is due more to those influences than directly to those based on class.[5]

The interaction of generation and socioeconomic status demonstrates some tendency for members of the sixties cohort from higher economic strata to be more involved, though this pattern is far from complete. In particular, the factors associated with childhood socialization and with self-per-

TABLE 13.10
Effects of Socioeconomic Factors on the Level of
Political Involvement within the Sixties Generation

Variables	Main	× Generation	Δ Structure	Hegemony	Total
Childhood class	.507	−.732*	.000	−.016	.082
Father	−.154**	−.053	−.002	−.007	−.036
Class	−.118	−.110	.009	−.040	−.091
Income	−.153**	.114	−.038	.034**	−.041
Ownership	−.179**	.127	.071	.126*	.041
Education	−.104*	.187*	.012	.112*	.055
Professional	−.160**	.217**	.025	.050**	.038
Service	.157**	−.138	−.020	−.030	.001
Union	−.137**	.240*	.016	.062*	.038

* = standard error ≤ B.
** = $p \leq .05$.

ceived class reinforce the noninvolvement shown in the main effects. The changing socioeconomic structure within the sixties generation also presented a mixed tendency, but one that leans slightly towards increased involvement.

The overall effects of the economic structure on how politically involved the sixties generation is (hegemony) closely parallel the interaction effects, with involvement again inconsistently related to the various measures of socioeconomic status. This applies as well to the total impact of the socioeconomic environment on the level of political involvement demonstrated by the population as a whole, indicating that the net result of the sixties generation's entrance into the class structure of the United States has been to change a generally negative relationship to a generally indeterminate one with positive (that is politically involved) leanings.

In Tables 13.11 to 13.14 the relationships between socioeconomic factors, generation, and decision-making cues are presented. The main effects of SES are split in terms of ideological decision making, but they are consistently related to the greater use of cue-specific decision making, party-based decision making, and, surprisingly, nonpolitical decision

The Political Impact of the Socioeconomic Environment

TABLE 13.11
Effects of Socioeconomic Factors on Ideological
Decision Making within the Sixties Generation

Variables	Main	× Generation	Δ Structure	Hegemony	Total
Childhood class	−.022**	−.060	.000	−.031**	−.034**
Father	−.035**	−.011*	.000	−.001*	−.008**
Class	−.060**	.028	.005	.009	−.015*
Income	.015**	−.034**	−.004	−.010**	−.009*
Ownership	−.008	−.007	.003	−.007	−.007
Education	.016**	−.035**	−.002	−.029**	−.015*
Professional	−.019**	.007	.003	−.004*	−.002
Service	.012*	−.045**	−.002	−.020**	−.014*
Union	.028**	.025	−.003	.002	.005

* = standard error ≤ B.
** = p ≤ .05.

TABLE 13.12
Effects of Socioeconomic Factors on Cue-specific
Decision Making within the Sixties Generation

Variables	Main	× Generation	Δ Structure	Hegemony	Total
Childhood class	−.204*	.095	.000	.013**	−.066*
Father	.034**	.082	.000	−.017**	.006*
Class	.027	.037	−.002	−.020	.011
Income	.074**	.058	−.019	−.024**	−.011
Ownership	.038**	−.021*	−.015*	−.057**	−.035**
Education	.158**	.006	−.019	−.012	.005
Professional	.076**	.013	−.012	−.031**	−.012
Service	.107**	−.012	−.014	−.034*	.008
Union	.113**	.059	−.013	−.025*	.003

* = standard error ≤ B.
** = p ≤ .05.

making. As usual, the interaction of generation and status disrupts most of these consistent patterns. Ideological decision making was slightly less likely, and both party-based and nonpolitical decision making was much less likely among higher SES members of this generation than among either their contemporaries or their economic peers. The changing economic composition of the sixties generation generally de-

TABLE 13.13
Effects of Socioeconomic Factors on Party-based
Decision Making within the Sixties Generation

Variables	Main	× Generation	Δ Structure	Hegemony	Total
Childhood class	.096**	.005	.000	.005	.045*
Father	.022	−.036	.000	−.002	−.001
Class	.026*	−.043	−.002	−.017	−.006
Income	.022**	−.103**	−.006	−.015**	−.018*
Ownership	.014	−.047**	−.006	−.025*	−.020*
Education	−.009	.017	.001	.013	.006
Professional	.018	−.025	−.003	.001	−.002
Service	.012	−.010	−.002	.001	.001
Union	.007	−.125**	−.001	−.021**	−.020*

* = standard error ≤ B.
** = $p \leq .05$.

TABLE 13.14
Effects of Socioeconomic Factors on Nonpolitical
Decision Making within the Sixties Generation

Variables	Main	× Generation	Δ Structure	Hegemony	Total
Childhood class	.050	.186	.000	.067*	.084*
Father	.034	−.101	.000	−.029	−.016
Class	.082*	.002	−.007	−.007	.031
Income	.021	−.093*	−.005	−.027**	−.021
Ownership	−.030	.032	.012	.012	.006
Education	.028	−.138**	−.003	−.085**	−.061*
Professional	.024	−.101**	−.004	−.027**	−.020
Service	−.042	−.003	.005	−.014	−.017
Union	.022	−.173*	−.003	−.044**	−.033

* = standard error ≤ B.
** = $p \leq .05$.

creased slightly the likelihood of cue-specific, party-based, and nonpolitical decision making. It also had a mixed effect on ideological decision making.

When the effect of the specific economic structure of the sixties generation is considered, the evidence points to a movement away from all forms of decision making except for that based on party cues, which showed a more mixed pat-

TABLE 13.15
Effects of Socioeconomic Factors on the Level of Political Participation within the Sixties Generation

Variables	Main	× Generation	Δ Structure	Hegemony	Total
Childhood class	−.057	−.090	.000	−.053	−.064
Father	−.052*	−.004	−.001	−.013*	−.016
Class	−.058	.073	.005	.027	.004
Income	.060*	−.043	.015	−.014*	.016
Ownership	.007	.006	−.003	−.008	.000
Education	.127**	−.011	−.015	.005	.049
Professional	.020	.039	−.003	.000	.004
Service	.195**	−.118*	−.025	−.045*	.007
Union	.068*	−.042	−.008	−.016	−.006

* = standard error ≤ B.
** = $p \leq .05$.

tern of effects. Finally, the net or total impact of socioeconomic status on decision making is generally to decrease the use of ideological, party-based, and nonpolitical criteria and to have a mixed impact on the use of the more cue-specific approaches.

Despite the negative effects of perceived class (both as an adult and as a child) and of socialization in a professional or managerial family, most measures of socioeconomic status have main effects positively related to political participation (Table 13.15). This is not true for the interaction of generation and socioeconomic status, however, where the results are again mixed. The changing economic structure of the sixties generation also had various effects, though both these generation-based measures indicate some decrease in participation.

The impact of the overall economic structure of the sixties generation (hegemony) was also inconsistent, but, again, it leaned slightly toward nonparticipation. Despite this negative leaning produced by the generation-based measures, the positive main effects are too strong to be obscured, as was

Situations and Structures

TABLE 13.16
Effects of Socioeconomic Factors on Diffuse Party Support within the Sixties Generation

Variables	Main	× Generation	Δ Structure	Hegemony	Total
Childhood class	−.086	.126	.000	.059	.011
Father	.030	.227**	.000	.056**	.028
Class	.016	−.309**	−.001	−.158**	−.129**
Income	.015	.048	−.004	.010	.007
Ownership	−.016	.006	.006	.005	−.001
Education	.030	.078	−.004	.050*	.053*
Professional	.013	.018	−.002	.004	.003
Service	.072**	−.216**	−.009	−.082**	−.055*
Union	.060*	.140*	−.007	.030*	.030

* = standard error ≤ B.
** = $p \leq .05$.

TABLE 13.17
Effects of Socioeconomic Factors on Short-term Party Choice within the Sixties Generation

Variables	Main	× Generation	Δ Structure	Hegemony	Total
Childhood class	−.359	−.928	.000	−.430	−.508
Father	−.655**	.105	−.007	−.061*	−.134*
Class	−.933**	−.190	.075	−.141	−.492*
Income	−.304**	.107	.077	−.020	.022
Ownership	−.308**	.187	.121	.130	.023
Education	−.093	−.434*	.011	−.290*	−.273*
Professional	−.543**	.149	.084	−.049	−.273**
Service	.052	−.743**	−.007	−.303**	−.251**
Union	−.026	.623*	.003	.115	.103

* = standard error ≤ B.
** = $p \leq .05$.

indicated by the largely positive total effects of SES on political participation by the whole population.

The relationships among generation, the socioeconomic environment, and party choice and support are presented in Tables 13.16 to 13.18. The main effects of SES were, as usual, both consistent and interpretable. Higher status led to greater support for the party system and less support for the

The Political Impact of the Socioeconomic Environment

Democratic party in both the short- and the long-term measures. The interaction of generation and status reinforced diffuse support for the party system, but produced support for the Democrats on four of the measures associated with short-term support and on one measure for long-term support. The changing structure of the sixties generation, however, decreased the level of diffuse support and increased both short- and long-term support for the Democratic party.

The pressure of the overall socioeconomic structure of the sixties generation generally was consistent with the main effects, however, increasing support for the party system, and bringing about support for Republicans over both the long and short term. The net result of all of these forces ("Total") again reinforces the main effects by a two-to-one margin.

The last set of relationships examined were those concerning stability in participation (Tables 13.19 to 13.22). The main effects of socioeconomic status on stability in the level of participation are mixed. With an increase in status there was a decrease in stability in the long- and short-term party choice, and an increase in the stability of the allegiance to one candidate during a single campaign. That is, upper-status cohorts are more likely to remain committed to their original choice during a campaign, but less likely to support Democrats or Republicans consistently for different offices and during different elections. The interaction of generation and socioeconomic status reinforces the main effects for long-term instability and campaign stability, while obscuring SES-based distinctions in the stability of participation and (to a lesser degree) in short-term party choice. The effects of the changing economic structure of the sixties generation worked very much in opposition to the main effects. They slightly decreased stability in the level of participation and increased stability in partisan choice during campaigns, both in the short run and in the long run.

TABLE 13.18
Effects of Socioeconomic Factors on Long-term Party Choice within the Sixties Generation

Variables	Main	× Generation	Δ Structure	Hegemony	Total
Childhood class	−.282*	−.464*	.000	−.208	−.295*
Father	−.196**	−.127*	−.002	−.042**	−.065*
Class	−.307**	−.335**	.025	−.176*	−.278**
Income	−.098**	.003	.025	−.005	.005
Ownership	−.065*	.031	.026	.029	.023
Education	−.091*	−.178*	.011	−.120**	−.133**
Professional	−.166**	−.048	.026	−.029*	−.018
Service	.076*	−.247**	−.010	−.093**	−.064
Union	.020	.354*	−.002	.076*	.066

* = standard error ≤ B.
** = p ≤ .05.

TABLE 13.19
Effects of Socioeconomic Factors on Stability in the Amount of Political Participation within the Sixties Generation

Variables	Main	× Generation	Δ Structure	Hegemony	Total
Childhood class	.707**	−1.48**	.000	−.649**	−.240
Father	−.252**	.048	−.003	−.030*	−.054
Class	−.424**	.211	.034	.086	−.107
Income	.087	−.092	−.022	−.024	−.025
Ownership	−.051	−.060	−.020	.024	−.060
Education	.020	.050	−.002	.025	.032
Professional	−.175**	.150*	.027	.005	.013
Service	.162**	−.256*	−.021	−.098	−.048
Union	.118*	−.405*	−.014	−.091	−.067

* = standard error ≤ B.
** = p ≤ .05.

The impact of the overall economic structure of the sixties generation was to decrease the stability in long-term choice and to increase it during a single campaign. The effect of such hegemony on short-term stability and on the level of participation is much more mixed. Finally, the net effect of the socioeconomic structure of the whole population on political stability was to make both the amount of participation and long-term choices less stable, and to make choices within

The Political Impact of the Socioeconomic Environment

TABLE 13.20
Effects of Socioeconomic Factors on Stability in the Long-term Choice of Party within the Sixties Generation

Variables	Main	× Generation	Δ Structure	Hegemony	Total
Childhood class	.330**	−1.22**	.000	−.535*	−.307*
Father	−.451**	−.331**	−.005	−.106**	−.158**
Class	−.566**	−.792**	.045	−.416**	−.591**
Income	−.267**	−.416*	.067	−.099**	−.122*
Ownership	−.299**	.071**	.118*	.074	.030
Education	−.113	−1.38**	.013	−.795**	−.741**
Professional	−.428**	−.410**	.066	−.124**	−.093
Service	−.232**	−.589**	.029	−.236**	−.258**
Union	−.147*	.838*	.017	.167	.134*

* = standard error ≤ B.
** = $p \leq .05$.

TABLE 13.21
Effects of Socioeconomic Factors on Stability in the Short-term Choice of Party within the Sixties Generation

Variables	Main	× Generation	Δ Structure	Hegemony	Total
Childhood class	.320	−1.20**	.000	−.535**	−.308
Father	−.318**	−.070	−.003	−.056**	−.087*
Class	−.389**	−.103	.031	−.063	−.212**
Income	−.204**	.159*	.051	.019	.036
Ownership	−.184**	.182*	.072*	.124	.053
Education	−.094	−.044	.011	−.041	−.066
Professional	−.339**	.229**	.052	.015	.021
Service	−.066	.046	.008	.010	−.004
Union	−.135**	.161	.016	.027	.016

* = standard error ≤ B.
** = $p \leq .05$.

a single campaign more stable (the effects on short-term choices were inconsistent).

SUMMARY AND CONCLUDING REMARKS

In this chapter we have explored the relationship between the socioeconomic environment of the United States, the sixties generation, and political orientations. The results of

TABLE 13.22
Effects of Socioeconomic Factors on Stability in the Choice of Party during a Campaign within the Sixties Generation

Variables	Main	× Generation	Δ Structure	Hegemony	Total
Childhood class	.448	−.294	.000	−.114	.092
Father	.138**	.231**	.002	.088**	.085*
Class	.213	.162**	−.017	.094	.165
Income	.000	.164	.000	.040*	.032
Ownership	.083	.072	−.033	.037	.058
Education	−.096**	.264**	.011	.146**	.092
Professional	.039**	.079	−.006	.025*	.016
Service	−.003	.343**	.000	.140**	.118*
Union	−.100	.776**	.012	.163**	.132*

* = standard error ≤ B.
** = p ≤ .05.

these analyses suggest a complex pattern of interrelationships that defies a simple explanation. Yet, despite this complexity, some systematic strands run through these findings. First, the main effects of the various dimensions of socioeconomic status examined in this analysis were generally consistent both across measures and in terms of their interpretability. The measures that were inconsistent most often were childhood class, which is largely perceptual and which evaluates a past rather than present status, and union membership, which is less easily considered in status terms. Both of these "errant" measures suggest that the inconsistencies are in measurement rather than in the effects of status. In addition, except for the negative relationship with political involvement, and part of the pattern of decision making, the main effects of socioeconomic status were intuitively reasonable. They resulted in greater support for the system, an agenda that emphasized economic issues at the expense of others, stands on issues that could be termed domestically conservative and hawkish on foreign policy; decision making that focused on specific cues such as the preferences of groups, issues, the nature of the times and party; higher rates of participation; support for the party system generally

The Political Impact of the Socioeconomic Environment

and for the Republican party in particular; and independent behavior in candidate or party choice, but stability once a decision has been reached.

Second, the interaction of the sixties generation with SES reflected the status inconsistency generated by the unusual mixture of cultures that we argued was occurring within this cohort's middle class (Chapter Two). The interaction terms reflected a hybrid of class and generation that more often than not contained elements of both main effects; this was clearly the case for the selection of agendas, stands chosen on issues, political involvement, political decision making, participation, party choice, and certain aspects of stability. Occasionally, the effects of generation dominated this interaction, as with political support. In other situations (several of the stability dimensions, for example), socioeconomic status dominated. Taken together, this adds to the impression of tension between class and generation that resulted in an unusual composite of both.

Third, the changing socioeconomic structure of the sixties generation, downwardly mobile relative to the prior population, consistently worked to counteract the main effects of SES, regardless of the main effects of generation. This negation of the effects of socioeconomic status represented a different process based on economics rather than on generation. When these processes were complementary (as with political support), the effect of changing structure was to enhance the distinctive character of the sixties generation presented in previous chapters. When the processes were contradictory (as with the extent of political involvement), the changing economic structure diluted the distinctiveness of that generation. Overall, the two processes were more likely to complement than to offset each other since economic conditions were important in the initial development of the sixties generation's unique character.

Fourth, except for a slight liberalization on domestic issues, a decreased level of participation and a movement towards instability on some dimensions, the overall socioeconomic environment within which the sixties generation existed generally induced that generation to conform to the values of an advanced industrial democratic society: supportive of the system (and the party system in particular), primarily concerned about the traditional issues of economics and foreign policy, in favor of the involvement of the United States in foreign affairs, marginally interested in politics, and dependent on party cues for making political decisions. These characteristics fit remarkably well with the profile of the citizen presented in Berelson's revision of democratic theory (1952) that emphasized the importance of stability. In fact, the two clearest exceptions to this pattern of hegemony—the decrease in participation and the instability in certain aspects of participation—are generally regarded as the two areas where the current political system has failed to work as it was designed to. They are viewed as serious threats to the legitimacy and stability of that system (Burnham, 1970).

Fifth, and finally, the net effect of the socioeconomic environment on the political orientations of the whole population depends upon the relative strengths of those forces working to distinguish the sixties generation and those pulling back towards more traditional mass politics. By and large the latter forces outweigh the former, reducing the impact of the sixties generation on the larger political impacts of socioeconomic status to minor inconsistencies in otherwise consistent relationships.

What do these findings suggest about the political impact of the sixties generation in particular, and about the nature of mass-based, evolutionary political change more generally? While we address this issue in greater detail in the final chapter, a few points should be made here. The previous chapter

The Political Impact of the Socioeconomic Environment

suggested that change in mass behaviors and attitudes can arise from structural change or from unusual circumstances or events, but lasting and constructive change requires a supportive environment that will allow the replication of new orientations both within the group that first develops them and within other groups and future generations. In our analysis of political orientations throughout this book, we have found evidence of generational change, but it has been either less dramatic than anticipated (as in the case of issue stands or agendas) or destructive rather than constructive (as in the case of support, involvement, or participation). In this chapter we can begin to see why this is the case. The socioeconomic environment in which the sixties generation lived is more or less the same as that in which preceding generations had lived. It is a system that has evolved (consciously or not) to replicate the political orientations of those preceding generations, and undoubtedly, of generations before them. In addition, changes in this environment are not actively planned or structured to preserve or eliminate particular attitudes, opinions, or behaviors but, are instead passively and incrementally brought about by larger social and economic successes and failures. As a result, there is no coherent environment in which any seeds that may have been present in this new generation can be nurtured and grow. The socioeconomic environment that does exist results either in conformity, alienation, or inconsistency, none of which are particularly good bases for systematic and progressive political change.

NOTES

1. As the reader will soon see, the analyses presented in this chapter are intricate and, because of the complexity of the relationships, often difficult to interpret systematically. To prevent making the chapter even more cumbersome, we focus exclusively on the main effects of generation

and the interaction of generation with the socioeconomic environment. While the interaction of this environment with period effects, as well as the more detailed three- and even four-way interactions would no doubt provide additionally useful information, it falls beyond the scope of this study and, most probably, beyond the scope of the data being used. For the same reason, we did not explore the effects of subgeneration in this regard. The reader should note, however, that the effects of period, life cycle, and interactions are removed from the measures of political orientations used in this chapter so as not to confound the generational analysis.

2. This estimation procedure occasionally results in a measure that will range slightly above 1. As a result, and because of the limited variance in several of the measures used, the unstandardized coefficients are occasionally greater than 1.

3. While ideally these demographic variables and their interaction with generation would be included in a single regression equation, the limited number of cases in this kind of aggregate analysis and the high correlation among the measures of socioeconomic status would quickly lead to a serious identification problem. As a result, we must be content with this separate analysis and focus on overall patterns rather than on individual dimensions.

4. Several of the variables to be analyzed in the next chapter under the heading of "sociocultural environment" might be considered economic as well (certain aspects of sex, race, houseperson, or head of household for example). While we acknowledge this, we ultimately made our "cut" based on a narrower definition of economic concerns. We will consider the economic element in the next chapter where appropriate as well, however.

5. It is important to note that given the aggregate nature of this analysis, these findings should not be interpreted as demonstrating that lower SES *individuals* follow politics at a greater rate than higher SES *individuals*. Also, the exploratory nature of the analysis and the counterintuitive nature of these particular findings suggest that they *could* be a methodological artifact rather than a substantive fact.

REFERENCES

Achen, Christopher H. *Interpreting and Using Regression*. Beverly Hills: Sage Publications, 1982.

Berelson, Bernard R. "Democratic Theory and Public Opinion." *Public Opinion Quarterly,* 16 (Fall, 1952), pp. 313–330.

Burnham, Walter Dean. *Critical Elections and the Mainspring of American Politics*. New York: Norton, 1970.

Claggett, William. "Partisan Aquisition vs Party Intensity: Life Cycle, Generational and Period Effects." *American Journal of Political Science*, 25 (1981), pp. 193–214.

CHAPTER 14

The Political Impact of the Sociocultural Environment

We have examined the relationship between the socioeconomic environment and changing political orientations within the sixties generation, and found that socioeconomic status seems antithetical to the profile of the sixties generation developed over the previous eight chapters. Higher status members of the sixties generation displayed political orientations that combined the effects of both these socializing agents, often inconsistently. In addition, the overall socioeconomic environment, which was unchanged in any constructive, systematic way with the entrance of the sixties generation, caused that generation to adopt the political attitudes, opinions, and behaviors of the more-stable (from the viewpoint of the existing political system) norm. As a result of this tension, the most identifiable impact of the sixties generation on the relationship between mass politics and socioeconomic status was to make it more inconsistent and unpredictable.

In this chapter we build upon the analyses of the past two chapters, looking now at the sociocultural environment in which the sixties generation was maturing politically. The analysis in Chapter Twelve uncovered evidence both of stability and of change in sociocultural situations, roles, and institutions, resulting from the effects both of period and generation. Using the same summary measures developed in the last chapter (as well as the same method of analysis and form of presentation), the connection between this environment and the political orientations of the sixties generation is the subject of this chapter.

THE SOCIOCULTURAL ENVIRONMENT, POLITICAL ORIENTATIONS, AND THE SIXTIES GENERATION

The results of the analysis for the level of political support are presented in Table 14.1. Again, "Main" refers to the main effect of the demographic variable in question and measures the general effect of that variable on the level of political support. "X Generation" refers to the interaction effect of being a member of the sixties generation and having the social characteristic in question, therefore measuring the unique reaction of certain segments of the sixties generation. The "Δ Structure" column measures the change in political orientations due to the different situations in which members of the sixties generation found themselves relative to previous generations (and documented in Chapter Twelve). "Hegemony" estimates the effect of the social structure in question on the development of unique political orientations within the sixties generation. Finally, "Total" measures the overall or net effect of the sociocultural environment on the political orientations of the population as a whole.

The main effects of the various dimensions of the sociocultural environment on the level of support for the political system are more difficult to interpret than the SES measures discussed in the previous chapter. This is hardly surprising

The Political Impact of the Sociocultural Environment

since we are not examining a single dimension in this case, as we were with economic status. Males, married persons, heads of households, and residents of the South and West were somewhat more supportive of the political system than the norm, while all the remaining characteristics are, to varying degrees, associated with less support for the system. Although these relationships do not suggest a readily discernible pattern, there is some indication that roles or institutions that could be considered "dominant" (males, those employed outside the home, heads of households) were more supportive of the system, while "subordinate" ones (women, housepersons, dependents, students) were less supportive. Only race does not fit this characterization: whites demonstrated less support than blacks (again, recall that period effects have been removed). "Traditional" roles and institutions such as those revolving around the family structure or religion surprisingly produced a generally nonsupportive attitude towards the political system.

The interaction of generation and culture was most notable in that, with the exception of living in the South, it is essentially the mirror image of the main effects—roles that led to support by the population as a whole were less likely to do so by the sixties generation, and vice versa. As a result, within the sixties generation, it was the more subordinate cohorts that were more supportive, indicating a possible reaction to the greater visibility of subcultural norms during this generation's socialization and development. It is interesting to note that this reversal also led to slightly greater support for the system among those involved with most traditional institutions (parents, housepersons, churchgoers), although being married does not conform to this characterization.

The changing sociocultural norms of the sixties generation were as likely to lead to decreased as to increased support,

TABLE 14.1
Effects of Sociocultural Factors on Political Support within the Sixties Generation

Variables	Main	× Generation	Δ Structure	Hegemony	Total
Sex	.030	−.152	.000	−.019	−.024
Race	−.197**	.000	.008	.011**	−.155**
Head	.289**	−.243**	−.057	.054	.142**
Dependent	−.329**	.279**	−.043	.005	−.044
Student	−.890**	.432**	−.077	.000	−.088
Houseperson	−.181**	.162**	−.027	.055**	−.032
Marital status	.045*	−.019	−.011	−.017	.015
Children	−.032**	.044*	.017	.023*	.022*
Attendance	−.091**	.030	.012	.028	−.021
Northeast	−.069	−.068	.005	−.009	−.021
Midwest	−.070	.109	.001	.004	−.005
South	.084*	.111	.007	.042	.069
West	.113	−.089	.003	−.004	.009

* = standard error ≤ B.
** = $p \leq .05$.

though the extent of either is relatively small. Changes in the dominant or subordinate roles of the generation led generally to weakened support (due largely to the growth in the number of subordinate roles among this generation as documented in Chapter 12). Movements relative to the more-traditional institutions are less uniform in their impact because of the inconsistency of the main effects and the inconsistency of the generation's changing relationships with such institutions. Finally, regional shifts away from the Northeast and Midwest and to the South and West resulted in very small but consistent increases in support, due, we assume, to differences in regional cultures.

Perhaps most interesting of all, and despite the complex and seemingly disparate effects shown by different elements of culture and across the main, interaction, and structural change measures, the two summary measures revealed more internally uniform effects. Within the sixties generation, co-

The Political Impact of the Sociocultural Environment

horts within each particular sociocultural institution were twice as likely to be supportive of the system as not, indicating social pressure to conform akin to that due to socioeconomic status. Despite this, the more negative effects of the three prior measures (main, interaction and Δ structure) are strong enough overall to render the net impact of the culture on the level of political support in the population mixed, but with a slightly negative bias.

Tables 14.2 to 14.5 present the relationships among culture, generation, and agenda selection. On balance, cohorts in "dominant" positions were more likely to emphasize the economic agenda at the expense of both the sixties and the social-welfare agendas. The foreign agenda does not show a consistent relationship with this "dimension." The traditional institutions or roles of marriage, family, houseperson, and church again show relatively untraditional main effects, leading frequently to a focus on the sixties and the social-welfare agendas and away from the economic agenda (the foreign-policy agenda is again inconsistently related to these characteristics). Finally, the regional measures suggest that residents of the Northeast were more likely to emphasize foreign-policy agendas, those in the Midwest, social welfare, those in the South, economic and social welfare, and those in the West, the sixties agenda.

The interaction of generation and socioculture, where such relationships exist, partly reinforced or paralleled that of the main effects, with dominant groups concerned with economic issues, much less concerned with social welfare and issues of the sixties, and having mixed views on foreign policy. The interaction of generation and culture in terms of the traditional institutions was less consistent, however. Housepersons selected relatively nontraditional agendas, while married persons, parents, and church goers demonstrated mixed agendas. Finally, interactions of region and generation

TABLE 14.2
Effects of Sociocultural Factors on Selection of a
Sixties Agenda within the Sixties Generation

Variables	Main	× Generation	Δ Structure	Hegemony	Total
Sex	−.397	.690	.000	.303	.089
Race	−.988**	−.757*	.040	−.628*	−.989*
Head	−.073	.000	.015	.011	−.048
Dependent	−1.70**	1.58**	−.611	.027	−.623
Student	.277	.000	.024	.021	.040
Houseperson	.509*	.676*	.077	.155*	.314
Marital status	.393	−.361	−.098	−.344	−.026
Children	−.177**	.059	.093	.153**	.108
Attendance	.039	.945**	−.005	.633*	.507*
Northeast	−.638*	.958**	.047	.362**	.154
Midwest	−.145	−.989**	.003	−.825**	−.538
South	−.229	.601	−.018	.027	.002
West	.985**	−.971**	.026	−.184*	.006

* = standard error ≤ B.
** = p ≤ .05.

TABLE 14.3
Effects of Sociocultural Factors on Selection of an
Economic Agenda within the Sixties Generation

Variables	Main	× Generation	Δ Structure	Hegemony	Total
Sex	.069	.634**	.000	.216*	.242*
Race	.477**	1.11**	−.019	.822**	1.15**
Head	.104**	.000	−.021	−.068**	.046
Dependent	−1.25**	1.23**	−.293	−.043**	−.364
Student	−.191*	.000	−.016	.069**	.009
Houseperson	−.465**	−.372**	−.070	−.108**	−.265**
Marital status	−.061	.078	.015	.013	−.006
Children	.043	.298*	−.023	−.028	.019
Attendance	−.642**	−.449**	.082	−.233**	−.433**
Northeast	−.044	−.390	.003	−.145*	−.108
Midwest	−.123	.698**	.002	.162*	.128
South	.164	.048	.013	−.021	.065
West	−.220	.407	−.006	−.009	−.012

* = standard error ≤ B.
** = p ≤ .05.

TABLE 14.4
Effects of Sociocultural Factors on Selection of a
Social Welfare Agenda within the Sixties Generation

Variables	Main	× Generation	Δ Structure	Hegemony	Total
Sex	−.103	−.435*	.000	−.204*	−.215*
Race	−.345**	−.119	.014	−.114	−.373**
Head	.096*	.000	−.019	−.027*	.058
Dependent	1.44*	−1.58**	.187	−.042**	.168
Student	−.238*	.000	−.020	−.031*	−.039
Houseperson	.103	.249*	.016	.029	.077
Marital status	−.010	.121	.003	.078	.070
Children	.136**	−.050	−.070*	−.033*	−.046*
Attendance	.476**	−.256	−.119	−.194*	.009
Northeast	−.171	.624**	.013	.124**	.089
Midwest	.291	−.429	−.005	−.154	−.038
South	.077	−1.30**	.006	−.441**	−.342**
West	−.298	1.03**	−.008	.115**	.068

* = standard error ≤ B.
** = p ≤ .05.

TABLE 14.5
Effects of Sociocultural Factors on Selection of a
Foreign Agenda within the Sixties Generation

Variables	Main	× Generation	Δ Structure	Hegemony	Total
Sex	.552**	−.872*	.000	−.349*	−.075
Race	.338*	−.665*	−.016	−.493	−.145
Head	−.044	.000	.009	.034*	−.017
Dependent	1.25**	−1.15**	.943*	−.013	.970*
Student	−.049	.000	−.004	.026	.006
Houseperson	.103	−.207	.016	−.011	.017
Marital status	−.401*	.361	.100	.378	.036
Children	−.054*	.125	.028	.069*	.057
Attendance	.599**	−.391	−.077	−.229	.075
Northeast	.899**	−1.39**	−.067	−.285**	−.123
Midwest	−.169	1.29**	.003	.655**	.506*
South	−.151	1.23**	.012	.431**	.322
West	−1.68**	−.533	−.043	−.098	−.319

* = standard error ≤ B.
** = p ≤ .05.

Situations and Structures

mirrored the main effects, indicating sizable generational differences within regional cultures concerning political agendas.

The changing sociocultural structure of the sixties generation also had an impact on that generation's political agenda. In terms of dominance or subordination, changes have resulted in greater emphasis on the sixties and (less consistently) social-welfare agendas, less emphasis on economic issues, and mixed emphasis on foreign policy. Changes in the prevalence of traditional roles and institutions also showed mixed effects. Only church attendance showed effects that consistently related to the main pattern demonstrated by the sixties generation (with reductions in church attendance weakening this generation's emphasis on the sixties and social-welfare agendas and increasing its emphasis on economic matters). Finally, the regional mobility of the sixties generation did not consistently relate to the generation's main profile, further obscuring its distinctiveness.

When we turn to the effects of the culture's hegemony, we found, compared to our previous findings, an unusual pattern. The dominant and the subordinate measures indicated support for the sixties agenda (a non-mainstream agenda). In addition, interest in the economic agenda was inconsistently related to these measures, contrary to the usual emphasis on this kind of traditional issue. The impact of the sociocultural environment on the social-welfare agenda conformed to the hegemony argument, however, as did (to a lesser extent) the impact on the foreign-policy agenda.

The hegemony thesis also does not apply to the traditional institutions: the overall impact on members of the sixties generation increased their emphasis on the sixties agenda, decreased emphasis on the economic agenda, and divided them over issues of social welfare and foreign policy. Finally, the overall effect of regional cultures on the agendas that mem-

The Political Impact of the Sociocultural Environment

bers of the sixties generation selected was mixed, being as likely to encourage non-mainstream as mainstream agendas. In short, there is no evidence of sociocultural pressure upon the sixties generation to behave according to the norm in the case of agenda building.

What, then, is the net impact of the sociocultural environment on the agenda-building process? For the dominant and subordinate dimension of culture, the effect is, at best, to disturb the pattern established prior to the sixties generation's entrance into the electorate: attention to issues associated with the sixties or to foreign policy are less consistently associated with this dimension than are the simple main effects. On the other hand, this dimension clearly distinguished the dominant and the subordinate in their emphasis on the economy and social welfare. Again, there was little evidence of systematic change that is consistent with the profile of the sixties generation developed in Chapter Five and that has continued to have a measurable impact on the overall relationship between culture and politics.

We now turn from general agendas to specific stands on issues (Tables 14.6 and 14.7). A clear relationship existed between the dominant or subordinate aspects of the culture and stands on domestic issues, with dominant groups taking conservative stands on these issues and subordinate groups taking liberal ones. This relationship prevailed in the area of foreign policy as well, though less clearly. The measures of traditional institutions were not as consistent overall. Being married and having children resulted in a conservative outlook in both issue areas, and being a houseperson or churchgoer resulted in a liberal outlook. Finally, (and surprisingly) the cultures of the South and the West produced liberal main effects on domestic issues, as well as a desire for less intervention in foreign affairs.[1]

The interaction of generation and socioculture disturbs the

TABLE 14.6
Effects of Sociocultural Factors on Domestic-issue Stands within the Sixties Generation

Variables	Main	× Generation	Δ Structure	Hegemony	Total
Sex	−.028	−.136	.000	−.060	−.064
Race	−.372**	−.044	.015	−.028	−.330**
Head	−.590**	.599**	−.120	.574**	−.190
Dependent	.387 *	−.394*	.050	−.008	.048
Student	.047	−.070	.004	−.004	.002
Houseperson	.036	.003	.005	−.003	.013
Marital status	−.217	.234*	−.055	.219*	−.070
Children	−.029**	.043	.015	.012	.016
Attendance	.175**	−.011	−.022	−.025	.064
Northeast	−.268**	.536**	.020	.123**	.065
Midwest	−.088	.580**	.002	.178**	.131*
South	.184**	−.843**	.015	−.274**	−.161**
West	.234*	−.530**	.006	−.069*	−.035

* = standard error ≤ B.
** = $p \le .05$.

TABLE 14.7
Effects of Sociocultural Factors on Foreign-issue Stands within the Sixties Generation

Variables	Main	× Generation	Δ Structure	Hegemony	Total
Sex	.039	1.10**	.000	.460*	.423*
Race	.847**	1.58**	−.034	1.18**	.782**
Head	.317	−.551*	−.064	−.385	−.146
Dependent	.002	.329	.000	.027	.026
Student	.694	−.452	.060	.005	.068
Houseperson	−.202	−.189	−.031	−.030	−.111
Marital status	.055	−.206	−.014	−.175	−.122
Children	.054 *	−.021	−.028	−.003	−.014
Attendance	−.776**	−1.02**	.099	−.451**	−.766**
Northeast	.172	−.827*	−.013	−.197*	−.141
Midwest	.073	1.03*	−.001	.306	.297
South	−.110	1.45**	−.009	.465**	.360*
West	−.215	−1.00*	−.006	−.161*	−.162

* = standard error ≤ B.
** = $p \le .05$.

relationship between dominance or subordination and issue stands, but not consistently. Males and whites in this generation were even more conservative. Housepersons were slightly more liberal. Heads of households were more liberal. Both dependents and students were more conservative. The fact that dependents and students were generally liberal, but less so within the sixties generation suggests that it was the increased numbers within these categories in the sixties rather than an increased liberalism among students and young people of the sixties generation that was behind the student and youth movements. This interpretation is supported by the findings concerning changes in the sociocultural structure of the generation. With the exception of the relationship between church attendance and stands on domestic issues, the interaction of traditional institutions and generation indicated a consistent liberalization concerning both domestic and foreign matters. Finally, it is members of the sixties generation from the Northeast and Midwest who were the most liberal on domestic issue stands, and those from the Northeast and West were most likely to oppose government intervention in foreign affairs.

The changing structure of the sociocultural environment of the sixties generation consistently augmented its support of liberal domestic policies and its concern over the involvement of the United States abroad. This is especially true for changes in the subordinate and dominant measures and for the regional shifts. Nevertheless, the measure of cultural hegemony indicates a conservative effect on the choice of both domestic and foreign issues for most of the measures of subordination and domination. However, this sociocultural pressure was not evident for regional measures, which showed a mixed effect, or for the traditional institutions, which showed a decidedly liberal influence on issues.

Finally, the net effect of the sociocultural environment on

TABLE 14.8
Effects of Sociocultural Factors on the Level of
Political Involvement within the Sixties Generation

Variables	Main	× Generation	Δ Structure	Hegemony	Total
Sex	.126*	−.260*	.000	−.096	−.036
Race	−.274**	−.074	.011	−.043	−.268**
Head	−.035	.154	.007	.154	.100
Dependent	−.208	.062	−.027	.002	−.033
Student	−.210**	.000	−.018	.004	−.022
Houseperson	−.176**	.297**	.027	.089**	.051
Marital status	−.079	.164	.020	.157	.075
Children	−.054**	.105**	.028*	.049**	.045**
Attendance	.273**	−.068	−.035	−.044	−.085*
Northeast	−.264**	.453**	.020	.119**	.056
Midwest	−.115	.265	.002	.101*	.045
South	.293**	−.776**	.023	−.241**	−.093
West	−.022	.100	−.001	.030	.015

* = standard error ≤ B.
** = $p \le .05$.

issue stands is to reinforce the existent pattern for the main effects of the dominant or subordinate roles, to lead to a more consistently liberal association with the traditional institutions, and to add to the already mixed effects of region.

Whether one considers the dominant or subordinate dimension, the traditional dimension, or regional culture, the general impact of the main effects of the sociocultural environment on the level of political involvement is to decrease it (Table 14.8). In contrast, the interaction of generation and culture is only slightly less consistent in its positive association with involvement (column two), again cutting across the specific dimensions underlying the sociocultural environment. This increased involvement was supplemented by the effects of the changing structure of the sixties generation's cultural environment, which also led to greater political involvement. Even the hegemonic nature of the cultural environment was consistent in this regard, further strengthening this tendency towards involvement within the sixties generation.

The Political Impact of the Sociocultural Environment

For the first time since beginning the examination of the structural environment, we encountered a situation in which all three generational measures were working consistently in a single direction: in this case towards increasing the generation's level of political involvement. The result of this uniform impact is evident in the total effect of the relationship between the sociocultural environment and involvement. Eight of the 13 measures of the environment indicated an increased association with involvement resulting from the entry of the sixties generation into the electorate (this despite the negative main effect of generation found in Chapter Seven).

The relationships among the sociocultural environment, generation, and political decision making are presented in Tables 14.9 to 14.12. Cohorts in positions of cultural dominance were more likely to use ideological and party-based cues, slightly less likely to use cue-specific approaches, and consistently less likely to use nonpolitical cues. The effects of traditional institutions and of regional cultures are much less consistent. The political decision-making process is not systematically related to these dimensions.

The interaction of generation and culture for the dominant and subordinate measures reversed the results found in the main effects. Dominant members of the sixties generation were less likely to depend on ideological or party cues and more likely to focus on cue-specific or nonpolitical approaches. The interaction of generation and traditional institutions, like the main effects, produced less consistent results, although there is some movement away from cue-specific approaches and towards party-based decision making. Regional interactions, while often sizable, again were not very informative concerning the more general patterns of decision making within the sixties generation.

The changing structure of the sociocultural environment of the sixties generation did not significantly affect its deci-

Situations and Strucures

TABLE 14.9
Effects of Sociocultural Factors on Ideological Decision Making within the Sixties Generation

Variables	Main	× Generation	Δ Structure	Hegemony	Total
Sex	.029**	−.012	.000	−.010*	.006
Race	−.049**	−.040**	.002	−.036**	−.070**
Head	.020*	−.010	−.004	−.014	.005
Dependent	−.003	−.010	.000	−.005**	−.003
Student	−.261**	.239**	−.022	−.005**	−.025
Houseperson	−.016**	.041**	−.002	.007**	.001
Marital status	.012**	−.002	−.003	−.007	.004
Children	−.003**	.013**	.002**	−.002*	.002**
Attendance	.042**	−.006	−.005	−.011*	.013*
Northeast	.014	.042**	−.001	.005	.008
Midwest	−.020*	.018	.000	.002	−.003
South	−.005	−.030	.000	−.014*	−.012*
West	.049**	−.140**	.001	−.021**	−.011

* = standard error ≤ B.
** = $p \le .05$.

TABLE 14.10
Effects of Sociocultural Factors on Cue-specific Decision Making within the Sixties Generation

Variables	Main	× Generation	Δ Structure	Hegemony	Total
Sex	.009	.360**	.000	.115**	.121**
Race	−.187**	.225**	.007	.159**	.000
Head	.184**	−.192**	−.037	−.222**	−.090*
Dependent	−.141*	.168*	−.018	−.034**	−.032
Student	−.466	.452	−.040	−.040**	−.058
Houseperson	−.120**	.000	−.018	−.030**	−.060**
Marital status	.085**	−.104**	−.021	−.132**	−.039*
Children	−.016**	−.017	.008	−.035**	−.015**
Attendance	−.004	−.279**	.001	−.182**	−.143**
Northeast	−.038	−.061	.003	−.052**	−.034
Midwest	−.175**	.534**	.003	.133**	.078*
South	.078*	.109	.006	−.003	.046
West	.214**	−.602**	.006	−.115**	−.054

* = standard error ≤ B.
** = $p \le .05$.

The Political Impact of the Sociocultural Environment

TABLE 14.11
Effects of Sociocultural Factors on Party-based Decision Making within the Sixties Generation

Variables	Main	× Generation	Δ Structure	Hegemony	Total
Sex	.009	−.124**	.000	−.050**	−.041**
Race	.016	−.028	−.001	−.021	−.007
Head	.063**	−.046*	−.013	−.042*	.010
Dependent	−.055*	.027	−.007	.002	−.008
Student	−.314*	.297*	−.027	.004*	−.026
Houseperson	−.007	.042**	−.001	.014**	.007
Marital status	.011	−.001	−.003	.002	.007
Children	−.004**	.004	.002	.005*	.003
Attendance	.004	.004	−.001	.006	.005
Northeast	.022	.049*	−.002	.015*	.014
Midwest	.021	−.180**	.000	−.053**	−.041*
South	−.015	−.110**	−.001	−.032**	−.032*
West	−.046	.211**	−.001	.032**	.020

* = standard error ≤ B.
** = p ≤ .05.

TABLE 14.12
Effects of Sociocultural Factors on Nonpolitical Decision Making within the Sixties Generation

Variables	Main	× Generation	Δ Structure	Hegemony	Total
Sex	−.056*	−.136*	.000	−.069*	−.080*
Race	.086**	−.120*	−.003	−.115*	−.024
Head	−.157**	.127**	.032	.114**	−.016
Dependent	.234**	−.210**	.030	−.011**	.027
Student	1.19**	−1.10**	.102	−.006*	.102
Houseperson	.046*	−.003	.007	−.014	.012
Marital status	−.024	.138	.006	−.004	.030
Children	.046**	−.058**	−.024*	−.037**	−.032*
Attendance	−.048	.266**	.006	.132**	.096*
Northeast	.020	−.052	−.001	−.021	−.011
Midwest	.070*	−.264**	.001	−.094**	−.054
South	−.054*	.004	−.004	−.009	−.025
West	−.016	.366**	.000	.041**	.038

* = standard error ≤ B.
** = p ≤ .05.

sion making, nor could the effects that were produced be interpreted according to dominance, tradition, or region. There was, however, a slight tendency away from ideological and party-based decision making and towards nonpolitical cues as a result of this changing structure.

The effects of cultural hegemony are evident for political decision making, in that cue-specific, ideological, and nonpolitical approaches are all reduced by the overall sociocultural structure of the sixties generation, while the use of party-based cues increased in importance. Finally, the net impact of the relationship between socioculture and decision making generally was to reinforce the main effects found for ideological and cue-specific approaches and to unsystematically disturb the main effects for party-based and nonpolitical decision making.

The main effects of the dominant and subordinate measures of culture consistently indicate that dominant groups participated in politics more than subordinate ones did (Table 14.13). In addition, traditional institutions also tended to increase the rate of participation. Finally, participation was increased by the culture of the Northeast and slightly by the Midwest, while it was decreased in the South and West. These main effects are, for the most part, reversed by the interaction of generation and culture, however, and this holds true across all three dimensions of the sociocultural environment. The very characteristics associated with greater participation in the population as a whole are usually associated with decreased participation in the sixties generation. In addition, the changing structure of the sociocultural environment decreased the level of participation across the board for this generation.

The overall impact of the sociocultural structure of the sixties generation also demonstrated a general pattern of reduced participation rates, indicating that the hegemonic

TABLE 14.13
Effects of Sociocultural Factors on the Level of
Political Participation within the Sixties Generation

Variables	Main	× Generation	Δ Structure	Hegemony	Total
Sex	.126**	−.113	.000	−.059*	.008
Race	.006	.118	.000	.091	.088*
Head	.234**	−.197**	−.048	−.200**	.007
Dependent	−.037	.003	−.005	−.012**	−.012
Student	−1.72**	1.63**	−.148	−.011*	−.155
Houseperson	−.168**	.170**	.025	.042**	.018
Marital status	.029	−.004	−.007	−.015	.011
Children	.011	.039*	−.006	.007	.006
Attendance	.085**	−.213**	−.011	−.125**	−.065*
Northeast	.162**	−.008	−.012	−.012	.019
Midwest	.008	−.017	.000	−.014	−.006
South	−.044	−.147*	−.004	−.022	−.040
West	−.244**	.188	−.006	.008	−.020

* = standard error ≤ B.
** = p ≤ .05.

culture failed to maintain this element of the political system at an acceptable level (a pattern similar to that found with the socioeconomic environment, in Chapter Thirteen). The net effect of these generational and cultural forces, however, was again to reinforce the main effects of all three dimensions of the sociocultural environment.

The effects of generation and culture on party support and partisan choice are presented in Tables 14.14 to 14.16. The dominant and subordinate dimensions indicate an inconsistent tendency for subordinate groups to be more supportive of the system than dominant ones, but nothing from this dimension can be applied to predict their short- or long-term support of a particular party. Adherence to traditional institutions was associated with decreased support for the party system, and except for church attendance, increased support for the Republican party. Finally, residence in the South resulted in slightly less support for the party system, and living

TABLE 14.14
Effects of Sociocultural Factors on Diffuse Party Support within the Sixties Generation

Variables	Main	× Generation	Δ Structure	Hegemony	Total
Sex	.014	−.033	.000	−.015	−.007
Race	−.003	−.165*	.000	−.143*	−.007
Head	−.046	.040	.009	.038	−.002
Dependent	.073	−.061	.009	.000	.026
Student	1.24**	−1.23**	.107	.002	.108
Houseperson	−.041*	−.002	−.006	.003	−.015
Marital status	−.002	−.010	.001	−.008	.000
Children	−.011	−.005	.006	−.003	−.008
Attendance	−.024	−.024	.003	−.010	−.020
Northeast	.058	−.164**	−.004	−.037*	−.023
Midwest	.042	.114	−.001	.033	.043
South	−.069*	.311**	−.006	.102*	.059**
West	.043	−.391**	.001	−.052**	−.040

* = standard error ≤ B.
** = p ≤ .05.

in the South and West produced the greatest long-term and short-term support for the Democratic party.

The interaction of generation and culture reduced the level of diffuse party support for all the measures of the dominant and subordinate dimension (except heads of household) and for all measures of traditional institutions. Regional interactions were split, with members of the sixties generation from the Northeast and West less supportive, but those from the Midwest and South more supportive of political institutions. The interactions for both short- and long-term party choice were almost completely the reverse of the main effects. They indicated a leaning towards the Democratic party across most of the cultural roles for members of the sixties generation (the exceptions were males, whites, and residents of the South or West).

The changing socioculture of the sixties generation generally had a small impact on the level and direction of party

The Political Impact of the Sociocultural Environment

TABLE 14.15
Effects of Sociocultural Factors on Short-term Party Choice within the Sixties Generation

Variables	Main	× Generation	Δ Structure	Hegemony	Total
Sex	.306**	−.975**	.000	−.452**	−.246*
Race	−.716**	−.647**	.029	−.534**	−.977**
Head	−.153	.000	.031	−.020	−.120
Dependent	.349	−.228	.045	−.022	.042
Student	−1.72*	1.42*	−.234	−.036*	−.282
Houseperson	−.158*	.351*	−.024	−.075*	−.062
Marital status	−.027	.274	.007	.224	.174*
Children	−.034	.048	.018	−.013	.007
Attendance	.802**	.168	−.103	−.001	.388**
Northeast	−.354**	.593**	.026	.120*	.056
Midwest	−.362**	1.34**	.007	.723**	.526**
South	.358**	−1.29**	.029	−.445**	−.226*
West	.396*	−.872*	.010	−.118**	−.046

* = standard error ≤ B.
** = p ≤ .05.

TABLE 14.16
Effects of Sociocultural Factors on Long-term Party Choice within the Sixties Generation

Variables	Main	× Generation	Δ Structure	Hegemony	Total
Sex	.069	−.180	.000	−.078	−.038
Race	−.211**	−.511**	.008	−.426**	−.545**
Head	−.002	.000	.000	.001	−.001
Dependent	−.043	.202	−.006	.007	.004
Student	−1.21**	.84**	−.190	−.003	−.201
Houseperson	−.093**	.137*	−.014	.039*	−.007
Marital status	−.026	.113	.007	.102*	.067*
Children	−.030**	.043	.016	.012	.017
Attendance	.220**	.138*	−.028	.051	.139**
Northeast	−.018	.316**	.001	.075*	.061
Midwest	−.309**	1.21**	.006	.389**	.241**
South	.154**	−.562**	.012	−.180**	−.094*
West	.136	−.717**	.004	−.088**	−.061

* = standard error ≤ B.
** = p ≤ .05.

support. Where effects existed, they increased diffuse support across most measures of dominance, subordination, and tradition, but decreased support related to regional distinctions. Both short- and long-term support for the Democratic party also was increased by these changing cultural patterns, although this generalization did not hold for changes in housepersons, students, church attendance, and (for short-term choice only) dependents.

The overall impact of the sociocultural structure on the levels of party choice and support (hegemony) was quite mixed. It was as likely to increase as decrease diffuse support, fairly consistently resulted in a trend towards the Republicans in short-term choices, and was erratic in its effect on long-term choices (with a slight Democratic bias). These inconsistencies were present in dominant and subordinate roles, traditional roles, and regional cultures. The total impact, when these separate effects are combined, is generally to reinforce the main effects on diffuse party support and in so doing to decrease the level of such support within most of the roles examined. The net impact on long- and short-term party choice was as likely to counteract as to reinforce the main effects, however, and as likely to lead to increased Republican as Democratic support. The exceptions to this were the regional measures, where the net effects worked in opposition to the main effect, decreasing Democratic support in the South and West and increasing it in the Northeast and Midwest.

The final set of political orientations examined are the stability measures (Tables 14.17 to 14.20). Dominant groups appear to be more stable in the amount of their participation but less stable in both long- and short-term party choices (stability during a campaign is inconsistent). Beyond this, the various dimensions of the sociocultural environment seemed as likely to increase as to decrease the stability across all types

The Political Impact of the Sociocultural Environment

of behavior and across the regional and the traditional measures.

Consideration of the interaction of generation and culture does little to clarify the picture. There was some tendency for the sixties generation to react to the sociocultural environment in the opposite way of previous generations concerning stability of both their short-term and campaign choice, but, beyond this, the interactions showed no systematic or easily interpretable pattern. However, the changing structure of the sociocultural environment of the sixties generation did appear to increase both its long- and short-term choice stability consistently within most situations and structures and to decrease stability in the amount of participation.

The overall structure of the sixties generation's cultural environment consistently led to decreased stability in the amount of participation and in both long- and short-term party choice. Finally, the net impact of the sociocultural environment reflects the erratic effects of the specific factors, demonstrating contradictory patterns across measures of stability as well as across dimensions of culture.

SUMMARY, DISCUSSION, AND CONCLUDING REMARKS

In this chapter we have explored the relationships among the sixties generation, political orientations, and several components of the sociocultural environment. The results of this analysis have demonstrated an often bewildering array of interrelationships and patterns. While discussing aspects of this environment in terms of general dimensions such as dominant, subordinate, traditional, and regional cultures has, in some instances, helped to clarify some of the forces at work in shaping the political orientations of the sixties generation, the only consistent conclusion that can be made is that the effects are inconsistent. Yet despite this (and in

TABLE 14.17
Effects of Sociocultural Factors on Stability in the Amount of Political Participation within the Sixties Generation

Variables	Main	× Generation	Δ Structure	Hegemony	Total
Sex	.327**	−.644**	.000	−.295**	−.107
Race	−.020	−.193	.001	−.171	−.233*
Head	.463**	.000	−.094	−.008	.078
Dependent	−.133	−.084	−.017	−.014	−.033
Student	−.995**	.707**	−.086	−.022*	−.103
Houseperson	−.222**	.297**	−.034	.077*	−.027
Marital status	.071*	.105	−.018	.084	.117**
Children	.011	.113*	−.006	.038	.029*
Attendance	.460**	−.311**	−.059	−.214**	.039
Northeast	.493**	.014	−.036	−.010	.073
Midwest	−.021	.070	.000	.014	.009
South	−.194**	−.277	−.016	−.103*	−.164*
West	−.494**	.112	−.011	−.004	−.056

* = standard error ≤ B.
** = p ≤ .05.

TABLE 14.18
Effects of Sociocultural Factors on Stability in the Long-term Choice of Party within the Sixties Generation

Variables	Main	× Generation	Δ Structure	Hegemony	Total
Sex	.110	−1.11*	.000	−.498**	−.376**
Race	−.301**	−1.10**	.012	−.895**	−.989**
Head	−.515**	.000	.118	−.004	−.361**
Dependent	.612**	−.527	.080	−.013	.081
Student	1.07*	−1.83**	.169	−.028	.110
Houseperson	.215**	.587**	.032	.157*	.207**
Marital status	−.050	.558*	.013	.496*	.376**
Children	−.012	−.079	.006	−.085*	−.046*
Attendance	.385**	.950**	−.049	.480**	.591**
Northeast	−.341**	.565**	.025	.131*	.060
Midwest	−.066	1.90**	.005	.586**	.499**
South	.287**	−1.18**	.023	−.391**	−.217**
West	−.124	−.268	−.003	−.03	−.050

* = standard error ≤ B.
** = p ≤ .05.

TABLE 14.19
Effects of Sociocultural Factors on Stability in the Short-term Choice of Party within the Sixties Generation

Variables	Main	× Generation	Δ Structure	Hegemony	Total
Sex	.077	−.143*	.000	−.066	−.022
Race	−.327**	−.170	.013	−.134	−.386**
Head	−.232**	.262**	.047	.244**	.037
Dependent	.261*	−.260*	.034	−.008	−.056
Student	−.705	.591	−.061	−.009	−.068
Houseperson	.053	−.013*	.008	−.010	.015
Marital status	−.050	.077	.013	.041	.013
Children	−.015	.047	.008	.020*	.020
Attendance	.379**	−.248**	−.049	−.170**	.036
Northeast	−.051	.135	.004	.028	.018
Midwest	−.074	.854**	.001	.265**	.210*
South	.071	−.290*	.006	−.099*	−.054
West	.045	−.720**	.001	−.096**	−.079

* = standard error ≤ B.
** = p ≤ .05.

TABLE 14.20
Effects of Sociocultural Factors on Stability in the Choice of Party during a Campaign within the Sixties Generation

Variables	Main	× Generation	Δ Structure	Hegemony	Total
Sex	−.048	1.04**	.000	.455**	.371**
Race	.104	.826**	−.004	.707**	.696**
Head	.050	−.122	−.010	−.102	−.054
Dependent	−.111	.238	.014	.023**	.029
Student	1.38**	−1.35**	.119	.006	.123
Houseperson	.031	−.267**	.005	−.054*	−.036
Marital status	.005	−.059	−.001	−.039	−.034
Children	−.001	.083**	.001	.057**	.037*
Attendance	−.170**	−.669**	.022	−.314**	−.361**
Northeast	.027	−.187	−.002	−.035	−.029
Midwest	.055	.426*	−.001	.138*	.135
South	.038	.073	.003	.031	.039
West	−.376*	.092	−.010	.005	−.047

* = standard error ≤ B.
** = p ≤ .05.

some cases because of this), there are still some generalizations that can be drawn from this analysis.

First and foremost, the heterogeneity of the sociocultural environment, especially when compared to the socioeconomic environment, is reflected in the heterogeneous impact it had on political orientations. Unlike the more-structured, class-based nature of the economic system, the culture of the United States is less easily categorized into mutually exclusive divisions. The socializing effects of race, sex, religion, region, the family structure, etc., because such characteristics and institutions exist or develop with some degree of autonomy, are less likely to have a uniform impact. In addition, cultural institutions are often more permeable than those based on class, allowing a greater variety of combinations to exist in a society. Finally, cultural institutions are often more likely to undergo change than economic institutions, decreasing further the likelihood of consistent, reinforced socialization. This diversity, in turn, is reflected in the relatively chaotic impact the sociocultural environment has on political orientations: It is not that effects do not exist but that they often pull in contrary directions.

A second generalization, which in many ways is a corollary of the first, is that within specific aspects of the sociocultural environment are some identifiable and interpretable political impacts. Males, for example, present a very consistent pattern: they generally support the system; they are more likely to focus on the traditional agendas of the economy and foreign policy; they are more conservative on both domestic- and foreign-policy issues; they are more involved politically; they are more likely to use ideological cues and less likely to use nonpolitical ones; they are more likely to participate; they are more likely to support the party system generally; and they are more likely to be stable in their party support. Students are less supportive of the system, more likely to focus on the sixties agenda, more liberal on domestic issues, less involved in politics and more likely to make decisions based on nonpolitical cues, and they are less likely to participate. Church goers are more suspicious of the political system, less interested in the economic agenda, more supportive of government involvement in solving domestic problems and less supportive of government involvement abroad. They are also more likely to use political cues in decision making, more likely to participate, less supportive of the party system, and more likely to support the Democratic party and more likely to be stable in that support. Not every political orientation fits consistently with the rest, and not every measure of culture is equally consistent in its characterization, but, given the generally low level of constraint found in the United States, and the cross pressures that underlie many of these measures, sufficient consistencies have been found to indicate that a clear socialization effect was at work.

Third, of the various ways in which one might arrange the individual measures of culture, the dominant and subordinate dimension appears to be most useful in interpreting political effects. While not absolutely consistent, there are indications that cohorts situated in dominant structures and roles are similar in their political orientations to the characterization presented for males above (in relative degree if not always in absolute relationships). Traditional institutional structures and regional breakdowns were, in general, less useful in characterizing the effects of culture, though some consistencies were found here as well. Again, while these patterns were neither complete nor overwhelming, as a whole they do indicate the presence of some underlying dimensions to the socializing effects of culture.

Fourth, the single most-consistent impact of the interaction of generation and the socioeconomic environment is to reduce the distinctiveness among cohorts with different experiences or characteristics. Every measure of politics except for the selection of the economic agenda demonstrates this, as do 72 percent of the relationships between the political measures and the individual components of culture. This interaction occasionally leads to a particular result (such as greater system support, increased attention to the sixties agenda, or a loss of diffuse party support), but this appears to be more the result of a reaction to consistent main effects than to the political orientation per se. In short, the sixties generation was *internally* less distinctive along cultural lines in its political orientations than were previous generations.

Fifth, the effects of a changing sociocultural environment on the sixties generation were generally small (in part because the changes are small). They are also as likely to be in contrast to the main tendencies of the sixties generation as to reinforce them (both within and across the political measures). Because the sociocultural environment is heterogeneous and permeable, and because changes are seldom systematic, the overall political impact of a changing structure is inconsistent.

Sixth, while there was evidence of hegemonic cultural pressure to adhere to conservative and mainstream political orientations on some of the summary measures (most clearly for political support, the foreign-policy agenda, political involvement, and all forms of political decision making), it was almost as common for the overall structure of the sociocultural environment to increase the distinctiveness of the sixties generation (as with the sixties agenda, levels of participation, and the stability of both the amount and partisan direction of that participation). In short, the sociocultural environment is much less able than the socioeconomic to reproduce the specific elements of a stable political system (at the mass level). This should not surprise us, given that the cultural environment is less closed and less structured than the economic one and therefore less likely to shape attitudes, opinions, and behaviors in a consistent manner.

We do not mean to imply that the sociocultural environment is not involved in the reproduction of political orientations from generation to generation. The "Total" column indicates that when one focuses on individual components of that environment, it can be seen that the net impact on the population as a whole is twice as likely to reinforce a majority of main effects on political orientations as to weaken them, with the absolute reversal of main effects rarer still. In short, the culture is relatively effective at reproducing the relationships between specific aspects of itself and political orientations. Because of the heterogeneous nature of the culture, however, this process does not always result in a consistent, system-supportive and stabilizing whole. Nor, however, does it add up to consistent change, either generally or specifically within the sixties generation.

NOTE

1. The main effect indicating that the South is liberal on domestic issues seems an anomaly and may in fact be a methodological artifact of the estimation procedure. It is also possible, however, that the general conservatism of the South is more the result of the effects of life cycle, period, generation, and interaction (which have been removed or controlled for) than of other components of regional culture.

CHAPTER 15

Generations, Periods, and Political Change

Throughout this book we have taken a detailed look at mass political change in the United States over the past three decades: detailed both in the dissection of political attitudes, opinions, and behaviors, and in the dissection of the generational, life-cycle, period and interactive sources of political change. In this concluding chapter we step back from the detail and present a more general overview of our findings and their significance. The next three sections present summaries of the respective impacts of the life cycle, periods, and the sixties generation on recent trends in mass politics. Section five is a discussion of the role of the economic, social, political, and cultural structure of society on generational change. This is followed by a discussion of how these findings contribute to our understanding of political trends since 1980, as well what they portend for the not-so-distant future. Finally, we end by considering what this examination of generational change tells us about the more-general issue of mass political change in advanced industrial societies such as the United States.

Generations, Periods, and Political Change

THE LIFE CYCLE AND POLITICAL CHANGE

The process of growing older has shown itself to be an important element in the development of political orientations. While the relationship between aging and mass politics is complex and not easily characterized, three effects consistently appeared throughout the previous chapters. First, aging has an independent effect on the development of most political attitudes, opinions, and behaviors. This effect is consistent across generations, though not always consistent for all political orientations. In general, as cohorts grow older, they become gradually more cynical about the political system, more conservative in their issue stands, more likely to register and vote, more likely to support the Republican party, and more stable in their partisan support. The effects of aging on political agendas, political involvement, and decision making are more complex and less easily summarized.

In addition to this main effect, aging also seems to bring with it a certain insulation from the political pushes and pulls of specific periods. Throughout our analysis it was found that older cohorts were most resistant to period-driven change, regardless of the substantive or ideological direction of that change. This finding suggests that political orientations that have been developed and refined over time are less susceptible to relatively short-term forces than those less firmly grounded in experience.

As important as both these findings are, we believe that the most important (and in some ways most surprising) effect of aging is the pressure it imposes on people to adhere to the political norm. Repeatedly it was found that, as the sixties generation aged, its political distinctiveness slowly eroded. As with aging's insulation from short-term trends, this return to the hegemonic center occurs regardless of the ideological or substantive nature of the generational distinctiveness or of the more general impact of aging. This suggests that individual or group change that runs counter to the *de facto* norms of society and that has no structural or institutional basis, is extremely difficult to maintain over time (a point we elaborate on below).

PERIOD-BASED POLITICAL CHANGE

One of the major themes running through this book is the discussion of the inconsistent trends that characterized the decades under examination. Political protest and declining support during years of economic prosperity. Decreasing political involvement and participation during an era of increased information and education, and so on. One of the most common findings of this research has been that most of the consistent impact of the changing social and economic environment resides in the general effects of period. Once the effects of generational replacement (and the life cycle) are removed, political orientations in the years from the 1950s through the 1980s are seen to parallel much more closely the more-general environmental changes. Diffuse support for the system remained strong during the three decades. The political agenda reacted dramatically to changes in the nation and the world. Stands on issues became increasingly conservative as a majority of the population entered the middle class and as the economy's downturn put an end to the country's altruistic mood. The three dimensions of political engagement—involvement, ideological decision making, and participation—all showed increases during these decades of expanding political resources. Only in the direction of partisan support, where the period effects are inconsistent, and in the stability of support, where they are consistently unstable, do these effects fail to show a coherent picture. And even this indecisiveness is consistent with the nature of the times, given the demise of the New Deal coalition, the growing conservatism and the increased independence of the electorate.

In short, the period effects suggest that the part of the electorate that existed prior to the advent of the sixties generation reacted to the events of the late fifties, the sixties, and the seventies as a loyal, involved and somewhat self-interested citizenry; as a citizenry that benefitted from environmental changes and that rewarded the status quo with its relatively consistent support. This is not to say that this portion of the electorate was unaffected by the "darker" or more conflictual side of the sixties, nor is it to say that they did not waver from established attitudinal and behavioral norms. Rather, the conclusion is made that such wavering is outweighed by the more dominant pattern of political support, moderate conservatism, and growing political sophistication and involvement in mainstream electoral politics.

MASS POLITICS AND THE SIXTIES GENERATION

In as much as the sixties generation was part of the electorate in the sixties and seventies, they too were affected by the main period effects described above. At the same time, however, they demonstrated a unique generational character that in many ways ran counter both to those period effects and to the political profile of prior generations. Part of this distinct profile revolves around an alternative political worldview. The sixties generation is slightly more liberal than its predecessors. It had a political agenda that, in a small way, more closely reflected the issues of the 1960s and early 1970s. It is more likely to vote Democratic and to persist in this party allegiance across elections and across individual races. All of these characteristics are consistent with our impressions of this generation and the times in which members of the generation became politically aware.

Despite these real tendencies of the sixties generation, one cannot help but be struck as much by the smallness of these distinctions (relative to earlier generations) as by their existence. Yes, this generation is more liberal, but not dramatically so. Yes, its members emphasize a slightly different agenda, but overall the differences are outweighed by the similarities with the agendas of older generations. Yes, they are more Democratic in their vote, but not in their deep-seated nor their long-term support for that party. When the erosion of these characteristics over the life cycle are considered, these differences seem even less remarkable.

It is the *rejection* of mainstream politics rather than the development of an alternative political direction that most clearly distinguishes the sixties generation from preceding cohorts. This generation is substantially less supportive of the political system. Despite its having greater educational opportunities and being raised in an information-rich environment, it is remarkably less likely to follow politics. It rejects most traditional forms of decision-making cues (including ideological ones), but offers no evidence of replacing them with other politically relevant cues. It participates in elections at a greatly reduced rate. It is decidedly less supportive of the party system generally, and of the Democratic party specifically, than its collective vote choice would lead one to expect. In short, it is a generation which, relative to earlier generations, rejects the norms and institutions that are central to the political system of which they are a part. What distinguishes this generation most is what it does not like or does not do, and not what it likes or does.

Our examination of the three cohorts that comprise the sixties generation adds to our understanding of the process of generational development. First, it is clear that the simi-

Generations, Periods, and Political Change

larities shared by the three subgenerations indicated that they do comprise a political generation with basically similar orientations: the profile described above is generally true for all three cohorts. Second, within this general profile there are some important differences that result from each cohort's unique juncture of age and environment. These differences vary depending on the particular orientation involved. For example, each cohort emphasizes a different aspect of the sixties agenda. The ambivalent cohort is the most Democratic in its voting behavior; the socialized cohort is most likely to participate in mainstream politics beyond voting. While a number of these patterns are not easily explained and do not fit together into consistent subgenerational profiles, taken as a whole there are general tendencies that can be explicated. The ambivalent cohort often reflects the conflicting pressure that its duel heritage exerts. This conflict manifests itself sometimes by a less distinctive generational character (less distinctive, that is, than the younger two cohorts), sometimes by an erratic pattern across the individual measures of political orientations, and sometimes by a greater tendency to return to the status quo over time. However, the conflict fairly consistently reflects the ambivalence that we originally anticipated. The experienced subgeneration, the cohort that most clearly was at the center of the tumult of the 1960s, most often typifies the overall generational profile. In addition, it is the subgeneration that, in its interaction with both period and life-cycle effects, most often resisted pressure to adhere to the status quo.

The socialized cohort is the most difficult to characterize, in part because of the inconsistency of the evidence uncovered in these pages, in part because of the difficulty in knowing what one should expect from its members, and in part because of the short time they have been part of the electorate. In many ways they resemble the ambivalent cohort—a subgeneration with only one foot clearly planted in the 1960s. Unlike the ambivalent cohort, however, it was the formative years rather than the young-adult years that were affected by that period. This particular experience seems to have resulted in a generational character that often is the most distinctive of the three cohorts in terms of the main effects, but that is also the most likely to rapidly return towards the norm with age. Again, we must emphasize that the relative youth of this subgeneration means that it is still in the process of forming its distinct character. It will be a while before its political personality is established in any clear way. It will also, therefore, be more susceptible to being fundamentally affected by future period effects.

Despite subgenerational differences, however, we must end by emphasizing that, as a whole, the sixties generation has consistently rejected involvement in and support of the political norms and institutions of the political system in the United States. In fact, it is not inappropriate to say that the recent indications of political malaise and disinterest in the United States are due, on the whole, to the process of generational replacement and not to changes within cohorts that were in the electorate prior to the 1960s. In many ways the last three decades would have been highpoints in political support, involvement, and participation were it not for this process of generational replacement.

THE IMPACT OF STRUCTURE

It is from the examination of structural change and its interaction with political orientations that we begin to see why generational replacement has the particular effect that it does. Political attitudes, opinions, and behaviors are not formed or maintained in a vacuum. They are developed and sustained within the context of a sociopolitical environment. Short-term change either in institutions or in mass political orientations can occur in isolation, resulting from unusual environmental disturbances (such as those that took place in the 1960s). For such change to be lasting and meaningful, however, it must be integrated into the larger institutions, attitudes, and behavior of the society. Our analysis of the political institutions of mass politics (Chapters Four through Eleven) and of the socioeconomic and sociocultural institutions (Chapters Twelve through Fourteen) indicates clear evidence of marginal change, but little evidence of any major restructuring of society during the three decades examined. More specifically, the political, social, and economic design of the United States is fundamentally the same now as it was in 1952. Mass politics is still defined by electoral politics generally, and voting for either the Democrats or the Republicans more specifically. Social learning is still imparted by the institutions of the family, the school, the workplace, and the church, all of which have maintained essentially the same internal structures as well as the same interrelationships with the larger social structure over many years. The economic system and class structure in the United States remains largely unaltered from that of the presixties era, with the exception that financially and personally unrewarding service sector jobs have replaced some of the financially and personally unrewarding manufacturing sector jobs. The few attempts at structural change that arose out of the sixties—communal living, alternative religious or moral codes, experimental, nonhierarchical educational structures, four-day work weeks, more humane, fulfilling work experiences, etc.—could not be maintained for any length of time or on a significant scale. In part this was due to the poor conception or execution of many of these ideas, but in part their failures were the inevitable result of being set in a larger and integrated set of institutions that were built upon a different set of norms and values.

Planted in such a hostile environment, whatever seeds of

change may have been sown in the sixties were unlikely to grow to maturity, let alone bear fruit. The sixties "revolution" lacked coherence or direction from the start, and never really developed it. That it never captured any particular aspect of the socioeconomic or sociocultural environment is clear from the analysis of Chapters Thirteen and Fourteen. As a result, with the passage of time, members of this generation found it difficult to resist the attitudes and behavior of mainstream society. Not having been able (or willing) to devise alternative institutional structures, this generation is slowly making the only choices they see available to them. That those choices are increasingly similar to past generations should not be surprising, given that they are increasingly being made from the same social, economic and political perspective of those prior generations.

THE 1980S AND BEYOND

Relating the past to the future is a risky business, especially given what we now know about the potential effects of period-based change. And yet, after tracing the political development of the sixties generation over two decades, it is impossible to resist speculating on some aspects of its potential impact. One thing is certain: this generation will, in numerical terms, dominate American politics for the next half century. They are already of an age to dominate middle-level management positions in business, to fill most of the lower prestige manual labor and service jobs, to be a majority of the teachers in grade schools and high schools, and to be swelling the ranks of assistant and associate college professors. They are making the movies and television shows America watches and writing the news we read and see. They are even becoming the candidates we vote for at the same time they make up a majority of the eligible electorate.

Generations, Periods, and Political Change

In addition, they are increasingly becoming the heads of households and raising children of their own, beginning to socialize the next generation of Americans. In short, the sixties generation is entering a period in which they are in a much better position to affect the institutional structure of society than they have ever been before.

What does this portend for politics in the next decade? What about politics beyond that? The potential impact of the sixties generation lies in four areas: their impact as a group on electoral politics; their impact on the social structure in which the next generation is being and will be socialized; their impact as a group on nonelectoral politics; and their impact on social and political leadership. We can talk about the first two areas based, in part at least, on the information presented in this book. We must depend upon more ephemeral evidence to speculate on the latter two.

It is ironic (though probably not coincidental) that the profile of the sixties generation that we have developed in this book suggests that it was most substantively distinctive (in terms of issue stands, agendas, and support for the political institutions of the United States) when it was a minority in the electorate and when it was least likely to participate in or be involved in mainstream politics. As members of the sixties generation became a larger part of the electorate, and as they became somewhat more willing to vote, their political views have become increasingly similar to those of the rest of the population. They are still more independent as a group, still more volatile in their political participation as a group, and, according to other research (Yankelovich, 1981, 1984; Ladd, 1984), more liberal on certain social issues that we have not been able to examine in this study (gay rights, the ERA, abortion, decriminalization of marijuana, etc.). Our analysis suggests, however, that they are not remarkably different from older generations (and becoming less so with time) in either their agenda (economics and foreign policy dominate) or their stands on nonsocial issues (with the possible exception of their attitudes toward a Vietnam-like action).

Considering this profile of the generation, we would expect electoral politics in the near future to be relatively unstable. That is, neither party will be able to develop a permanent majority coalition in either government or the mass population. Increasingly, shifts in support will be between candidates who are both economically and socially conservative and those who are economically conservative and socially liberal. More specifically, it seems likely that the sixties generation will base its vote choice predominantly on personal economic considerations during times of economic uncertainty, and be somewhat more willing to consider social issues if economic conditions indicate that they can be paid for without adversely affecting one's personal economic condition. Support for a New Deal type candidate seems increasingly unlikely for this generation as a whole. Stands on foreign-policy issues are more difficult to predict, though the analysis presented in this book suggests a growing conservative attitude towards involvement of the United States abroad, as long as the specifics of that involvement do not take on the look of another Vietnam (unclear goals, noneconomic or defensive justifications, protracted fighting, large draft, etc.).

Beyond this general characterization, it will still be subgroups in the population that dominate electoral politics. Cleavages of region, race, education, income, etc., which have traditionally been the basis for the formation of electoral coalitions, will undoubtedly continue to do so. This will become increasingly so as situational and structural differences within the sixties generation continue to erode any sense of common consciousness that may have existed within it.

Generations, Periods, and Political Change

The role which future generations will play is difficult to determine, though the key clearly lies in the failure of the sixties generation, to this point, to fundamentally alter the structure of social, political, or economic institutions. The institutions through which future generations learn about the world and their role in it remain the same. Where they have been changed, it has been either in relatively insignificant ways, or in random, unplanned ways, but not in ways that fit together into a coherent whole. This in turn makes even these few changes difficult or undesirable to maintain. Thus low scores in standardized tests are blamed on the permissive nature of educational experiments developed in the sixties; increased drug use, sexual promiscuity, or juvenile delinquency is blamed on the "breakup" of the family unit (translated as the fact that women now often work outside the home); child abuse is the result of children being cared for outside the home and by disreputable strangers; economic woes are blamed on political experiments to aid the socially, economically, and politically disadvantaged. What few structural changes that were made possible by the environment of the sixties have come under continual attack because they are perceived as having failed. And yet it is possible the changes failed because they were isolated within a basically hostile overarching structure. That they failed not because they went too far, but because they did not go far enough. Whatever the reasons, the institutional legacy of the sixties and, it seems increasingly clear, of the sixties generation itself to future generations, is small and dwindling. Given this fact, it seems unlikely that the next generation will benefit in any direct way from this generation's experience. While it may be members of the sixties generation who raise, or teach, or train, or manage the next generation, they will be doing so in roles and from positions essentially unaltered from those filled by prior generations. Maintaining countercultural norms and values in this situation is difficult: transmitting them to a new generation is all but impossible. In short, it seems clear that the political character of the next generation will be shaped by the social, cultural, economic, and political events its members experience or by which they are socialized, much as the character of the sixties generation was. And, barring an environment even more politically and socially charged than the sixties, and a generation even larger than the baby boom cohort, new generations will find their profiles either consistent with the larger social institutions right from the start, or, much as the sixties generation has, slowly conforming over time.

The final two predictions concerning the future impact of the sixties go even further beyond the data of this study. It is possible that the sixties generation has been involved in the development of an alternative political structure, but that this structure is outside of electoral politics, and therefore, not uncovered in this research. For example, it is possible that the generation is more directly involved in grassroots politics through neighborhood associations, or makes up the heart of national movements such as the nuclear freeze, or still engages in protest politics. In considering this, we must distinguish between the form of participation and the substance of that participation. If the sixties generation is engaged in liberal, progressive politics in any sizable way, our findings on agendas and on issue stands should have been sensitive to this, regardless of whether or not these views were expressed in electoral politics. Since the evidence of new agendas and liberal stands is minimal at best in this study, it seems unlikely that (with the possible exception of social issues viewed by both the overall population and the sixties generation as peripheral concerns) we would find that the generation developed alternative agendas and took unusual stands on issues at other levels.

In terms of the type of participation, however, it is possible that the sixties generation has moved away from electoral politics but into other forms of participation. While we cannot dismiss this possibility, several aggregate patterns make it unlikely that this is typical of the generation. First, protest behavior is still an extremely rare occurrence, as is, to a lesser extent, participation in demonstrations and rallies. Even if members of the sixties generation are disproportionately likely to engage in such activity, this would not allow us to argue that such behavior is typical of or even common among members of the generation. And we are concerned in this book with the profile of the generation as a whole and not of extremely small subsets within it. While participation in grassroots political organizations is somewhat more common than protest behavior (and, according to some researchers, is increasing in recent years) it is still an activity engaged in by at most only one of five citizens, and even then with no regularity. In addition, it is not at all clear that members of the sixties generation are much more likely to participate in this way than are members of other generations (see Table 9.6). Again, in terms of a generational profile, dropoffs in electoral participation do not seem to be offset by gains in nonelectoral participation, even if one is willing to make the most generous assumptions. Finally, it remains the case that protests, demonstrations, and even most forms of grassroots participation are still secondary to electoral politics in terms of how the public as a whole performs its civic obligation. In 1985, as in 1952, mass politics in the United States still means voting. Even allowing that members of the sixties generation participate in nonelectoral politics at unusual rates (something not clearly established), it would simply be further evidence of the failure of this generation to successfully redefine the meaning of the status quo.

The issues raised above lead us to a consideration of the

last area of concern: leadership. Throughout this book we have studied the impact of the 1960s on the sixties generation *as a whole*. This is not the same as trying to determine whether or not that period has affected the political views and behaviors of select individuals or groups of individuals. It is clear from the conclusions presented in Chapters Thirteen and Fourteen that whole economic or social strata within the generation were not fundamentally changed in politically constructive ways. However, it is unquestionably the case that individual members of the generation have been. These individuals are perhaps members of a subset of those who were active in the social movements of the sixties, perhaps a subset of those who were socialized by such movements, or perhaps a combination of both. If a constructive legacy seems increasingly unlikely to be developed by the sixties generation as a whole, perhaps it will develop out of individual leaders that the generation produces. While our study does not allow us to confirm this supposition, a cursory look at the evidence to date is not particularly encouraging in this regard (at least at the national level). The leaders of the sixties (Jerry Rubin, Stokely Carmichael, Bobby Seals, Abbie Hoffman, H. Rapp Brown, Tom Hayden, Angela Davis, Daniel and Philip Berrigan, and Eldridge Cleaver, among others) are either out of politics, involved in rather traditional, mainstream politics, have moved politically to the right of center, or are unable to attract the attention of much more than small groups of supporters and curiosity seekers today. True, there is little systematic evidence at the state and local level concerning the leadership role of members of the sixties generation (though Broder, 1981, does examine this issue). Nor has the generation matured enough to eliminate the possibility that new leaders will develop out of its ranks. To this point, however, it is the absence of visible and nontraditional leaders that seems most distinctive about the generation. In more mainstream party politics, the new generation of leadership in both the Democratic and the Republican parties is dominated by the philosophy of high technology, conservative economic policy, moderate-to-liberal stands on most social policies, and a strong defense coupled with a non-interventionist foreign policy. A political philosophy not inconsistent with the picture we have painted of the generation as a whole. In the most comprehensive analysis of generational change in leadership, Broder concludes that, despite some evidence of nontraditional leaders, "those who are 'outsiders' today will remain on the fringes of power, and not at the center, for the balance of their political lives" (p. 476).

THE POSSIBILITY OF GENERATION-BASED POLITICAL CHANGE

We began this book by suggesting that an examination of the sixties generation would tell us not only about its specific contribution to mass political change, but also about the nature of generational change more generally. While undoubtedly each generation and each historical period contains its own unique pattern, the analysis presented in these chapters suggests that there are certain limits to generation-based political change which face any generation in any political environment.

In Chapter Twelve we distinguished between change that was situational or structural, change that maintained the system, adjusted it, or challenged it and change that was "restructive," "instructive," "destructive" or "astructive." We argued that the most fundamental, long-term kind of change was structurally based, system challenging, and restructive. Generational change is often "triggered" by structural change. In the case of the sixties generation, for instance, the new role of the mass media and the increased availability of advanced education clearly helped shape the political profile of its members. However, since generational change, by its very nature, involves the gradual replacement of one age cohort with a younger one, the structural sources of change will inevitably be of this sort. That is, they will involve reactions of a new generation to the structural change introduced by older generations. This is so because institutions are usually controlled (to the extent that anyone controls them) by already established generations. This also suggests that much of the uniqueness of any generation will be situational-based, and not structurally-based. One's situation as college student, or draft-aged citizen, or middle-class dependent, and the interaction of that situation with historical events is often the key to generational distinctiveness.

The research on the sixties generation also demonstrates how difficult it is to sustain system-challenging change without some form of institutional support. Despite the apparent shift in the flow of norms and values, and despite the anti-system rhetoric of the times and of the generation, the attitudinal and behavioral changes that seem likely to persist as a part of the political system at best bring about an adjustment of the existing system. That is, a modified set of opinions and behaviors develop that are necessary for the system to adjust to uncontrollable changes in the environment, without a fundamental restructuring of power relationships. And since the inability to develop institutional support seems a likely problem for any new generation, the inability to maintain system-challenging views seems likely to be part of the process of generational-based change.

Given a lack of autonomous structural sources of generational change, and an inability to maintain truly challenging opinions and behaviors, it should not be surprising that we also conclude that restructive change (or change that ultimately leads to the development of new or altered institutions that both reflect the new norms and values and that serve to reproduce this order in future generations) is highly unlikely to ever develop out of generational replacement. The institutional legacy of the sixties generation is a certain amount of destructive change (the weakening of certain established institutions such as electoral politics, parties, etc.), a certain amount of astructive change (superficial changes in lifestyle, fashion, leisure activities, etc.) and a good deal of instructive change (change such as the rise of the service sector which allows institutions to replicate basic power relationships in new environments). And, we would suggest, this may very well be the limit of generational-based change.

Given this pattern, it is easy to see how this part of the cycle of generational replacement fits into the larger process. If, when the smoke clears, even a generation that vigorously challenged the system (and was large enough to make its feelings known) winds up replicating, with minor adjustments, the institutions of prior generations, then what this generation passes on to a subsequent one will also help ensure that future change will be minimal and reformist rather than fundamental.

All of this suggests that a political system is extremely unlikely to undergo radical change as a result of generational replacement. New generations may provide the raw materials for change (discontent with old institutions and structures, an uncommitted voting block, support for unusual programs or experimental institutions, etc.), but their members are unlikely to provide the ideological or institutional coherence to transform opposition to one thing into support for something else. This kind of planning requires both experience and power, and so must necessarily be developed from a generation already established in the population. But here again we run smack into our "Catch 22": In order to be part of the empowered structure, members of a generation are likely to

Situations and Structures

have come to accept its rules (or at least to have stopped resisting them).

For someone who prefers the predictability of stable politics or who is genuinely satisfied with social, economic, and political relations as they currently exist in the United States, this process of generational replacement will provide some comfort. During periods of political calm, new generations replace old ones with little more than the most cosmetic of changes. At times of generational discontent and challenge, the system is capable of adjusting itself so that, in the end, its underlying structure remains essentially unaltered.

If one is less content with the prevailing distribution of power, with the nature of the political agenda, or with the institutions that serve to implement democratic politics (or if one is more generally uncomfortable with a system that is so insulated from political change), then the apparent failure of the sixties generation to provide fundamental new direction to American politics, and the possibility that this was inevitable, is cause for great disappointment. And yet while this is the final chapter of this book, the final chapter for the generation itself has not yet been written. If there is any reason to continue to look to this generation as a potential catalyst for political change, it lies in the facts that, first, it represents a majority of the adult population and will continue to do so for some time to come. Second, it will, for the next few decades, be in positions of institutional power. Third, the evidence of discontent found in this book suggests that they are still not completely integrated into mainstream, normal politics. Fourth, and most important, this discontent (as well as some of the more substantive indicators of political distinctiveness) may still prove to be politically relevant through some kind of interaction between generation and period in the future. While the specifics of this interaction are not easy to imagine, should it occur, the generation would now be in a position of relative power. This would, of course, mean that my conclusions concerning the inability of generational-based change to alter a political system fundamentally would be wrong, but it is a recantation I would gladly make.

REFERENCES

Broder, David S. *The Changing of the Guard*. New York: Penguin Books, 1981.
Ladd, Everett Carl. "Opinion Roundup: Values." *Public Opinion* 6 (December, 1984), pp. 21–40.
Yankelovich, Daniel. *New Rules*. New York: Random House, 1981.
——. "American Values: Change and Stability." *Public Opinion* 6 (December, 1984), pp. 2–8.

APPENDIX A

Variable Means

1. PROPORTION OF SAMPLE CONSTITUTED BY GENERATIONS AND SUBGENERATIONS (AND MEAN AGE FOR SAMPLE, SIXTIES GENERATION, AND PREDECESSORS)

	1952	1956	1960	1964	1968	1972	1976	1980	Total
Predecessors	1.0	.94	.94	.80	.66	.58	.48	.39	.70
Sixties[1]	0.0	.13	.22	.29	.39	.48	.55	.65	.33
Ambivalent	0.0	.06	.06	.20	.26	.22	.22	.20	.16
Experienced	0.0	0.0	0.0	0.0	.08	.20	.26	.29	.11
Socialized	0.0	0.0	0.0	0.0	0.0	0.0	.05	.12	.02
Age (Sample)	42	43	47	45	44	44	44	43	44
Age (Sixties)	**	22	25	27	28	28	30	32	29
Age (Pred.)	42	46	53	52	54	59	61	63	51

2. MEAN SCORES OF INDEPENDENT VARIABLES IN REGRESSION EQUATIONS

LC: 28	GEN: .33	P50: .22	P60: .37
P70: .28	LC × GEN: 3.8	LC × P50: 5.9	LC × P60: 9.9
LC × P70: 7.2	GEN × 60: .14	GEN × 70: .17	AMB: .16
EXPER: .11	SOC: .03	LC × AMB: 2.1	LC × EXPER: .82
LC × SOC: .08	AMB × P60: .08	AMB × P70: .06	EXPER × P70: .08

[1]Percent of the population which is constituted by the SIXTIES generation as a whole does not precisely equal the sum of the three subgenerations because of differences in the estimating procedures (for details, see Chapter Three).

APPENDIX B

Question Wording and Coding

1. POLITICAL SUPPORT[1]

VOTE CARE: "If a person doesn't care how an election comes out he shouldn't vote in it" (disagree = 1; depends = .5; agrees = 0).

OFFICIALS: "I don't think public officials care much what people like me think" (disagree = 1; depends = .5; agrees = 0).

VOTE ONLY: "Voting is the only way that people like me can have any say about how the government runs things" (agree = 1; depends = .5; disagree = 0).

LOCAL: "A good many local elections aren't important enough to bother with" (disagree = 1; depends = .5; agree = 0).

VOTE MATTERS: "So many other people vote in the national elections that it doesn't matter much to me whether I vote or not" (disagree = 1; depends = .5; agree = 0).

HAVE SAY: "People like me don't have any say about what the government does" (disagree = 1; depends = .5; agree = 0).

Appendix B

VOTE WIN: "It isn't so important to vote when you know your party doesn't have any chance to win" (disagree = 1; depends = .5; agree = 0).

COMPLEX: "Sometimes politics and government seem so complicated that a person like me can't really understand what's going on" (disagree = 1; depends = .5; agree = 0).

¹All items were used in the SUPPORT summary index.

---

2. POLITICAL AGENDA

"What do you think are the most important problems facing this country?" (Only first response coded.)

ICPSR provides several standard categories into which responses are grouped. Several of these categories (Social Welfare,[1] Labor,[2] Government,[3] and Other) were used as clustered. The remaining categories were more finely distinguished so as to allow discriminating among agendas of potential importance in the sixties and to the sixties generation. More specifically, the following modifications were made:

Agricultural issues[2] (farm economics, surplus food, etc.) were separated from environmental issues[3] (conservation, pollution, etc.).

Race issues[3] (black civil rights, voting rights, etc.) were separated from more-general issue of public order[3] (campus unrest, antiwar protests, violence in streets, etc.).

General economic issues[2] (inflation, taxes, interest rates, etc.) were separated from issues of consumer protection[3] (truth in labeling, control of harmful products, mass transportation, etc.).

Question Wording and Coding

Issues relating to Vietnam[3] were separated from other foreign-affairs concerns.[4]

Issues of arms control[3] (nuclear proliferation, the arms race, etc.) were separated from more-general issues of defense.[4]

[1]Used in SOCIAL WELFARE AGENDA summary index.
[2]Used in ECONOMIC AGENDA summary index.
[3]Used in SIXTIES AGENDA summary index.
[4]Used in FOREIGN AFFAIRS AGENDA summary index.

3. ISSUE STANDS

EDUCATION:[1]

(Pre-1964): "If cities and towns around the country need help to build more schools, the government in Washington ought to give them the money they need. Do you have an opinion on this or not?" (strongly agree = 1; agree = .75; depends/don't know = .5; disagree = .25; strongly disagree = 0).

(1964 and after): "Some people think the government in Washington should help towns and cities provide education for grade and high school children; others think this should be handled by the states and local communities. Have you been interested enough in this to favor one side over the other? (IF YES) Which are you in favor of?" (help from Washington = 1; depends, no interest = .5; handle at state/local level = 0).

HEALTH:[1]

(Pre-1964): "The government ought to help people get doctors and hospital care at low cost. Do you have an opinion on this or not?" (strongly agree = 1; agree = .75; depends/don't know = .5; disagree = .25; strongly disagree = 0).

Appendix B

(1964 and after): "Some say the government in Washington ought to help get doctors and hospital care at a low cost; others say the government should not get into this. Have you been interested enough in this to favor one side over the other?" (IF YES) What is your position? (government should help = 1; depends, no interest = .5; government should stay out of this = 0).

JOBS:[1]

(Pre-1964): "The government in Washington ought to see to it that everybody who wants to work can find a job. Do you have an opinion on this or not?" (strongly agree = 1; agree = .75; depends/don't know = .5; disagree = .25; strongly disagree = 0).

(1964 and after): "In general, some people feel that the government in Washington should see to it that every person has a job and a good standard of living. Others think the government should just let each person get ahead on his own. Have you been interested enough in this to favor one side or the other? (IF YES) Do you think that the government. . ." (government should get involved = 1; depends, no interest = .5; government should stay out = 0).

INTEGRATION:[1]

(Pre-1964): "The government in Washington should stay out of the question of whether white and colored children go to the same school. Do you have an opinion on this or not?" (strongly agree = 0; agree = .25; depends/don't know = .5; disagree = .75; strongly disagree = 1).

(1964 and after): "Some people say that the government in Washington should see to it that white and Negro children are allowed to go to the same schools. Others claim this is not the government's business. Have you been concerned enough about this question to favor one side over the other? (IF YES) Do you think the government in Washington should. . ." (should see to it = 1; depends, no interest = .5; government should stay out = 0).

BLACK WELFARE:[1]

(Pre-1964): "If Negroes are not getting fair treatment in jobs and housing, the government should see to it that they do. Do you have an opinion on this or not?" (strongly agree = 1; agree = .75; depends/don't know = .5; disagree = .25; strongly disagree = 0).

(1964 and after): "Some people feel that if Negroes are not getting fair treatment in jobs the government in Washington should see to it that they do. Others feel that this is not the federal government's business. Have you had enough interest in this question to favor one side over the other? (IF YES) How do you feel?" (government should get involved = 1; depends, no interest = .5; government should not get involved = 0).

INTERVENTIONISM:[2] The country would be better off if we just stayed home and did not concern ourselves with problems in other parts of the world (disagree = 1; depends = .5; agree = 0).

FOREIGN AID:[2]

(Pre-1964): "The United States should give economic help to the poorer countries of the world even if those countries can't pay for it." (strongly agree = 1; agree = .75; depends/don't know = .5; disagree = .25; strongly disagree = 0).

(1964 and after): "We now come to a few questions about our dealings with other countries. Some people say that we should give aid to other countries if they need help, while

Appendix B

others think each country should make its own way as best it can. Have you been interested enough in this to favor one side over the other? (IF YES) Which opinion is most like yours?" (give aid = 1; depends, no interest = .5; don't give aid = 0).

INVOLVEMENT: "Do you think we did the right thing in getting into the fighting in (Vietnam/Korea) or should we have stayed out?" (did right thing = 1; depends = .5; stay out = 0).

SOLUTION: "Which of the following do you think we should do now in (Vietnam/Korea)?" (military solution = 1; middle ground = .5; withdraw = 0).

[1]Used in DOMESTIC ISSUE STANDS summary index.
[2]Used in FOREIGN AFFAIRS ISSUE STANDS summary index.

4. POLITICAL INVOLVEMENT[1]

PAPERS: "Did you read about the campaign in any newspaper? (IF YES) How much did you read newspaper articles about the election—regularly, often, from time to time, or just once in a great while?" (regularly = 1; often = .75; time to time = .5; once in a great while = .25; never = 0).

TV: "How about television—did you watch any programs about the campaign on television? (IF YES) How many television programs about the campaign would you say you watched—a good many, several, or just one or two?" (a good many = 1; several = .66; one or two = .33; none = 0).

RADIO: "How about Radio—did you listen to any programs about the campaign on the radio? (IF YES) How many programs about the campaign did you listen to on the radio—a

Question Wording and Coding

good many, several, or just one or two?" (a good many = 1; several = .66; one or two = .33; none = 0).

MAGAZINES: "How about magazines—did you read about the campaign in any magazines? (IF YES) How many magazine articles about the campaign would you say you read—a good many, several, or just one or two?" (a good many = 1; several = .66; one or two = .33; none = 0).

CAMPAIGN: "Some people don't pay much attention to the political campaigns. How about you, would you say that you have been very much interested, somewhat interested, or not much interested in following the political campaigns so far this year?" (very much interested = 1; somewhat interested = .5; not much interested = 0).

POLITICS:

(Pre-1964): "We'd also like to know how much attention you pay to what's going on in politics generally. I mean, from day to day, when there isn't any big election campaign going on, would you say you follow politics very closely, fairly closely, or not much at all?" (very closely = 1; fairly closely = .5; not much at all = 0).

(1964 and after): "Some people seem to follow what's going on in government and public affairs most of the time, whether there's an election going on or not. Others aren't that interested. Would you say you follow what's going on in government and public affairs most of the time, some of the time, only now and then, or hardly at all?" (most of the time = 1; some of the time = .66; now and then = .33; hardly at all = 0).

MAJORITY I: "Do you happen to know which party had the most Congressmen in Washington before the election this

Appendix B

month? Which one?" (1 = correct answer; .5 = don't know; 0 = wrong answer).

MAJORITY II: "Do you happen to know which party elected the most Congressmen in the election this month? Which one?" (1 = correct answer; .5 = don't know; 0 = wrong answer).

TOTALS: Summary measure of total number of evaluations offered concerning the parties. (8–12 = 1; 4–7 = .5; 0–3 = 0).

[1]All items were used in INVOLVEMENT summary index.

5. DECISION-MAKING CUES

All decision-making cues were derived from the responses to the following four questions. "Now I'd like to ask you about the good and bad points of the two major candidates for president. Is there anything in particular about (Democratic/Republican candidate) that might make you want to vote (for/against) him? What is that? Anything else?"

Each of the twelve responses (three responses for each of the four questions) was then coded according to the scheme developed originally by Campbell, et al. (1964) and standardized by Nie, et al. (1976). Responses are coded to range from zero to one, with the actual score representing the percentage of total responses falling into each category. The actual categories used are explicit ideological references,[1] implicit ideological references,[1] group references,[2] policy mentions,[2] reference to the nature of the times,[2] party-based evaluations,[3] and a residual category that is mainly contentless.[4] For actual coding of original responses, see Nie, et al., 1976, Appendix 2C (pp. 403–404).

Question Wording and Coding

[1] Used in IDEOLOGICAL DECISION-MAKING summary index.
[2] Used in CUE-SPECIFIC DECISION-MAKING summary index.
[3] Used in PARTY-BASED DECISION-MAKING summary index.
[4] Used in NON-POLITICAL DECISION-MAKING summary index.

6. ELECTORAL PARTICIPATION[1]

ALWAYS VOTE: "In the elections for president since you have been old enough to vote, would you say that you have voted in all of them, most of them, some of them, or none of them?" (all = 1; most = .66; some = .33; none = 0).

REGISTER: "Now, how about the election this November? Are you registered (eligible to vote) so that you could vote in the November election if you wanted to?" (yes, definitely = 1; think so = .75; no, but intend to = .50; no, probably won't = .25; no, definitely = 0).

PRESIDENT: "Did you vote for president this year?" Adapted from vote choice question if not asked directly. (yes = 1; no = 0).

CONGRESS: "How about the vote for Congressman? Did you vote for a candidate for Congressman?" Adapted from vote choice question if not asked directly. (yes = 1; no = 0).

MEETING: "Did you go to any political meetings, rallies, dinners, or things like that?" (yes = 1; don't know = .5; no = 0).

ORGANIZATION: "Do you belong to any political clubs or organizations?" (yes = 1; don't know = .5; no = 0).

DISPLAY: "Did you wear a campaign button or put a campaign sticker on your car?" (yes = 1; don't know = .5; no = 0).

Appendix B

WORK: "Did you do any work for one of the parties or candidates?" (yes = 1; don't know = .5; no = 0).

INFLUENCE: "During the campaign did you talk to any people and try to show them why they should vote for one of the parties or candidates?" (yes = 1; don't know = .5; no = 0).

CONTRIBUTE: "Did you give any money to a political party (or candidate) this year?" (yes = 1; don't know = .5; no = 0).

[1]All items were used in PARTICIPATION summary index.

7. PARTISAN SUPPORT

ID STRENGTH:[1] (IF DEMOCRAT OR REPUBLICAN) "Would you call yourself a strong (Democrat/Republican) or a not very strong (Democrat/Republican)?" (IF INDEPENDENT) "Do you think of yourself as closer to the Republican or Democrat party?" (strong partisan = 1; weak partisan = .66; leaning independent = .33; true independent = 0).

CARE WIN:[1] "Generally speaking, would you say that you personally care a good deal which party wins the presidential election this fall or that you don't care very much which party wins?" (care very much = 1; care pretty much = .75; depends = .5; care a little = .25; don't care = 0).

PARTY DIFFERENCES:[1] "Do you think there are any important differences between the Republican and Democratic parties?" (yes = 1; don't know = .5; no = 0).

INTENTIONS:[2] "Whom do you plan to vote for in the election for president?" (definitely Democratic = 1; probably Demo-

Question Wording and Coding

cratic = .75; don't know = .5; probably Republican = .25; definitely Republican = 0).

PRESIDENT:[2] "Whom did you vote for in the election for president?" (Democratic = 1; other = .5; Republican = 0).

CONGRESS:[2] "Whom did you vote for in the election for Congressman?" (Democratic = 1; other = .5; Republican = 0).

LOCAL:[2] "How about the elections for other state and local offices, did you vote a straight ticket, or did you vote for candidates from different parties? (IF STRAIGHT TICKET) Which party? (IF DIFFERENT PARTIES) How did you split it?" (straight Democratic = 1; mostly Democratic = .75; about even = .5; mostly Republican = .25; straight Republican = 0).

LAST TIME:[2] "Do you remember for sure if you voted (in the last presidential election)? (IF YES) Which one did you vote for?" (Democratic = 1; don't know/other = .5; Republican = 0).

USUAL VOTE:[3] "Have you always voted for the same party or have you voted for different parties for president? (IF SAME) Which party was that?" (always Democratic = 1; mostly Democratic = .75; about even = .5; mostly Republican = .25; always Republican = 0).

PARTY ID:[3] "Generally speaking do you usually think of yourself as a Republican, Democrat, or what? (IF DEMOCRAT OR REPUBLICAN) Would you call yourself a strong (Democrat/Republican) or a not very strong (Democrat/Republican)? (IF INDEPENDENT) Do you think of yourself as closer to the Republican or Democrat party?" (strong Democrat = 1; weak Democrat = .83; leaning Democrat = .66;

true independent = .5; leaning Republican = .33; weak Republican = .16; strong Republican = 0).

PARTY EVALUATION:[3] "Is there anything in particular that you (like/dislike) about the (Democratic/Republican) party? What is that?" (three possible responses for each question) (total number of positive Democratic statements were subtracted from total number of negative Democratic statements. This is replicated for Republicans. Net Republican statements then subtracted from net Democrat statements. This number is then recoded as follows: one or greater = 1; zero = .5; less than zero = 0).

[1] Used in DIFFUSE PARTY SUPPORT summary index.
[2] Used in SHORT-TERM PARTY SUPPORT summary index.
[3] Used in LONG-TERM PARTY SUPPORT summary index.

8. PARTISAN STABILITY

ROLLOFF:[1] Index of voting for president, congressman, AND all local races during a single election (1 = complete voting; 0 = incomplete voting).

REGULARITY:[1] Index of voting for president in consecutive elections (1 = votes in both; 0 = skips at least on race).

ID DIFFERENT:[2] "Was there ever a time when you thought of yourself as a (Democrat/Republican) rather than a (Republican/Democrat)?" (if never different = 1; if different at some point = 0).

LOYALTY:[2] Index of voting for candidate for president, congressperson, or local office of different party than the one to which respondent is affiliated (not voting for candidate of party different than personal affiliation = 1; voting for such a candidate = 0).

Question Wording and Coding

ALWAYS:[2] "Have you always voted for the same party or have you voted for different parties for president?" (always same party = 1; usually same party = .5; split about equally = 0).

LOCAL SPLIT:[3] "How about the elections for other state and local offices, did you vote a straight ticket, or did you vote for candidates from different parties?" (always the same = 1; usually the same = .5; split about equally = 0).

NATIONAL SPLIT:[3] Index of splitting ticket in presidential and congressional races (straight ticket = 1; split = 0).

OTHER:[3] Voting for third-party candidate for president (voting major party = 1; voting minor party = 0).

TIMING:[4] "How long before the election did you decide that you were going to vote (for president) the way you did?" (knew all along = 1; during conventions = .75; after convention/during the campaign = .5; last two weeks of campaign = .25; election day = 0).

SUREDNESS:[4] Index of actually voting for presidential candidate respondent planned to vote for during first interview (vote for same candidate = 1; vote for different candidate = 0).

[1]Used in BEHAVIORAL STABILITY summary index.
[2]Used in LONG-TERM STABILITY summary index.
[3]Used in SHORT-TERM STABILITY summary index.
[4]Used in CAMPAIGN STABILITY summary index.

9. DEMOGRAPHICS

CHILDHOOD CLASS: "What [social class] would you say your family was when you were growing up?" (upper = 1; middle = .66; working = .33; lower = 0).

Appendix B

FATHER: "What kind of work did your father do for a living while you were growing up?" (professional/manager = 1; other = 0).

CLASS: "What social class do you consider yourself a member of?" (upper = 1; middle = .66; working = .33; lower = 0).

INCOME: "About what do you think your total income will be this year for yourself and your immediate family?" (adjusted for inflation) (greater than 40,000 = 1; 30,000–39,999 = .75; 20–29,999 = .50; 10,000–19,999 = .25; under 10,000 = 0).

OWNERSHIP: "Do you (does your family) own your own home, pay rent, or what?" (own = 1; other = .5; rent = 0).

EDUCATION: "How many grades of schooling did you finish?" (college degree = 1; some college = .75; high-school degree = .25; less than high-school degree = 0).

PROFESSIONAL: "What kind of work do you do? (IF NECESSARY) What exactly do you do on your job?" (professional/manager = 1; other = 0).

SERVICE: "What kind of work do you do? (IF NECESSARY) What exactly do you do on your job?" (service workers, except private household = 0; other = 0).

UNION: "Does anyone in this household belong to a labor union? (IF YES) Who is it that belongs?" (respondent = 1; other family member = .5; no one = 0).

RACE: Determined by interviewer (white = 1; other minority = .5; black = 0).

SEX: Determined by interviewer (male = 1; female = 0).

Question Wording and Coding

HEAD: "What is your relationship to the head of household?" (head or spouse of head = 1; dependent = 0).

DEPENDENT: "What is your relationship to the head of household?" (dependent = 1; head or spouse of head = 0).

STUDENT: "Are you presently employed; or are you unemployed, or retired, or a housewife, or a student, or what?" (student = 1; other = 0).

HOUSEPERSON: "Are you presently employed; or are you unemployed, or retired, or a housewife, or a student, or what?" (houseperson = 1; other = 0).

MARITAL: "Are you married now and living with your (wife/husband) or are you widowed, divorced, separate or single?" (married now = 1; formerly married = .5; single = 0).

CHILDREN: "Are there children under 18 years old in this family? (How many?)" (have children = 1; no children = 0).

ATTENDANCE: "Would you say you go to church regularly, often, seldom, or never?" (regularly = 1; often = .66; seldom = .33; never = 0).

NORTHEAST: (respondent lives in New England or Middle Atlantic state = 1; other = 0).

MIDWEST: (respondent lives in East North Central or West North Central state or Mountain state = 1; other = 0).

SOUTH: (respondent lives in Border South or Solid South state = 1; other = 0).

WEST: (respondent lives in Pacific state = 1; other = 0).

APPENDIX C

Model Parameters

Diffuse Support

	Generational Model				Subgenerational Model			
	Constant	r	r2	p	Constant	r	r2	p
Vote care	.40	.86	.74	.001	.40	.92	.85	.001
Officials	.76	.93	.86	.001	.76	.94	.88	.001
Vote only	.24	.87	.75	.001	.24	.89	.79	.001
Local	.89	.79	.62	.001	.89	.81	.66	.001
Vote matters	.91	.69	.48	.001	.91	.74	.54	.001
Have say	.76	.61	.37	.001	.76	.63	.39	.001
Vote win	.94	.80	.63	.001	.94	.82	.67	.001
Complex	.32	.62	.39	.001	.32	.64	.40	.001

Agendas

	Generational Model				Subgenerational Model			
	Constant	r	r2	p	Constant	r	r2	p
Social welfare	.09	.60	.36	.001	.09	.74	.47	.001
Agriculture	.04	.84	.70	.001	.04	.85	.71	.001
Environment	.002	.52	.27	.001	.002	.57	.33	.001
Labor	.04	.69	.48	.001	.04	.71	.51	.001
Race	.08	.79	.62	.001	.08	.85	.73	.001
Public order	.002	.64	.41	.001	.002	.67	.44	.001
Economy	.06	.92	.85	.001	.06	.95	.90	.001
Consumer	.000	.87	.75	.001	.000	.92	.84	.001
Vietnam	.000	.80	.64	.001	.000	.82	.67	.001
Foreign	.61	.83	.69	.001	.61	.88	.79	.001
Defense	.07	.42	.17	.05	.07	.54	.30	.01
Arms race	.01	.42	.18	.05	.01	.61	.38	.001
Government	.000	.55	.30	.001	.000	.65	.42	.001
Other	−.004	.44	.19	.01	−.004	.52	.27	.05

Model Parameters

Issue Stands

	Generational Model				Subgenerational Model			
	Constant	r	r2	p	Constant	r	r2	p
Education	.76	.97	.94	.001	.76	.98	.96	.001
Health	.54	.78	.61	.001	.55	.81	.66	.001
Jobs	.56	.94	.86	.001	.58	.95	.90	.001
Integration	.59	.81	.66	.001	.60	.82	.68	.001
Black welfare	.47	.96	.91	.001	.47	.96	.92	.001
Interventionism	.47	.74	.54	.001	.47	.81	.67	.001
Foreign aid	.55	.80	.65	.001	.57	.85	.73	.001
Involvement	.64	.94	.89	.001	.64	.95	.90	.001
Solution	.69	.84	.70	.001	.69	.83	.70	.001

Involvement

	Generational Model				Subgenerational Model			
	Constant	r	r2	p	Constant	r	r2	p
Papers	.54	.82	.67	.001	.54	.85	.73	.001
TV	.51	.89	.78	.001	.51	.90	.80	.001
Radio	.45	.86	.74	.001	.45	.87	.76	.001
Magazines	.29	.72	.52	.001	.29	.79	.62	.001
Campaign	.55	.73	.53	.001	.55	.76	.57	.001
Politics	.63	.72	.52	.001	.63	.79	.62	.001
Majority I	.69	.69	.48	.001	.69	.78	.60	.001
Majority II	.70	.57	.32	.001	.70	.66	.43	.001
Totals	.34	.88	.77	.001	.34	.88	.77	.001

Decision-making Cues

	Generational Model				Subgenerational Model			
	Constant	r	r2	p	Constant	r	r2	p
Ideology I	.005	.78	.61	.001	.005	.80	.64	.001
Ideology II	.022	.82	.67	.001	.022	.83	.68	.001
Groups	.029	.66	.43	.001	.029	.73	.53	.001
Policy	.029	.69	.48	.001	.029	.82	.67	.001
Times	.015	.40	.16	.05	.015	.47	.22	.05
Party	.155	.92	.84	.001	.155	.94	.88	.001
Nonpolitical	.746	.66	.44	.001	.746	.79	.63	.001

Appendix C

Participation

	Generational Model				Subgenerational Model			
	Constant	r	r2	p	Constant	r	r2	p
Always vote	.54	.87	.76	.001	.54	.88	.77	.001
Register	.72	.91	.82	.001	.72	.92	.85	.001
President	.69	.88	.77	.001	.69	.89	.79	.001
Congress	.60	.88	.78	.001	.60	.91	.82	.001
Meeting	.07	.51	.26	.001	.07	.61	.37	.001
Organization	.02	.56	.31	.01	.02	.62	.38	.01
Display	.19	.49	.24	.01	.19	.71	.50	.001
Work	.04	.69	.47	.001	.04	.69	.48	.001
Influence	.31	.78	.61	.001	.31	.81	.66	.001
Contribute	.04	.72	.52	.001	.04	.77	.59	.001

Partisan Support

	Generational Model				Subgenerational Model			
	Constant	r	r2	p	Constant	r	r2	p
ID strength	.62	.90	.81	.001	.62	.92	.85	.001
Care win	.63	.80	.65	.001	.63	.82	.67	.001
Party differ	.38	.81	.65	.001	.38	.82	.67	.001
Intentions	.50	.41	.16	.05	.50	.44	.19	.05
President	.48	.44	.20	.01	.48	.46	.21	.01
Congress	.56	.53	.28	.001	.56	.55	.30	.001
Local	.54	.53	.28	.001	.56	.55	.30	.001
Last time	.67	.72	.52	.001	.67	.75	.56	.001
Usual vote	.73	.67	.45	.001	.73	.69	.48	.001
Party ID	.65	.63	.40	.001	.65	.65	.42	.001
Party evaluate	.61	.45	.20	.01	.61	.47	.22	.01

Model Parameters

Partisan Stability

	Generational Model				Subgenerational Model			
	Constant	r	r2	p	Constant	r	r2	p
Rolloff	.48	.89	.80	.001	.48	.91	.82	.001
Regularity	.45	.84	.71	.001	.45	.85	.71	.001
ID different	.83	.68	.46	.001	.83	.76	.57	.001
Loyalty	.57	.80	.63	.001	.57	.82	.67	.001
Always	.84	.76	.58	.001	.84	.84	.71	.001
Local split	.67	.86	.73	.001	.67	.88	.77	.001
National split	.84	.71	.51	.001	.84	.73	.53	.001
Other	.99	.50	.25	.05	.99	.67	.45	.001
Timing	.53	.61	.38	.001	.53	.78	.61	.001
Suredness	.92	.54	.30	.001	.92	.63	.40	.001

Demographics

	Generational Model				Subgenerational Model			
	Constant	r	r2	p	Constant	r	r2	p
Childhood class	.46	.85	.73	.001	.46	.87	.75	.001
Father	.04	.77	.59	.001	.04	.80	.65	.001
Class	.41	.77	.59	.001	.41	.80	.65	.001
Income	.11	.87	.76	.001	.11	.89	.79	.001
Ownership	.40	.92	.86	.001	.40	.93	.87	.001
Education	.48	.94	.88	.001	.48	.95	.91	.001
Professional	.05	.85	.72	.001	.05	.88	.77	.001
Service	.31	.77	.58	.001	.31	.77	.59	.001
Union	.24	.83	.69	.001	.24	.83	.69	.001
Race	.93	.63	.40	.001	.93	.66	.43	.001
Head	.86	.82	.67	.001	.86	.97	.93	.001
Dependent	.12	.82	.68	.001	.12	.98	.96	.001
Student	.01	.84	.71	.001	.01	.96	.92	.001
Houseperson	.34	.80	.64	.001	.34	.84	.71	.001
Marital	.97	.88	.77	.001	.97	.97	.95	.001
Children	1.1	.88	.78	.001	1.1	.90	.81	.001
Attendance	.61	.77	.60	.001	.61	.81	.66	.001
Northeast	.25	.53	.28	.01	.25	.56	.31	.05
Midwest	.37	.58	.33	.001	.37	.61	.37	.001
South	.30	.63	.40	.001	.30	.68	.46	.001
West	.09	.66	.44	.001	.09	.70	.49	.001

APPENDIX D

Description of Methods Used in Part III

1. In order to analyze the relationship between generational and demographic change more efficiently, the individual items analyzed in Chapters Four through Eleven were recombined into 20 summary measures. Each measure is a simple additive index, rescaled to run from zero to one. Items were combined based upon both assumed underlying substantive similarities and the patterns found in the empirical analysis presented in Part II. The specific items which were used in each summary scale are noted in Appendix A. Each scale was then used as the dependent variable in the same equation described in Chapter Three. The model parameters for these equations are as follows.

	Constant	r	r^2	p
Support	.65	.88	.77	.001
Sixties agenda	.02	.88	.77	.001
Economic agenda	.05	.92	.84	.001
Social welfare agenda	.09	.60	.36	.001
Foreign affairs agenda	.23	.79	.62	.001
Domestic issue stands	.59	.91	.82	.001
Foreign affairs issue stands	.47	.74	.54	.001
Political involvement	.57	.80	.64	.001

Description of Methods Used in Part III

Ideological decision making	.01	.84	.71	.001
Cue-specific decision making	.02	.73	.53	.001
Party-based decision making	.15	.92	.84	.001
Nonpolitical decision making	.75	.66	.44	.001
Electoral participation	.35	.87	.76	.001
Diffuse party support	.54	.90	.82	.001
Long-term party support	.66	.58	.34	.001
Short-term party support	.56	.52	.27	.001
Behavioral stability	.48	.87	.75	.001
Long-term stability	.75	.70	.49	.001
Short-term stability	.84	.85	.72	.001
Campaign stability	.72	.63	.40	.001

2. Since our concern in Chapters Thirteen and Fourteen is the relative effects of "pure" generational change and demographic factors, it is necessary to remove the effects of period, life cycle and all interactions. This is done by creating new summary variables with such effects removed (Claggett, 1981). These variables are created through the use of the following general equation:

$$SUM2 = SUM1 - (b_1 * LC) - (b_2 * P50) - (b_3 * P60) - (b_4 * P70) - (b_5 * LC \times 50) - (b_6 * LC \times 60) - (b_7 * LC \times 70) - (b_8 * G \times LC) - (b_9 * G \times P60) - (b_{10} * G \times P70)$$

where
  SUM2 = New summary variables;
  SUM1 = Old summary variable;
  LC = Age (in years after 18);
  G = Sixties generation;
  P50 = The fifties;
  P60 = The sixties;
  P70 = The seventies;
  LC × G = Age × sixties generation;
  LC × P50 = Age × P50;
  LC × P60 = Age × P60;
  LC × P70 = Age × P70;

Appendix D

G × P60 = Sixties generation × P60;
G × P70 = Sixties generation × P70; and
b_1 through b_{10} = Unstandardized regression coefficients from models using SUM1 and described in Appendix C1.

These new summary variables are then used as the dependent variables in the equations used to estimate the relative effects of the sixties generation, selected demographic characteristics, and their interactions. These equations take the general form:

$$SUM2 = b_0 + b_1 DEM + b_2 GEN + b_3 D \times G$$

where
b_0 = the constant term;
DEM = The demographic characteristic under consideration; and
D × G = Demographic characteristic × the sixties generation; and
b_1 through b_3 = Estimates of effects of above variables.

These regression estimates are then used, in conjunction with estimates from the models described in Appendix C1, to arrive at the more-detailed effects described in Chapters 13 and 14.

Index

Abramson, Paul, 13, 21, 58, 71, 178, 191, 193, 202, 217
Achen, Christopher H., 67, 69, 71, 274, 294
Afghanistan: Soviet invasion of, 48
Age cohort: definition of, 7
Agenda (political), 43–44, 95–119, 243; aggregate trends in, 98–105; economic agenda measure, 270–272; foreign agenda measure, 271–272; and the life cycle, 105–106, 108–109, 110, 114, 116; and period effects, 107–108, 109–110, 115, 116, 117; and political parties, 198, 202; the process of building, 95–97, 115–116; and the sixties, 97–98; sixties agenda measure, 270–272; and the sixties generation, 106–107, 108–110, 112, 116–117; social welfare agenda measure, 270–272; and the sociocultural environment, 299–303, 318–321; and the socioeconomic environment, 277–278, 290–293
Aging. See Life cycle
Agriculture, 99, 100, 105–117
Aldrich, John H., 178, 191, 193
Alienation (political), 41–43, 46, 48, 51, 85, 86, 89, 144, 162, 178, 216, 223, 276, 293. See also Support
Andersen, Kristi, 7, 21, 97, 118, 165, 176
Aristotle, 142
Arms race, 99, 104, 105–117

Attitudes (political), 40, 41–43, 51, 57. See also Support

Barnes, Samuel, 144, 157
Beatles, the, 16–17, 26, 40
Beck, Paul Allen, 122, 139, 143, 157
Behavior (political), 40, 44–46, 51, 57. See also Participation, Protests
Behr, Roy L., 199, 218
Bell, Daniel, 34, 53, 107, 118, 122, 140, 143, 157, 223, 238
Bem, Daryl J., 41, 53
Bengston, Vern L., 58, 71
Benjamin, Roger, 143, 157
Bennett, Stephen, 125, 139
Bennett, W. Lance, 41, 43, 53
Berelson, Bernard, 42, 53, 93, 94, 143, 144, 157, 162, 175, 238, 292, 294
Berrigan, Daniel and Philip, 40, 336
Binstock, Robert H., 13, 22, 180, 194
Bishop, George, 125, 139
Black Panthers, the, 39
Black welfare, 124–139. See also Blacks
Blacks: Black Panthers, 39; culture of, 25–26, 42; and diffuse support, 78–80; and issue stands, 122; and political attitudes, 42; and political behavior, 45; and political decision making, 163; and political violence, 39; and the Vietnam War, 37. See also Race
Blake, J. Herman, 25, 53

Index

Bolingbroke, Henry Saint-John, 196, 217
Boskin, Joseph, 25, 53
Boyte, Harry C., 49, 53, 165, 176
Brecht, Bertolt, 41
Broder, David, 178, 193, 223, 239, 336, 337, 341
Brody, Richard, 178, 191, 193
Brown, H. Rapp, 336
Burke, Edmund, 197, 217
Burnham, Walter Dean, 4, 5, 21, 96, 118, 178, 194, 199, 200, 217, 221, 223, 229, 239, 292, 294

Campbell, Angus, 13, 21, 57, 71, 141, 157, 164, 176, 180, 194, 222, 239
Cantril, Albert, 143, 157, 179, 194
Carmichael, Stokely, 336
Carter, Jimmy, 48, 202, 223
Change (political), 244; "astructive," 248, 337, 339; "constructive," 247, 293, 336; "destructive," 247–248, 293, 337, 339; individual versus aggregate, 6–11, 20; individual versus structural, 245–246; "instructive," 247, 337, 339; and the political agenda, 95–97; and political parties, 198; and political stability, 222; rates of, 3–6, 20; "restructive," 247, 264, 337, 338; situational versus structural, 246–248, 264–265, 267, 293, 337–340; and the sixties, 248, 264; and socialization, 245–246; system-adjusting, 247, 264, 337, 338, 340; system-challenging, 247, 264, 337, 338; system-maintaining, 247, 337; trends in situational and structural conditions, 248–256, 264, 328–330
Children, 248–266. See also Sociocultural environment
Church attendance, 248–266. See also Sociocultural environment
Civil liberties: as a political issue, 124–139
Civil-rights movement, 15, 38, 43, 44, 45, 96, 98, 112–113, 121, 201. See also Blacks, Race
Claggett, William, 58, 60, 65, 71, 202, 209, 217, 222, 239, 273, 294

Class: and childhood, 248–266; and culture, 27–30; and diffuse support, 78–80; and evidence of institutional change, 248–256; and interaction effects, 259–261, 263–264, 265; and issue stands, 122–123; and the life cycle, 256–258, 259–261, 262, 265; and period effects, 257, 259, 260–261, 263–264, 265; and the political agenda, 97; and political attitudes, 42; and political decision making, 163; and political involvement, 143–144; and political opinions, 44; and the sixties generation, 257, 258–261, 265–267; and the Vietnam War, 37. See also Economics
Cleaver, Eldridge, 336
Cobb, Roger, 39, 53, 96, 118
Conservatism, 121–123, 129–139, 154, 209; aggregate trends in, 123–128; nonideological, 110, 132, 152, 171–172, 188, 212, 232–233, 261. See also Issue stands, Liberalism
Consumer affairs, 99, 102, 105–117
Converse, Philip E., 13, 21, 57, 58, 65, 71, 141, 144, 151, 157, 164, 176, 178, 179, 180, 194, 202, 209, 217, 222, 239
Cues. See Decision making
Culture: black, 25–26, 33–34, 48, 49, 51; and class, 27, 33–34, 44; and economics, 32–35, 44; evidence of institutional changes in, 243–268; hegemonic, 24–25, 50–51; and issue stands, 121; and opinions, 43–44; oriental, 26–27; and the political agenda, 98; and political attitudes, 41–43; and political behavior, 44–45; and political involvement, 143, 144, 150; of the sixties, 24–30, 51, 245; subcultures, 24–25, 33–34, 48, 49, 51, 98; youth, 27, 42, 43, 44, 51, 98, 123
Cutler, Neil, 58, 71

Data: coding of, 67; demographic change, 248–249; description of, 55–58, 69–70; interpretation of findings, 66–69; issue stands, 123–124, 135–136; participation, 180; partisan support, 203–204; political agenda, 98–99;

Index

political decision making, 163–165; political involvement, 163–165; political stability, 224–225; political support, 80, 83; reliability and validity of, 57

Davis, Angela, 336

Dawson, Karen S., 13, 21, 246, 268

Dawson, Richard E., 13, 21, 246, 268

Decision making (political): aggregate trends in, 163–169; cues, 160–162, 173–174, 244; cue-specific measure, 271–272; elements of, 159–162, 173–174; ideological measure, 271–272; and interaction effects, 170–172, 172–173, 174–175; and the life cycle, 163, 169–170, 171–172, 172–173, 174–175; measurement of, 163–165; nonpolitical measure, 271–272; party-based measure, 271–272; and period effects, 162–163, 170, 171–172, 173, 174–175; and the sixties, 162–169, 171, 174–175; and the sixties generation, 162–163, 170, 171, 173, 174–175; and the sociocultural environment, 307–310, 318–321; and the socioeconomic environment, 282–285, 290–293; and subgenerations, 172–173, 174–175

Delli Carpini, Michael X., 161, 176

Demographic change, 243–268; aggregate trends in, 248–256; and interaction effects, 259–261, 263–264, 265; and the life cycle, 256–258, 259–261, 262, 265; measurement of, 248–249; and period effects, 257, 259, 260–261, 263–264, 265; and the sixties generation, 257, 258–261, 265–267; and subgenerations, 261–264. See also Sociocultural environment, Socioeconomic environment

Dennis, Jack, 13, 22, 76, 94, 199, 217

Dependents, 248–266. See also Sociocultural environment

Dickstein, Morris, 38, 53

Draft, the, 15, 35–36, 37

Dylan, Bob, 16, 40

Earth Day, 40

Easton, David, 76, 94

Economics: and culture, 32–33; and demographic change, 243–268; and diffuse support, 78–80; and issue stands, 121–122, 124–139; and participation, 177, 179; and party support, 201; and the political agenda, 99, 102, 105–117; and political attitudes, 43; and political decision making, 162; and political involvement, 143; and the seventies, 84; and the sixties, 30–35, 51, 245; and subcultures, 33–35; and subgenerations, 46. See also Class

Edelman, Murray, 96, 119

Education: changes in (due to life cycle, periods, and generation), 248–266, 338; and culture, 29–30; and economics, 34; and issue stands, 121, 122; and participation, 177, 179, 324; and party support, 202; and the political agenda, 97; and political decision making, 162, 170; and political involvement, 143, 324, 326; and political opinions, 44; as a public issue, 124–139; rise in, 8, 29–30, 248–256, 264

Efficacy (political), 42, 51, 178. See also Support

Eisen, Jonathan, 30, 53

Eisenhower, Dwight, 221

Elder, Charles D., 39, 53, 96, 118

Elections, 177, 178; stability and, 220–222, 225. See also Participation, Voting

Entman, Robert, 125, 140

Environment, the, 99, 100, 105–117

Epstein, Jay E., 39, 53

ERA (Equal Rights Amendment), 49, 96

Erikson, Erik H., 9, 22

Erikson, Robert, 42, 53, 136, 139

Evers, Medgar, 39

Existentialism, 41

Factions, 196–197. See also Parties

Fiorina, Morris, 160, 176, 202, 217

Flacks, Richard, 33, 53

Flanigan, William, 178, 194

Ford, Gerald R., 48, 202, 223

Foreign affairs, 99, 103, 105–117, 201. See also Vietnam War

Index

Foreign aid, 124–139
Foreign intervention, 124–139. See also Vietnam War
Frankovic, Kathleen, 125, 140
Freud, Sigmund, 9, 22
Friedenberg, Edgar Z., 27, 53

Gaudet, Hazel, 144, 157
Generations: critical years, 9–12; definition of, 7–8, 20; measurement of, 58–70; and political change, 337–341; and the transmission of values, 333–334; underlying assumptions of, 8–11. See also Sixties generation, Subgenerations
Ghandi, Mahatma, 40
Gilmour, Richard, 45, 53, 144, 157, 162, 176, 178, 194
Ginsberg, Benjamin, 93, 94, 97, 119, 177, 194, 221, 239
Gitlin, Todd, 24, 29, 53, 163, 176
Glenn, Norval D., 58, 71
Goel, M. L., 13, 22, 144, 157, 180, 194
Gold, Frank, 77, 94
Goldwater, Barry, 201, 223
Gordon, Thomas, 196, 218
Government: expansion of, 78, 143, 144, 222; involvement in solving the nation's problems, 124–139; running of, 99, 104, 105–117
Graber, Doris, 178, 179, 194, 201, 217
Gramsci, Antonio, 24, 53
Group identity: as a decision-making cue, 164–175

Hagstrom, Jerry, 121, 140, 268
Hamilton, Alexander, 197
Hayden, Tom, 336
Hbrenner, Ronald J., 200, 201, 217
Head of household, 248–266. See also Sociocultural environment
Health care, 124–139
Hefner, Ted, 58, 71
Hegemony: cultural, 24–30, 50–51, 263; economic, 33–34; and political orientations, 274–293, 296–321, 323
Hendrix, Jimmi, 39
Hirschman, Albert, 34, 48, 53, 143, 157

Hoffman, Abbie, 336
Hofstadter, Richard, 196, 197, 218
Home ownership, 248–266. See also Socioeconomic environment
Hoskin, Marilyn Brookes, 10, 22, 77, 94
Houseperson, 248–266. See also Sociocultural environment
Hudson, Robert H., 13, 22, 180, 194
Hume, David, 197, 218

Identification problem: defined, 58–59; and the model used, 64–66; solution to, 59–64
Ideology, 243; as a decision-making cue, 161–175. See also Conservatism, Liberalism
Income, 248–266. See also Socioeconomic environment
Information (political). See Involvement
Inglehart, Ronald, 5, 22, 32, 53, 97, 106–107, 118, 119, 121, 122, 140, 143, 144, 157, 162, 170, 176, 178, 185, 194
Integration, 124–139
Interaction effects: defined, 14–15, 21; and demographic change, 259–261, 263–264, 265; and diffuse support, 86–90, 91–93; and issue stands, 130–132, 134–135, 136, 138; and participation, 180, 187–188, 189–190, 191–192; and party support, 211–212, 213–214, 216; and the political agenda, 108–110, 114–115, 116–117; and political decision making, 170–172, 172–173, 174, 175; and political involvement, 144, 151–152, 152–154, 155–156; and political stability, 232–233, 235–236; summary of, 265, 323–328
Interest (political). See Involvement
Involvement (political), 144–158, 201, 202, 243; aggregate trends in, 145–148, 155; importance of, 141–143, 154; and interaction effects, 144–145, 151–152, 152–154, 155–156; and the life cycle, 144–145, 149–150, 151, 152, 153–154, 155–156; measurement of, 145–146; and period effects, 144–145, 150–151, 151–152, 153–154, 155–156; and political stability, 220, 222; and the six-

368

Index

ties, 143–144, 154; and the sixties generation, 144–145, 150, 151–152, 153–154, 155–156; and the sociocultural environment, 306–307, 318–321; and the socioeconomic environment, 281–282, 290–293; summary measure of, 271–272
Iranian hostage crisis, the, 48
Issue stands, 120–140, 243; aggregate trends in, 123–128; domestic stands measure, 271–272; foreign stands measure, 271–272; interaction effects, 130–132, 134–135, 136, 138; and the life cycle, 123, 129, 130–131, 132, 134, 135, 136, 137, 138; measurement of, 123–124, 135; and period effects, 130, 131–132, 135, 136, 138–139; and political parties, 198, 202, 203; and political stability, 219, 220; and the sixties, 120–123, 137–139; and the sixties generation, 121–123, 129–130, 130–132, 135–136, 138–139; and the sociocultural environment, 303–306, 318–321; and the socioeconomic environment, 278–281, 290–293

Jackson, Andrew, 197
Jackson, George, 39
Jackson State, 39
Jefferson Airplane, the, 40
Jennings, M. Kent, 9, 13, 22, 58, 71, 122, 123, 139, 140, 143, 157
Johnson, Lyndon B., 38, 112, 122, 144, 201, 202
Jones, Landon Y., 16, 22, 31–32, 35, 37, 54, 121, 140, 266, 268
Joplin, Janice, 39

Kasse, Max, 144
Keeter, Scott, 201, 218
Keniston, Kenneth, 35, 54
Kennedy, John F., 38, 201; assassination of, 8, 16, 38, 39
Kennedy, Robert, 39, 121
Kent State, 39
Key, V. O., Jr., 4, 22
Kim, Jae-On, 13, 22, 180, 194
King, Martin Luther, Jr., 39, 40

Knutson, Jeanne, 121, 140
Koeppen, Sheilah R., 45, 54
Korean War, the, 36, 135–137
Kritzer, Herbert M., 58, 60, 62, 71

Labor, 99, 101, 105–117
Ladd, Everett Carl, 28, 54, 121, 140, 331, 341
Lamb, Richard, 45, 53, 144, 157, 162, 176, 178, 194
Lambert, T. Allen, 8, 9, 22
Laufer, Robert S., 29, 54
Lazarsfeld, Paul F., 93, 94, 144, 157, 162, 175, 238
Lazarus, Edward H., 199, 218
Levitan, Teresa, 122, 140
Liberalism, 120–139, 243. See also Conservatism, Ideology, Issue stands
Life cycle, the: definition of, 12, 20; and demographic change, 256–258, 259–261, 262, 265; and diffuse support, 84–85, 86–88, 89–90, 91–93; ecological life cycle, 63–64, 70; and issue stands, 123, 129, 130–131, 132, 134, 135, 137, 138; measurement of, 58–70; and participation, 180, 185, 187–188, 189–190; and party support, 202, 203, 208–209, 211–212, 213, 215–216; and the political agenda, 105–106, 108–109, 110, 114, 116; and political decision making, 163, 169–170, 171–172, 172–173, 174–175; and political involvement, 144–145, 149–150, 151, 152, 153–154, 155–156; political relevance of, 13–14, 49–50; and political stability, 222, 229–230, 232–233, 235; summary of effects, 323–324
Lipset, Seymour Martin, 28, 54
Luttbeg, Norman, 42, 53, 136, 139

Madison, James, 197
Malcolm X, 39
Mannheim, Karl, 7, 8, 9, 22
Marital status, 248–266. See also Sociocultural environment
Markus, Gregory B., 58, 71
Marsh, Alan, 144, 157
Maslow, Abraham, 9, 22, 32, 54

Mass media: and diffuse support, 79; and generational change, 337; and issue stands, 122; and participation, 178, 179; and party support, 201–202; and the political agenda, 95–97; and political decision making, 162; and political involvement, 143–156; and political socialization, 246; and political stability, 222, 223; television, 28–29, 36–37
McCarthy, Eugene, 39, 121, 223
McCloskey, Herbert, 128, 140
McCluhan, Marshall, 28, 54
McGinnis, Joe, 201, 218
McGovern, George, 39, 121, 201, 215, 223
McPhee, William N., 93, 94, 144, 157, 162, 175, 238
Methods, 58–70; coding, 67; estimation of sociocultural and socioeconomic effects, 273–275; identification problem, 58–64; interpretation of findings, 66–69; justification of, 58–64, 70; model used, 64–66; removing life cycle, period, and interaction effects, 273; significance levels, 69
Migration patterns, 248–266. See also Sociocultural environment
Milbrath, Lester W., 13, 22, 144, 157, 180, 194
Miller, Warren E., 13, 21, 57, 71, 122, 140, 141, 157, 164, 176, 180, 194, 222, 239
Mills, C. Wright, 96, 119
Morrison, Jim, 39
Myerhoff, Barbara G., 26, 54

National defense, 99, 104, 105–117
National Election Studies, the, 55–58, 68–70, 98; benefits of, 55–56; drawbacks to, 56–57
Nature of the times: as a decision-making cue, 164–175
New Republic, The, 266–267, 268
Nie, Norman, 5, 13, 22, 78, 107, 119, 121, 123, 140, 141, 143, 158, 162, 164, 165, 168, 176, 177, 179, 180, 194, 195, 198, 199, 200, 201, 218, 222, 223, 229, 239
Niemi, Richard, 9, 13, 22, 58, 71, 123, 140
Nixon, Richard M., 16, 47–48, 144, 201, 202

Oldendick, Robert, 125, 139
Opinions (political), 40, 43–44, 45, 51. See also Agenda, Issue stands
Orient, the: effects on U.S. culture, 26–27
Orman, John, 38, 54

Paletz, David, 125, 140
Participation, 141–142, 154–155, 177–195, 223, 244; aggregate trends in, 180–185; attending meetings, 180–193; belonging to an organization, 180–193; contributing money, 180–193; and democracy, 177, 190; displaying slogans, 180–193; influencing another's vote, 180–193; and interaction effects, 180, 187–188, 189–190, 191, 192; and the life cycle, 180, 185, 187–188, 189–190; measurement of, 180; nonelectoral, 179, 192–193, 331, 334–335; and period effects, 186–188, 190, 192; and political stability, 219–239; and the sixties, 177–178; and the sixties generation, 179–180, 186–188, 190–193; and the sociocultural environment, 310–311, 318–321; and the socioeconomic environment, 285–286, 290–293; and subgenerations, 188–190, 191, 192–193; summary measure, 271–272; working for party, 180–193
Parties (political): ambivalence toward, 198–199, 211, 215; in democratic theory and practice, 196–198, 214–215; as a decision-making cue, 161–175; fifth party system, 200–201; number of opinions about, 145–146, 148; and participation, 178; and the sixties, 201–203; third parties, 198–199, 225, 228, 229, 230, 234; two-party system, 197–198. See also Partisanship, Support

Index

Partisanship: decline in, 178; direction of, 196–218; stability of, 219–239. See also Support
Party identification. See Partisanship, Support
Patrick, Robert, 39, 54
Patterson, Thomas, 141, 158, 201, 218
Period effects: defined, 14, 20; and demographic change, 257, 259, 260–261, 263, 264, 265; and diffuse support, 85–86, 87–88, 89–90, 91–93; and issue stands, 130, 131–132, 135, 138–139; measurement of, 58–70; and participation, 186–188, 190, 192; and party support, 210–211, 212, 214, 215–216; and the political agenda, 107–108, 109–110, 115, 116, 117; and political decision making, 162–163, 170, 171–172, 173, 174–175; and political involvement, 144–145, 150–151, 151–152, 153–154, 155–156; and political stability, 222, 229–230, 232–233, 236, 237; summary of effects, 324–325
Petrocik, John, 5, 22, 78, 107, 119, 121, 123, 140, 141, 143, 158, 162, 164, 165, 168, 176, 179, 180, 194, 198, 199, 200, 201, 218, 223, 229, 239
Phillips, Kevin, 200, 218
Pinter, Harold, 41
Podhoretz, Norman, 125, 140
Policy stands: as a decision-making cue, 164–175
Pollock, John C., 77, 94
Pomper, Gerald R., 143, 158, 162, 176, 199, 200, 218
Postmaterialism, 32–33, 97, 106, 121, 259
Prewitt, Kenneth, 13, 21, 246
Prezeworski, Adam, 93, 94
Primaries, 199, 202. See also Elections, Voting
Professional occupation, 248–266. See also Socioeconomic environment
Protests, 15–16, 33–35, 36–38, 39, 40, 43, 44, 45, 48, 78, 79, 192–193, 201, 223, 324–325, 334–335. See also Participation, Public order, Violence
Public order, 99, 101, 105–117, 143, 201, 223

Race, 97–118, 248–266. See also Blacks, Class, Culture, Sociocultural environment
Race relations, 99, 101, 105–117, 143, 223
Ranney, Austin, 178, 194, 198, 199, 211, 218
Reagan, Ronald, 49, 201, 215, 223
Realignments, 4–6, 7, 199, 201, 203, 214, 216. See also Change, Elections, Parties, Support, Voting
Regional culture, 248–266. See also Sociocultural environment
Registration (voting), 180–193
Reich, Charles A., 121, 140
Renshon, Stanley, 121, 140
Robinson, Michael, 179, 194
Rock music, 16–17, 26–27, 38, 40; and economics, 34
Rogers, Carl, 32, 54
Roll, Charles W., 143, 157, 179, 194
Rosenstone, Robert A., 38, 54
Rosenstone, Steven J., 13, 22, 180, 195, 199, 218
Rubin, Jerry, 336
Rusk, Jerrold, 178

Sahlins, Marshall, 24, 54
Sartre, Jean-Paul, 41
Scammon, Richard M., 125, 140
Schattschneider, E. E., 178, 194, 197, 218
Schulman, Mark, 199, 200, 218
Schumpeter, Joseph, 143, 158
Schwartz, Sandra Kenyon, 76, 94
Scott, Ruth K., 200, 201, 217
SDS (Students for a Democratic Society), 16, 163
Seals, Bobby, 336
Service sector, the, 248–266. See also Socioeconomic environment
Shankar, Ravi, 26
Shingles, Richard, 165, 176
Shively, W. Phillips, 160, 162, 176, 202, 218
Shogan, Robert, 121, 140
Sigel, Roberta, 10, 22, 77, 94
Sixties, the: culture of, 24–30; defined, 15–16, 21; and diffuse support, 78–80, 85–88, 91–93; economics of, 30–35;

371

Index

Sixties, the (*Continued*)
  and participation, 177–178; and party support, 201–202; and the political agenda, 97–98, 100–105, 107–108, 112–115, 116, 138–139; and political attitudes, 40–43; and political behavior, 44–45; and political decision making, 162–169, 171, 174–175; and political involvement, 143–144; and political opinions, 43–44; and political stability, 222–223; politics of, 35–40, 43; and Watergate, 47–48. See also Period effects, Sixties generation

Sixties generation, the: definition of, 16–19, 21; and demographic change, 257, 258–261, 265–267; and diffuse support, 78–80, 86–87, 89, 90, 91–93; and economics, 31–35; and the future, 330–337; and issue stands, 121–123, 129–130, 130–132, 135–136, 138–139; and participation, 179–180, 186–188, 190–193; and party support, 202–203, 209–210, 211–212, 216; and the political agenda, 98, 106–107, 108–110, 112, 116–117; and political attitudes, 40–43; and political behavior, 44–45; and political decision making, 162–163, 170, 171–172, 173, 174–175; and political involvement, 144–145, 150, 151–152, 153–154, 155–156; and political leadership, 336–337; and political opinions, 43–44; and political stability, 223–224, 230–231, 232, 233, 234, 235, 236, 237; and politics, 35–40; and the seventies, 49–50; size of, 28, 31–32, 49–50; and the sociocultural environment, 295–321, 326–328; and the socioeconomic environment, 269–294, 326–328; summary of effects, 325–328; and Watergate, 47–48

Snyder, Robin, 28, 54

Social welfare, 99, 100, 105–117

Socialization: and diffuse support, 76–77; and generations, 7–11, 33; and institutions, 245–248; and the sociocultural environment, 318, 319; and structural change, 245–246

Sociocultural environment, the, 295–321, 326–328; and diffuse support, 296–299; and issue stands, 303–306; and participation, 310–311; and party support, 311–314; and the political agenda, 299–303; and political decision making, 307–310; and political involvement, 306–307; and political stability, 314–317; summary of political effects, 318–321. See also Demographic change

Socioeconomic environment, the, 269–294, 326–328; and diffuse support, 273–276; and issue stands, 278–281; and participation, 285–286; and party support, 286–287; and the political agenda, 277–278; and political decision making, 282–285; and political involvement, 281–282; and political stability, 287–290; summary of political effects, 290–293. See also Demographic change

Sorauf, Frank, 201, 218

Stability (political), 219–239, 244; aggregate trends in, 224–229; behavioral summary measure, 271–272; campaign summary measure, 271–272; decline in, 220–222; function of, 220–221; and interaction effects, 232, 235–236; and the life cycle, 222, 229–230, 232–233, 235; long-term summary measure, 271–272; measurement of, 224–225; and period effects, 222–223, 231–232, 232–233, 236, 237; short-term summary measure, 271–272; and the sixties, 222–223; and the sixties generation, 223–224, 230–231, 232, 233, 234, 235, 236, 237; and the sociocultural environment, 314–317, 318–321; and the socioeconomic environment, 287–290, 290–293; and subgenerations, 233–238

Steinberg, David, 30, 53

Steinfels, Peter, 121, 140

Stokes, Donald E., 13, 21, 57, 71, 141, 157, 164, 176, 180, 194, 222, 239

Students, 248–266. See also Sociocultural environment

372

Index

Subgenerations: and attitudes, opinions, and behaviors, 45–46; definition of, 17–19, 21; and demographic change, 261–264; and diffuse support, 88–90, 91–93; and issue stands, 132–135, 136–137, 138–139; and participation, 188–190, 191, 192–193; and party support, 212–214, 216; and the political agenda, 110–115, 116–117; and political decision making, 172–173, 174–175; and political involvement, 152–154, 155–156; and political stability, 233–238; summary of political effects, 326–328

Sundquist, James L., 4, 22, 96, 119, 199, 218

Support (party), 196–218, 219, 244; aggregate trends in, 203–208; diffuse, 198–200, 201, 203–216, 271–272; and interaction effects, 211–212, 213–214, 216; and the life cycle, 202, 203, 208–209, 211–212, 213, 215–216; logic of, 198–200, 223; long-term summary measure, 271–272; measurement of, 203–204; and period effects, 210–211, 212, 214, 215–216; short-term summary measure, 271–272; and the sixties, 201–202; and the sixties generation, 202–203, 209–210, 211–212, 216; specific, 198–200, 201, 203–216; and the sociocultural environment, 311–314, 318–321; and the socioeconomic environment, 286–287, 290–293; and stability, 219–239; and subgenerations, 212–214, 216; weakening of, 199–200, 204–208, 215

Support (political), 41–43, 45, 51, 57, 203, 243; aggregate trends in, 80–84; development of, 76–77; diffuse, 57, 75–94; and interaction effects, 86–90, 91–93; and the life cycle, 84–85, 86–88, 89–90, 91–93; measurement of, 80, 83; and period effects, 85–86, 86–88, 89–90, 91–93; and the sixties generation, 78–80, 86–87, 89–90, 91–93; and the sociocultural environment, 296–299, 318–321; and the socioeconomic environment, 273–276, 290–293; specific, 76; and subgenerations, 88–90, 91–93; summary measure of, 270–272; theoretical importance of, 76–77

Symbionese Liberation Army, the, 39

Technology, 8. See also Mass media, Television

Tedin, Kent, 42, 53, 136, 139

Television: increased availability of, 28–29; and political involvement, 143–156; and Vietnam, 36–37

Trenchard, John, 196, 218

Triandis, Harry C., 41, 54

Trust (political), 41–43, 44, 51, 178; toward parties, 199, 201, 202. See also Alienation, Efficacy, Support

Tuchfarber, Alfred, 125, 139

Tufte, Edward R., 165, 176

Union membership, 248–266. See also Socioeconomic environment

Van Buren, Martin, 197

Verba, Sidney, 5, 13, 22, 78, 107, 119, 121, 123, 140, 141, 143, 158, 162, 164, 165, 168, 176, 177, 179, 180, 194, 195, 198, 199, 200, 201, 218, 222, 223, 229, 239

Vietnam War, the, 8, 15, 16, 35–38, 43, 332; and diffuse support, 78; and issue stands, 128, 130, 135–137, 138; and party support, 201; and the political agenda, 97, 98, 103, 105–117; and political involvement, 143; and political opinions, 44, 46, 47; and political stability, 223

Viguerie, Richard, 121, 140

Violence: and participation, 179; and party support, 201; and political decision making, 162; and political involvement, 144; and politics, 34–35, 39, 43, 45, 97. See also Protests

Voting, 177, 178, 180–193; choice, 203–216; stability of, 219–239. See also Elections, Participation

Wallace, George, 223

Washington, George, 197

373

Watergate, 14, 16, 47–48, 85, 96, 223
Wattenberg, Ben, 125, 140
Weathermen, the, 39
Weber, Max, 122, 140
Weissberg, Robert, 97, 119
White, Dan, 77, 94
Who, the, 40
Williams, Raymond, 24, 54
Wolfinger, Raymond, 13, 22, 180, 195

Women's movement, the, 49
Woodstock, 17, 40

Yankelovich, Daniel, 121, 140, 331, 341
Yumpies. See Yuppies
Yuppies, 265–267, 268

Zingale, Nancy, 178, 194
Zukin, Cliff, 28, 54, 201, 218